USING GAMES AND SIMULATIONS FOR TEACHING AND ASSESSMENT

Using Games and Simulations for Teaching and Assessment: Key Issues comprises a multidisciplinary investigation into the issues that arise when using games and simulations for educational purposes. Using both theoretical and empirical analyses, this collection examines cognitive, motivational, and psychometric issues with a focus on STEM content. Unlike other research-based volumes that focus solely on game design or the theoretical basis behind gaming, this book unites previously disparate communities of researchers—from civilian to military contexts as well as multiple disciplines—to critically explore current problems and illustrate how instructionally effective games and simulations should be planned and evaluated.

While computer-based simulations and games have the potential to improve the quality of education and training, *Using Games and Simulations for Teaching and Assessment: Key Issues* shows how the science of learning should underlie the use of such technologies. Through a wide-ranging yet detailed examination, chapter authors provide suggestions for designing and developing games, simulations, and intelligent tutoring systems that are scientifically-based, outcomes-driven, and cost-conscious.

Harold F. O'Neil is Professor of Education Psychology and Technology at the University of Southern California and Project Director at the National Center for Research on Evaluation, Standards, and Student Testing (CRESST).

Eva L. Baker is Distinguished Research Professor at the Graduate School of Education and Information Studies, University of California, Los Angeles. She is also co-director of CRESST.

Ray S. Perez is Program Officer at the Office of Naval Research (ONR), where he manages a cognitive science of learning research program.

USING GAMES AND SIMULATIONS FOR TEACHING AND ASSESSMENT

Key Issues

Edited by
Harold F. O'Neil
Eva L. Baker
Ray S. Perez

Routledge
Taylor & Francis Group

NEW YORK AND LONDON

First published 2016
by Routledge
711 Third Avenue, New York, NY 10017

and by Routledge
2 Park Square, Milton Park, Abingdon, Oxon OX14 4RN

Routledge is an imprint of the Taylor & Francis Group, an informa business

Library of Congress Cataloging in Publication Data
Names: O'Neil, Harold F., 1943– editor. | Baker, Eva L., editor. | Perez,
Ray S., editor.
Title: Using games and simulations for teaching and assessment : key issues /
edited by Harold F. O'Neil, Eva L. Baker, Ray S. Perez.
Description: New York : Routledge, [2016] | Includes bibliographical
references and index.
Identifiers: LCCN 2015040972| ISBN 9780415737876 (hardback) |
ISBN 9780415737883 (pbk.) | ISBN 9781315817767 (ebk)
Subjects: LCSH: Educational games. | Education—Simulation methods. |
Educational tests and measurements.
Classification: LCC LB1029.G3 U748 2016 | DDC 790.1—dc23
LC record available at http://lccn.loc.gov/2015040972

ISBN: 978-0-415-73787-6 (hbk)
ISBN: 978-0-415-73788-3 (pbk)
ISBN: 978-1-315-81776-7 (ebk)

Typeset in Bembo and Stone Sans
by Florence Production Ltd, Stoodleigh, Devon, UK

MIX
Paper from
responsible sources
FSC FSC® C013056
www.fsc.org

Printed and bound in Great Britain by
TJ International Ltd, Padstow, Cornwall

CONTENTS

CONTRIBUTORS

Eva L. Baker
National Center for Research on Evaluation, Standards, and Student Testing (CRESST)/ University of California, Los Angeles
Eva L. Baker is a Distinguished Research Professor of Education in the UCLA Graduate School of Education & Information Studies and is Co-Director of the National Center for Research on Evaluation, Standards, and Student Testing (CRESST). Dr. Baker's research focuses on the integration of standards, instruction, and measurement, including design and empirical validation, and new measures of complex human performance, particularly in technology. Baker initiated and served as president of the World Education Research Association, following her tenure as president of the American Educational Research Association (AERA). She was president of the Educational Psychology Division of the American Psychological Association, where she is a fellow, a status also held in American Psychological Society and AERA. She was Chair of the Board on Testing and Assessment of the National Research Council and Co-Chair of the Joint Committee on the Revision of the Standards for Educational and Psychological Testing (1999).

John T. Behrens
Pearson
John Behrens is the Vice President of the Advanced Computing and Data Science Lab at Pearson and an Adjunct Assistant Research Professor (by courtesy) in the Department of Psychology at the University of Notre Dame. John promotes, creates, and researches learning experiences that integrate digital activities with statistical methods to foster learning. John has applied these concepts to the development of emerging genres including simulation and

game-based assessment, comprehensive learning ecosystems, and articulation of the emerging "Digital Ocean." His methodological interests focus on the logical foundations of data analysis, technological implications for assessment, and multidisciplinary approaches to personalization.

Li Cai

National Center for Research on Evaluation, Standards, and Student Testing (CRESST)/ University of California, Los Angeles

Li Cai is a Professor of Education and Psychology at the University of California, Los Angeles (UCLA). He also serves as a Co-Director of the National Center for Research on Evaluation, Standards, and Student Testing (CRESST). His research focuses on measurement, methodology, and statistical applications in education and behavioral sciences.

Paul Chatelier

Naval Postgraduate School

Paul Chatelier, a retired Naval Medical Service Corps Captain, served as a Navy Aviation Psychologist for over 24 years. His responsibilities included managing and directing research, development, and application of human factors, modeling and simulation and education and training programs for the DoD science and technology R&D. He is currently a Research Associate Professor at the Naval Postgraduate School's Modeling and Simulation Institute (MOVES). He brings a broad base of experience through his work at DARPA, the White House Office of Science and Technology Policy, the DoD Education Activity, the Office of Naval Research, and as a current USA NATO delegate to the Human Factors and Medical Panel (HFMP). Much of his current work is on strategic analysis and planning of the DoD technical and organizational programs related to simulation and training. He continues to serve as a technical expert and analyst on NATO and DoD overseas human factors, medical, and M&S programs.

Kilchan Choi

National Center for Research on Evaluation, Standards, and Student Testing (CRESST)/ University of California, Los Angeles

Kilchan Choi is an Assistant Director/Principal Scientist for Statistical and Methodological Innovations at the National Center for Research on Evaluation, Standards, and Student Testing (CRESST). His expertise is in the development and application of advanced statistical methodologies and hierarchical modeling to applied problems in multisite evaluation, growth modeling, and school effectiveness/accountability in large-scale assessment systems.

Gregory K. W. K. Chung

National Center for Research on Evaluation, Standards, and Student Testing (CRESST)/ University of California, Los Angeles

Greg Chung is Assistant Director for Research Innovation at the National Center for Research on Evaluation, Standards, and Student Testing (CRESST). His current work at CRESST involves developing games and assessments, and conducting validation and evaluation studies for technology-based tools in K-16 environ-ments. He has experience in developing Web-based assessment tools for diagnostic and embedded assessment purposes using Bayesian networks, domain ontologies, and other advanced computational tools.

Joseph V. Cohn

Office of the Undersecretary of Defense, Human Performance Training and BioSystems Directorate

Dr. Joseph V. Cohn holds a Ph.D. in neuroscience from Brandeis University and a B.S. in biology from the University of Illinois-Urbana Champaign and is a Commander in the United States Navy's Aerospace Experimental Psychology community. He co-edited a three-volume book series focusing on training system development, a book on enhancing human performance in high risk environments, and is working on a book entitled *Modeling Sociocultural Influences on Decision Making*. He is the recipient of numerous awards, including the United States Naval Aerospace Experimental Psychology Society's Michael G. Lilienthal Leadership Award; the Association of Medical Service Corps Officers of the Navy's "Best in Innovation" Awards for developing a portable traumatic brain injury diagnosis tool and for developing neurocognitive technologies to ensure Warfighter resilience; and the Admiral Jeremy M. Boorda Award for Outstanding Integration of Analysis and Policy-Making.

Zoë B. Corwin

University of Southern California

Zoë B. Corwin is Associate Research Professor with the University of Southern California's Pullias Center for Higher Education. She has conducted research on college preparation programs and access to financial aid for underserved students, college pathways for foster youth and the role of social media and games in postsecondary access and completion. She is co-editor of *Postsecondary Play: Games, Social Media and Higher Education* with Johns Hopkins Press and *Preparing for College: Nine Elements of Effective Outreach* with SUNY Press.

Robert W. Danielson

University of Southern California

Robert W. Danielson is a doctoral student studying Education at the University of Southern California and has a B.A. in psychology and an M.A. in psychological science from California State University, Chico. He is interested in promoting conceptual change across various controversial science topics using metaphorical graphics, digital media, and refutation texts in both formal and informal learning environments. He is also interested in the public's understanding (and misunderstanding) of science and the implications on educational policy.

Girlie C. Delacruz
National Center for Research on Evaluation, Standards, and Student Testing (CRESST)/ University of California, Los Angeles
Girlie Delacruz is an experienced applied research scientist in the areas of assessment, learning, education, cognitive and learning science, and developmental psychology. Her primary research goals lie at the intersection of theories of assessment and learning in educational, training, and military contexts, with a focus on the design and use of various forms of technology including computers, Web- and mobile-based applications, video games, and sensor-based networks. In the area of assessment, her research focuses on issues of validity, effective and efficient assessment design, and the use of advanced computational models to support formative assessment and adaptive learning. Dr. Delacruz is a MacArthur Foundation/ETS Edmund W. Gordon Fellow—awarded to emerging scholars concerned with the impact of new technologies, recent advances in the learning sciences, and the broader impact of assessment and learning on society in the 21st century.

Kristen E. DiCerbo
Pearson
Kristen DiCerbo is a Principal Research Scientist and Lead of the Center for Learning Science and Technology at Pearson. Her research program centers on the use of interactive technologies in learning and assessment. Specifically, Dr. DiCerbo investigates the use of evidence from learner activity in games and simulations to understand what learners know and can do. She has also engaged with teachers to understand how to best communicate information about student performance to inform instructional decisions.

Arthur C. Graesser
University of Memphis
Dr. Arthur C. Graesser is a professor in the Department of Psychology and the Institute of Intelligent Systems at the University of Memphis and is an Honorary Research Fellow at the University of Oxford. His primary research interests are in cognitive science, discourse processing, and the learning sciences. He served as editor of the journal *Discourse Processes* (1996–2005) and *Journal of Educational Psychology* (2009–2014). His service in professional societies includes president of the Empirical Studies of Literature, Art, and Media (1989–1992), the Society for Text and Discourse (2007–2010), the International Society for Artificial Intelligence in Education (2007–2009), and the Federation of Associations for

Behavioral and Brain Sciences Foundation (2012–2013). In addition to receiving major lifetime research achievements awards from the Society for Text and Discourse and University of Memphis, he received an award in 2011 from the American Psychological Association on Distinguished Contributions of Applications of Psychology to Education and Training.

Noelle C. Griffin

National Center for Research on Evaluation, Standards, and Student Testing (CRESST)/ University of California, Los Angeles

Noelle Griffin is Associate Director of the National Center for Research on Evaluation, Standards, and Student Testing (CRESST) at UCLA. Through her work at CRESST she has led program evaluations in a variety of educational settings, including evaluations of professional development, science instruction, math instruction, and social services programs. Dr. Griffin has particularly focused on the evaluation of arts-based education and its integration into the K–12 curriculum and, in addition to her work with the Webplay program, she also led the national evaluation of the Leonard Bernstein Center Artful Learning Model. Prior to returning to CRESST in 2006, she served as director of assessment for Loyola Marymount University and has a continued interest in assessment and evaluation issues at the higher education level.

Xiangen Hu

University of Memphis

Dr. Xiangen Hu is a professor in the Department of Psychology and Department of Electrical and Computer Engineering at The University of Memphis (UofM) and senior researcher at the Institute for Intelligent Systems (IIS) at the UofM and visiting professor at Central China Normal University (CCNU). Dr. Hu received his MS in applied mathematics from Huazhong University of Science and Technology, MA in social sciences and Ph.D. in Cognitive Sciences from the University of California, Irvine. Dr. Hu is the Director of the Advanced Distributed Learning (ADL) center for Intelligent Tutoring Systems (ITS) Research & Development, and senior researcher in the Chinese Ministry of Education's Key Laboratory of Adolescent Cyberpsychology and Behavior. Dr. Hu's primary research areas include mathematical psychology, research design and statistics, and cognitive psychology. More specific research interests include general processing tree (GPT) models, categorical data analysis, knowledge representation, computerized tutoring, and advanced distributed learning.

Markus R. Iseli

National Center for Research on Evaluation, Standards, and Student Testing (CRESST)/ University of California, Los Angeles

Dr. Markus Iseli is a Senior Research Associate at CRESST/UCLA with a focus on integration of engineering and technology for educational purposes. Dr. Iseli holds a Ph.D. and MS degrees in electrical engineering from UCLA and from ETH Zürich, Switzerland. His specialization is in digital signal processing, speech and image analysis, pattern recognition, acoustics, and natural language processing. He has 15+ years of practical expertise as a technology and engineering consultant applying data analysis and artificial intelligence algorithms for technology-based learning and knowledge assessment systems. Currently, he is involved as a knowledge engineer in various private and publicly funded projects.

Rajesh Jha

SimInsights Inc.

Rajesh Jha is founder and CEO at SimInsights Inc. He has 15+ years of software industry experience designing and developing simulations and games. He has led the development of the SimInsights collaborative simulation platform SimPhysics, the early-learning platform KinderTouch, and various other games. Prior to SimInsights, he worked in the computer-aided engineering software industry for 9 years helping build the HyperWorks simulation platform used by thousands of companies to accelerate product innovation via virtual prototyping and optimization. Mr. Jha holds BS and MS degrees in engineering from IIT Varanasi and Ohio State University, respectively, and an MBA degree from UCLA.

Megan Kuhfeld

University of California, Los Angeles

Megan Kuhfeld is a Ph.D. candidate in the Graduate School of Education & Information Studies at the University of California, Los Angeles (UCLA). Her research interests are in the fields of educational measurement, multilevel item factor models, and teacher evaluation.

John J. Lee

National Center for Research on Evaluation, Standards, and Student Testing (CRESST)/ University of California, Los Angeles

Dr. Lee's current research is related to technology-based assessments in a variety of military, medical, and civilian contexts. He is working on the development of computer-based tools for the assessment of tactical action officers (TAOs), shiphandlers, damage control personnel, and engineering plant technicians for the Navy. He is involved with an evaluation of tools that process honest signals with relation to stress and depression with veterans, and curriculum analysis and development tools for the Educational Framework Initiative (EFI). He is also working on a number of technical projects for the Smarter Balanced Assessment Consortium.

Ayesha Madni

National Center for Research on Evaluation, Standards, and Student Testing (CRESST)/
University of California, Los Angeles

Ayesha Madni is a senior researcher at the National Center for Research on Evaluation, Standards, and Student Testing (CRESST). Her research interests include educational games, student motivation, social and emotional learning, and human learning and memory. Her current work involves students' self-efficacy and social and emotional learning within educational games and evaluation of technology-based assessments and tools. She also has experience in working as a learning specialist targeting student learning and motivation across a variety of student populations.

Richard E. Mayer

University of California, Santa Barbara

Richard E. Mayer is Professor of Psychology at the University of California, Santa Barbara, where he has served since 1975. His research is at the intersection of cognition, instruction, and technology, with current projects on multimedia learning, computer-supported learning, and computer games for learning. He is the winner of the Thorndike Award for career achievement in educational psychology, the Scribner Award for outstanding research in learning and instruction, and the American Psychological Association's Distinguished Contribution of Applications of Psychology to Education and Training Award. He is the author or co-author of more than 500 publications including 30 books.

Robert J. Mislevy

ETS

Robert Mislevy is the Frederic M. Lord Chair in Measurement and Statistics at Educational Testing Service. He is Professor Emeritus of Measurement, Statistics, and Evaluation at the University of Maryland, with affiliations with Second Language Acquisition and Survey Methods. Dr. Mislevy's research applies developments in statistics, technology, and cognitive science to practical problems in educational assessment. His projects have included a multiple-imputation approach to integrate sampling and psychometric models in the National Assessment of Educational Progress (NAEP), an evidence-centered framework for assessment design, and simulation- and game-based assessment with the Cisco Networking Academy and GlassLab.

Allen Munro

University of Southern California Center for Cognitive Technology

Allen Munro serves as emeritus research professor at the University of Southern California's Rossier School of Education. He conducts research on learning in the context of simulations, games, and interactive visualizations. Under the sponsorship of the Office of Naval Research (ONR), he and his colleagues created

RIDES, VIVIDS, and iRides—software systems for authoring and delivering simulation-centered training. He is interested in teaching, learning, practice, and assessment using simulation learning environments.

James Niehaus
Charles River Analytics

Dr. James Niehaus is a Senior Scientist at Charles River Analytics. Dr. Niehaus's areas of expertise include artificial intelligence, training systems, and health technology. He is currently leading projects to develop and run clinical trials on a mobile application to accompany a cognitive behavioral therapy for anger management, enhance physical therapy with video games and virtual coaches, create games to teach science, technology, engineering, and math (STEM) and entrepreneurship to high school students, and investigate the neural, cognitive, and behavioral relationship between implicit learning and intuition.

Benjamin D. Nye
University of Southern California

Dr. Benjamin D. Nye is the Director of Learning Sciences at the University of Southern California Institute for Creative Technologies. His research interests include modular intelligent tutoring system designs, modeling social learning and memes, cognitive agents, and educational tools for the developing world and low-resource communities. He received his Ph.D. in Systems Engineering from the University of Pennsylvania in 2011 and previously served as a Research Assistant Professor at the University of Memphis Institute for Intelligent Systems. Ben's major research interest is to identify barriers and solutions to development, adoption, and social intelligence for ITS so that they can reach larger numbers of learners, which has traditionally been a major roadblock for these highly effective interventions.

Harold F. O'Neil
University of Southern California

Harold F. O'Neil is a Professor of Educational Psychology and Technology at the University of Southern California's Rossier School of Education. His research interests include the computer-based teaching and assessment of 21st century skills, for example adaptive problem solving; the teaching and assessment of self-regulation skills, such as metacognition and self-efficacy; and the effectiveness of computer simulations and games to solve education and training problems, for example medical simulations. A prolific writer, Dr. O'Neil has recently co-edited four books on the following topics: what works in distance learning; assessment of problem solving using simulations; computer games and team and individual learning; and teaching and measuring cognitive readiness. He is a fellow of the American Psychological Association (APA), the American Educational Research Association (AERA), and the Association for Psychological Sciences (APS).

Ray S. Perez

Office of Naval Research

Dr. Ray S. Perez is a senior scientist and Program Officer at the Office of Naval Research (ONR) in Arlington, VA. In this capacity, he is responsible for managing ONR's Cognitive Science of Learning Program. This program has three major multidisciplinary and highly intertwined thrusts. Specifically, he is responsible for (1) training/education research and their core technologies, (2) individual differences research, and (3) neuro-biology of learning research. He also serves as the Service training lead for the Human Systems Community of Interest for DoD. Dr. Perez's research in the areas of technology-based education and training spans over 30 years. Throughout his career, he has received numerous awards for his work in advanced learning technologies. He has edited six books on the use of technology in education and training. Recently, he co-edited a book with Drs. O'Neil and Baker entitled *Teaching and Measuring Cognitive Readiness*, published in 2014 by Springer.

Gisele Ragusa

University of Southern California

Gisele Ragusa is a Professor at the University of Southern California (USC) in the Viterbi School of Engineering's Division of Engineering Education. She co-directs USC's STEM Education Consortium. She has expertise in multimodal research design, assessment, psychometrics, advanced quantitative analyses, and impact focused pedagogy in STEM. She is active in engineering and science education, teacher education, distance learning, program evaluation, and special education fields. She has been principal investigator on more than 25 federal grants through the US Department of Education, the National Institute of Health, and the National Science Foundation. Dr. Ragusa is also a first generation college student.

Jason Ralph

Naval Undersea Warfare Center

Dr. Jason Ralph is a human factors scientist at the Naval Undersea Warfare Center in Newport, RI. Dr. Ralph recently received a Ph.D. in cognitive science from Rensselaer Polytechnic Institute where he studied variations in cognitive strategies due to interactions with task environments. He is currently developing training programs and investigating the neurological and cognitive dynamics of multitasking and task switching.

Robert Rueda

University of Southern California

Robert Rueda, Ph.D., is Professor Emeritus at the Rossier School of Education at the University of Southern California, where he taught in the area of Psychology in Education. His research has centered on the sociocultural basis of motivation, learning, and instruction, with a focus on reading and literacy in English learners, and students in at-risk conditions, and he teaches courses in learning and motivation. He is a member of the National Academy of Education, and is a fellow of the American Educational Research Association and the American Psychological Association.

Anna Skinner
AnthroTronix, Inc.

Anna Skinner, Ph.D. is the Human Factors Program Manager at AnthroTronix Inc. (ATinc), a small, woman-owned human factors engineering research and development (R&D) firm. Over the past 13 years, Dr. Skinner has led numerous R&D efforts at ATinc in the areas of human–computer interaction, human–robot interaction, human factors design and evaluation, training and education, and physiological assessment within the context of both training and operational settings. Dr. Skinner received her bachelor's degree in Biomedical Engineering from The Catholic University of America (CUA). She completed her Master's degree in Human Factors Psychology and Ph.D. in Applied Experimental Psychology at CUA.

Elena Son
University of Southern California

Elena Son is a research professor at the Brain and Motivation Research Institute at the Korea University, where she teaches undergraduate educational psychology courses. Her research interests center on students' academic motivation, particularly of students of color and English language learners, and its relationship to language learning and academic achievement; motivation interventions; and the bridge between theory and practice. She has co-authored chapters on second language learners' reading comprehension and motivation.

Robert A. Sottilare
U.S. Army Research Laboratory

Dr. Robert A. Sottilare leads adaptive training research within the U.S. Army Research Laboratory where the focus of his research is automated authoring, automated instructional management, and evaluation tools and methods for intelligent tutoring systems. Dr. Sottilare is a co-creator of the Generalized Intelligent Framework for Tutoring (GIFT), an open-source tutoring architecture, and he is the chief editor for the Design Recommendations for Intelligent Tutoring Systems book series. He is a visiting scientist and lecturer at the United States Military Academy and a graduate faculty scholar at the University of Central Florida. Dr. Sottilare received his doctorate in Modeling & Simulation from the University of Central Florida with a focus in intelligent systems. He is the inaugural recipient of the U.S. Army Research Development & Engineering Command's Modeling & Simulation Lifetime Achievement Award (2012).

Roy Stripling
National Center for Research on Evaluation, Standards, and Student Testing (CRESST)/
University of California, Los Angeles
Dr. Stripling is currently the Director for Student Success Dashboard Research
Initiatives at the California State University. Prior to this, he was the Assistant
Director for Assessment at the Center for Research on Evaluation, Standards,
and Student Testing (CRESST) at UCLA. Before joining CRESST, he served
as the program officer for Human Performance, Training, and Education
(HPT&E) in the Office of Naval Research's Expeditionary Maneuver Warfare
and Combating Terrorism department. Prior to serving as the HPT&E program
officer, he worked for the U.S. Naval Research Laboratory. Dr. Stripling received
his Ph.D. in Neuroscience from the University of Illinois at Urbana-Champaign.

William G. Tierney
University of Southern California
William G. Tierney is University Professor, Wilbur-Kieffer Professor of Higher
Education, Co-director of the Pullias Center for Higher Education at the
University of Southern California, and past president of the American Educational
Research Association (AERA). His research focuses on increasing access to
higher education, improving the performance of postsecondary institutions, and
analyzing the impact of privatization on postsecondary education. He is a Fellow
of AERA and has been elected to the National Academy of Education.

PREFACE

Harold F. O'Neil, Eva L. Baker, and
Ray S. Perez

Why simulations and games? Computer-based simulations, intelligent systems for education and training, and games have become increasingly prevalent in both education and training. Games, simulations, and intelligent systems can improve the quality of learning in three ways: (1) better organized and efficient learning systems because they use learning and usability data as part of development; (2) tailored learner interactions with instructional material and tasks to meet the learning needs and abilities of each person or subgroup of individuals; and (3) powerful strategies to increase motivation, attention, and engagement.

Through the everyday use of technology, such as smartphones, and by the widespread playing of commercial games, most adults by now have already been introduced to simulation and game technologies, a fact that eases their use in formal settings involving teachers where they are increasingly more welcome.

Background of Technologies

Simulations, for the most part, were used in training environments to help practice or make observable elements not easily found in normal instructional practice. Games using technology have involved casual games, such as solitaire or bridge. The explosion of roleplaying games was closely followed by game availability on apps and tablets in the latter part of the last decade. Although intelligent systems for education and training have had a long, arcane history linked to research and development in artificial intelligence (AI) methods (see Carbonell, 1970), they have emerged from the laboratory and continue to be found more frequently in classrooms or other more informal learning settings.

Across technologies, although a major challenge, major advances continue in platform development and software functions, enabling the release of new and astounding interfaces at regular intervals. However, the effective arrangement of content presents similar difficulties with less progress. There is comparable urgency to create verified design methods and elements derived from the allied field of the learning sciences so that platforms can yield their best impact. Of similar importance is the continued attempt to bridge the differences in goals, strategies, and incentives to integrate in a timely manner the best approaches to learning embodied in the most up-to-date and appealing platforms. Also important is the continued conduct and sharing of research findings in learning to make commercial and scientific development more valuable.

While everyone has some notion of hardware and software design from their smartphone, the development and composition of learning science are not as well known. The most succinct definition of learning science, conceptualized by Mayer (2011), is amazingly straightforward: It is the scientific study of how people learn. Yet, although this sounds simple, learning sciences has many component subdisciplines. Part of this domain depends on scientific findings from research tracing in detail elements of student encounters and their reaction to content. Closely related is research on how to arrange these encounters in instruction, or more simply, how to teach.

Similarly, assessments in technology are part of the learning sciences. They are used to determine what students know at particular points to guide students' next adaptive steps and as outcome measures to provide evidence of impact. How assessments can be staged, distributed, and embedded in the technology to reduce their salience, the increasing use of data analytics, and the technical quality of these measures contribute to learning sciences as well. Moving beyond the purely behavioral sciences, neuroscience is providing insights about structure, function, and stimulation of attention, metacognition, and other key elements of human learning. It and emerging versions of applications are part of the learning sciences as well.

The chapters in this book focus on the use of games, simulations, and intelligent systems to report the uses of learning science to investigate the content domains of science, technology, engineering, and math (STEM). A critical STEM issue is to find a way to bring closer together different research communities in the game, intelligent systems for education and training, and simulation R&D areas. For example, there are rare interactions among researchers addressing both different content and level of learners. Math researchers may not interact much with those interested in biology or engineering. Scholars address different ages and sectors of learners, including children in K-12 schools, postsecondary students, medical trainees, and adults preparing for careers and military training. These R&D communities unfortunately have only intermittent scholarly contact. For example, researchers in disparate areas have their own specific professional identities contextualized in either civilian or military research organizations and read and contribute to different journals and conferences. Although there are bridging groups such as the American Association for the Advancement of Science (AAAS), the American Psychological Association (APA), the American Educational Research Association (AERA), and their foreign and international counterparts, they subdivide their membership into separate topical groups.

A similar separation occurs among those who wish to commercialize technology and those committed to producing tools to integrate the science of learning perspective into games, simulations, or intelligent tutors for education and training. Separation between academic R&D and the often more applied technology developers and commercial entities results in misunderstandings and more importantly lags in widespread applications from the sites of R&D and the commercial enterprises. As described above, there are few forums to share lessons learned about the design, use, and effectiveness of games and simulations across different communities and other technologies.

These groups also differ in terms of their perception of time available to make products. Academics invest in sensitivity, accuracy, and utility, to obtain a thoroughly vetted understanding of the phenomenon under study. On the other hand, the commercial world focuses on rapid scaling of "good enough" products. Although these differences are oversimplified for clarity, we are happy to note greater integration between academics and commercial enterprises. From the academic side, academics have an opportunity to see their findings scaled and sustained. From the commercial side, scientific or other empirical findings can improve the effectiveness of commercial ventures.

Chapters in this book represent a range of these views. In addition, the content reported in this volume varies in form. We include original scientific studies, reports from applied research and development, studies focused on evaluation, reviews of topics of key importance, and conceptual analyses of emerging options. Moreover, our authors come from multiple disciplines and are logically integrated by their expertise in investigating new ways to teach or assess in schools, in the workplace, and in informal settings. Experts from both civilian and military organizations are represented.

So who should be interested in this book? We suggest computer scientists interested in the scientific and practical approach to computation and its application (e.g., AI systems or analytics). Other readers should include teachers or designers of instructional systems, measurement experts concerned with assessing learning, and entrepreneurs who plan to make usable and effective products. Taken together, the book serves as a small signpost that says "Share here." In the best case, we will learn from one another about topics such as the importance of validity, the centrality of usability, and the next horizons ripe for research in the learning sciences. If we can leverage the best of these technologies to develop improved and appealing education and training, we will have made an impact.

Now to the details. The chapters in this volume vary from the articulation of broad theory or frameworks (Chapters 1–4) to more narrow in-depth descriptions of the following topics: Assessment (Chapters 5–8), Cognitive/Motivational

Issues (Chapters 9–11), and Psychometric Issues (Chapters 12–13). In the opening section, authors provide rich descriptions of various models and theories for designing, teaching, and assessing with games, intelligent systems for education and training, and simulations. The chapters in the assessment section include assessment theory, measures, and new methods, for instance, using crowdsourcing, lessons learned from intelligent tutoring systems, learning in team-based simulations, and the role of neurobiology in evaluating games/simulation strategies. The cognitive/motivational section provides chapters based on empirical studies focused on metacognition, cognitive process and outcomes, motivation and engagement, and the role of games to facilitate college access. The psychometric section authors address theoretical and practical insights regarding inference and the use of multilevel item response models.

In summary, the goal of this book is to integrate key theoretical and empirical issues arising from the use of computer games, intelligent systems for education and training, and simulations to teach and assess the learning and motivation of both children and adults.

Author Note

The work reported herein was supported under the DARPA ENGAGE Program (N00014-12-C-0090), and by the Office of Naval Research (N00014-08-C-0563), the Corporation for Public Broadcasting (20114720), the U.S. Dept. of Education (R305C080015), and the Bill and Melinda Gates Foundation (OPP1088937) with funding to the National Center for Research on Evaluation, Standards, and Student Testing (CRESST). The findings and opinions expressed here do not necessarily reflect the positions or policies of the Defense Advanced Research Projects Agency, the Office of Naval Research, the U.S. Department of Defense, the Corporation for Public Broadcasting, the U.S. Department of Education, or the Bill and Melinda Gates Foundation.

References

Carbonell, J. R. (1970). AI in CAI: An artificial-intelligence approach to computer-assisted instruction. *IEEE Transactions on Man-Machine Systems, 11*(4), 190–202.
Mayer, R. E. (2011). *Applying the science of learning*. Boston: Pearson Education.

PART I

Theory/Framework/Context

1

A FRAMEWORK TO CREATE EFFECTIVE LEARNING GAMES AND SIMULATIONS

Eva L. Baker and Girlie C. Delacruz

This chapter presents a broad framework for ways to consider the design and evaluation of games and simulations. The design rubric is overarching. From our perspective, design means the planning and re-planning of elements to be executed in a product designed for learning. We will describe the information that is included in the initial design and the elements that trigger revisions. Our own experience covers the development and evaluation of learning games and simulations created by academic, nonprofit research, and commercial firms. The framework we provide is intended to be flexible enough to encompass a wide range of potential development, and we have selected our emphases to highlight importance, innovation, and durable features not so affected by changes in interface or platform. The orientation we take is largely conceptual, with guidance on how these ideas might be made into procedures, but without any notion that there is one right procedural way to do this design and evaluation work.

The Centrality of Design—What Is Under the Hood

Our framework is grounded in the essential but fundamentally unsexy topic of designing the infrastructure that supports rapid and iterative R&D areas and simulations. When an important goal of the game is to meet an educational objective, much of the front-end game design efforts should be on clearly operationalizing those educational goals at different levels of specificity (Baker, Chung, & Delacruz, 2008; Delacruz, 2014). There are differences in approaches to the design and development of games. For example, in commercial settings, design is focused on how to make games within constraints (time and budget) and their aesthetic or marketing value. Agile development approaches support progress tracking of game software, and the asset development needed for integration. They emphasize timely releases during the creation of the game. They may stop at playtesting rather than accumulate evidence of the attainment of learning outcomes. We have observed and have participated in sprints (incremental development), stand-ups (daily coordination meeting), and a/b testing (contrast of different variations). This "agile" approach that derives from general software development is contrasted in the literature with so-called "waterfall" approaches, which are inaptly characterized as goal-focused, single-track development, involving minimal data collection and quality control, but without iteration or comparative version testing (Dybå & Dingsøyr, 2008).

In the current state of the practice, commercial games may not have learning outcomes paramount or clear evidence about their effectiveness, but despite the fact that they are not intentionally instructional in the school learning sense, they do support the development of some skill sets that can be applied in academic learning and in the workforce. Similarly, many games designed to be educational (or serious games) have aped the structure and strategy of commercial "play" games and are games with highly compelling engagement that simultaneously report evidence of consistent learning, particularly of difficult skills and concepts (Clark, Tanner-Smith, & Killingsworth, 2015; Delacruz, Baker, & Chung, 2013).

In our own design work we use a combination of the agile and waterfall approaches. We use a model-based engineering process to design and develop games and simulations (Delacruz, 2014)—a simultaneous top-down and bottom-up design process that goes beyond the typical design document or storyboards. In this approach, a set of explicit models are developed and revised to produce the game/simulation instructional framework and assessment architecture—a transparent and externally represented coordinated system to guide game design development and evaluation activities (Baker, 2012; Baker & Delacruz, 2013; Delacruz, 2014). There is a focus on goals, ontologies, feature analysis, instructional strategies, assessment, and evaluation. We will discuss each of these foci in the remainder of the chapter.

Goals

In this approach, a general slate of learning goals is articulated. This goal set includes the desirable outcomes to be achieved by the player, including potential optional goals that might be anticipated at the outset of development. One clear responsibility is to describe learning clearly and explicitly, without reverting to the empty set of response format, such as passing a multiple-choice test on troubleshooting disasters aboard a naval ship, which tells the designer almost nothing important about how to build the intervention. Instead, at this point, the emphasis is on getting more operational about what situations or tasks will be presented to the learner and a specified set of conditions or constraints that will define the nature of the tasks, in addition to the expected range of behaviors, actions, or decisions that could (and should) be made.

For example, when designing games to train naval officers on surface warfare tactics (e.g., Iseli, Koenig, Lee, & Wainess, 2010), the designer should be given detailed specifications of the class of problems the learner should be able to solve (e.g., mitigating communication failures due to poor data transmission), under what conditions and the context (e.g., equipment and personnel available), and information provided (e.g., a few pieces of high-quality information versus a lot of low-quality information). It is important that the designer also be given operational descriptions of what the learner should consider or attend to (e.g., is communication completely lost or intermittent, proximity to other members of the fleet) when making various choices and decisions to meet the objective or solve the problem.

At this point the work is about saying what the learning is to accomplish and how the designer will likely know. This set of decisions presages important choices to be made during the process of designing instructional options, as well as for developing the set of checkpoints or formative assessment options for the instructor to tell how well the student is learning. Finally, the goals, as fleshed out, present the core elements of the evaluation frame, the way effectiveness is to be gauged, and impact and return on investment calculated. What is not decided yet is how the learning is to take place. It has been the practice in game development to begin with an opposite point of entry, that is, storyboarding the sequence that the learning goes through and making the assumption that such a sequence will be optimal for learning.

To add depth to goals, we need to create options to be considered and reviewed. For example, we developed a game for the Defense Advanced Research Projects Agency (Delacruz et al., 2013). Our program manager had a general idea of developing STEM (science, technology, engineering, and math) games for children ages 5 to 9 in Grades K–4. We took that idea and moved it to a more specific goal premise: We wanted to teach children physics concepts that they could use in a game environment, and as a consequence of play, that they would learn. The first set of ideas was generated by knowledge and confirmation about what these learners were likely to be able to do. Some of our design principles driven by goals were as follows:

- Children would need to have ways to see the concepts in action rather than as abstractions.
- They might be able to be successful with nine or so concepts in a short 40-minute game.
- No child would be asked to deal with more than three concepts simultaneously (e.g., mass, velocity, friction).
- The cognitive process on which we focused was problem solving in a game scenario. Using a structure created by inviting cognitive scientists to give us their structure of problem solving (Mayer, 2011) and subsequently revised in versions by Delacruz (2013) and Baker (Baker & Delacruz, 2013), we

defined the elements of the problem-solving scenario (e.g., obstacles in the game).

- We also recognized that children at ages 5 to 9 might not have strong reading skills, so we needed to plan for scenarios with rebuses or pictures to convey words, or with audible supports.

Ontologies

At our institution, the Center for Research on Evaluation, Standards, and Student Testing (CRESST), we have used ontologies in math (Phelan, Vendlinski, Choi, Herman, & Baker, 2011), physics (Delacruz et al., 2013), communication (Baker, 2011), problem solving (Baker & Delacruz, 2013), situation awareness (Baker, 2011), and decision making (Baker, 2011), to name some examples. The ontologies are represented in different ways (e.g., network graph, matrices, text descriptions) to provide operational definitions at different levels of granularity to support the needs of designers, game developers, programmers, and data analysts.

In the course of our work, beginning with simulations of M-16 rifle marksmanship (Baker, 2012) and moving through math learning for middle school (Baker, 2012), we have used our model of ontology development. Ontologies are usually content driven and represent the relationship of elements to one another (Baker, 2012). They are developed often as vertical "part-of" sequences, for instance, when it is clear that if the goal were to identify a vector, then a part of that task is to be able to identify the marker showing direction. There are also ontologies that are less hierarchical but show relationships. For example, in solving a balance problem, the student does not need to address either the right or the left side of the fulcrum first. The process can begin on either side, so long as the result is achieved (Baker, 2012).

Specifically, we use ontologies for at least four purposes: First, they depict key elements to be learned. For example, in a network representation, the nodes with the most links may indicate a level of importance and criticality that should be considered in deciding on outcomes. They also display the range of the domain to be learned and support the idea of comprehensiveness. If it is decided that it is not possible to be comprehensive, the decision to exclude certain areas is made clear. This approach contrasts with a strategy that says the goal is to improve learners' performance on the construct of math achievement, consisting of rational numbers, geometry, and algebra, with items sampled for each but not explicitly weighted to reflect importance or relationships among major topics.

Second, because of their focus on relationships, visual ontologies can help decide the components of content that are prerequisite to learning particular goals. The prerequisites follow the notion of venerable educational psychologist Robert Gagné (Gagné, 1968; Gagné & Medsker, 1996), who suggested we ask a simple but important question: What does the learner need to be able to do before he or she can begin to tackle the next question? Gagné called his work "task analysis," and like ontologies they were created by experts with the expectation that they would be empirically verified. A variant on this procedure (Clark, Feldon, van Merriënboer, Yates, & Early, 2008) is cognitive task analysis, which involves interrogating an expert during the process of completing a task or answering a particular question to elicit what the experts are thinking. A set of student responses could then be compared to determine whether the designer was on target for estimating what elements were needed in instruction.

Third, the ontologies can help generate a best case or set of alternative sequences of learning, sometimes called learning progressions (to connote increasing learning requirements) or learning trajectories (to show individual or group patterns to various standards of achievement; Confrey & Maloney, 2012). As with component knowledge elements, these ideally need empirical verification for the types of learners and settings in which the product will be used. This verification process is expensive in terms of time and dollars. As a less expensive alternative to verification, we have used two other approaches. One is to use crowdsourcing (Law & von Ahn, 2011) as a verification tool to see the extent to which others, presumably knowledgeable in the domain, would identify the same components and sequences. A second approach is to consider the use of expert versus novice comparisons (Acton, Johnson, & Goldsmith, 1994). For example, one could look at how learners who presumably have mastered the tasks perform on what are thought to be subsets of needed tasks. These performances are contrasted with learners who have not yet succeeded in the skill area.

As ontologies based on problem solving only have meaning as they are embedded in the domain, for every major content node it is possible to extract elements of the cognitive ontology. For example, to succeed, a learner must be able to recognize or describe the concept and distinguish it from other members of its set (for instance, to know the difference between "<" and ">") before responding to certain probabilistic statements. Thus an important task is integrating the cognitive demands with the content ontology (Koenig, Iseli, Wainess, & Lee, 2013; Koenig, Lee, Iseli, & Wainess, 2010).

A fourth use of ontologies is in the design of assessments or other measures to be used during the various trials of the intervention. These assessments may focus on prerequisites identified in the ontologies, or in-game or in-simulation requirements intended to suggest that the learner is ready to progress, and in the outcome measures themselves, whether they are given immediately or following instruction to assess retention or transfer. We strongly recommend the use of transfer measures. Success on the measures means that the learner can take what has been learned and apply it in a new way, that is, transfer (Perkins & Salomon, 1988). The transfer may be relatively simple like a minor change in the scenario of the question or the objects the students are to manipulate. More difficult examples of transfer require applying a similar strategy (e.g., deploying something in multiple directions simultaneously) to problems that appear very different on the surface (e.g., military and radiation problems) (Gick & Holyoak, 1983). The transfer might involve modality, that is, solving problems on the screen and then solving the same circuitry problems on a board. In any case, the type of transfer depends upon the extent to which you expect the learner to apply learning in other environments.

Feature Analysis

Feature analysis, as we use the term, is a qualitative, low-inference rating system that is used to characterize elements or features of either assessments or interventions (Baker, 2015a, 2015b). The approach, derived from the much earlier work of Tatsuoka (1983), requires that components of an item, a level, or a task in a simulation be decomposed into its elements. These elements do include subject matter and cognitive elements that are represented or extracted from the ontologies in use. The idea is that the features are unlikely to be nested within any one task, item, or level, but will recur as the learner proceeds to completion.

In the early stages of our work, features were analyzed for test item elements only (Cai, Baker, Choi, & Buschang, 2014). For example, both stimulus and response options of test items were considered. Four major classes of elements were used: subject matter, cognitive demands, linguistic requirements, and task demands (Baker, 2015b; Baker, Cai, Choi, & Madni, 2015; Cai et al., 2014). Subject matter is taken to mean knowledge, including concepts and subconcepts, procedures and their principles, and examples thereof. Cognitive demands also include components of problem solving (e.g., problem identification) and conceptual learning tasks (e.g., discriminating concepts from close approximations, procedural learning, reasoning, and judgment). These elements are always embedded in the task and content elements. In addition, task features focus on the details of stimulus or material presented or available to the learner. These include directions, that is, what to do, as well as guidance on how to do it, and components that are presented to the learner, such as graphics, maps, charts, pictures, or a combination thereof. Tasks will also vary in regard to the number of steps a student needs to engage in, whether the task is linear or requires circling back, whether interim performance is required, that is showing progress, and the range of other response options. Some characterizations of the data have been binary (the element is there or it isn't) whereas others record the judgment of the raters, based on detail or frequency within the unit under examination. In our research raters have attained inter- and intra-rater agreements in the .90s (Madni et al., 2014).

The final major category of feature analysis involves the language or linguistic requirements for the respondent. These include type, amount, and density of discourse, and syntactic or world level elements. While it is possible that no written text is given for math items, if language is used to enable performance, for instance, through audio, then the elements are reviewed and classified. Our experience is that the more language is used, the more difficult the math test items. However, it can be particularly useful if academic discourse or words are used, with language specialized to the domain, such as math or biology.

Stepping back from surface features, we have also used student think-aloud elicitations, where we note any particular troubles or issues that can be inferred. Two additional sources of features exist. One is drawn from background information about the learner, for instance, language, instructional history, and evidence of prior knowledge, and so on. These may be considered separately, or based on data analyses, integrated in subsets of description.

The uses of feature analysis involve design and analysis. Presumably based on prior studies, designers or developers of interventions and assessments would systematically select features that traverse student requirements. For example, if it were important to develop skill in the use of particular terminology associated with a task, then the instruction would support the understanding of such terminology, using models, graphics, or synonyms to assist the learner's skill acquisition. Such assistance would extend across levels or test items if the terms were important in themselves or necessary to succeed at the task.

The features have a number of roles to play. In our work in testing (Cai et al., 2014), features were tagged for all test items used and those that were associated significantly with performance (item difficulty) were identified. Features could either be associated with higher levels or features or could be systematically related to lower levels (or in other words, with performance difficulty). Overall, we have obtained results that show that the features we have identified account for between 50% and 80% of the variation in test item performance, a surprisingly high contribution. Another obvious role of feature analysis is to use these features as partially comprising the model that we expect to emerge through the analysis of big data. This information could be supplemented by more exploratory uses of data mining. In upcoming work, we intend to include metacognitive and motivational features, both those appearing on the surface of the implementation and those identified through the use of sensors.

Instructional Interventions

Much has been written about instruction. By instruction, we are focusing on information to be learned embedded in the game or simulation. While it is well known that many of these interventions work in concert with teachers, the range of their behaviors will depend largely on what is required by the intervention. Hattie (2009, 2012) has synthesized a set of meta-analyses, which effectively provide support based on effect sizes, for various types of instructed strategies. The information that is proposed below for consideration, for the most part focuses on three attributes of instruction, the overall instructional strategy, the use of instructional variables as systematic elements in the overall instructional plan, and elements of instruction through technology that may need attention, for instance, how the system adapts to the learner.

On the overall instructional strategy level, there are at least two major but nonexclusive approaches. One addresses the overall scheme of instruction intended to be delivered through the system. Common elements that are addressed here involve the type of narrative (Dickey, 2006), or the type of role the learner has (e.g., independent, part of a real-time team, part of a virtual but human team, part of a computer team) (Garris, Ahlers, & Driskell, 2002). Other important strategies involve whether the system itself seeks to engage students in tracing their own learning, through the use of metacognitive strategies that prompt or model tasks such as planning or monitoring one's behavior (Mayer, 2016; Veenman, Van Hout-Wolters, & Afflerbach, 2006).

The purpose of including these strategies is twofold: to assist the learner to accomplish the desired goals in view, and to promote the routinization of such self-activating learning so as to improve the likelihood that they will be used in other systems or settings. This latter perspective was a driver in reciprocal learning (Brown & Palincsar, 1987). Common notions of instructional strategies—inductive, exploratory, deductive, didactic—depend in strong measure on the type of game mechanics and vision the developer has for learning. While summaries of studies have shown that there are relatively low effect sizes for inductive and inquiry types of learning, direct instruction shows considerably more power (Hattie, 2009, 2012).

In contrast there is little or no empirical support for the view that there exist specific learning styles for students and that by matching up student preferences with alternative models of instruction efficient and effective learning will result (Clark, 1982). De Bruyckere, Kirschner, and Hulshof (2015) summarize studies that largely undermine this learning styles approach. For learning styles to work, they note that people have to be clustered in definable groups and second, a disordinal interaction is needed, that is, a method that is good for one group depresses performance in the other, and the reverse. They go on to clarify that they are not implying that students don't vary, but that they do so in many unique ways.

A subdivision of the general instructional strategy has been investigated to determine whether different modalities work better for some students than for others. There have been many studies dating back more than 50 years, of learning through different modalities or channels, for instance, through visual or auditory channels (Murdock & Walker, 1969). There is also research (Mayer, 2009) suggesting that even the use of visual learning, whether pictures or other graphs are involved with text, can vary with alternative ways of placing the material on the page. Even though it may seem like common sense, recent research suggests that redundancy (same information conveyed visually and through auditory approaches) does not result in greater learning. But there is fairly strong evidence that students who lack strong skill sets or particularly relevant prior knowledge do not do well in conditions where they are in control of their instructional options

(Clark & Mayer, 2011). Instead, highly structured sequences result in better learning (Hattie, 2009; Lawless & Brown, 1997).

Far easier to manage and understand are a set of instructional variables that can be included in a variety of simulations and games. While the exact and appropriate instance of such variables remains an issue for the designer, the variables themselves can be easily described, and because they are supported by scientific evidence, can be employed with some confidence. The variables of most utility are determined by the effect size obtained of a series of independent comparisons with and without the variable. For example, among the variables with strong support is feedback, that is, letting learners know both that they are wrong and how they may specifically improve (Shute, 2008).

Implicit feedback is common is many games and simulations. The player may blow up, go off the rails, or run out of time before achieving a desired end. Their typical fate is to start over until chance, obtained tools, or a special insight allows them to progress. This start-over or reset is different from the view of individualized or adaptive learning, in which instructional decisions are based on moment-to-moment interactions with a student as in one-on-one tutoring or in computer-based situations that monitor and respond to ongoing progress (Glaser, 1977; Park & Lee, 2003).

We will consider it here under the rubric of how to improve learning, that is, the kind of elaborated process a student receives to catch up. On the one hand, students may see models or help complete examples of the problem they have just failed. In others, they may be given verbal or graphical hints on where to put their efforts. Still other systems drop the student back to an easier problem, and then advance them upon success, without ever explaining or helping them find reasons for their inadequate performance. There are insufficient studies of methods of adaptivity to improve student learning. Depending upon the criterion, level correct, complexity of correct performance, speed to criterion, or a combination, increasing adaptivity may be a good approach. But designers need to think through the range and options of adaptivity and fully test their effects in their own systems.

A negative finding that surprises game and simulation designers is the failure of "help" options in promoting learning. They seem to fail for a number of reasons. First, students don't use them voluntarily, without incentives (Delacruz, 2011a, 2011b), and second, reading through help or adjunct tutorials may be distractions, breaking up the rhythm of the game or simulation. Third, they simply add time and may inhibit completion in some timed interventions.

The major lesson of this instruction section should be that the games or simulation instruction should map back to the goals and ontologies that provide its framework, that instructional metastrategies are less important than one might think, and strategies that use specific variables that have scientific bases can be added to almost any format or set of goals in a way that strengthens the offering to the player. Finally, a/b testing is often invoked when there seem to be arbitrary or preferential options in game development. Creating a testbed that allows easy manipulation of important variables, for example, adding elaborated, different, or more frequent feedback, is really worth the time as measured by student growth (Chung, 2012).

Assessment

The entire development process is iterative, starting with goals and hypothetical learning sequences, which are sure to change as a function of experience in developing, testing, and finally evaluation of the product. Evaluation is the gathering of information to determine the merit, worth, or value of something to make programmatic decisions, which often requires quality assessment tools and practices (Scriven, 1967). Nonetheless, the assessment part of the cycle deserves its own section, as it is a major component of evaluation.

Assessment is defined as "a process of reasoning from evidence" (Pellegrino, Chudowsky, & Glaser, 2001) using tools "designed to observe students' behavior and produce data that can be used to draw reasonable inferences about what students know" (p. 42). Assessments designed for administration at the outset, during, and after instruction have shared and distinct properties. At minimum, they all should find a home on some part of the networks that make up the ontologies. Additionally, there need to be enough tasks or items to gauge a reliable score, to get to the point where it is likely true the learner should advance, get some help, or blessedly move on to the next system, with his or her own stamp of proficiency. A common statistical approach to determining the number of tasks needed is to conduct a generalizability study to estimate variance underlying the assessments as a function of number of tasks (Brennan, 1992; Shavelson, Webb, & Rowley, 1989).

Common Attributes of Assessments That Can Be Applied to Games and Simulations

- Assessments should reflect the cognitive and content demands of the goals.
- They should include different levels of complexity, or the elaboration of concepts and procedures to promote understanding of their core properties and support transfer to different settings or constraints.
- They should be completed independently.
- They should minimize cheating to discern as much as possible about the learner's true understanding.
- They should be objectively scored, which means open-ended items can be judged by trained raters with high levels of agreement, until artificial intelligent scoring can address meaning as well as syntactic features.

- Good assessments may be developed using a parameterized approach, where item or task models, content, scenarios, and problems can be rotated to provide a wide range of comparable options, subjected to human curation.
- Assessments need to be validated before they are used as outcome measures. This premise is to avoid the notion that they are linked inextricably to the system. They need to be validated, using data again from expert versus untrained people to see that they can be learned. Validation as repeatedly discussed (American Educational Research Association, American Psychological Association, & National Council on Measurement in Education, 2014) requires data relevant to the purpose of the assessment and the inferences to be made (Mislevy, Almond, & Lukas, 2003). Thus if the purpose of the assessment in process is to identify student needs for improvement, the utility of the item as a diagnostic tool is assessed. If the purpose is to use the items for certification of individuals, then these certification data may be compared to others certified through different means.
- Assessment is rarely used without a decision purpose. As indicated, some assessments, when properly designed, should guide the developer and ultimately the player to occasions where their learning might be improved or even advanced at a different rate. Some assessments are for the adaptation of instruction to student performance, that is, the learner model. Others used for certification, comparative effectiveness studies, or accountability have technical requirements, such as reliability or scaling that may conflict with understanding the performance itself.
- Assessments take many surface forms but should be chosen for the intellectual process and command of subject matter they measure.
- Often, assessment serves the process of evaluation (Scriven, 1967).

Evaluation

One of the purposes of assessment is that it provides a core for evaluating the product, both for formative and summative purposes. Formative evaluation is the process of gathering information to determine whether goals are being met, with the intent that the information may be used to improve the design of something if necessary. In contrast, a summative evaluation is used to describe the merits or value of a product (Stake, 1967).

The evaluation design may require that assessments be used often at the outset, during, and at the conclusion of the learning sequence. The content of the assessment will vary depending upon its use in the design or evaluation of products within the universe of specified goals, ontologies, and so on. When competing products are compared, as is often the case with technology-enhanced learning, the issues of research design need to be considered. Although currently a focus of commercial and governmental evaluations, a randomized controlled design has merit because the probability of differences can be estimated from the findings, assuming appropriate power analyses have been done. Currently, the emphasis is on the effect size, the difference in standard deviation units among the products being compared. Cohen (1992) describes effect size indices for small (.20), medium (.50), and large (.80) effects. This statistic has supplanted the necessary but now insufficient use of "significance," an estimate based on the unlikelihood of differences found on outcome measures.

Without elaborating here, it is a clear requirement for any evaluation that the design, with or without randomized controlled trials, should be specified well and that the outcome measures and other measures of process should be clear and valid for the purpose. For instance, many designs may suggest the use of a commonly used measure, for example, a standardized test, as the dependent variable for performance on products that themselves are only directed to a small portion of the test content. Because these tests often sample domains very lightly in their attempt to "cover" a domain, it is usually unlikely to find differences on them. If specially designed measures are used, then it is important that the outcome measures include tasks or components that are fair to the products being compared. It is also the case that pretests, sometimes intended to discern levels of general or product-specific prior knowledge, also represent products to be compared. This is especially so if the premeasure is used to adjust scores statistically.

In addition, the generally accepted sampling procedures used in research studies apply. These will include sampling students and other units to which the results are expected to generalize. To the extent possible, it is desirable to specify important contextual elements. What are characteristics of the learners? Are instructors involved? What is required of them? Have they been trained to use, facilitate, or simply oversee the learners' interactions with the product?

There have been long-standing evaluation notions associated with implementation issues derived from experimental research (O'Donnell, 2008). One focuses on whether the "treatment" has been used (or implemented) as intended. In technology products, such implementation issues would consist of topics such as the appropriate availability of learning platforms, the absence of disruption, and that the individuals participating interact as intended, that is, as individuals or teams.

However, in technology products there may be value in implementing the products in different ways, that is, in allowing the students and/or instructors to distribute participation as it makes most sense. If this approach is taken, then evaluation implementation issues become a process of documenting what happens, when, and if possible, why, rather than holding up the actual activity to a prespecified method by which the product should be used. It is likely, however, in the latter stages of development and evaluation cycles, a decision will be made about the importance of adherence to an implementation plan or the desire to allow flexibility on the part of the users.

With respect to reports of games and simulations evaluations, these reports vary by use. External or in-house evaluators will report to developers or to management, usually under a nondisclosure agreement that forbids the sharing of information without permission. When the evaluation is contracted by a funding agency, perhaps one that supported the development itself, there are usually rules and expectations for broader publication. In this case, it is important that any claims or problems are well documented rather than simply a high-level judgment of the evaluator. Second, it is desirable to include examples of what is referenced in the evaluation report. Third, consider the matter of differentially pitched reports for different audiences, for example, marketers, instructor users, and funders. Although it is usually desirable to have reports adjusted to the interests of the audience, special care needs to be taken that the inferences drawn from reports for different audiences converge.

An Example Game

To give an instructional game example, consider the educational physics video game, Go Vector Go (GVG) (Baker, 2015a; Baker, Delacruz, Chung, Madni, & Griffin, 2014). Subject matter experts (SMEs) with a background in physics generated the force and motion ontology that was used to design GVG by defining the higher-level concepts involved, including their relations. The SMEs and the science educators then worked out a suggested learning progression that outlined the sequence of instructional goals and the associated required background knowledge, plus concrete examples of these goals. These goals were then mapped to the high-level concepts in the force and motion ontology. Example instructional goals of GVG included that students should be able to identify specific elements such as the different forces acting on an object or which forces cause a change in the object's motion, and to manipulate the forces to produce a desired result.

We then used our specified instructional goals as the basis for designing the mechanics of GVG. To our knowledge, Go Vector Go is unique compared to other existing physics games because it uses a free body diagram (FBD) as the main game mechanic to elicit measures of the learning outcomes. FBDs use vector arrows to depict the magnitude and direction of forces acting on an object. We chose the FBD as our representation for two reasons. First, FBDs are standard models used by physicists to represent and analyze forces and motion. Second, the FBD seemed to be the best way to represent many of the underlying concepts conveyed in the game.

In GVG, students are asked to use physics concepts to help Vector the Train reach his destination, and along the way, to collect stars and to avoid obstacles such as dynamite (see Figure 1.1). As may be seen in the figure, to help Vector move, students manipulate various physics concepts (nine in total) such as force, magnitude and direction, mass, slope, and friction. Before deciding what actions to take, students must formulate the problem. They need to consider how

FIGURE 1.1 Screenshot of Go Vector Go.

far Vector is from his destination, any potential obstacles to overcome, and whether Vector is moving at a fast or slow speed.

We are currently analyzing gameplay data using a set of problem-solving features, such as the number of constraints a student must consider, how explicit the problem is as given to the student, and whether or not there are single or multiple solutions to the problem, as a way of understanding the variance in performance in the game.

We implemented a testbed where we could reskin or easily change the context of the problem, the degree of friction, and the mass–gravity relationship, all in the service of developing usable levels that reflected parameterization of the game assets as well as complexity involved in the students' successful responses (Delacruz et al., 2013). This testbed also supports the ability to implement different instructional and assessment approaches. For example, relevant instructional media (e.g., videos or graphical pictures) can be interwoven among the game levels, the sequence of game levels can be varied, and guided exploration can be made available. Data will be collected in a crowdsourced context to compare various pedagogical designs (formative evaluation), with the goal of designing the most effective version of the game to be tested in the classroom for efficacy trials (summative evaluation).

Summary

This chapter was intended to provide a tour through needed phases of work when considering the design and evaluation of games and simulations. Areas reserved for other chapters involve clear treatment of motivation and engagement, metacognitive learning, data mining, and topics directly related to training or to educational outcomes. As claimed at the outset, we have presented a flexible framework, built on broad principles, rather than a recipe. It is our intention that this can be used by designers, developers, and evaluators of all persuasions.

Author Note

The work reported herein was supported under the DARPA ENGAGE Program (N00014-12-C-0090), and by the Office of Naval Research (N00014-08-C-0563), the Corporation for Public Broadcasting (20114720), the U.S. Dept. of Education (R305C080015), and the Bill and Melinda Gates Foundation (OPP1088937) with funding to the National Center for Research on Evaluation, Standards, and Student Testing (CRESST). The findings and opinions expressed here do not necessarily reflect the positions or policies of the Defense Advanced Research Projects Agency, the Office of Naval Research, the U.S. Department of Defense, the Corporation for Public Broadcasting, the U.S. Department of Education, or the Bill and Melinda Gates Foundation.

References

Acton, W. H., Johnson, P. J., & Goldsmith, T. E. (1994). Structural knowledge assessment: Comparison of referent structures. *Journal of Educational Psychology, 86*(2), 303.

American Educational Research Association, American Psychological Association, & National Council on Measurement in Education. (2014). *Standards for educational and psychological testing.* Washington, DC: Author.

Baker, E. L. (2011, November). *Learning and assessment: 21st century skills and content ontologies.* Paper presented at the International Symposium of Organization for the Study of College Admissions, National Center for University Entrance Examinations, Tokyo, Los Angeles, CA.

Baker, E. L. (2012). *Ontology-based educational design: Seeing is believing* (Resource Paper No. 13). Los Angeles: University of California, National Center for Research on Evaluation, Standards, and Student Testing (CRESST).

Baker, E. L. (2015a, April). *Design issues regarding the use of games and simulations for learning and assessment: Feature analysis as a technology design and evaluation tool.* Presentation at the annual meeting of the American Educational Research Association, Chicago, IL.

Baker, E. L. (2015b, April). *The design and validity of new assessments: Windows on architecture, art, & archaeology.* Paper presented at the annual meeting of the American Educational Research Association, Chicago, IL.

Baker, E. L., Cai, L., Choi, K., & Madni, A. (2015, June). *Functional validity: Extending the utility of state assessments.* Presentation at the 2015 National Conference on Student Assessment (NCSA), San Diego, CA.

Baker, E. L., Chung, G. K. W. K., & Delacruz, G. C. (2008). Design and validation of technology-based performance assessments. In J. M. Spector, M. D. Merrill, J. J. G. van Merriënboer, & M. P. Driscoll (Eds.), *Handbook of research on educational communications and technology* (3rd ed., pp. 595–604). Mahwah, NJ: Erlbaum.

Baker, E. L., & Delacruz, G. C. (2013, April). *Learning and assessment ontologies of cognitive processes: Step 1: Problem-solving.* Paper presented at the annual meeting of the American Educational Research Association, Vancouver, Canada.

Baker, E. L., Delacruz, G. C., Chung, G. K. W. K., Madni, A., & Griffin, N. C. (2014, April). *Children's games for learning physics and social and emotional skills.* Presentation at the annual meeting of the American Educational Research Association, Philadelphia, PA.

Brennan, R. L. (1992). Generalizability theory. *Educational Measurement: Issues and Practice, 11*(4), 27–34.

Brown, A. L., & Palincsar, A. S. (1987). *Reciprocal teaching of comprehension strategies: A natural history of one program for enhancing learning.* Norwood, NJ: Ablex.

Cai, L., Baker, E., Choi, K., & Buschang, R. (2014, April). *CRESST functional validity model: Deriving formative and summative information from Common Core assessments.* Presentation at the annual meeting of the American Educational Research Association, Philadelphia, PA.

Chung, G. K. W. K. (2012, February). *A testbed approach to game development, testing, and validation.* Poster presentation at the DARPA Engage PI Summit Meeting, Los Angeles, CA.

Clark, D. B., Tanner-Smith, E. E., & Killingsworth, S. S. (2015). Digital games, design, and learning: A systematic review and meta-analysis. *Review of Educational Research.* Advance online publication. doi:10.3102/0034654315582065

Clark, R. C., & Mayer, R. E. (2011). *E-learning and the science of instruction: Proven guidelines for consumers and designers of multimedia learning.* San Francisco, CA: John Wiley & Sons.

Clark, R. E. (1982). Antagonism between achievement and enjoyment in ATI studies. *Educational Psychologist, 17,* 92–101.

Clark, R. E., Feldon, D. F., van Merriënboer, J. J. G., Yates, K. A., & Early, S. (2008). Cognitive task analysis. In J. M. Spector, M. D. Merrill, J. J. G. van Merriënboer, & M. P. Driscoll (Eds.), *Handbook of research on educational communications and technology* (3rd ed., pp. 577–593). Mahwah, NJ: Erlbaum.

Cohen, J. (1992). A power primer. *Psychological Bulletin, 112*(1), 155.

Confrey, J., & Maloney, A. (2012). A next generation digital classroom assessment based on learning trajectories. *Digital Teaching Platform,* 134–152.

De Bruyckere, P., Kirschner, P. A., & Hulshof, C. D. (2015). *Urban myths about learning and education.* London: Academic Press/Elsevier.

Delacruz, G. C. (2011a). The impact of incentivizing the use of feedback on learning and performance in educational videogames. *NASA Conference Publication of the MODSIM World Conference & Expo, Virginia Beach.*

Delacruz, G. C. (2011b). *Games as formative assessment environments: Examining the impact of explanations of scoring and incentives on math learning, game performance, and help seeking* (CRESST Report 796). Los Angeles, CA: University of California, National Center for Research on Evaluation, Standards, and Student Testing.

Delacruz, G. C. (2013, April). *Front-end efforts to support game-based learning, standardization, and IP.* Presentation at the Global 3D Standards & IP Forum 2013, Seoul, Korea.

Delacruz, G. C. (2014, July). *Setting up learning objectives and measurement for game design.* Workshop presentation at the Serious Games Conference, Los Angeles, CA.

Delacruz, G. C., Baker, E. L., & Chung, G. K. W. K. (2013, June). *Solving the puzzle: Designing games and assessment for young children's physics learning.* Presentation at the meeting of the Council of Chief State School Officers National Conference on Student Assessment, National Harbor, MD.

Dickey, M. D. (2006). Game design narrative for learning: Appropriating adventure game design narrative devices and techniques for the design of interactive learning environments. *Educational Technology Research and Development, 54*(3), 245–263.

Dybå, T., & Dingsøyr, T. (2008). Empirical studies of agile software development: A systematic review. *Information and Software Technology, 50*(9), 833–859.

Gagné, R. M. (1968). Learning hierarchies. *Educational Psychologist, 6*(1), 1–9.

Gagné, R. M., & Medsker, K. L. (1996). *The conditions of learning: Training applications.* Orlando, FL: Harcourt Brace & Company.

Garris, R., Ahlers, R., & Driskell, J. E. (2002). Games, motivation, and learning: A research and practice model. *Simulation & Gaming, 33*(4), 441–467.

Gick, M. L., & Holyoak, K. J. (1983). Schema induction and analogical transfer. *Cognitive Psychology, 15*(1), 1–38.

Glaser, R. (1977). *Adaptive education: Individual diversity and learning.* New York, NY: Holt, Rinehart and Winston.

Hattie, J. A. C. (2009). *Visible learning: A synthesis of over 800 meta-analyses relating to achievement.* New York, NY: Routledge/Taylor & Francis.

Hattie, J. A. C. (2012). *Visible learning for teachers: Maximizing impact on learning.* New York, NY: Routledge/Taylor & Francis.

Iseli, M. R., Koenig, A. D., Lee, J. J., & Wainess, R. (2010). *Automated assessment of complex task performance in games and simulations* (CRESST Report 775). Los Angeles: University of California, National Center for Research on Evaluation, Standards, and Student Testing.

Koenig, A., Iseli, M., Wainess, R., & Lee, J. J. (2013). Assessment methodology for computer-based instructional simulations. *Military Medicine, 178*(10S), 47–55. doi:10.7205/MILMED-D-13-00217

Koenig, A. D., Lee, J. J., Iseli, M. R., & Wainess, R. (2010). *A conceptual framework for assessing performance in games and simulations* (CRESST Report 771). Los Angeles, CA: University of California, National Center for Research on Evaluation, Standards, and Student Testing.

Law, E., & von Ahn, L. (2011). Human computation. *Synthesis Lectures on Artificial Intelligence and Machine Learning, 5*(3), 1–121.

Lawless, K. A., & Brown, S. W. (1997). Multimedia learning environments: Issues of learner control and navigation. *Instructional Science, 25*(2), 117–131.

Madni, A., Buschang, R. E., Michiuye, J. K., Griffin, N., Baker, E. L., Choi, K., & Cai, L. (2014). *CCSSO cognitive lab qualitative study results: Fourth grade* (Interim report to funder). Los Angeles: University of California, National Center for Research on Evaluation, Standards, and Student Testing.

Mayer, R. E. (2009). *Multimedia learning* (2nd ed.). New York, NY: Cambridge University Press.

Mayer, R. E. (2011). *Thinking, problem solving, cognition* (3rd ed.). New York, NY: WH Freeman/Times Books/Henry Holt & Co.

Mayer, R. E. (2016). Role of metacognition in STEM games and simulations. In H. F. O'Neil, E. L. Baker, & R. S. Perez (Eds.), *Using games and simulations for teaching and assessment: Key issues.* Routledge/Taylor & Francis.

Mislevy, R. J., Almond, R. G., & Lukas, J. F. (2003). *A brief introduction to evidence-centered design* (Research Report RR-03-16). Princeton, NJ: Educational Testing Service.

Murdock, B. B., & Walker, K. D. (1969). Modality effects in free recall. *Journal of Verbal Learning and Verbal Behavior, 8*(5), 665–676.

O'Donnell, C. L. (2008). Defining, conceptualizing, and measuring fidelity of implementation and its relationship to outcomes in K–12 curriculum intervention research. *Review of Educational Research, 78*(1), 33–84.

Park, O.-C., & Lee, J. (2003). Adaptive instructional systems. In D. H. Jonassen & M. P. Driscoll (Eds.), *Handbook of research on educational communications and technology* (2nd ed., pp. 651–684). Mahwah, NJ: Erlbaum.

Pellegrino, J. W., Chudowsky, N., & Glaser, R. (Eds.). (2001). *Knowing what students know: The science and design of educational assessment.* Washington, DC: National Academies Press.

Perkins, D. N., & Salomon, G. (1988). Teaching for transfer. *Educational Leadership, 46*(1), 22–32.

Phelan, J., Vendlinski, T., Choi, K., Herman, J., & Baker, E. L. (2011). *The development and impact of POWERSOURCE©: Year 5* (CRESST Report 792). Los Angeles: University of California, National Center for Research on Evaluation, Standards, and Student Testing.

Scriven, M. (1967). The methodology of evaluation. In R.W. Tyler, R M. Gagné, & M. Scriven (Eds.), *Perspectives of curriculum evaluation* (pp. 39–83). Chicago, IL: Chicago: Rand McNally.

Shavelson, R. J., Webb, N. M., & Rowley, G. L. (1989). Generalizability theory. *American Psychologist, 44*(6), 922.

Shute, V. J. (2008). Focus on formative feedback. *Review of Educational Research, 78,* 153–189.

Stake, R. (1967). The countenance of educational evaluation. *The Teachers College Record, 68*(7), 523–540.

Tatsuoka, K. K. (1983). Rule space: An approach for dealing with misconceptions based on item response theory. *Journal of Educational Measurement, 20*(4), 345–354.

Veenman, M. V. J., Van Hout-Wolters, B. H. A. M., & Afflerbach, P. (2006). Metacognition and learning: Conceptual and methodological considerations. *Metacognition and Learning, 1*(1), 3–14.

2

COMPUTATIONAL ISSUES IN MODELING USER BEHAVIOR IN SERIOUS GAMES

Markus R. Iseli and Rajesh Jha

The main challenge when modeling user in-game behavior in serious games is to accurately infer the users' knowledge, skills, and attributes (KSAs) from their actions in a game. The definition of the "A" in the KSA acronym in the literature varies from abilities, to attitudes, to attributes. We define the "A" in KSA to be user attributes that are not knowledge or skills, but are properties of the user that can be changed, such as attitudes, affect, interests, and preferences. This allows us (1) to include other attributes, such as, for example, mental or physical health, (2) to resolve some of the ambiguity between abilities and skills, and (3) to include various changeable factors of learning or mental or physiological change in our models. These factors are important, since games present a highly nonlinear assessment or learning experience and thus require an accurate validation, not just of the resulting computational models, but more importantly, of the process and assumptions used to generate these models. There are many possible issues and pitfalls in this process. Several recommendations to address these issues are given.

The accurate and valid modeling of human in-game behavior provides valuable information about the game properties, the user KSAs, and their interaction in a given context or environment. When analyzing the issues of user in-game behaviors we will focus on games rather than on simulations, since we see games as extensions of simulations where simulated real or imaginary environments are extended by incentive and reward structures that trigger human behavior and responses. Such extensions are capable of producing engagement as reflected in the success of the game industry. Leveraging engagement for learning has received considerable attention in recent years. In particular, games have been found to provide opportunities for authentic and appropriate knowledge representation of complex ideas, many of which seem underrepresented in traditional assessments (Behrens, Frezzo, Mislevy, Kroopnick, & Wise, 2007; Mislevy et al., 2014).

The objective of the modeling activity is to measure progress toward and to help achieve the overall goals of the game–user interaction. Overall goals often revolve around user engagement, performance, and learning outcomes which address different learning objectives, whether related to education, policy, or business. In addition to engagement and outcomes, models can also provide insights into other aspects of a player's experience and behavior such as emotional and physiological states, group behaviors, and patterns based on geographic, demographic, gender, and other characteristics. If models are used to guide business decisions that have an impact on revenues and other business objectives, companies often demand an evaluation of a training intervention program in terms of return on investment or increase in company value.

The four-level training evaluation model (Kirkpatrick & Kirkpatrick, 2006) is often used in the evaluation of long-term value added. This model, when applied to training using serious games, would evaluate the four levels by measuring (1) the user's reaction to the game, mostly done by using self-reports; (2) the user's learning that has taken place based on previously defined learning objectives, done by inferring knowledge and skills through observation of in-game behavior, before and after playing the game; (3) the user's real-life behavioral changes due to playing the game, done by observing if the user applies the gained knowledge and skills on the job; and (4) the results, that is, the value added by the training to the company.

We claim that user behavior models can contribute to computational analysis and inference making of both in-game and real-life user behavior (Level 2 of the Kirkpatrick model). This chapter will focus on in-game behavior models only, claiming, however, that the underlying computational framework for in-game models will be very similar—if not the same—for real-life models. The analysis and prediction of transfer from in-game to real-life behavior as well as the discussion of value-added issues are outside the scope of this chapter.

In order to define and delimit the different entities, such as KSAs and user and game properties, that play a role in the modeling of user in-game behavior, we use ontologies. Ontologies, as the term is used by the computer science and artificial intelligence community, can be used to represent, store, organize, assess, and convey information about entities and about relations between these entities. Graphically, entities can be shown as nodes, and relations between entities can be represented as links between the nodes. Applied to learning, entities can be replaced with KSA definitions, or simply KSAs. Relations (links) between KSAs can be of a temporal, locational, or spatial, taxonomic, causal, or dependency nature, to name a few. Taxonomic relations help define and delimit the domain and are useful for object-oriented implementations that use inheritance of object properties and methods. By adding semantic structure to the ontology, nodes and links can be expanded to also contain verbs or whole sentences, or by allowing nodes to be user IDs or people, ontologies can become representations for social networks (Lecocq, Martineau, & Caropreso, 2013). The graphical, networked nature of ontologies lends itself to the delineation, visualization, communication, comparison, and processing of KSAs, and domains or subdomains of KSAs. Thus, ontologies can be used as representation, storage, and organization models that can be combined with probability, graph, and network theory to form graph-based computational models such as neural networks, structural equation models, and probabilistic graphical models, such as dynamic Bayesian networks and derivatives such as state-space models and hidden Markov models (Koller & Friedman, 2009). The implementation of ontologies is simple, since many different ontology description frameworks, languages, and tools exist, such as the Resource Description Framework (RDF), the Web Ontology Language (OWL), and the Protégé tool, to name the currently most prominent. These resources simplify ontology accessibility and the interchange of information. See Jain and Singh (2013) for more details.

Out of the many game genres, we will focus on the modeling of user in-game behavior in serious games, since these games often require real-time adaptive assessment of the user's KSAs given observed user behavior, and thus need highly sophisticated user behavior modeling. The primary purpose of the serious game genre is about learning with engagement as a secondary purpose. Thus these games usually involve problem-solving tasks with clearly defined learning objectives and can address any domain from education, science and engineering, healthcare, management, planning, and others. It should be noted, however, that modeling in-game behavior might prove valuable for understanding the user–game interaction in other intelligent or adaptive game genres as well.

In-game behavior is dependent on many factors, such as game scenario, user KSAs, and other user-intrinsic or extrinsic factors. We claim that when modeling user in-game behavior it is important to account for possible factors that can influence this behavior and to know which factors will have to be neglected in the modeling process, whether for computational constraints, lack of viable modeling strategies, or lack of evidence, such as observations or measurements.

Validity

Most of the issues described in this chapter are related to validity. It is evident that interpretation of in-game user behavior should always be evaluated in the context of the task, the game situation, and game mechanics, the environment where the game is played, the user's assumed prior knowledge and skills, and other user attributes. The *Standards for Educational and Psychological Testing* (American Educational Research Association, American Psychological Association, & National Council on Measurement in Education, 2014) define validity as:

> The degree to which accumulated evidence and theory support a specific interpretation of test scores for a given use of a test. If multiple interpretations of a test score for different uses are intended, validity evidence for each interpretation is needed.
>
> (p. 225)

Messick (1994, p.16) formulates the delineation of learning domain and learning objectives and their instantiations as tasks and situations as questions:

> What complex of knowledge, skills, or other attributes should be assessed, presumably because they are tied to explicit or implicit objectives of instruction or are otherwise valued by society. Next, what behaviors or performances should reveal those constructs, and what tasks or situations should elicit those behaviors?

These questions have become an integral part of many subsequent approaches to assessment design and validation (e.g., American Educational Research Association et al., 2014; Kline, 2010; Mislevy & Riconscente, 2006). In Baker, Chung, and Delacruz (2008), validity criteria for the validation of technology-based performance assessments include the accurate specification of the user's KSAs and domain content, evidence of scoring stability and consistency, clear criterion performance standards, evidence of the user's knowledge transfer and generalization, and fairness of results. Herman and Choi (2012) offer an additional set of validity criteria related to assessment attributes (domain representation, fairness, value, utility, credibility) and related to validity of score interpretation (reliability, fairness, model fit, generalizability, sensitivity, comparability, consequences). All these criteria (Baker et al., 2008; Herman & Choi, 2012) are possible factors that influence overall validity.

Computational issues when modeling user in-game behavior are often rooted in missing or inaccurate user KSAs, vague delineation of the learning domain, ill-defined assessment or learning objectives, badly designed instantiations of these objectives as learning experiences (e.g., games and tasks), unreliable or incomplete measurement of observed behavior, and choice of inappropriate—and thus inaccurate—computational models. However, from a practical perspective, where the implementation of an accurate model of user in-game behavior is the objective, we think it is important to consider all possible factors that influence this objective. Because the achievement of this practical objective can be seen as a process that starts with the definition of the game users and ends with the interpretation of the outcomes and the ensuing consequences of game play, all design and implementation steps on the way will contribute to final model validity. This validity can be compared to *process validity*, as used in the validation of manufacturing processes, where process validation is done in stages from design to final monitoring and improvement—see, for example, the new process validation guidelines of the Food and Drug Administration (Long, Baseman, & Henkels, 2011).

Brown (2010) describes a "validity chain" for the process of assembling validation evidence for assessment, where the weakest link in the chain will undermine the validity of the overall claims. From this it can be seen that the different validity criteria are often dependent on each other, whether linearly as a process or some sort of chain, or nonlinearly with more complex dependency patterns. We thus propose to depict the dependencies of the validity criteria graphically as a validity ontology, where each node represents a validity criterion (or a possible threat to overall validity) and where directed links denote the dependencies between validity criteria. Figure 2.1 shows an example of a validity ontology that draws on the *Standards for Educational and Psychological Testing* (American Educational Research Association et al., 2014). For the purpose of modeling in-game user behavior the terms "test" and "population" were replaced respectively with "game" and "user," and since the standards do not mention computational factors, the nodes "Analysis and Modeling" and "Methods and Models Choice" were added. The figure highlights the main process of game-based instruction or assessment as a validity chain starting with the node "User Definition" and ending with "Outcome Interpretation" (bold nodes and dependency arrows in the center of the figure). It can be seen that validity criteria later in the process depend on

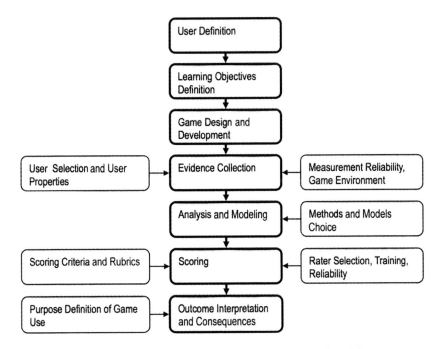

FIGURE 2.1 An example of a validity ontology for the process of modeling in-game user behavior. This ontology is based on terminology and validity criteria mentioned in the *Standards for Educational and Psychological Testing* (American Educational Research Association et al., 2014). The validity chain starting with the definition of users and ending with the interpretation of outcomes and resulting consequences for the user is highlighted in the center of the figure. Nodes represent validity criteria or factors that influence validity. Arrows indicate dependencies between nodes, e.g., scoring is influenced by scoring criteria, by the way analysis and modeling were performed, and by the selection of raters.

earlier criteria, which indicates that earlier criteria will influence the overall validity the most. The criteria in Figure 2.1 are as follows: the precise definition of the potential users of the game (node "User Definition"), the clear and concise definition of the learning objectives ("Learning Objectives Definition"), the design and development of tasks and game situations given the user properties and learning objectives ("Game Design and Development"), the reliable and accurate measurement of user behavior in a potentially distracting environment such as a classroom (nodes "Evidence Collection" and "Measurement Reliability, Game Environment"), the computational analysis and modeling of the data ("Analysis and Modeling"), which depends on the appropriate choice of methods and models ("Methods and Models Choice"), the scoring ("Scoring"), which depends on scoring criteria ("Scoring Criteria and Rubrics") and on how reliable raters are selected and trained ("Rater Selection, Training, Reliability"), and finally the interpretation of the outcomes and the ensuing consequences ("Outcome Interpretation and Consequences"), which depend on the overall purpose of the game for learning or assessment ("Purpose Definition of Game Use").

Since the determination of model validity (see node "Analysis and Modeling") is an important criterion in the overall validity chain, we recommend several ways to detect evidence-based model validity: (1) Model fit: Different model-fit formulae exist that calculate how well a chosen model and its parameters fit to the collected data (see also Iseli, Koenig, Lee, & Wainess, 2010). Note: If the data set is not large enough, a round-robin method can be used to select model training, testing, and evaluation data sets; (2) Model stability or consistency: If the same latent variable is calculated in different models or with the same model over different time instances, calculation differences for that variable will indicate either a model validity issue or a user outlier (e.g., the user was distracted at some instance in time); (3) Model inference accuracy: If the model can deal with missing data—as, for example, Bayesian networks do—the model can be tested by randomly leaving out evidence to see if the model accurately fills in the missing evidence. These are the main strategies used for model validation and, given an actual application, many theoretical and engineering approaches can certainly be derived. Depending on the choice of model, several validation approaches exist. We refer the reader to explore the publications for these models; for example, for Bayesian network models, Darwiche (2009) provides several formulae on model validation and model fit.

The following sections will focus on validity issues regarding the following criteria: "Definition of Users, Objectives, and Purpose," "Game Design and Development," "Evidence Collection," and "Analysis and Modeling."

Definition of Users, Objectives, and Purpose

An incomplete or inaccurate definition for assessment or learning objectives is one of the biggest factors that influence the modeling of in-game user behavior.

The definition of these objectives requires clear descriptions of who the users are, what the purpose of the assessment is, and what the learning domain should comprise. Ideally, assessment of learning objectives should be defined at the beginning of serious game design. If this is not the case, the specification of these objectives in retrospect will still be needed to build accurate and valid models of user behavior. Thus a clear and concise delineation of the domain in question is required. We define the domain knowledge, the skills, and user attributes (KSAs) that should be addressed for a given task and situation. These KSAs can be organized as proposed by Baker (1997), who lists content understanding, problem-solving skills, teamwork/collaboration skills, communication skills, and self-regulation as model components for a model-based performance assessment. Given the task at hand, other skills, such as psychomotor skills, or user attributes, such as persistence and resilience, might also be involved. Clearly written learning objectives greatly assist data collection and modeling, in addition to promoting student learning by giving students feedback on past and current learning performance and by recommending next steps. Once game assessment and learning objectives are clearly captured—for example, written down in natural language—the next step is to translate/represent them in a format suitable for computation.

While full-fledged domain ontologies can be time-consuming and expensive to create since they may require expert interviews, cognitive task analyses, and review of existing research and curricula, the authors believe that smaller ontologies, capturing the required KSAs specific to a game, can be created with a reasonable amount of effort. These game-specific ontologies can later be reused and assembled to form more complete ontologies, thus saving time and expense. Over recent years, ontologies that can be accessed online have become increasingly available; the mathematical modeling ontology (http://sourceforge.net/projects/mamo-ontology/) or the gene ontology (http://www.geneontology.org/GO.downloads.shtml) are just two examples. In addition to these online resources, ontologies can be constructed by analyzing textual information about the domain, including the written learning objectives, using natural language processing algorithms (Mousavi, Kerr, & Iseli, 2013).

An example ontology for the subdomain of force and motion in physics is shown in Figure 2.2 which shows physical constructs as nodes and their relations as links (arrows). It also contains a proposed teaching sequence that is shown as the path starting at node "matter" and ending at node "collision," going clockwise along the outer boundary of the ontology. This path, or any other proposed path, can later be used in computational models for adaptive instruction. This ontology was designed for kindergarten and first- and second-grade students to illustrate elastic collision of balls with their incidental and accidental angles of impact. Given these low grade levels, important physical concepts, such as acceleration, gravity, or momentum, were implicit in the realistic modeling of the game and were not mentioned explicitly. Thus, only a small subset of this ontology was addressed.

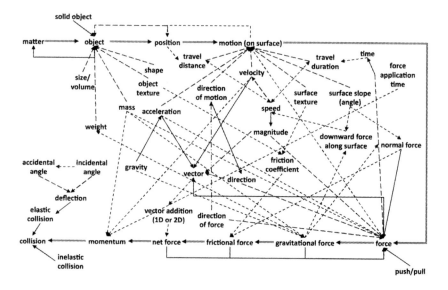

FIGURE 2.2 Example KSA ontology for the subdomain of force and motion in physics. Double arrows indicate a proposed teaching sequence, solid arrows represent *type-of* relations, dashed arrows *property-of* relations, dotted arrows *influences* relations, and dash-dotted arrows *opposes* relations.

Figure 2.2 shows an example of one particular way in which a learning domain could be described using an ontology. A proposed learning path starts with the definition of matter and then moves on to objects, which have properties such as size, weight, structure, and shape. Then the path continues by changing the object's position, resulting in the object's motion which can be described with the properties of travel distance and duration, velocity, and acceleration (acceleration was only added to illustrate the concept of gravity). Since motion was only imagined to take place on a surface, the properties of the surface were introduced as texture and slope. Then the construct of force was introduced and its influence on motion. By adding gravitational force and thus being able to calculate the normal force of the object onto the surface, frictional force could be determined. Combining all the forces, net force could then be determined using vector addition (with vector magnitude and direction). As mentioned above, momentum, though a very important construct in force and motion physics, was not defined further for this example. Finally, the construct of collision is introduced. Note that in reality there are many possible teaching sequences that need to be evaluated using user in-game performance data. The determination of optimal teaching sequences is an unsolved problem because even a suboptimal sequence depends on many factors, such as user attributes (interests, state of mind, etc.) and user prior knowledge and skills, game properties (game mechanics, teaching style), and learning objectives (domain knowledge and skills). Since "optimal" teaching sequences will depend on many factors, such as individual KSAs of the user, task properties, and situation, it is unclear if such an optimal sequence could ever be determined. We thus recommend dealing with this unsolved problem on a case-by-case basis and evaluating user in-game behavior using collected evidence and user feedback, until future research provides more insight.

Game Design and Development

In this section we discuss the issues with instantiating assessment and learning objectives—as defined by KSA ontologies—as tasks and situations in learning experiences (e.g., games). This requires the linking of latent (not directly observed) KSAs to observable behavior and performance in a game context or situation. For this purpose, it is assumed that the constructed domain and KSA models (e.g., the ontologies) are accurate and appropriate for the intended assessment or learning objectives.

Latent KSAs are called latent because they cannot be measured directly but have to be inferred by user behavior, given a task and a situation. The linking of latent KSAs to observable measures of behavior is important to create the computational models discussed in the next section. Using these models, the mastery of KSAs can be inferred from observed user behavior. As a simple example, consider errors observed during game play. These errors inform the level of mastery of KSAs. A common issue with errors is the definition of the latent KSAs that are missing: Shall the missing KSAs be formulated negatively as misconceptions such as "user doesn't understand . . ." or positively as "user understands . . ."? Our approach is to define all KSAs positively and indicate bad performance as low performance probabilities of the KSA nodes. Observations can range from simple measures such as the response correctness of multiple-choice items to more complex measures such as the ordering of a sequence via drag-and-drop events, to user in-game behavior to a problem-solving task. As one KSA node can be linked to multiple items or responses from the same or from different games, a more complete picture of a user's performance on similar KSAs can be created. Note that learning content such as instructions or feedback can also be linked to a KSA node, and depending on the user's performance can be presented to the user. The description of this procedure, however, is outside the scope of this chapter.

To illustrate some of the problems that can occur when linking latent ontological KSAs to observable behavior, we present an example using the force and motion ontology from Figure 2.2. Assume a multiple-choice item as part of a test assesses a student's knowledge (K1) on "what variables are needed to calculate the angle of a slope so that an object resting on the slope starts moving downward along the surface, overcoming static friction?" The student's multiple-choice answer will be a selection of variables from a list. The interesting and correct answer is that the slope angle only depends on the friction coefficient between the object and the inclined surface and not on the gravitational force on the object or its mass. What behavior would we expect that indicates some knowledge of K1? We would expect students exhibiting K1 to only select "friction coefficient," as opposed to students not having K1, who would likely declare other variables. How would we embed this behavior in a game? There are many options for how to accomplish this and several pitfalls to avoid. One possible scenario is to show a physical model of a slope and an object resting on it, to give the user the goal to get the object to start moving down the slope, and finally to allow the user to manipulate several properties, for example, mass, size, and density of the object, and the friction coefficient of the surface but not its slope. If a combination of property changes is allowed, we may never know if the user understands that only the last property change was required or if the user thinks that multiple properties need to change in order for the object to move. Additionally, if the game mechanics are unclear or complicated such that the user doesn't know where to click to change the slope friction coefficient, an incorrect answer might be evoked which should not be used to infer the user's understanding of K1. If other factors, such as time constraints, or obstacles are introduced, the correct answer might also not be the first response, even if the knowledge is present.

Some of these issues can be solved rather simply. For example, we advise to define clearly formulated, *atomic* KSA. We use the term atomic in the sense of the smallest necessary KSA definition granularity needed so that it will not need to be further split into sub-KSAs. Atomic KSA definitions must be sentences that contain at least a verb and an object, since they describe what a user is expected to do. When defining atomic KSAs, it is important to understand where and why basic errors happen, because these errors can reveal the thinking processes that are involved in solving a particular problem, whereas correct answers don't necessarily show the thinking processes, unless the answers show the solution steps. Finally, as a rule of thumb, atomic KSA definitions should be as broad as possible and as specific as needed.

Given above statements about atomic KSA definitions, here are a few examples: The nodes in the force and motion ontology of Figure 2.2 are non-atomic since they only represent concepts and their relationships but contain no verbs. However, the node "matter" could be made atomic by adding the verb "define" and additional qualifiers to form "Define the term 'matter' as it is used in the context of this physics class." Just adding verbs to the objects might also not be specific enough, as, for example, the KSA "add numbers" is most likely non-atomic, because there is no mention of how many numbers and what kind of numbers (e.g., integer/rational/irrational numbers, number of digits and size, positive/negative) are added. Without such qualifiers, the KSA "add numbers" is too broad to be considered atomic. However, depending on the application or game, the KSA "add integer numbers resulting in a sum smaller than 100" might be considered atomic, even though it doesn't specify how many numbers are added, the number of digits of the addends, and the sign of the addends.

As another example, analysis of user result data on addition problems involving two-digit positive integers might show that the problem 12 + 17 was answered correctly by most of the users, but that the problem 12 + 18 was incorrectly answered most of the time. Since the latter problem involves a carryover operation, adding the atomic KSA "perform carryover operation in addition problems" might be advisable. This situation shows the iterative nature of the overall process, where we have to backtrack to update the KSA ontology. Once the atomic KSAs are defined and to avoid the above-mentioned combination of multiple KSAs, we recommend designing in-game measures solely for the atomic KSAs. More interesting and more complex problems and in-game measures that are based on atomic KSAs can then be built. Finally, note that the definition of atomic KSAs is not absolute but always relative to the user, the assessment and learning objectives, and the overall purpose of the game/assessment.

Over recent years, the use of game design elements in nongame contexts to motivate and increase user engagement and retention has rapidly gained traction in interaction design and digital marketing. Termed *gamification*, this idea has started to gain traction in many business, marketing, finance, sustainability, productivity, health, news and entertainment, and last but not least, educational applications. Although the term gamification has its roots mostly outside of educational science, it is still important to see how it fits into game design. The term is defined by the Oxford Dictionaries as "The application of typical elements of game playing (e.g., point scoring, competition with others, rules of play) to other areas of activity, typically as an online marketing technique to encourage engagement with a product or service." Several vendors now offer gamification as a software service layer that can be added to existing nongame contexts and that provides rewards and reputation indicators such as points, badges, levels, and leader boards. Seamless integration of this additional layer with existing content is not guaranteed and there are intense debates about the viability and usefulness of this approach (Deterding, Dixon, Khaled, & Nacke, 2011). Generally, adding game design elements to existing nongame content and context or adding nongame learning context to existing games can negatively affect game play flow, user acceptance, learning outcomes, and, last but not least, assessment validity. Game mechanics can interfere with assessment or instruction, for example having to click on the correct answer for a given target KSA and at the same time having to dodge other game obstacles may result in failed attempts where it is hard to tell if the user failed because of a lack of target KSAs or because of a lack of experience with the game mechanics. Unless there is another measure that can be used to distinguish between the two outcomes, this measure of game success will fail to inform of the user's target KSA mastery. Note that pregame training modules on complex game mechanics still will not completely resolve the issue of added cognitive load during game play and the resulting potential interference with assessment or instruction has to be accounted for.

Besides the above criticism of gamification, there are many good ways of intelligently adding game design elements to existing assessment and learning content and contexts by exploring the positive motivational, visualization, and even social aspects that games can add (Simões, Redondo, & Vilas, 2013). Finally, we believe that awareness of factors that add to the cognitive load and affect learning outcomes is important: Low, Jin, and Sweller (2010) present a cognitive load framework and instructional procedures and implications for the design of serious games, and consequently, Huang and Tettegah (2014) analyze the relationship between users' cognitive load and empathy development capacity during serious game play and state that "the design of serious social games must consider the equilibrium between cognitive loads that engage players in the learning process and the cognitive allowance that supports empathy development" (p. 26). Cognitive load can be understood as the amount of cognitive information processing in short-term working memory. Cognitive load theory differentiates between three types of cognitive load: intrinsic (inherent level of difficulty of a topic), extraneous (load generated by the design of instructional materials, e.g., a serious game), and germane (the load related to the construction and automation of organized thought or behavior). Extraneous load has to be minimized, since it is not relevant to the user's attempt to solve a problem. See also Low et al. (2010).

In order to address validity issues that are influenced by game design, we recommend to (1) use game training modules to get the user trained in the required game mechanics before any in-game assessment takes place; (2) use small assessment modules where the game context (or frame) is clearly defined and where user actions clearly map to latent variables; (3) gradually proceed to more complex scenarios where more than two latent variables are involved; (4) be aware of problems with more than one solution or more than one solution path; and (5) try to get answers as to why users did what they did, which is not an easy accomplishment to integrate seamlessly into any assessment. Here, one possible approach could include multimodal data collection such as audio or video recordings of think-aloud tasks. These recommendations should ensure that the collected data will be interpretable, accurate, and ready to be used.

Evidence Collection

In-game behavior can be measured in different dimensions and modalities, resulting in additional information that can help improve inference making and model parameter training. This additional multimodal/multidimensional data can be collected using audio or video recordings of the user, electroencephalography (EEG), eye tracking, motion data, and other user-related activity. Since data can be collected at different time points, with different amounts and frequencies, and as different types (e.g., EEG, eye tracking, motion data) with different units (e.g., metric vs. imperial), their fusion can be a challenge. However, using appropriate models and data processing, it is possible to fuse very rich information, such as text, physiological measures, voice recordings, and body language, to, for example, detect affect (Calvo & D'Mello, 2010). Khaleghi, Khamis, Karray, and Razavi (2013) provide a good review of the state of the art of multisensor data fusion.

In order to understand and model human in-game behavior, user actions and reactions in the game need to be observed and reliably recorded for online or offline analysis, model training and updates, and model validation. According to the *Standards for Educational and Psychological Testing* (American Educational Research Association et al., 2014), reliability is defined as:

> The degree to which test scores for a group of test takers are consistent over repeated applications of a measurement procedure and hence are inferred to be dependable and consistent for an individual test taker; the degree to which scores are free of random errors of measurement for a given group.
>
> (p. 222)

Since the topic of reliability could fill a whole book alone, we refer the reader to existing literature on reliability in domains such as psychometrics, measurement theory, and engineering, to name a few domains.

In addition to reliability, data relevance is important. As outlined in Koenig, Lee, Iseli, and Wainess (2010), only relevant in-game measures need to be logged to get an understanding of user behavior. The definition of "relevant" data depends on the overall objective of the game, as well as whether the game is adaptive. For example, recording every mouse movement and mouse click event might be appropriate when analyzing psychomotor skills but would be considered irrelevant when determining correctness of task performance. In general, adaptive games require more data to be collected and faster processing to be performed so that real-time changes can be made and feedback to user actions can be given if needed. Protocols for offline data analysis, such as the format of log-file construction (Chung & Kerr, 2012), can inform the protocol design for online data collection. Despite the ease with which data can be collected and stored, inferring appropriate knowledge, skills, or attributes remains a challenge (Ash, 2011).

Analysis and Modeling

As mentioned in the introduction, user in-game behavior cannot be modeled on its own, since it depends on the choice of method and models and on various user-intrinsic and extrinsic factors that govern the user's in-game behavior (see also Figure 2.1). In systems engineering, which involves system design and identification, as well as in statistical analysis, it is necessary to know the possible factors that influence model fit. If some of the factors cannot be measured, they can either be estimated or inferred from other observables, be accounted for as random noise (with assumed distributions), or be declared as ignored if assumed to be small in influence. Unaccounted factors that are important but not declared will weaken any research study's published results. Thus, being aware of and declaring possible factors that have either been inferred, assumed, or neglected, is an important part of modeling and reporting results.

We distinguish between informational and computational models, where informational models provide an overview of the domain or subdomain, which then can be used to design and implement the computational models, which integrate the users' observable behavior. An example for an informational model is the KSA ontology for the subdomain of force and motion in physics shown in Figure 2.2.

Our computational models are derived from our informational models and build on models used in educational research. For example, evidence-centered design, or ECD (Mislevy, 2013; Mislevy & Riconscente, 2006; Rupp, Gushta, Mislevy, & Shaffer, 2010), provides a formal framework for designing assessments in line with Messick's (1994) guiding questions and contains three main model components: the student model, the evidence model, and the task model. The student model contains the user's KSAs which are inferred from the evidence model, which in turn maps observed evidence to the KSAs. Finally, the task model puts the evidence into context by creating a task.

In the assessment context, KSAs are the knowledge, skills, and attributes required to master or solve a task. Also, KSAs are latent variables that cannot be measured directly and have to be inferred from observed evidence (e.g., user behavior). This connection between learning, behavior, and context provides support for the validity of what is being assessed. See also Rupp et al. (2010) and Behrens et al. (2007). Koenig et al. (2010) developed a conceptual framework for analyzing the data from interactive games that relies on dynamic Bayesian networks to represent students' real-time actions and decisions. This representation can feed both formative and summative assessments of student performance to provide information about their knowledge, skills, and attributes.

We believe that it is crucial to model user behavior holistically, and to address the complexity of the user, the learning process, and the context of the learning experiences. Figure 2.3 shows a general computational model of the assessment and learning process where information flow or dependencies are shown as arrows between nodes that can represent states of user KSAs, states of the game, states of learning objectives, and so on. Because this model is general and doesn't show particular KSAs, it is thus domain-independent and can be applied to various modeling scenarios. The model represents user traits that usually do not change or only change slowly over time (node "User Demographics, Gender, Culture, Social Norms"), user attributes that can change over time, such as preferences,

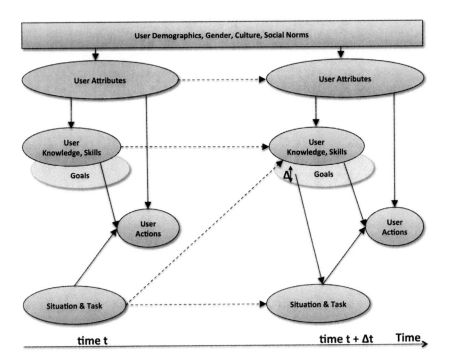

FIGURE 2.3 A proposed general, computational model of the process of assessment and learning. Solid arrows indicate dependencies or data flow, dashed arrows stand for time dependencies or data flow.

interests, personal objectives, attitudes, rapport, emotions, values, ethics, faith, and beliefs, which in turn can be influenced by persuasion, authority, or coercion (node "User Attributes"), user knowledge and skills (node "User Knowledge, Skills"), as well as user actions and responses (node "User Actions") to tasks and situations (node "Situations and Task").

Comparing Figure 2.3 to the ECD student model, we see that (1) the subgraph including nodes "User Attributes" and "User Knowledge, Skills" could be expressed with an ECD student model; (2) the subgraph including the student model nodes and the node "User Actions" align with the ECD evidence model; and (3) the subgraph including nodes "User Actions" and "Situation and Task" could be represented with an ECD task model. In addition to the ECD model, the model shown in Figure 2.3 adds a time-dependency component (dashed arrows), which allows for modeling processes that evolve over time. For example, the longitudinal evolution of KSA states could be imagined as a path through an N-dimensional space, where each KSA state along this path represents knowledge, skills, and attributes at a certain instant in time. The number of dimensions would in this case be equivalent to the number of latent variables that describe a user's state. Employing control theory to this example, we can now define a learning goal function and by defining a distance metric on the given state-space, we can then calculate the distance from the current KSA state to the goal KSA state, and decide on future "Situation and Task" states that would potentially address these discrepancies, minimizing the distance between current KSA and objective KSA states. This minimization can be achieved using several state-of-the-art linear or nonlinear optimization techniques (see, for example, Nise, 2010).

Though Figure 2.3 seems to show a monolithic computational model similar to a state-space model, its parts can be implemented using different models, such as the ECD approach. We have used dynamic Bayesian networks (DBNs) as instantiations of state-space models (Iseli et al., 2010; Koenig et al., 2010). While DBNs are well grounded in theory, they also have high computational complexity, since they have to update probabilities throughout all observed time slices. To reduce the complexity of having to process DBNs, we connect (static) Bayesian networks that model the time-slices of a dynamic Bayesian network, and where posterior probabilities from a previous time-slice are used as priors for the next time-slice. A time-domain representation of state-space models is well suited to implement methods of control theory. We believe that combinations of probabilistic graphical models (Koller & Friedman, 2009), item–response-theory models (e.g., Cai, 2010), diagnostic classification models (Rupp, Templin, & Henson, 2010), Bayesian knowledge tracing (BKT) models (see a review of BKT and other models in Desmarais & Baker, 2012), and more general state-space models from domains such as engineering (Friedland, 2005; Nise, 2010) may also be possible. In the end, model validation and performance will show which combination of theoretical and computational models will work best for which situations, tasks, actions, and KSAs.

Conclusions and Outlook

In conclusion, rapid adoption of games in education is creating opportunities for leveraging model-based assessment and instruction. We discussed issues related to user in-game behavior modeling, an endeavor that if accurate and valid provides valuable information about game properties, user attributes, and their interaction in a given context or environment. However, development and implementation of good models remains a challenging task with many issues involved. This chapter described many key issues and offered recommendations for addressing several of them, and thus is expected to be useful to practitioners engaged in model building and implementation.

We provided a definition of KSA (knowledge, skills, and attributes) that distinguishes itself from other definitions: We define the "A" in KSA as user attributes, properties of the user that can be changed, such as attitudes, affect, interests, and preferences. This allows us (1) to distinguish from ingrained user traits; (2) to resolve some of the ambiguity between abilities and skills; and (3) to include various factors of user learning or change in our models. We also introduced the term atomic KSA in the sense of the smallest necessary KSA granularity needed. The definition of atomic KSAs is not absolute but always relative to the user, the assessment and learning objectives, and the overall purpose of the game/assessment.

We stated that (1) accurate representations and delineations of KSAs and domain content are needed in order to inform the construction of viable computational models; (2) possible factors that influence game behavior, and thus learning outcomes, have to be stated and their omission reported; and (3) overall validity of game performance can be evaluated as a validity chain where validities of the realization of different game components and game design stages influence each other.

To depict the dependencies of validity criteria graphically we proposed a validity ontology in which each node represents a validity criterion or a factor that influences a criterion, and in which directed links denote the dependencies between these nodes. The structure of these graphs may indicate the relative importance of validity criteria: Because incomplete or inaccurate definitions for users, objectives, and purpose are at the root of the presented dependency graph, we consider them as the biggest factors that influence the modeling of in-game user behavior.

We proposed the use of ontologies as informational models to represent, store, organize, assess, and convey information. For computational models we proposed probabilistic graphical networks, such as Bayesian networks and state-space models, since they all share a graphical structure with the ontologies and can be derived from them. These models are very well grounded in theory and by research in different domains, such as control theory, graph theory, and probability (Darwiche, 2009; Koller & Friedman, 2009; Nise, 2010). However, since not all theoretical models work well in practice we also presented a few engineering approaches to make these models more viable in practice.

Looking ahead, we are inspired by the possibility of borrowing modeling approaches developed in fields other than education and psychometrics, such as physics, engineering, signal processing, control systems, and graph theory, to name a few. Researchers in these fields have developed techniques for modeling systems composed of many complex interacting subsystems and those techniques hold promise for modeling the serious game, the learner, and the game-learner interaction.

Author Note

The work reported herein was supported by the Office of Naval Research, grant numbers N00014-08-C-0563, N00014-08-1-0126, and N00014-14-1-0664, the Bill and Melinda Gates Foundation, grant number OPP1003019, the U.S. Department of Education, grant number R305C080015, the U.S. Army/Medical

Research Acquisition Activity, grant number W8IXWH-11-C-0529, and the Roddenberry Foundation, grant number 20150038, with direct or indirect funding to the National Center for Research on Evaluation, Standards, and Student Testing (CRESST). The findings and opinions expressed in this chapter are those of the authors and do not necessarily reflect the positions or policies of the funding agencies.

References

American Educational Research Association, American Psychological Association, & National Council on Measurement in Education. (2014). *Standards for educational and psychological testing*. Washington, DC: Author.

Ash, K. (2011). Digital gaming goes academic. *Education Week, 30*(25), 24–28. Retrieved from http://static.ow.ly/docs/Gaming Goes Academic_cth.pdf

Baker, E. L. (1997). Model-based performance assessment. *Theory Into Practice, 36*(4), 247–254.

Baker, E. L., Chung, G. K. W. K., & Delacruz, G. C. (2008). Design and validation of technology-based performance assessments. In J. M. Spector, M. D. Merrill, J. J. G. van Merriënboer, & M. P. Driscoll (Eds.), *Handbook of research on educational communications and technology* (3rd ed., pp. 595–604). Mahwah, NJ: Erlbaum.

Behrens, J. T., Frezzo, D., Mislevy, R., Kroopnick, M., & Wise, D. (2007). Structural, functional, and semiotic symmetries in simulation-based games and assessments. In E. L. Baker, W. Wulfeck, & H. F. O'Neil (Eds.), *Assessment of problem solving using simulations* (pp. 59–80). New York, NY: Erlbaum.

Brown, G. T. L. (2010). Assessment: Principles and practice. In R. Cantwell & J. Scevak (Eds.), *An academic life: A handbook for new academics* (pp. 35–44). Melbourne, Australia: ACER Press.

Cai, L. (2010). A two-tier full-information item factor analysis model with applications. *Psychometrika*, 581–612.

Calvo, R., & D'Mello, S. (2010). Affect detection: An interdisciplinary review of models, methods, and their applications. *IEEE Transactions on Affective Computing, 1*(1), 18–37. Retrieved from http://ieeexplore.ieee.org/xpls/abs_all.jsp?arnumber=5520655

Chung, G. K. W. K., & Kerr, D. S. (2012). *A primer on data logging to support extraction of meaningful information from educational games: An example from Save Patch* (CRESST Report 814). Los Angeles: University of California, National Center for Research on Evaluation, Standards, and Student Testing.

Darwiche, A. (2009). *Modeling and reasoning with Bayesian networks*. New York, NY: Cambridge University Press.

Desmarais, M. C., & Baker, R. S. J. d. (2012). A review of recent advances in learner and skill modeling in intelligent learning environments. *User Modeling and User-Adapted Interaction, 22*, 9–38. doi:10.1007/s11257-011-9106-8

Deterding, S., Dixon, D., Khaled, R., & Nacke, L. (2011). From game design elements to gamefulness: Defining "gamification." In *Proceedings of the 15th International Academic MindTrek Conference: Envisioning Future Media Environments* (pp. 9–15). New York, NY: ACM. Retrieved from http://dl.acm.org/citation.cfm?id=2181040

Friedland, B. (2005). *Control system design: An introduction to state-space methods*. Mineola, NY: Dover Publications.

Gamification. (2015). In *Oxford Dictionaries*. Retrieved from www.oxforddictionaries. com/us/definition/american_english/gamification

Herman, J. L., & Choi, K. (2012). *Validation of ELA and mathematics assessments: A general approach*. Los Angeles: University of California, National Center for Research on Evaluation, Standards, and Student Testing.

Huang, W.-H. D., & Tettegah, S. (2014). Cognitive load and empathy in serious games: A conceptual framework. In J. Bishop (Ed.), *Gamification for human factors integration: Social, education, and psychological issues* (pp. 17–30). Hershey, PA: Information Science Reference.

Iseli, M. R., Koenig, A. D., Lee, J. J., & Wainess, R. (2010). *Automated assessment of complex task performance in games and simulations* (CRESST Report 775). Los Angeles: University of California, National Center for Research on Evaluation, Standards, and Student Testing.

Jain, V., & Singh, M. (2013). Ontology development and query retrieval using Protégé tool. *International Journal of Intelligent Systems and Applications, 5*(9), 67–75. doi:10.5815/ ijisa.2013.09.08

Khaleghi, B., Khamis, A., Karray, F. O., & Razavi, S. N. (2013). Multisensor data fusion: A review of the state-of-the-art. *Information Fusion, 14*(1), 28–44. doi:10.1016/j.inffus. 2011.08.001

Kirkpatrick, D. L., & Kirkpatrick, J. D. (2006). *Evaluating training programs: The four levels* (3rd ed.). San Francisco: Berrett-Koehler.

Kline, P. (2010). *The handbook of psychological testing* (2nd ed.). New York, NY: Routledge.

Koenig, A. D., Lee, J. J., Iseli, M. R., & Wainess, R. (2010). *A conceptual framework for assessing performance in games and simulations* (CRESST Report 771). Los Angeles, CA: University of California, National Center for Research on Evaluation, Standards, and Student Testing.

Koller, D., & Friedman, N. (2009). *Probabilistic graphical models: Principles and techniques*. Cambridge, MA: MIT Press.

Lecocq, R., Martineau, E., & Caropreso, M. F. (2013). An ontology-based Social Network Analysis prototype. *IEEE International Multi-Disciplinary Conference on Cognitive Methods in Situation Awareness and Decision Support (CogSIMA)*, 149–154. doi:10.1109/Cog SIMA.2013.6523839

Long, M., Baseman, H., & Henkels, W. D. (2011). FDA's new process validation guid-ance: Industry reaction, questions, and challenges. *Pharmaceutical Technology, 35*, s16–s23.

Low, R., Jin, P., & Sweller, J. (2010). Learners' cognitive load when using educational technology. In R. Van Eck (Ed.), *Gaming and cognition: Theories and practice from the learning sciences* (pp. 169–188). Hershey, PA: Information Science Reference.

Messick, S. (1994). The interplay of evidence and consequences in the validation of performance assessments. *Educational Researcher, 23*(2), 13–23. doi:10.3102/0013189X 023002013

Mislevy, R. J. (2013). Evidence-centered design for simulation-based assessment. *Military Medicine, 178*(10S), 107–114. doi:10.7205/MILMED-D-13-00213

Mislevy, R. J., Oranje, A., Bauer, M. I., von Davier, A., Hao, J., Corrigan, S., ... John, M. (2014). *Psychometric considerations in game-based assessment*. Redwood City, CA: GlassLab. Available from http://glasslabgames.org/research/

Mislevy, R. J., & Riconscente, M. M. (2006). Evidence-centered assessment design. In S. Downing & T. Haladyna (Eds.), *Handbook of test development* (pp. 61–90). Mahwah, NJ: Erlbaum.

Mousavi, H., Kerr, D., & Iseli, M. R. (2013). *Unsupervised ontology generation from unstructured text* (CRESST Report 827). Los Angeles: University of California, National Center for Research on Evaluation, Standards, and Student Testing.

Nise, N. S. (2010). *Control systems engineering* (6th ed.). New York, NY: John Wiley & Sons.

Rupp, A. A., Gushta, M., Mislevy, R. J., & Shaffer, D. W. (2010). Evidence-centered design of epistemic games: Measurement principles for complex learning environments. *Journal of Technology, Learning, and Assessment, 8*(4). Retrieved from www.jtla.org

Rupp, A., Templin, J., & Henson, R. A. (2010). *Diagnostic measurement: Theory, methods, and applications.* New York, NY: The Guilford Press.

Simões, J., Redondo, R. D., & Vilas, A. F. (2013). A social gamification framework for a K-6 learning platform. *Computers in Human Behavior, 29*(2), 345–353. doi:10.1016/j.chb.2012.06.007

3

A FRAMEWORK FOR VALIDATING 21ST CENTURY ASSESSMENT TOOLS

Roy Stripling, John J. Lee, and Joseph V. Cohn

Our world is becoming increasingly connected through mobile digital technologies. As of June 2014, Internet World Stats estimated that around 87% of the North American population and around 70% of the European population is connected in some way to the web. Outside of these regions the numbers are smaller but rapidly growing: Internet usage in Africa has grown by close to 6,000% over the past 15 years, while Internet usage in other regions has shown similar growth ranging from over 1,600% in Latin America to over 3,000% in the Middle East (Internet World Stats, 2014). In mid-2014, mobile devices replaced desktop and laptop computers as the single most common method to access the Web in the United States (Perez, 2014). Of additional interest, Cisco (2015) predicts that by 2019, 89% of mobile devices in North America will be smart devices, defined as "having advanced computing and multimedia capabilities with a minimum of 3G connectivity" (p. 8). Likewise by 2019, 70% of Europe's mobile devices will be smart, 61% in Latin America, 56% in the Asia Pacific region, and 41% in the Middle East and Africa (Cisco, 2015). This shift away from the tethered connections afforded by laptops and PCs toward untethered connections afforded by low-footprint smart devices (Horowitz, 2010) is accompanied by advances in data collection capabilities which enable multimodal and real-time sharing of information (Uti & Fox, 2010).

As mobile devices become more capable and more powerful, they will become increasingly embedded in our daily patterns of life (Atzori, Iera, Morabito, & Nitti, 2012; Gershenfeld, Krikorian, & Cohen, 2004). In 2014, 57% of smartphone users reported using apps on their phone every single day, while 79% reported using apps at least 26 days per month (Perez, 2014). Consequently, mobile devices may represent a novel and more natural means for collecting long-term data about an individual's behaviors, which has long been a barrier to progress in the behavioral sciences. Because of the difficulties inherent in collecting these pattern-of-life data, most behavioral studies require practitioners to use relatively constrained test instruments, validated against a large population, from which to draw their conclusions. Drawing these inferences is always statistically risky, and thus, a natural tendency in the behavioral sciences is to eagerly adopt new technologies that afford new or improved capabilities for gathering human performance data "in the wild" (Hutchins, 1995; Stanney, Mourant, & Kennedy, 1998). Mobile devices, which are fast becoming an internalized part of our personal actions and our social interactions, offer a tantalizing alternative to current methods and promise to provide entirely new ways of exploring human behavior over the long term. For educational purposes, for example, these tools could provide much needed data to address the total effectiveness of any games and simulation training system.

Kirkpatrick (1998) described a framework with four levels of program assessment that are a useful point of comparison. The first assessed how users liked the training. The second assessed immediate learning effects. The third assessed learning transfer, or whether learners were able to apply their new knowledge in the real world. The fourth assessed the impact of the learner's application of their new knowledge in the real world on organizational objectives (e.g., increased productivity, profit, etc.). The kinds of data being collected and assessed through mobile devices may provide evidence capable of supporting Kirkpatrick's third level of assessment (Kirkpatrick, 1998).

Yet, while the education community continues to adopt, to varying degrees, new technologies like intelligent tutors, game-based simulations, and even massive open online courses (MOOCs), it has been slower to adopt the kinds of methodologies that would help definitively prove that these and other interventions have a meaningful and long-term effect on human performance as described by Kirkpatrick's framework (see, for example, Cook et al., 2013; Steenbergen-Hu & Cooper, 2013; Yousef, Chatti, Schroeder, & Wosnitza, 2014). Here the educational community can benefit from lessons learned in the medical community, which has been focusing on using mobile devices to capture epidemiological data (Klasnja & Pratt, 2012) and related behavioral changes (Madan, Cebrian, Lazer, & Pentland, 2010; Wac, 2012), as well as to provide detailed statistics regarding individual patient progress using online patient communities (Little, Wicks, Vaughan, & Pentland, 2013; Wicks, Vaughan, Massagli, & Heywood, 2011). These initial forays into collecting longitudinal pattern-of-life data have revealed several key challenges that must be resolved before applying mobile devices and other novel sources of pattern-of-life data to the task of better understanding human behavior. A key challenge is to ensure the validity, reliability, and accuracy (or *rigor* as we sometimes collectively refer to these concepts) of longitudinally-collected data, particularly when using novel data sources to assess constructs previously assessed through noncomputational methods (e.g., via self-report surveys and diagnostic interviews). A further challenge is to develop a priori approaches for predicting the relative contributions of unique data streams in advance of their actual incorporation.

In this chapter we leverage the work being done in the medical domain to extract a useful framework and set of practices suitable for addressing these challenges in education and training applications. The example use case focuses on our experience evaluating a mobile system designed to capture pattern-of-life longitudinal data in order to produce a risk assessment for difficult-to-measure symptoms of post-traumatic stress disorder (PTSD). It's worth noting that the collection of medically-related information through smartphone devices that can capture data without the explicit awareness of the user creates important ethical and privacy issues that are beyond the scope of this chapter, but that nonetheless merit serious consideration. For discussion of such matters, see Appelbaum (2002), Gray and Thorpe (2015), and Thorpe and Gray (2015).

PTSD is a condition that may develop in an individual following exposure to one or more traumatic events. Its symptoms may take months, if not years, to fully develop and may manifest in different ways, unique to each individual being monitored and the contexts in which they find themselves (Horowitz & Solomon, 1978; Solomon & Mikulincer, 2006; Van Dyke, Zilberg, & McKinnon, 1985). PTSD is currently assessed through completion of self-report questionnaires such as the PTSD Checklist (PCL) (Weathers, Huska, & Keane, 1991), or more rigorously through structured interviews with trained diagnostic clinicians. These traditional methods have the advantage of having a clear mapping between the specific items they incorporate and the symptoms that are required for diagnosis of PTSD according to the Diagnostic and Statistical Manual of Mental Disorders (DSM), the American Psychiatric Association's standard reference for the classification of mental disorders (First, Spitzer, Gibbon, & Williams, 2007). However, these methods are limited by the recall accuracy and truthfulness of the patient as well as the skill of the diagnostic interviewer (in the case of structured interviews) in interpreting responses. Certain items, such as those related to quality of sleep, are notoriously difficult for people to accurately self-track and report. For these reasons, smartphone-based tools have recently been developed to collect data and make automated inferences of psychological status from indirect sources of evidence in order to provide independent and objective measures predictive of psychological symptoms of interest. As such, these new tools represent an entirely new means of collecting and assessing behaviors relevant to inferring constructs of interest.

The work we reference in this chapter was performed by us in our role as independent evaluators for the Detection and Computational Analysis of Psychological Signals (DCAPS) program sponsored by the Defense Advanced Research Projects Agency (DARPA) and the Office of Naval Research (ONR). The goal of that program was to develop novel tools and technologies that could assist veterans and active duty service personnel in the tracking and assessment of their mental and emotional well-being. Among the tools being developed under this program were two smartphone apps and two web-based assessment systems—all planning to use novel methods for psychological assessment and each being developed by a different set of independent technology developers.

Once such tools are developed, the question becomes, how do we know they work? How do we determine their validity (i.e., evidence and theory supporting the proposed tool use), reliability (i.e., consistency of measurements over repeated measures), and accuracy (in this case, correct classification of individuals with regards to the presence or absence of any psychological illnesses or related underlying symptoms) without the benefit of similar tools against which to compare them (Natamba et al., 2014; Stinchfield, 2003)? The only option left is to compare them to current best practices—clinical surveys and structured clinical interviews. However, that presents us with a daunting "apples-to-oranges" comparison. Faced with this very challenge, we developed and followed a five-step process to design what we believe to be a fair and rigorous evaluation of smartphone and other novel computational tools designed to assess PTSD symptoms via novel passive, pattern-of-life data collection methods. In brief, our steps were to:

1. Identify a relevant and meaningful use case.
2. Develop an "information flow model" that graphically maps the path of data from individuals using the tool, through the various intervening processing steps, to the final outcome measures produced by the tools.
3. Conduct an analysis of the information flow model to verify that the derivation of the desired outcome measure(s) from the sources of data and intervening processing steps is logically feasible.
4. Identify the best alternative, independent method(s) for outcome measure validation (given available resources and knowledge of "gold-standard" practices in the appropriate domain).
5. Address other concerns such as how the tool will address outlier behaviors/responses relative to human raters, and whether the tool use itself is likely to affect behavior in intended and/or unanticipated ways.

Use Cases

The goal of a valid evaluation is well served when the process begins with identification of use cases that provides a narrative description of who will use the tool(s), how they will interact with it, and toward what ends or purposes they will use it (American Educational Research Association, American Psychological Association, & National Council on Measurement in Education, 2014; Kulak & Guiney, 2003).

"Who will use the tool(s)" should address parameters such as age, gender, ethnicity, socioeconomic factors, and any other specialty affiliations (e.g., veterans, physicians, teachers, etc.) or prior experience requirements (e.g., trauma exposure, job certifications, years of experience, etc.). The tool developers should have identified these user parameters early in the development process. However, when comparing independently developed tools, variations in targeted user populations will need to be reconciled. As with all aspects of an evaluation, the earlier in the tool development process this can be done, the better for all parties involved.

Next, the use case should address "how they will use the tool(s)." At a minimum, this question seeks to identify the location, duration, frequency, and nature of the interaction. Interactions may be passive, but come with requirements (such as users are expected to carry their smartphone with them most or all of the time), or it may be active in any number of ways (complete online surveys, participate in interviews, conduct exercises, etc.).

Finally, the use case describes, "Toward what end or purposes will they use it?" This question covers a lot of territory, but is critical for developing valid evaluation test(s) and a valid evaluation plan. Will the tool(s) be used in an initial assessment (as just one part of it, or as the entire assessment), in conjunction with ongoing treatment, in support of the user or of the treatment administrator (e.g., counselor, teacher, physician, etc.), or as a training tool for student clinicians? In short, is the immediate and end-user of the tool's output measures the one actually using the tool, someone else (e.g., the counselor), or both? Whatever the answers are, more questions arise. How will the outcome measures be used? How important are the decisions that it will be used to make? Will there be other sources of evidence to inform these decisions as well? Answers to these questions may determine in part the valuation placed on such considerations as minimizing false positive outcomes versus achieving the highest overall accuracy.

When conducting evaluations of tools whose use cases are not in agreement with respect to who will use the tool(s), how they will interact with it, and toward what ends or purposes they will use it, effort must be made to identify common and core elements that can or must be preserved in the development of a common use case. Part of this consideration should include an agreement on what elements are essential for success and that have not been previously evaluated in relevant contexts. For example, in the program in which we evaluated smartphone and other novel computational tools as a means of assessing PTSD symptoms, several use cases were discussed including using the tools for identifying early onset of psychological disorders, using the tools to support therapists with users in treatment, using the tools to keep family members informed, and using the tools to train therapists.

Each of the use cases described above contains elements that potentially conflict with each other, making a combined and comprehensive evaluation unwieldy. However, all cases required that the tools be able to accurately, reliably, and validly assess the psychological status of the user. So the tool developers and the evaluators were able to come to agreement on a common evaluation use case that focused on user assessment, and stripped many of the different feedback channels that the other use cases would require. This limits the validity of the comparative evaluation to the assessment aspects of the tools. However, that aspect is critical to any other use of the tools—and, as it makes use of the novel element of collecting and processing pattern-of-life data to make automated assessments, it was also the least tested aspect of the tools, so the evaluation still remained relevant and meaningful.

Information Flow Model

Once the characteristics of the tools' users and the parameters and purposes of the tools' uses are identified, a detailed, structured map, which we refer to as the information flow model, should be constructed for each tool (Bewley & O'Neil, 2013; Cai, 2013; Koenig, Iseli, Wainess, & Lee, 2013). This structured map is divided into four layers: the Background layer, the Event layer, the Indicator layer, and the Construct layer.

The Background layer simply identifies the source or sources of data—indicating in brief the "who" from the use case. It should also indicate the context of the tool's use, which may also be derived from the use case, or may be a practical constraint for the evaluation (such as limiting the geographic area from which the test population will be recruited). For example, a background layer representation for tools purporting to measure specific PTSD symptoms might look like that shown in Figure 3.1. (Note in these and subsequent figures, we follow the convention of visually representing observable elements in rectangles and unobservable, or *latent*, constructs and subconstructs in ovals.)

Next, the Event layer (Figure 3.2) identifies the lowest level behavioral and system state data that the tool will capture. A smartphone tool seeking to characterize locational behavior of an individual, for example, may capture location data from GPS, cell-tower, Bluetooth, and/or Wi-Fi signals. It may also capture the on/off status of these components in order to internally verify the data before processing it. And more generally, it may capture data on the "health" of the phone that might affect the accuracy of the locational sensors, such as battery charge status or on/off state of the phone itself. Elements in the Event layer should be behaviors or states (either of the individual user or of the tool) that can be independently observed, quantified, and verified.

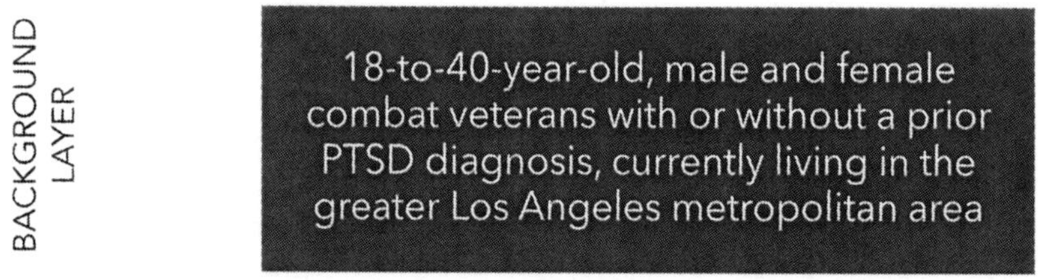

BACKGROUND LAYER

18-to-40-year-old, male and female combat veterans with or without a prior PTSD diagnosis, currently living in the greater Los Angeles metropolitan area

FIGURE 3.1 Background layer: Brief description of use case population.

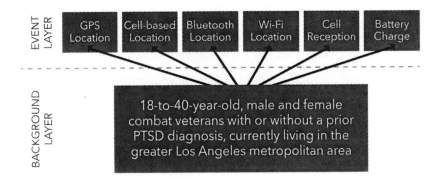

FIGURE 3.2 Event and background layers.

Above the Event layer is the Indicator layer (Figure 3.3). This layer identifies interim variables that are derived from the event layer data, but still reflect observable, quantifiable, and independently verifiable data. At the highest level within this layer will be variables that provide evidence for the inferences to be made at the Construct layer. Extending the above example, these could be duration of time spent at specific locations, frequency of location changes, and/or a change in these values over time. As discussed above, internal use of these and underlying variables may be moderated by other variables (e.g., location data may be ignored for periods of time when the phone is turned off, in airplane mode, or when the battery is too low).

Finally, above the Indicator layer is the Construct layer (Figure 3.4). This layer identifies all of the top-level constructs and underlying subconstructs that are part of the information flow model. Constructs and subconstructs are latent variables (Bollen, 2002) that are derived from indicator layer or lower subconstruct measures. As the term *latent variable* implies, they are not directly observable, but

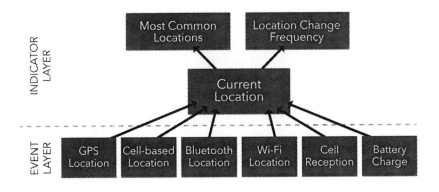

FIGURE 3.3 Indicator and event layers.

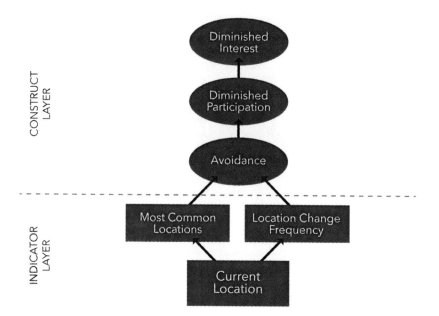

FIGURE 3.4 Construct and indicator layers.

are still quantifiable to some approximation (e.g., they may be represented as categorical values, such as "positive for PTSD," associated with a probability of being correct, such as "probability of .67 that the user is positive for PTSD"). Importantly, they are the primary objects of interest. Constructs and subconstructs are conceptual in nature and can only be estimated through inference (Cai, 2013).

Examples of constructs derived from locational data might be increased avoidance behaviors, or diminished participation or interest in activities. These constructs may have a locational element to them, but also require assumptions about the internal motivation driving the observable location-based behaviors.

In these visual depictions, the actual calculations used to derive higher-level values are not explicitly represented. These graphic representations could, however, form the basis of an actual computational model (Cai, 2013). For developing evaluation plans, the primary use of these models is to map the logical flow of data through the tool, and to identify elements that are missing or that are useful capabilities or important requirements that would have otherwise been neglected. When mapping novel sources of data (as might be derived from a smartphone) to established higher order constructs (such as the psychological symptom of avoidance), we find it useful to differentially represent constructs or subconstructs that cannot be validly inferred from the underlying sources of evidence available, such as when the collected sources of data do not suffice to meet the definition of the construct. Extending our example, a simple psychological definition of

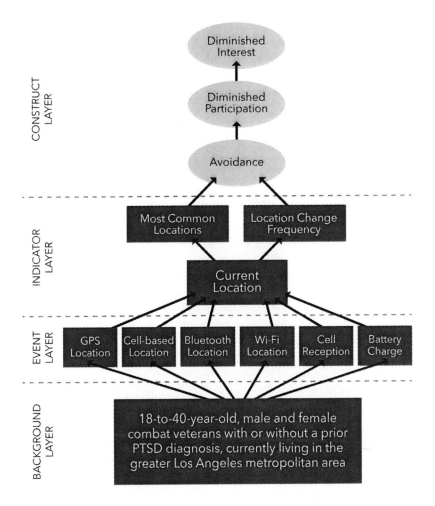

FIGURE 3.5 Full information flow model.

avoidance might include physical avoidance of a class of locations (such as marketplaces or other highly populated areas), but might also require additional evidence related to feelings of inadequacy, low self-esteem, or feelings of anxiety that the tool does not capture or infer from other sources of data. In this case, we would update the information flow model by reshading the elements (from dark gray to light gray as in Figure 3.5) that cannot be inferred by the tool based on the types of data it collects and interim measures it is able to derive. This makes gaps and limitations readily identifiable. In our example, this might produce the complete model shown in Figure 3.5, where we can readily identify who uses the tool (and therefore who should be recruited when testing it), what information is collected, how that information is transformed into desired information, and whether or not the desired information can feasibly be obtained. If it is determined that it cannot be, then the tool developers can be encouraged to address shortcomings and remedy them by either finding alternative means or paths to obtain the outcome metrics or by modifying their tool's purpose and/or the outcome measures it produces.

Identifying Methods for Independent Validation

The *Standards for Educational and Psychological Testing* (American Educational Research Association et al., 2014) outlines three thematic clusters of standards for assessing validity. They are establishing (a) intended uses and interpretations, (b) issues regarding sample and settings used in validation, and (c) specific forms of validity evidence. To see how these clusters apply to the challenge of evaluating new technologies or tools, we again consider the smartphone evaluation described in this chapter.

The intended use and interpretations of the pattern-of-life data collected passively through novel tools, such as the smartphone app described here, are to obtain and interpret objective evidence related to the everyday behavior patterns of an individual. Such tools may provide data in the form of phone use logs, through sensors (e.g., GPS) that provide location information over time, or from data collected through other apps on the device. For example, a planned interpretation might take the form of an expectation for "normal" locational behavior (revealed through GPS data) to include daily patterns of travel from home to work and back again most days of the week. However, an assumption underlying this interpretation is that the user lives in one location and works in another. This may be the case for most people, but some may work at home or travel throughout the day for work, and that may not be distinguishable from someone who is unemployed or avoiding work. Also, if a person leaves their phone at home, the GPS data alone would not be able to distinguish between the person being at home sick or other possible explanations. However, more sophisticated interpretations that incorporate additional evidence, like phone activity logs providing evidence that the person is with their phone, could help disambiguate alternate explanations for location data results. These more sophisticated interpretations would therefore increase the tool's validity for the purpose of using pattern-of-life data to identify individuals behaving in ways that suggest they may be at higher risk for suffering PTSD. The sophistication of interpretations made by the tool will have been captured in part by the information flow model. Any remaining uncertainty about how the tool handles potentially ambiguous situations, such as the example described above, should be clarified through deeper discussions with the tool developers.

For issues regarding samples and settings, useful validity arguments include detailed information about participant background (socioeconomic, demographic, and any other relevant characteristics that are pertinent to the constructs being tested) as well as information about the settings in which any empirical data is to be collected. Who is expected to use the tool and under what circumstances? How well do alternative sources of evidence being used to evaluate the tool match to these background characteristics? In our framework, this information is captured during the development of the use case(s). Care should be taken to avoid deviations in samples and settings between those used to create the tool and those used to test it.

Finally, to meet the need for specific validity evidence, we identify methods for assessing the tool's constructs (and possibly subconstructs, indicators, etc.) that are independent, valid, alternative measures of the constructs and other variables that the tools are purporting to measure. This begins by identifying alternative measures and metrics suitable for comparison. In our case, we looked to compare the results from these novel psychological assessment tools with measures that are recognized as being the current "gold standard" for psychological assessment. Specifically, for PTSD the gold standard is the Clinician-Administered PTSD Scale (CAPS) (Blake et al., 1997). The CAPS is designed on the criteria (symptoms) for differential diagnosis found in the DSM-IV (American Psychiatric Association, 1994) and DSM-5 (American Psychiatric Association, 2013). As discussed above, the tools we were to evaluate classified a user's risk for selected PTSD symptoms, and, as described in the evaluation use case, were to be used in early detection assessment.

In addition to identifying alternative measures of the construct of interest itself (PTSD and its underlying symptoms in our case), it is important to identify other conditions that could lead the new tools to score a tool user as positive for a symptom of PTSD or for PTSD itself. Other social anxiety disorders, for example, may produce symptoms in an individual that resemble those of PTSD closely enough that the new assessment tools could score them as at high risk while the CAPS interviewers scores the individual as not having PTSD. As part of the evaluation, it is important to understand how selective these tools are in assessing PTSD. In our case, we address this need by administering both the CAPS (Blake et al., 1997) and the full Structured Clinical Interview for DSM Disorders (SCID, First et al., 2007) as sources of evidence for "ground truth" in our test population and to maximize our ability to capture any instances where a tool's false positive for PTSD (or one of its underlying symptoms) is actually detecting another psychological condition from which the user is suffering.

More generally, multiple independent or corroborating sources of evidence can help to increase validity, reliability, and accuracy of an evaluation, and may provide greater explanatory power. Some of the tools under evaluation were developed using a self-report questionnaire for PTSD as its source of ground truth for PTSD symptoms. So in addition to collecting our gold-standard sources of evidence, it behooves us to collect data from the same sources used in development. This better enables us to explain potential sources of discrepancy between the tool outcomes and the interviewer findings, should there be notable differences between the two.

Conclusions

New scientific paradigms often arise as a direct result of enhancements to existing technologies, or the development of new technologies, which open new ways of understanding existing challenges, or which present entirely new challenges (Kuhn, 2012). In a sense, as new developments arise, scientists are required to re-examine their assumptions and beliefs against these new findings. A quick review of this volume's table of contents suggests that most, if not all, of the chapters focus in some way on addressing "old" problems associated with assessing teaching using "new" tools, technologies, and methodologies. Given recent advances in the learning sciences, which enable better framing of hypotheses for enhancing the effectiveness of specific interactions, combined with new developments in technology that allow for ever more complex testing of these hypotheses, this process of self-improvement is reasonable and necessary (Koedinger, Booth, & Klahr, 2013).

An enduring challenge in the field of education is to develop tools that can diagnose and remediate individual students' performance (Mislevy & Bock, 1989; Steenbergen-Hu & Cooper, 2013). Addressing this challenge requires the ability to capture longitudinal data about each student, in order to understand the degree to which an educational intervention leads—or fails to lead—to behavior change. Unlike other human behavior research areas, education brings with it some unique constraints on technology solutions: it's the need for acceptance by large numbers of practitioners (students and teachers), standardized approaches (core curriculum), and a quite reasonable need for clear demonstration of effectiveness prior to full-scale implementation (Klahr, 2013; Klahr & Li, 2005). Yet, other fields evolve through the integration of new technologies, so it seems reasonable to ask, what can the field of educational research learn from other fields to assist in its adoption of new technologies to better understand and improve educational effectiveness?

Medical research provides an interesting source of technology advances that may also be leveraged to enhance education research. By analogy to education, the need for new approaches for capturing long-term data about an individual is critical to understanding and managing certain types of cognitive challenges that require time to evolve. Post-traumatic stress disorder is one example of this type of cognitive challenge. PTSD is a condition that develops in an individual following exposure to one or more traumatic events. While PTSD may present soon after exposure to a stressful experience (Orcutt, Erickson, & Wolfe, 2004), it is also possible that the symptoms may take months, if not years, to fully develop (Horowitz & Solomon, 1978; Solomon & Mikulincer, 2006; Van Dyke et al.,

1985). This suggests that only through dedicated, long-term data collection approaches can accurate diagnoses be made, and effective treatments be provided.

In this chapter we provide a framework for validating the use of novel, but increasingly ubiquitous technologies, such as smartphones, for data collection in the wild (Hutchins, 1995; Stanney et al., 1998). Importantly, these devices are swiftly becoming a common channel for social interactions, oftentimes serving as a transparent interface between individuals and their environment, mediating social interactions, managing personal schedules, and providing guidance and information (Atzori et al., 2012). Because these devices are increasingly providing a natural and unique method for collecting long-term data about an individual's behaviors, they provide a nonthreatening capability for long-term data collection.

Smartphones' ubiquity makes them an ideal tool for also capturing long-term information about students. As online resources and tools for education continue to grow (Chamberlin & Parish, 2011; Daniel, 2012; Emanuel, 2013) and their implementation on smart devices rises (Graham, 2013) the framework presented here should provide an easy-to-follow map for the education technology community.

A key goal of education and training is to effect lasting and positive behavior changes at both the individual and organizational levels (Kirkpatrick, 1998). The importance of quantifying the long-term impact of educational interventions cannot be overemphasized. Significant resources are devoted by the government, as well as by large and small corporations, to develop more effective educational technologies. A valid criticism of these efforts (Cohn & Fletcher, 2010) is that they rarely demonstrate cost and performance effectiveness. This is often due to a lack of ability to conduct long-term follow-up assessments that track long-term behavior changes resulting from exposure to these technologies (Kirkpatrick, 1998). The approaches discussed in this chapter provide a means for addressing the performance effectiveness part of this criticism by ensuring that novel tools claiming to be capable of providing useful information are truly valid, accurate, and reliable for the intended purpose.

The applications for the approaches outlined in this chapter extend beyond medicine and education. As marketing efforts become increasingly web-based, the ability to determine the extent to which any single marketing effort induces long-term changes in consumer behavior would allow advertisers unique insight into how to tailor their efforts. Similarly, crowdsourcing approaches, which enable the harnessing of the intelligence of crowds (Belleflamme, Lambert, & Schwienbacher, 2014; Brabham, 2008; Surowiecki, 2005), can use the framework here to validate and develop new ways of blending data from different types of smart devices, on a massive scale. In a broader sense, the approaches discussed in this chapter provide a means of validating new and generalizable solutions to the challenge of capturing long-term data, of different types, for the express purpose of gaining deeper insights into an individual's behavior patterns.

Author Note

The DCAPS work reported herein was supported by grant number N00014 1110089 from the Office of Naval Research and the Defense Advanced Research Projects Agency to the National Center for Research on Evaluation, Standards, and Student Testing (CRESST). The findings and opinions expressed in this chapter are those of the authors and do not necessarily reflect the positions or policies of the Office of Naval Research or the Defense Advanced Research Projects Agency.

References

American Educational Research Association, American Psychological Association, & National Council on Measurement in Education. (2014). *Standards for educational and psychological testing.* Washington, DC: Author.

American Psychiatric Association. (1994). *Diagnostic and statistical manual of mental disorders* (4th ed.). Washington, DC: Author.

American Psychiatric Association. (2013). *Diagnostic and statistical manual of mental disorders* (5th ed.). Washington, DC: Author.

Appelbaum, P. S. (2002). Privacy in psychiatric treatment: Threats and responses. *American Journal of Psychiatry, 159,* 1809–1818.

Atzori, L., Iera, A., Morabito, G., & Nitti, M. (2012). The Social Internet of Things (SIoT)—When social networks meet the Internet of things: Concept, architecture and network characterization. *Computer Networks, 56*(16), 3594–3608.

Belleflamme, P., Lambert, T., & Schwienbacher, A. (2014). Crowdfunding: Tapping the right crowd. *Journal of Business Venturing, 29*(5), 585–609.

Bewley, W. L., & O'Neil, H. F. (2013). Evaluation of medical simulations. *Military Medicine, 178*(10S), 64–75.

Blake, D., Weathers, F. W., Nagy, L. M., Kaloupek, D. G., Charney, D. S., & Keane, T. M. (1997). *Clinician administered PTSD scale* (revised). Boston: Behavioral Science Division, Boston National Center for Post-Traumatic Stress Disorder.

Bollen, K. A. (2002). Latent variables in psychology and the social sciences. *Annual Review of Psychology, 53*(1), 605–634.

Brabham, D. (2008). Crowdsourcing as a model for problem solving: An introduction and cases. *Convergence: The International Journal of Research into New Media Technologies, 14*(1), 75–90.

Cai, L. (2013). Potential applications of latent variable modeling for the psychometrics of medical simulation. *Military Medicine, 178*(10S), 64–75.

Chamberlin, L., & Parish, T. (2011, August). MOOCs: Massive Open Online Courses or Massive and Often Obtuse Courses? *eLearn Magazine.* Retrieved from http://elearnmag. acm.org/archive.cfm?aid=2016017

Cisco. (2015). *Cisco visual networking index: Global mobile data traffic forecast update, 2014–2019.* San Jose, CA: Author. Retrieved from www.cisco.com/c/en/us/solutions/collateral/service-provider/visual-networking-index-vni/white_paper_c11-520862.pdf

Cohn, J., & Fletcher, J. D. (2010). What is a pound of training worth? Frameworks and practical examples for assessing return on investment in training. In *Proceedings of the*

Interservice/Industry Training, Simulation & Education Conference (I/ITSEC) (Vol. 2010, No. 1). Arlington, VA: National Training Systems Association.

Cook, D. A., Hamstra, S. J., Brydges, R., Zendejas, B., Szostek, J. H., Wang, A. T., . . . & Hatala, R. (2013). Comparative effectiveness of instructional design features in simulation-based education: Systematic review and meta-analysis. *Medical Teacher, 35*(1), e867–e898.

Daniel, J. (2012). Making sense of MOOCs: Musings in a maze of myth, paradox and possibility. *Journal of Interactive Media in Education, 2012*(3), 18. doi: dx.doi.org/10.5334/2012-18

Emanuel, E. (2013). MOOCs taken by educated few. *Nature, 503,* 342.

First, M. B., Spitzer, R. L., Gibbon, M., & Williams, J. B. W. (2007). *Structured clinical interview for DSM-IV-TR Axis I disorders, research version, patient edition (SCID-I/P).* New York, NY: Biometrics Research, New York State Psychiatric Institute.

Gershenfeld, N., Krikorian, R., & Cohen, D. (2004). The Internet of things. *Scientific American, 291*(4), 76–81.

Graham, J. (2013, December 17). Duolingo: Apple's choice for App of the Year. *USA Today.* Retrieved from www.usatoday.com/story/tech/columnist/talkingtech/2013/12/17/duolingo-apples-iphone-app-of-the-year/4042469/

Gray, E. A., & Thorpe, J. H. (2015). Comparative effectiveness research and big data: balancing potential with legal and ethical considerations. *Journal of Comparative Effectiveness Research, 4*(1), 61–74.

Horowitz, B. T. (2010, December 30). Mobile health apps to triple by 2012, presenting challenges for mobile networks: Report. *eWeek.* Retrieved from www.eweek.com/c/a/Health-Care-IT/Mhealth-Apps-to-Triple-by-2012-Presenting-Challenges-for-Mobile-Networks-Report-869725

Horowitz, M. J., & Solomon, G. F. (1978). Delayed stress response syndromes in Vietnam veterans. In C. R. Figley (Ed.), *Stress disorders among Vietnam veterans: Theory, research, and treatment* (pp. 268–280). New York, NY: Brunner/Mazel.

Hutchins, E. (1995). *Cognition in the wild.* Cambridge, MA: MIT Press.

Internet World Stats. (2014). *Internet usage statistics: The Internet big picture: World Internet users and 2014 population stats.* Retrieved from http://internetworldstats.com/stats.htm

Kirkpatrick, D. (1998). *Evaluating training programs: The four levels.* San Francisco: Berrett-Koehler.

Klahr, D. (2013). What do we mean? On the importance of not abandoning scientific rigor when talking about science education. *Proceedings of the National Academy of Sciences, 110*(Supplement 3), 14075–14080. doi:10.1073/pnas.1212738110

Klahr, D., & Li, J. (2005). Cognitive research and elementary science instruction: From the laboratory, to the classroom, and back. *Journal of Science Education and Technology, 14*(2), 217–238. doi:10.1007/s10956-005-4423-5

Klasnja, P., & Pratt, W. (2012). Healthcare in the pocket: mapping the space of mobile-phone health interventions. *Journal of Biomedical Informatics, 45*(1), 184–198.

Koedinger, K. R., Booth, J. L., & Klahr, D. (2013). Instructional complexity and the science to constrain it. *Science, 342*(6161), 935–937.

Koenig, A., Iseli, M., Wainess, R., & Lee, J. J. (2013). Assessment methodology for computer-based instructional simulations. *Military Medicine, 178*(10S), 47–54.

Kuhn, T. S. (2012). *The structure of scientific revolutions.* Chicago: University of Chicago Press.

Kulak, D., & Guiney, E. (2003). *Use cases: Requirements in context* (2nd ed.). Boston, MA: Addison-Wesley.

Little, M., Wicks, P., Vaughan, T., & Pentland, A. (2013). Quantifying short-term dynamics of Parkinson's disease using self-reported symptom data from an Internet social network. *Journal of Medical Internet Research, 15*(1), e20.

Madan, A., Cebrian, M., Lazer, D., & Pentland, A. (2010, September). Social sensing for epidemiological behavior change. In *Proceedings of the 12th ACM International Conference on Ubiquitous Computing* (pp. 291–300). New York, NY: ACM.

Mislevy, R. J., & Bock, R. D. (1989). A hierarchical item-response model for educational testing. In R. D. Bock (Ed.), *Multilevel analysis of educational data* (pp. 57–74). San Diego, CA: Academic Press.

Natamba, B. K., Achan, J., Arbach, A., Oyok, T. O., Ghosh, S., Mehta, S., . . . Young, S. L. (2014). Reliability and validity of the center for epidemiologic studies-depression scale in screening for depression among HIV-infected and -uninfected pregnant women attending antenatal services in northern Uganda: A cross-sectional study. *BMC Psychiatry, 14*(1), 303. doi:10.1186/s12888-014-0303-y

Orcutt, H. K., Erickson, D. J., & Wolfe, J. (2004). The course of PTSD symptoms among Gulf War veterans: A growth mixture modeling approach. *Journal of Traumatic Stress, 17*, 195–202. doi:10.1023/B:JOTS.0000029262.42865.c2

Perez, S. (2014, August 21). Majority of digital media consumption now takes place in mobile apps. *Techcrunch*. Retrieved from http://techcrunch.com/2014/08/21/majority-of-digital-media-consumption-now-takes-place-in-mobile-apps/

Solomon, Z., & Mikulincer, M. (2006). Trajectories of PTSD: A 20-year longitudinal study. *American Journal of Psychiatry, 163*(4), 659–666.

Stanney, K. M., Mourant, R. R., & Kennedy, R. S. (1998). Human factors issues in virtual environments: A review of the literature. *Presence: Teleoperators and Virtual Environments, 7*(4), 327–351.

Steenbergen-Hu, S., & Cooper, H. (2013). A meta-analysis of the effectiveness of intelligent tutoring systems on K–12 students' mathematical learning. *Journal of Educational Psychology, 105*(4), 970–987.

Stinchfield, R. (2003). Reliability, validity, and classification accuracy of a measure of DSM-IV diagnostic criteria for pathological gambling. *American Journal of Psychiatry, 160*(1), 180–182.

Surowiecki, J. (2005). *The wisdom of crowds*. New York, NY: Anchor Books.

Thorpe, J. H., & Gray, E. A. (2015). Big data and ambulatory care: Breaking down legal barriers to support effective use. *The Journal of Ambulatory Care Management, 38*(1), 29–38.

Uti, N. V., & Fox, R. (2010, August). Testing the computational capabilities of mobile device processors: Some interesting benchmark results. In *Proceedings of the 2010 IEEE/ACIS 9th International Conference on Computer and Information Science (ICIS)* (pp. 477–481). New York, NY: IEEE.

Van Dyke, C., Zilberg, N. J., & McKinnon, J. A. (1985). Posttraumatic stress disorder: A thirty-year delay in a World War II veteran. *The American Journal of Psychiatry, 142*, 1070–1073.

Wac, K. (2012). Smartphone as a personal, pervasive health informatics services platform: Literature review. *IMIA Yearbook of Medical Informatics, 7*(1), 83–93. arXiv:1310.7965.

Weathers, F. W., Huska, J. A., & Keane, T. M. (1991). *PCL-C for DSM-IV*. Boston: National Center for PTSD-Behavioral Science Division.

Wicks, P., Vaughan, T. E., Massagli, M. P., & Heywood, J. (2011). Accelerated clinical discovery using self-reported patient data collected online and a patient-matching algorithm. *Nature Biotechnology, 29*(5), 411–414.

Yousef, A. M. F., Chatti, M. A., Schroeder, U., & Wosnitza, M. (2014, July). What drives a successful MOOC? An empirical examination of criteria to assure design quality of MOOCs. In *Proceedings of the 2014 IEEE 14th International Conference on Advanced Learning Technologies (ICALT)* (pp. 44–48). New York, NY: IEEE.

4

INTELLIGENT TUTORING SYSTEMS, SERIOUS GAMES, AND THE GENERALIZED INTELLIGENT FRAMEWORK FOR TUTORING (GIFT)

Arthur C. Graesser, Xiangen Hu,
Benjamin D. Nye, and Robert A. Sottilare

Many of us have had the vision of learners acquiring STEM subject matters by being immersed in motivating learning environments (such as games) that advance learners to new levels of mastery. Concepts in STEM (science, technology, engineering, and mathematics) are complex and difficult, and require learning at deeper levels than merely memorizing facts, rules, and procedures. Learners would ideally be challenged and motivated to improve on mastering complex topics that might not be acquired with traditional training methods. They would spend hundreds of hours in a hunt for a solution to a problem that few have solved, for the sweet spot in a trade-off between two or more factors, or for a resolution to a set of incompatible constraints. This is precisely the vision of progress for training in the 21st century. How can deep learning be achieved in a motivating learning environment? Games provide a good first place to look for answers because well-designed games are motivating and some meta-analyses have reported positive impacts of games on learning (Mayer, 2011; O'Neil & Perez, 2008; Ritterfeld, Cody, & Vorderer, 2009; Shute & Ventura, 2013; Tobias & Fletcher, 2011; Wouters, van Nimwegen, van Oostendorp, & van der Spek, 2013).

This chapter explores the prospects of integrating games with intelligent tutoring systems (ITSs). The hope is that there can be learning environments that optimize both motivation through games and deep learning through ITS technologies. Deep learning refers to the acquisition of knowledge, skills, strategies, and reasoning processes at the higher levels of Bloom's (1956) taxonomy or the Knowledge-Learning-Instruction (KLI) framework (Koedinger, Corbett, & Perfetti, 2012), such as the application of knowledge to new cases, knowledge analysis and synthesis, problem solving, critical thinking, and other difficult cognitive processes. In contrast, shallow learning involves perceptual learning, memorization of explicit material, and mastery of simple rigid procedures. Shallow knowledge may be adequate for near transfer tests of knowledge/skills but not for transfer tests to new situations that have some modicum of complexity.

There have been some attempts to develop game–ITS hybrids (Adams & Clark, 2014; Halpern et al., 2012; Jackson & McNamara, 2013; Johnson & Valente, 2008; McNamara, Jackson, & Graesser, 2010; McQuiggan, Robison, & Lester, 2010; Millis et al., 2011; Sabourin, Rowe, Mott, & Lester, 2013). However, it is too early to know whether the marriage between games and ITSs will end up celebrating a multidecade anniversary or will end up in a divorce because of incompatible constraints between the two worlds. Deep learning takes effort, is often frustrating, and is normally regarded as work rather than play (Baker, D'Mello, Rodrigo, & Graesser, 2010; D'Mello, Lehman, Pekrun, & Graesser, 2014). Indeed, the correlation between liking and deep learning tends to be negative in current ITS research without game attributes (Graesser & D'Mello, 2012; Jackson & Graesser, 2007). Perhaps game features can turn this work into play with sufficient entertaining features, learner freedom, and self-regulated activities (Lepper & Henderlong, 2000), and thereby shift the correlation from negative to positive (Sabourin et al., 2013). If not, then games may be reserved for the acquisition of shallow knowledge and skills, such as memorization of facts, simple skills, and rigid procedures. In contrast, games may not be suited for the acquisition of deep knowledge and strategies, such as understanding complex systems, reasoning about causal mental models, and applying sophisticated quantitative algorithms.

This chapter will not unveil the secrets of building a successful ITS in a game environment. It is too early to tell that story. Instead, we hope to achieve three goals. First, we will review successes and challenges in ITS research and development. Second, we will describe the components of ITSs in the Generalized Intelligent Framework for Tutoring (GIFT). GIFT has recently been developed by the U.S. Army Research Laboratory as a stable blueprint and guide for developing ITSs in the future (Sottilare, Graesser, Hu, & Goldberg, 2014; Sottilare, Graesser, Hu, & Holden, 2013). Third, we will reflect on how these efforts might be integrated with games. An adequate understanding of ITS components and the underlying research is a necessary prerequisite to formulating a meaningful courtship between ITSs and games.

It is important to point out two areas of research and application that will not be addressed in this chapter. This chapter does not address the role of games in the acquisition and mastery of shallow learning. The empirical evidence has convinced us that a well-designed game can effectively enhance shallow learning, whereas there is uncertainty in the literature on whether deep learning can benefit from games. This chapter also does not address learning and problem solving in the context of teams. Our focus is on deep learning in individuals who interact with an ITS.

Successes and Challenges in ITS Research and Development

This section briefly defines what we mean by an ITS, reviews the successes of ITS technologies, and identifies the chief challenges in scaling up these systems for more widespread use. Meta-analyses and landmark systems support the claim that ITSs are a promising solution to achieving deep learning. However, there are four categories of challenges which we place under the umbrellas of motivation, measurement, materials, and money. These challenges can be mitigated, if not conquered, by some recommended efforts.

What Is an Intelligent Tutoring System?

We define an ITS as a computer learning environment that helps the student master deep knowledge/skills by implementing powerful intelligent algorithms that adapt to the learner at a fine-grained level and that instantiate complex principles of learning (Graesser, Conley, & Olney, 2012). We see ITS environments as a generation beyond conventional computer-based training (CBT). CBT systems also adapt to individual learners, but they do so at a more coarse-grained level with simple learning principles. In a prototypical CBT system, the learner (a) studies material presented in a lesson, (b) gets tested with a multiple-choice test or another objective test, (c) gets feedback on the test performance, (d) re-studies the material if the performance in (c) is below threshold, and (e) progresses to a new topic if performance exceeds threshold. The order of topics presented and tested typically follows a predetermined order, such as ordering on complexity (simple to complex) or ordering on prerequisites. The materials in a lesson can vary from organized text with figures, tables, diagrams, and multimedia to example problems to be solved. ITSs can be viewed as enhancements of CBT with respect to the adaptability, grain-size, and the power of computerized learning environments. In ITSs, the processes of tracking knowledge (called user modeling) and adaptively responding to the learner incorporate computational models in artificial intelligence and cognitive science, such as production systems, case-based reasoning, Bayes networks, theorem proving, and constraint satisfaction algorithms (see Graesser, Conley, & Olney, 2012; Woolf, 2009).

This chapter does not sharply divide systems that are CBT systems versus ITSs, but one useful dimension is the space of possible computer–learner interactions that can be achieved with the two classes of systems. For an ITS, every tutorial interaction is unique and the space of possible interactions is extremely large, if not infinite. Imagine hundreds of alternative states of the learner, hundreds of alternative responses of the tutor, and thousands/millions of alternative sequences of interaction. An ITS attempts to fill in very specific learning deficits, to correct very specific misconceptions, and to implement dynamic sequencing and navigation. For CBT, interaction histories can be identical for multiple students and the interaction space is finite, if not small (e.g., < 100 possible interactions).

Successful ITSs have been developed for mathematically well-formed topics, including algebra, geometry, programming languages (the Cognitive Tutors: Aleven, McLaren, Sewall, & Koedinger, 2009; Anderson, Corbett, Koedinger, & Pelletier, 1995; Koedinger, Anderson, Hadley, & Mark, 1997; Ritter, Anderson, Koedinger, & Corbett, 2007; ALEKS: Doignon & Falmagne, 1999), physics (Andes, Atlas, and Why/Atlas: VanLehn et al., 2002, 2007), electronics (SHERLOCK: Lesgold, Lajoie, Bunzo, & Eggan, 1992), and information technology (KERMIT: Mitrovic, Martin, & Suraweera, 2007). Some intelligent systems handle knowledge domains that have a stronger verbal foundation as opposed to mathematics and precise analytical reasoning. AutoTutor (Graesser, Chipman, Haynes, & Olney, 2005; Graesser, D'Mello, et al., 2012; Graesser et al., 2004; Nye, Graesser, & Hu, 2014) helps college students learn about computer literacy, physics, and critical thinking skills by holding conversations in natural language. Other natural language ITSs that have shown learning gains include DeepTutor (Rus, D'Mello, Hu, & Graesser, 2013), iSTART (McNamara et al., 2010), and My Science Tutor (Ward et al., 2013). The Intelligent Essay Assessor (Landauer, Laham, & Foltz, 2003) and e-Rater (Burstein, 2003) grade essays on science, history, and other topics as reliably as experts of English composition. These systems automatically analyze language and discourse by incorporating recent advances in computational linguistics (Jurafsky & Martin, 2008; McCarthy & Boonthum-Denecke, 2012) and information retrieval, notably latent semantic analysis (Landauer, McNamara, Dennis, & Kintsch, 2007).

Meta-analyses

Meta-analyses and reviews support the claim that ITS technologies routinely improve learning over classroom teaching, reading texts, and/or other traditional learning methods. These meta-analyses normally report effect sizes (sigma, σ), which refer to the difference between the ITS condition and a control condition in standard deviation units. The reported meta-analyses show positive effect sizes that vary from $\sigma = 0.05$ (Dynarsky et al., 2007) to $\sigma = 1.08$ (Dodds & Fletcher, 2004), but most hover between $\sigma = 0.40$ and $\sigma = 0.80$ (Fletcher, 2003; Graesser, Conley, & Olney, 2012; Ma, Adesope, Nesbit, & Liu, 2014; Steenbergen-Hu & Cooper, 2013, 2014; VanLehn, 2011). Our current best meta-meta estimate from all of these meta-analyses is $\sigma = 0.60$. This performance is comparable to human tutoring which varies from between $\sigma = 0.20$ and $\sigma = 1.00$ (Cohen, Kulik, & Kulik, 1982; Graesser, D'Mello, & Cade, 2011), depending on the expertise of the tutor. Human tutors have not varied greatly from ITSs in direct comparisons between ITSs and trained human tutors (Olney et al., 2012; VanLehn, 2011; VanLehn et al., 2007).

We are convinced that some subject matters will show higher effect sizes than others when comparing any intervention (e.g., computer trainers, human tutors, group learning) to a control. It is difficult to obtain high effect sizes for literacy and numeracy because these skills are ubiquitous in everyday life and habits are automatized. For example, Ritter et al. (2007) reported that the Cognitive Tutor for mathematics has shown an effect size of $\sigma = 0.30$ to 0.40 in environments with minimal control over instructors. Human interventions to improve basic reading skills typically report an effect size of $\sigma = 0.20$. In contrast, when the student starts essentially from ground zero, such as many subject matters in science and technology, then effect sizes are expected to be more robust. ITSs show effect sizes of $\sigma = 0.60$ to 2.00 in the subject matters of physics (Van-Lehn, 2011; VanLehn et al., 2007), computer literacy (Graesser et al., 2004; Graesser, D'Mello, et al., 2012), biology (Olney et al., 2012), and scientific reasoning (Halpern et al., 2012; Millis et al., 2011). As a notable example, the Digital Tutor (Fletcher & Morrison, 2012) improves information technology by an effect size as high as $\sigma = 3.70$ for knowledge and $\sigma = 1.10$ for skills. Such large effect sizes would never be expected in basic literacy and numeracy.

Motivation

ITS technologies that target deep learning have the challenge of keeping students motivated because, as mentioned earlier, the intrinsic tendency is for there to be an inverse relationship between liking a system and deep learning. Simply put, thinking and reasoning hurt. The hope is that games will fill the motivational gap for ITSs. Unfortunately, there have not been enough studies combining games with ITSs for a meta-analysis at this point. However, some successful game–ITS hybrids have been Crystal Island (McQuiggan et al., 2010; Sabourin et al., 2013), iSTART-ME (Jackson, Dempsey, & McNamara, 2012), and Operation ARIES and Operation ARA (Halpern et al., 2012; Millis et al., 2011). However, there is no adequate body of research reporting effect sizes that contrast the game versions versus those without game features in these ITSs.

Game elements take some time to master so there is the risk of short-term penalties from games (Adams, Mayer, McNamara, Koenig, & Wainess, 2012). Narrative, fantasy, competition, choice, feedback, challenge, and other distinctive characteristics of games (Ritterfeld et al., 2009) may help motivation but they are not often intrinsic to subject matter mastery. In essence, game elements may pose a non-germane load to working memory and be a distraction from deep learning. This problem could be circumvented if all game elements had tangible hooks to the subject matter, but it is very rare to have game affordances aligned with components of deep learning. Given this difficulty of mapping game features to serious subject matter, the central question is whether the game features will have a payoff in the long run. For example, the game features of iSTART-ME (Jackson et al., 2012) had a short-term penalty compared to an ITS without game features, but iSTART-ME showed advantages after 8–10 hours. Therefore, we would argue that an adequate test of game characteristics for deep learning should involve assessments for 10 or more hours. Short interventions of an hour or less are essentially irrelevant because deep learning by definition takes many hours of training until mastery.

An ideal assessment of the motivational influence of game features on an ITS would allow students a free choice on whether to interact with the system. In essence, there would be a racehorse comparison in the total amount of learning when the ITS does versus does not have the game features. A mathematical integral metric is needed to incorporate both time and learning (much like integral calculus). An hour of training might show the game version to be only .7 as effective as the standard version without the game, but what if the learner chooses to play the game version 10 times as long as the standard version? That would be a substantial long-term victory for the game version. There needs to be a learning gain metric that multiplies *learning efficiency* (e.g., learning-per-hour) times *time* (number-of-hours) that the learner voluntarily uses the learning environment in a free-choice or self-regulated learning scenario after a learning environment is exposed to the learner. However, such an integral metric is virtually never reported because studies attempt to equilibrate time on task between conditions. These studies ignore or diminish the motivational dimension of the Learning × Motivation equation.

Measurement

All learning systems need to be assessed by defensible measures of performance and learning. The validity and reliability of measures are a broad and important matter that is ubiquitously discussed among researchers ranging from laboratory scientists to stakeholders of international assessments. The standards vary among research communities, and this applies to those within the ITS field. Ideal metrics have not been identified within the ITS community, let alone those involved with high-stakes state, national, and international assessments. Since the goal is deep learning, there would ideally be a psychometrically validated metric of deep learning for each particular subject matter. Unfortunately, available psychometric measures are a mixture of deep and shallow learning, as well as relevant versus irrelevant knowledge/skills. This is because they are generic measures of a broad skill rather than a metric that targets the specific subject matter of the ITS. Therefore, there is rarely a defensible gold standard for assessment of an ITS. In the absence of a suitable psychometric measure, researchers turn to researcher-defined metrics. Unfortunately, there is a risk of tailoring the ITS to the test under these circumstances, which makes it difficult to compare performance across studies and ITS technologies.

Another measurement problem lies in identifying the correct performance parameter. The typical metric is a learning gain metric that compares performance in a post-test with a pretest; there is either a difference score [post-pre] or a statistical analysis of post-test scores that partials out contributions of pretest scores. The learning gains are compared for the ITS versus the comparison condition. Sometimes normalized learning gains are computed that adjust for the pretest level: [(post-pre)/(1 − pre)]. Researchers also occasionally collect learning gain data for specific principles and concepts (Forsyth et al., 2012; VanLehn et al., 2007) and average these gains for the total set of principles/concepts. Arguments are also made for collecting learning parameters, namely how fast the learning occurs.

One parameter that may be considered is learning efficiency, which computes the amount of learning per unit of study time, that is, learning gain per hour. We argue that such a metric is inappropriate for any ITS that is targeting deep learning and mastery of the subject matter, unless it is computed appropriately. There are two problems with any simple metric of learning efficiency. First, it does not guarantee mastery of the deep knowledge/skill. Learning environments suited for shallow learning may plateau for deep knowledge and never meet the threshold of mastery, even after hundreds of hours of training. Second, metrics often include a combination of shallow and deep knowledge/skills. When that occurs, the efficiency metric is excellent during the initial time window by virtue of shallow learning, but it never reaches the threshold of mastery for deep learning. An appropriate performance measure for an ITS that targets deep learning should include exclusively deep performance indicators. Of course, a separate performance measure could be computed for shallow learning, but it is the worry of acquiring the deep knowledge/skills that is the central bottleneck.

We argue that an appropriate learning metric for an ITS would satisfy a number of criteria. First, the researchers need to decide on a set of knowledge/skills to master and a threshold for each that specifies adequate mastery. Second, the researchers need to measure the amount of training time (and/or the rate of learning) until mastery is reached for each knowledge/skill. Third, the researchers need to measure the total training time to master the total set of knowledge/skills. Our conjecture is that a good ITS will eventually meet these criteria whereas conventional trainers will either fail to reach performance thresholds or will take much more time to reach mastery of deep knowledge/skills.

Materials

The developers of the materials in most of today's ITSs require at least three forms of expertise: Subject matter knowledge, computer science, and pedagogical strategies. Subject matter expertise will always be needed, but there has been the dream of creating authoring tools that minimize expertise in computer science (Ainsworth & Grimshaw, 2004; Aleven et al., 2009; Murray, Blessing, & Ainsworth, 2003). The authoring tools would be so easy to navigate and use that only modest expertise in information technologies would be adequate for a subject matter expert to create the learning materials. Imagine teachers in K12 and designers of MOOCs (massive open online courses) being able to develop materials for ITS environments. Imagine Nobel laureates creating materials in less than a month to be shared directly with the world through ITS technologies. Unfortunately, the complexity of current ITS technologies has been a major challenge to this lofty goal. With rare exception, those who create the materials for current ITSs have moderate to high computer science expertise. Moreover, their knowledge of pedagogy is unspectacular.

We argue that the authoring tool bottleneck is best confronted by developing a science of authoring processes that helps the field better understand what training and information resources are needed. Just as there are sciences of writing, engineering design, software development, and other creative endeavours, there needs to be a science of creating materials for advanced learning environments in the future. Without a systematic science of the cognitive processes, technologies, and metrics of assessment, the bottleneck will continue to exist.

Money

The expense of developing an ITS is often expressed as a concern of those who make budget decisions (Fletcher, 2014; Fletcher & Morrison, 2012). Graesser and King (2008) projected the following estimates of costs:

> Approximate costs for an hour training session with conventional computer-based training would be $10,000, for a 10-hour course with conventional computer-based training and rudimentary multimedia would be $100,000, for an information-rich hypertext-hypermedia system would be $1,000,000, for a sophisticated intelligent tutoring system would be $10,000,000, and for a serious game on the web with thousands of users would be $100,000,000.
>
> (p. 130)

Colleagues have raised questions and have sometimes disagreed with these estimates, but we would argue that the estimates are within an order of magnitude of being correct.

The Internet entirely changes the landscape on costs. A learning environment that costs 100 million dollars to develop is inexpensive if it can be delivered to 10 million people, but too expensive if only to 10 people. The population of course delivery is therefore very important in the consideration of costs. We would argue that it is also very important to consider the depth of the knowledge/skills. Higher cost is essential if it is the only way for the students to receive deep knowledge/skills. A one million dollar system is worthless if it never progresses students beyond shallow knowledge and if depth is required. Stakeholders need concrete answers on the costs for achieving the targeted levels of expertise in addition to planning, developing, testing, and scaling up any ITS.

A number of concrete answers have been identified to lower costs and meet the pedagogical requirements of deep learning. Four solutions are addressed here. First, standards are needed for reusing learning objects in different systems in a manner that supports smooth interoperability between systems. The military took the lead with their Advanced Distributed Learning initiative (Fletcher, 2009) and the development of SCORM (Shareable Content Object Reference Model) standards for learning objects. Suppose that a chestnut learning object of 1–10 minutes is developed by any creative instructor in the Internet universe. If it has the right structure and metadata, it can be shared with millions of others and incorporated in an ITS. It takes only one chestnut learning object to meet standards and once that is achieved it can go viral and save costs. Second, authoring tools can be used to develop new learning objects with the ideal content, constraints, and metadata to be shared with other learning management systems. The authoring tools will of course need to be designed to maximize interface design for those with minimal computer science experience. Third, a computational infrastructure is needed to support these goals of shareability, interoperability, reuse, and so on. And fourth, it is important to tap into the successful ITS technologies that have already been built. There have been three decades of ITS development for basic universal skills, such as mathematics, physics, engineering, reading, and scientific reasoning. We need to capitalize on these landmark investments.

Generalized Intelligent Framework for Tutoring (GIFT)

The Generalized Intelligent Framework for Tutoring (GIFT) architecture is a major initiative by the Army Research Laboratory that targets some of these core ITS roadblocks (Sottilare et al., 2014; Sottilare et al., 2013). From the standpoint of the present book, the hope is that a systematic architecture (such as GIFT) will help overcome obstacles in building serious games in a manner that minimizes costs and development time, but maximizes student learning and motivation. Two roadblocks that GIFT concentrates on are the lack of modularity and the lack of shared standards, in addition to the other challenges articulated in the previous section. GIFT has three high-level components that are widely acknowledged in computer-based learning communities:

1. Standards-based, modular ITS components (i.e., learner models, pedagogy modules) and authoring tools to support authoring for these components;
2. An instructional manager that facilitates selection from the best pedagogical strategies; and
3. A testbed to study the impact of different ITS components and pedagogical strategies on learning.

This section is pitched at a somewhat technical level that can accommodate a diverse set of learner models and pedagogical strategies. An architecture such as GIFT guides curriculum designers, empirical researchers, and software developers in a coordinated manner. GIFT has multiple complementary functionalities: a service specification for connecting ITS components, the specific ITS components implemented by the standard GIFT runtime, and authoring tool suites. GIFT fulfills these objectives by adhering to modular design principles. That is, it needs to separate components so that they can be substituted for others that perform similar functions. These principles are also important for integration with third-party systems (e.g., game worlds), as they impose a well-defined interface for communicating with new systems.

GIFT addresses a serious challenge for the ITS community that has been recognized for over a decade. As discussed earlier, a major blocking point for scaling up ITSs has historically been the cost of development. This is particularly important for game-based ITSs that must incorporate complex tutoring functionality into an often already complex gaming environment. One solution is to tightly integrate the game environment with tutoring. Well-established systems such as Crystal Island (Rowe, Shores, Mott, & Lester, 2011) and Operation ARIES and Operation ARA (Halpern et al., 2012; Millis et al., 2011) use tight integration, such that several ITS principles and algorithms impose significant constraints over the entire game. The good news is that both of these systems have shown learning gains at deeper levels. One potential liability of these complex systems is that they scale poorly whenever a custom solution is required for each new game, unless the system can be decomposed into functional pieces.

The GIFT architecture emphasizes a loose, service-based integration of tutoring systems into games (Sottilare, Goldberg, Brawner, & Holden, 2012). Thus, the game environment imposes most of the constraints, whereas ITS principles are woven into the game to enhance it. To date, this has been accomplished technically with two serious games (Nye, Hu, Graesser, & Cai, 2014): Virtual BattleSpace 2 (a first-person shooter game) and VMedic (a combat casualty care game, Engineering and Computing Simulations, 2012). There are advantages to having ITS components being sufficiently modular so that they can be migrated into many different games. It increases reuse of components, which has strong practical benefits. Direct development costs for transferring tutoring to new game platforms are reduced, since only platform-specific mechanisms need to be redesigned, rather than the entire pedagogical decision-making system. Unfortunately, however, empirical data are not available to assess whether Virtual BattleSpace 2 and VMedic help student learning or motivation, and also whether there are major reductions in development time and costs. Such assessments are currently underway.

It is important to emphasize that GIFT is designed to increase quality but simultaneously decrease development costs. Tutoring can be developed for one game, then ported to a second game with similar content. This is a general benefit of modularity and separation of components in software design: Building components and strategies that are highly portable allows researchers to design components and then have them tested and refined more effectively. The researchers who use the tools may vary in expertise, ranging from computer scientists to curriculum developers who have limited computer technology skills. Modularity also allows GIFT to use the same suite of authoring tools across multiple domains and learning environments. GIFT is a relatively new architecture, so the magnitude of such benefits remains unclear. We argue that the ability to build or modify an ITS "piece by piece" is an important avenue that could drastically reduce barriers to developing ITSs in the long term.

GIFT Real-Time Adaptive Components

The major GIFT real-time components are summarized in Nye, Sottilare, Ragusa, and Hoffman (2014, see Figure 4 of that article). There is a tutor–user interface that interprets the input of the learner and transmits system actions to the learner environment. A gateway module acts as a bridge to third-party environments, ranging from 3D gaming environments to productivity applications such as Microsoft PowerPoint. The gateway module allows the rest of the system to remain separate from the specific game or learning environment. Multiple modules may split this functionality, such as SIMILE (student information models for intelligent learning environments), a dedicated system for monitoring performance in a learning environment (Engineering and Computing Simulations, 2012). A sensor module acts as an interface to third-party sensors, such as biofeedback sensors and emotion classifiers. Such components are increasingly popular in ITS research as researchers explore the roles of motivation and affect in learning (Calvo & D'Mello, 2010; D'Mello & Graesser, 2010, 2012; McQuiggan et al., 2010). A domain module manages information about the specific domain of instruction (e.g., algebra, military medicine, etc.), which is read from a domain knowledge file (DKF) for the current tutoring domain. A learner module tracks learners' knowledge, performance, emotion, and social states and thereby determines how well they have mastered the material and estimates their capabilities for future interactions. Additional learner information may be communicated to the learner module by external systems, such as the learning record stores (LRS) that maintain biographical data and historical learning data. Finally, a pedagogical module contains instructional strategies that can be selected during a session. These strategies determine the strategies and skills that guide how GIFT intervenes to improve learning.

GIFT intervenes in a gaming environment by monitoring the states and shifts in the learner's state, and then using these shifts to select instructional strategies. The goals of GIFT strategies are intended to increase domain knowledge, but in a game environment there are also the goals of maintaining motivation and persistence. The representation of pedagogical strategies in GIFT consists of IF <state> THEN <action> production rules, a standard representation for strategically selecting instructional strategies. Rule-based tutoring strategies have a long history in ITSs (Anderson et al., 1995; Graesser, Conley, & Olney, 2012; Woolf, 2009). The system watches over the landscape of current states existing in the working memory. Then, if particular states exist or reach some threshold of activation, a production rule is fired probabilistically. Contemporary rules are never brittle, but rather are activated to some degree and probabilistically. GIFT strategies are intended to be domain independent and are later resolved via domain-dependent tactics that are specific to the instructional domain and that activate actions in the game environment (Nye, Sottilare, et al., 2014).

The general GIFT processes and components provide multiple levels of adaptivity to learners. The example described above focuses on microadaptive behavior, also sometimes referred to as the inner-loop or step-based tutoring (VanLehn, 2006). Microadaptivity occurs when a system supports the user in one or more ongoing tasks or goals. GIFT can also provide macroadaptive support for learning, sometimes called outer-loop adaptivity. Macroadaptivity includes selecting tasks or problems for the learner to solve, usually with the intention to keep problems within a learner's zone of proximal development.

GIFT Information Flow

A simplified view of GIFT information flow can be considered when providing real-time microadaptation. GIFT is under active development, so some of these functions are likely to evolve over time (the current version is GIFT 4.0). Rather than focusing on specific details or mechanisms, we trace how knowledge flows through the system in order to explore how data about the learner, the learning environment, and the domain are processed by instructional strategies in GIFT to produce meaningful pedagogical actions for a gaming environment. Table 4.1 gives a high-level overview of how GIFT uses strategies and tactics to select actions that impact the learner as they interact with a game. Each of these steps will be described briefly. Symbols are assigned to various information states and functions noted in Table 4.1 to facilitate referencing the information in each step.

Session Inputs: Sensors and the Learning Environment (Step 1)

GIFT strategies have three main sources of information: the learning environment for the user (1.A), the external sensor data streams (1.B), and the model of the learner based on accumulated events over time (1.C). The learning environment could include the user interface, the state of the game world, or possibly the state of an accompanying slideshow presentation. Events with information about user behavior (E_t) are sent in real time to GIFT from the communication module for the learning environment. External sensors may also provide information about the learner (D_t), such as biometrics and emotion classifiers. Each of these input sources reaches the learner module by a separate path. While learner behavior

TABLE 4.1 High-Level Summary of GIFT Strategy Evaluation

Step	Module	Description	Functional Expression
1.A	Communication	The learner interacts with user interface and game environment, which sends events to the domain module	E_t – Events from user behavior at time t
1.B	Sensor	Sensor data states (e.g., emotion classifications) are sent directly to learner module	D_t – Data from sensors at time t
1.C	Learner	Persistent learner model data, such as the contents of a learning management system	D_L – Persistent learner model data
2	Domain	Performance assessment rules estimate discrete performance (e.g., below, at, or above expectation) on low-level domain concepts (C_L)	$P_{c,t}$ – Performance on concept c at time t R_c = Rules to assess c $P_{c,t} = R_c(E_t) \; \forall \, c \in C_L$
3	Domain	Performance for higher-level concepts (C_H) "rolled up" (aggregated) from lower levels	F_c – Roll-up function for c $P_{c,t} = F_c(C_L) \; \forall \, c \in C_H$
4	Domain	Performance assessment states sent to pedagogical module and to learner module	P_t – Performance states for all concepts at t $P_t = [P_{c1,t}, P_{c2,t} \ldots]$
5	Learner	Learner state changes on domain performance (Step 5) or sensors (Step 1.B) trigger strategy evaluation	
6	Pedagogy	Instructional strategy selected based on the transition from the prior to current learner state	S_t – Strategy for time t F_S – Strategy selection code for pedagogy module $S_t = F_S(P_{t-1}, D_{t-1}, P_t, D_t, D_L)$
7	Pedagogy	Strategy selection is sent to the domain module	
8	Domain (Tactics)	A strategy selection is mapped to a domain-specific tactic (T)	T_t – Tactic selected $T_t = F_T(S_t)$
9	Communication	A tactic causes one or more actions (A) to occur in the game environment (e.g., hints, changes in difficulty, etc.)	A_t – Actions for time t F_A – Map of tactics (T) to environment actions (A) $A_t = F_A(T)$

from the communication module passes through the domain module (Steps 2–4), sensor information is directly fed to the learner module. Many sources of information are integrated into the learner module ($\mathbf{D_L}$), such as persistent learner data (i.e., data stored in a learning management system) or biographical data (e.g., gender, age, etc.). Considerable information is not likely to change during a single learning session, so they will be treated as invariant for this discussion and will reside in 1.C. However, in practice, their states may change during a session.

Assessing Performance: Domain Module (Steps 2–4)

The domain module uses the events and information from the learning environment to assess performance on a set of domain concepts ($\mathbf{C}$). Two types of concepts exist: low-level concepts ($\mathbf{C_L}$) that are evaluated based on performance assessment rules and higher-level concepts ($\mathbf{C_H}$) where performance is inferred from performance on lower-level ones. Thus, there is a hierarchical structure of grain size, with a threshold differentiating low from high. Assessment rules are stored in a domain-knowledge file (DKF), which contains all the domain-specific rules and concepts for the tutoring system. For each low-level concept, the performance assessment rules for each concept ($\mathbf{R_c}$) use the learning environment events to classify performance as "below expectation," "at expectation," "above expectation," or "unknown" (for when it is not yet assessed). For higher-level concepts, performance is derived from the performance of child concepts through an aggregation function that "rolls up" performance ($\mathbf{F_c}$). External performance assessments can also be received, such as those calculated by SIMILE, a dedicated system for monitoring performance in a learning environment (Engineering and Computing Simulations, 2012). Third-party systems such as SIMILE can calculate and transmit assessments from a game environment, acting as a bridge between GIFT and a specific gaming environment. After performance is assessed, these assessments are sent to the learner module and pedagogy module.

Strategy Selection: Learner and Pedagogy Modules (Steps 5–7)

Performance and sensor data are considered in either discrete or continuous states. A large enough change to any of these states in the learner module can trigger a search for an appropriate strategy to support the learning goals. This selection process is handled by the pedagogical module, which considers the current learner state (sensors and learning assessments) and the prior learner state. For any given transition, one instructional strategy may be selected by the pedagogy module. The strategy selection process ($\mathbf{F_S}$) is determined by functions in the pedagogy module, which may be rules (similar to the DKF) or more advanced Java functions. In general, rules are used and different transitions may be combined using Boolean operators (e.g., AND) to determine the conditions for selecting a domain-independent strategy decision. For many transitions, no strategy may be activated. In that case, the pedagogical module waits until the next strategy trigger occurs. When a strategy (S_t) is selected, it is sent to the Domain Module for evaluation. At this stage, the strategy decision may be referred to as an "abstract strategy" because it is not domain specific.

As a concrete example, consider the transition of a student being engaged in a task versus disengaged or bored. This is a transition that can be sensed from multiple channels with some degree of accuracy (Calvo & D'Mello, 2010; D'Mello & Graesser, 2010). One selected pedagogical strategy would be to increase or decrease the difficulty of the assigned next task (D'Mello & Graesser, 2012), which would depend on the performance level of the student in the session. For comparatively higher performers, more difficult tasks would be selected in order to increase the challenge level. For lower performers, easier tasks would be selected because the existing difficulty level is beyond what the student can handle. So the general abstract pedagogical strategy in this example is to adjust the difficulty level of the next task when there is a large discrepancy in engagement and the adjustment depends on specific knowledge states and performance of the learner. Production rules capture these contingencies in GIFT and there is empirical evidence for some of these production rules. An affect-sensitive AutoTutor has been shown to improve learning in comparison with an affect-neutral AutoTutor (D'Mello & Graesser, 2012) but it is too early to quantify effect sizes for particular strategies at this point in the science.

From Strategies to Tactics: Domain Module (Steps 8–9)

After a general strategy is selected, it must be translated into a more specific form that is suitable for the domain. For example, an abstract strategy decision might be: "Provide corrective feedback for concept A." The tactics component of the domain module must map each strategy to a domain-specific decision. At present, tactics (T) are mapped on a one-to-one basis to abstract strategy decisions (S) in GIFT. This mapping (F_A) is defined as part of the domain-specific information. As an example, a tactical decision for a math domain to "Provide corrective feedback for concept A" would be to inform the learner that the correct answer is 5, but their answer was 8. Alternatively, for a medical domain, concept A might be a diagnosis, so tactical design could inform the learner that their diagnosis of anemia was wrong and that the correct answer was scurvy. Once a tactical decision has been made, this decision (T_t) will be sent to the learning environment, which will take some actions that will implement the decision. So continuing the example of corrective feedback, the learning environment might provide a voiceover that speaks the corrective feedback. In a different learning environment, this feedback might be provided using a text hint instead. This modularity makes GIFT well-matched for integrating intelligent tutoring into a variety of game environments.

Closing Comments

The technical specifications of GIFT help organize the ITS side of the GIFT–ITS marriage. That is, all ITSs must somehow fit into the GIFT conception of ITSs. However, what about the motivating game elements? Our conjecture is that game components can fit in the same architecture with little or no problems other than understanding the essence of games. Game features are essentially like any other subject matter, namely complex, multifaceted, and ranging from brittle to probabilistic in their mechanisms. Just as math can be merged with physics, so can games. Angry Birds and Newton's Playground (Shute & Ventura, 2013) are success cases in illustrating the meshing of game constraints with formal systems.

But alas, games have some constraints that are very different than the components of deep learning and that will pose challenges to meshing the worlds (Adams & Clark, 2014; Graesser, Chipman, Leeming, & Biedenbach, 2009). We believe it is most feasible to embed ITS modules within existing game environments to enhance the game, such as intelligent dialogue, simulations, and so on. The native motivational features of a successful game will be minimally compromised by the embedded intelligent features. We believe it is possible to add game features to ITS and thereby attempt to enhance motivation (called gamification), but that may have limited success for reasons articulated below. Finally, we believe that it will be extremely difficult to develop a game that has components that are closely aligned with the constraints of an ITS because the constraints are very different. Below are some of the pressure points that may make it difficult, or even impossible, to design some game–ITS technologies that show benefits for deep learning.

1. **Non-germane load bloat**. The cognitive load from the game elements may not be germane to the mastery of the serious subject matter and ultimately reduce deep learning (Adams et al., 2012). For example, if the narrative, fantasy, and competition components take up too much time and are profoundly distracting, then an insufficient amount of deep learning may be achieved. The penalty may persist over and above the added time the game elements afford for intrinsic motivation and self-regulated learning. When this occurs, there are no payoffs for the game elements on any metric, including the integral learning-time metric discussed earlier.

2. **Feedback guideline clashes**. Feedback is an important aspect of both ITSs and games. However, the timing and nature of the feedback may be very different for the two worlds. Games often provide timely, if not quick, feedback to the learner about the quality of their contributions in order to keep the student in what Csikszentmihalyi (1990) called the state of psychological flow. Flow is intense engagement to the point where time and sometimes fatigue psychologically disappear. In ITS technologies, there needs to be time for thought and reflection over the depth of the material,

a timing pattern that might clash with the speedy tempo of games. In essence, there will be a clash in timing if online temporal dynamics are incompatible in games and ITSs. There may also be traffic jams among feedback, particularly in complex environments with many competing tasks. Prioritizing feedback in a dynamic, game-based environment is non-trivial. Similarly, there may be clashes in the qualitative feedback, such as justifications, explanations, and recommended actions. Qualitative feedback is perhaps the hallmark of ITS deep learning, but hardcore gamers may not appreciate technical content encroaching on their game experience. The serious content needs to be smuggled into games in slick ways that routinely stymie game designers that aspire to build serious games.

3. **Content collision between narrative and deep learning**. The ideal is a seamless harmony between the game narrative and the subject matter content. Unfortunately, the odds of that happening may be akin to a film director winning an Academy Award. What is the typical integration scenario? Either the narrative does not promote the difficulties of the subject matter, or the narrative is incoherently boring as it caters to the constraints of the subject matter. It is safe to assume that the two worlds are in collision unless a genius can find ways to connect them. That being said, there may be some realistic approaches in meshing narrative with ITSs to promote deep learning. Specifically, the ITS modules can be embedded within the game world to increase the intelligence of game components and to avoid interfering with the conceptual integrity of the game constraints.

4. **Control struggles**. The learners want to be in control and follow their whims in a capricious trajectory that is guided by intrinsic motivation or possibly self-regulated learning. The harbingers of deep knowledge want to be in control over the learning experience to satisfy the curriculum, pedagogy, and efficiency metrics. This is a power struggle.

5. **System engineering disconnections**. These various incompatible constraints might possibly be resolved by a cost–benefit analysis that maximizes progress. That will not happen if stakeholders wallow in their professional caves, guard their positions, and resist communication and compromise. A cost–benefit analysis needs to be quantified in monetary units.

It is very true that there are struggles in solving anything fundamental to society. However, we continue to be skeptically optimistic on promoting the game–ITS marriage because the lofty goal of turning work into play may be in sight with enough effort, coordination, science, and creativity. We need to see more success cases of systems that apply game features to intelligent tutoring systems, that weave ITS modules into game components, and that have successful dances between the constraints of games and subject matter domains. More success cases are needed before we can answer the question of whether serious games can promote deep learning of difficult academic material.

Author Note

The research was supported by the National Science Foundation (SBR 9720314, REC 0106965, REC 0126265, ITR 0325428, REESE 0633918, ALT-0834847, DRK-12-0918409, 1108845), the Institute of Education Sciences (R305H050 169, R305B070349, R305A080589, R305A080594, R305G020018, R305C 120001), Army Research Lab (W911INF-12-2-0030), and the Office of Naval Research (N00014-00-1-0600, N00014-12-C-0643). Any opinions, findings, and conclusions or recommendations expressed in this material are those of the authors and do not necessarily reflect the views of NSF, IES, or DoD. The Tutoring Research Group (TRG) is an interdisciplinary research team comprised of researchers from psychology, computer science, physics, and education at University of Memphis (visit www.autotutor.org, http://emotion.autotutor.org, http://fedex.memphis.edu/iis/).

References

Adams, D. M., & Clark, D. B. (2014). Integrating self-explanation functionality into a complex game environment: Keeping gaming in motion. *Computers & Education, 73,* 149–159.

Adams, D. M., Mayer, R. E., McNamara, A., Koenig, A., & Wainess, R. (2012). Narrative games for learning: Testing the discovery and narrative hypotheses. *Journal of Educational Psychology, 104*(1), 235–249.

Ainsworth, S. E., & Grimshaw, S. K. (2004). Evaluating the REDEEM authoring tool: Can teachers create effective learning environments? *International Journal of Artificial Intelligence in Education, 14,* 279–312.

Aleven, V., McLaren, B. M., Sewall, J., & Koedinger, K. (2009). A new paradigm for intelligent tutoring systems: Example-tracing tutors. *International Journal of Artificial Intelligence in Education, 19,* 105–154.

Anderson, J. R., Corbett, A. T., Koedinger, K. R., & Pelletier, R. (1995). Cognitive tutors: Lessons learned. *Journal of the Learning Sciences, 4,* 167–207.

Baker, R. S. J. d., D'Mello, S. K., Rodrigo, M. T., & Graesser, A. C. (2010). Better to be frustrated than bored: The incidence, persistence, and impact of learners' cognitive-affective states during interactions with three different computer-based learning environments. *International Journal of Human-Computer Studies, 68,* 223–241.

Bloom, B. S. (1956). *Taxonomy of educational objectives: The classification of educational goals. Handbook I: Cognitive Domain.* New York, NY: McKay.

Burstein, J. (2003). The E-rater scoring engine: Automated essay scoring with natural language processing. In M. D. Shermis & J. C. Burstein (Eds.), *Automated essay scoring: A cross-disciplinary perspective* (pp. 122–133). Mahwah, NJ: Erlbaum.

Calvo, R. A., & D'Mello, S. K. (2010). Affect detection: An interdisciplinary review of models, methods, and their applications. *IEEE Transactions on Affective Computing, 1,* 18–37.

Cohen, P. A., Kulik, J. A., & Kulik, C. C. (1982). Educational outcomes of tutoring: A meta-analysis of findings. *American Educational Research Journal, 19,* 237–248.

Csikszentmihalyi, M. (1990). *Flow: The psychology of optimal experience.* New York, NY: Harper-Row.

D'Mello, S., & Graesser, A. C. (2010). Multimodal semi-automated affect detection from conversational cues, gross body language, and facial features. *User Modeling and User-adapted Interaction, 20,* 147–187.

D'Mello, S. K., & Graesser, A. C. (2012). AutoTutor and affective AutoTutor: Learning by talking with cognitively and emotionally intelligent computers that talk back. *ACM Transactions on Interactive Intelligent Systems, 2*(23), 1–38.

D'Mello, S., Lehman, S., Pekrun, R., & Graesser, A. (2014). Confusion can be beneficial for learning. *Learning and Instruction, 29,* 153–170.

Dodds, P. V. W., & Fletcher, J. D. (2004). Opportunities for new "smart" learning environments enabled by next generation web capabilities. *Journal of Education Multimedia and Hypermedia, 13,* 391–404.

Doignon, J. P., & Falmagne, J. C. (1999). *Knowledge spaces.* Berlin, Germany: Springer.

Dynarsky, M., Agodina, R., Heaviside, S., Novak, T., Carey, N., Campuzano, L., . . . Sussex, W. (2007). *Effectiveness of reading and mathematics software products: Findings from the first student cohort.* Washington, DC: U.S. Department of Education, Institute of Education Sciences.

Engineering and Computing Simulations. (2012). *vMedic.* Retrieved October 2, 2013 from www.ecsorl.com/products/vmedic

Fletcher, J. D. (2003). Evidence for learning from technology-assisted instruction. In H. F. O'Neil & R. S. Perez (Eds.), *Technology applications in education: A learning view* (pp. 79–99). Mahwah, NJ: Erlbaum.

Fletcher, J. D. (2009). Education and training technology in the military. *Science, 323,* 72–75.

Fletcher, J. D. (2014). *Digital tutoring in information systems technology for veterans: Data report* (Document D-5336). Alexandria, VA: Institute for Defense Analyses.

Fletcher, J. D., & Morrison, J. E. (2012). *DARPA Digital Tutor: Assessment data* (IDA Document D-4686). Alexandria, VA: Institute for Defense Analyses.

Forsyth, C. M., Pavlik, P., Graesser, A. C., Cai, Z., Germany, M., Millis, K., . . . & Dolan, R. (2012). Learning gains for core concepts in a serious game on scientific reasoning. In K. Yacef, O. Zaïane, H. Hershkovitz, M. Yudelson, & J. Stamper (Eds.), *Proceedings of the 5th International Conference on Educational Data Mining* (pp. 172–175). Chania, Greece: International Educational Data Mining Society.

Graesser, A. C., Chipman, P., Haynes, B., & Olney, A. (2005). AutoTutor: An intelligent tutoring system with mixed-initiative dialogue. *IEEE Transactions on Education, 48,* 612–618.

Graesser, A. C., Chipman, P., Leeming, F., & Biedenbach, S. (2009). Deep learning and emotion in serious games. In U. Ritterfeld, M. Cody, & P. Vorderer (Eds.), *Serious games: Mechanisms and effects* (pp. 81–100). New York, NY and London: Routledge, Taylor & Francis.

Graesser, A. C., Conley, M., & Olney, A. (2012). Intelligent tutoring systems. In K. R. Harris, S. Graham, & T. Urdan (Eds.), *APA educational psychology handbook: Vol. 3. Applications to learning and teaching* (pp. 451–473). Washington, DC: American Psychological Association.

Graesser, A. C., & D'Mello, S. (2012). Emotions during the learning of difficult material. In. B. Ross (Ed.), *The psychology of learning and motivation* (Vol. 57, pp. 183–225). Amsterdam, Netherlands: Elsevier.

Graesser, A. C., D'Mello, S. K., & Cade, W. (2011). Instruction based on tutoring. In R. E. Mayer & P. A. Alexander (Eds.), *Handbook of research on learning and instruction* (pp. 408–426). New York, NY: Routledge Press.

Graesser, A. C., D'Mello, S. K., Hu, X., Cai, Z., Olney, A., & Morgan, B. (2012). AutoTutor. In P. McCarthy & C. Boonthum-Denecke (Eds.), *Applied natural language processing: Identification, investigation, and resolution* (pp. 169–187). Hershey, PA: IGI Global.

Graesser, A.C., & King, B. (2008). Technology-based training. In J. J. Blascovich & C. H. Hartel (Eds.), *Human behavior in military contexts* (pp. 127–149). Washington, DC: National Academy of Sciences.

Graesser, A. C., Lu, S., Jackson, G. T., Mitchell, H., Ventura, M., Olney, A., & Louwerse, M. M. (2004). AutoTutor: A tutor with dialogue in natural language. *Behavioral Research Methods, Instruments, and Computers, 36,* 180–193.

Halpern, D. F., Millis, K., Graesser, A. C., Butler, H., Forsyth, C., & Cai, Z. (2012). Operation ARA: A computerized learning game that teaches critical thinking and scientific reasoning. *Thinking Skills and Creativity, 7,* 93–100.

Jackson, G. T., Dempsey, K. B., & McNamara, D.S. (2012). Game-based practice in a reading strategy tutoring system: Showdown in iSTART-ME. In H. Reinders (Ed.), *Digital games in language learning and teaching* (pp. 115–138). Basingstoke, UK: Palgrave Macmillan.

Jackson, G. T., & Graesser, A. C. (2007). Content matters: An investigation of feedback categories within an ITS. In R. Luckin, K. Koedinger, & J. Greer (Eds.), *Artificial intelligence in education: Building technology rich learning contexts that work* (pp. 127–134). Amsterdam: IOS Press.

Jackson, G. T., & McNamara, D. S. (2013). Motivation and performance in a game-based intelligent tutoring system. *Journal of Educational Psychology, 105,* 1036–1049.

Johnson, L. W., & Valente, A. (2008). Tactical language and culture training systems: Using artificial intelligence to teach foreign languages and cultures. In M. Goker and K. Haigh (Eds.), *Proceedings of the Twentieth Conference on Innovative Applications of Artificial Intelligence* (pp. 1632–1639). Menlo Park, CA: AAAI Press.

Jurafsky, D., & Martin, J. H. (2008). *Speech and language processing: An introduction to natural language processing, computational linguistics, and speech recognition.* Upper Saddle River, NJ: Prentice-Hall.

Koedinger, K. R., Anderson, J. R., Hadley, W. H., & Mark, M. (1997). Intelligent tutoring goes to school in the big city. *International Journal of Artificial Intelligence in Education, 8,* 30–43.

Koedinger, K. R., Corbett, A. C., & Perfetti, C. (2012). The Knowledge-Learning-Instruction (KLI) framework: Bridging the science-practice chasm to enhance robust student learning. *Cognitive Science, 36*(5), 757–798.

Landauer, T. K., Laham, D., & Foltz, P. W. (2003). Automatic essay assessment. *Assessment in Education: Principles, Policy & Practice, 10,* 295–308.

Landauer, T. K., McNamara, D. S., Dennis, S., & Kintsch, W. (Eds.). (2007). *Handbook of latent semantic analysis.* Mahwah, NJ: Erlbaum.

Lepper, M. R., & Henderlong, J. (2000). Turning "play" into "work" and "work" into "play": 25 years of research on intrinsic versus extrinsic motivation. In C. Sansone & J. M. Harackiewicz (Eds.), *Intrinsic and extrinsic motivation: The search for optimal motivation and performance* (pp. 257–307). San Diego, CA: Academic Press.

Lesgold, A., Lajoie, S. P., Bunzo, M., & Eggan, G. (1992). SHERLOCK: A coached practice environment for an electronics trouble-shooting job. In J. H. Larkin & R. W. Chabay (Eds.), *Computer assisted instruction and intelligent tutoring systems: Shared goals and complementary approaches* (pp. 201–238). Hillsdale, NJ: Erlbaum.

Ma, W., Adesope, O. O., Nesbit, J. C., & Liu, Q. (2014). Intelligent tutoring systems and learning outcomes: A meta-analytic survey. *Journal of Educational Psychology, 106,* 901–918.

Mayer, R. E. (2011). Multimedia learning and games. In S. Tobias & J. D. Fletcher (Eds.), *Computer games and instruction* (pp. 281–305). Charlotte, NC: Information Age.

McCarthy, P., & Boonthum-Denecke, C. (Eds.). (2012). *Applied natural language processing: Identification, investigation, and resolution.* Hershey, PA: IGI Global.

McNamara, D. S., Jackson, G. T., & Graesser, A. C. (2010). Intelligent tutoring and games (ITaG). In Y. K. Baek (Ed.), *Gaming for classroom-based learning: Digital role-playing as a motivator of study* (pp. 44–65). Hershey, PA: IGI Global.

McQuiggan, S. W., Robison, J. L., & Lester, J. C. (2010). Affective transitions in narrative-centered learning environments. *Educational Technology & Society, 13,* 40–53.

Millis, K., Forsyth, C., Butler, H., Wallace, P., Graesser, A., & Halpern, D. (2011). Operation ARIES! A serious game for teaching scientific inquiry. In M. Ma, A. Oikonomou, & J. Lakhmi (Eds.), *Serious games and edutainment applications* (pp. 169–196). London, UK: Springer-Verlag.

Mitrovic, A., Martin, B., & Suraweera, P. (2007). Intelligent tutors for all: The constraint-based approach. *IEEE Intelligent Systems, 22,* 38–45.

Murray, T., Blessing, S., & Ainsworth, S. (2003). (Eds.). *Authoring tools for advanced technology learning environments.* Amsterdam: Kluwer.

Nye, B. D., Graesser, A. C., & Hu, X. (2014). AutoTutor and family: A review of 17 years of natural language tutoring. *International Journal of Artificial Intelligence in Education, 24,* 427–469.

Nye, B. D., Hu, X., Graesser, A. C., & Cai, Z. (2014). AutoTutor in the Cloud: A service-oriented paradigm for an interoperable natural language ITS. *Journal of Advanced Distributed Learning Technology, 2*(6), 49–63.

Nye, B. D., Sottilare, R. A., Ragusa, C., & Hoffman, M. (2014). Defining instructional challenges, strategies, and tactics for adaptive intelligent tutoring systems. In R. A. Sottilare, A. C. Graesser, X. Hu, & B. Goldberg (Eds.), *Design recommendations for intelligent tutoring systems: Vol. 2. Instructional management* (pp. xv–xxvi). Orlando, FL: Army Research Laboratory.

Olney, A., D'Mello, S. K., Person, N., Cade, W., Hays, P., Williams, C., . . . & Graesser, A. C. (2012). Guru: A computer tutor that models expert human tutors. In S. Cerri, W. Clancey, G. Papadourakis, & K. Panourgia (Eds.), *Proceedings of Intelligent Tutoring Systems (ITS) 2012* (pp. 256–261). Berlin, Germany: Springer.

O'Neil, H. F., & Perez, R. S. (Eds.). (2008). *Computer games and team and individual learning.* Amsterdam, Netherlands: Elsevier.

Ritter, S., Anderson, J. R., Koedinger, K. R., & Corbett, A. (2007). Cognitive Tutor: Applied research in mathematics education. *Psychonomic Bulletin & Review, 14,* 249–255.

Ritterfeld, U., Cody, M., & Vorderer, P. (Eds.). (2009). *Serious games: Mechanisms and effects.* New York, NY and London: Routledge, Taylor & Francis.

Rowe, J. P., Shores, L. R., Mott, B. W., & Lester, J. C. (2011). Integrating learning, problem solving, and engagement in narrative-centered learning environments. *International Journal of Artificial Intelligence in Education, 21,* 115–133.

Rus, V., D'Mello, S., Hu, X., & Graesser, A. C. (2013). Recent advances in intelligent systems with conversational dialogue. *AI Magazine, 34,* 42–54.

Sabourin, J. L., Rowe, J. P., Mott, B. W., & Lester, J. C. (2013). Considering alternate futures to classify off-task behavior as emotion self-regulation: A supervised learning approach. *Journal of Educational Data Mining, 5,* 9–38.

Shute, V. J., & Ventura, M. (2013). *Measuring and supporting learning in games: Stealth assessment.* Cambridge, MA: MIT Press.

Sottilare, R. A., Goldberg, B. S., Brawner, K. W., & Holden, H. K. (2012). A modular framework to support the authoring and assessment of adaptive computer-based tutoring systems (CBTS). In *Proceedings of the Interservice/Industry Training, Simulation & Education Conference (I/ITSEC) 2012* (12017). Arlington, VA: National Training Systems Association.

Sottilare, R., Graesser, A., Hu, X., & Goldberg, B. (Eds.). (2014). *Design recommendations for intelligent tutoring systems: Vol. 2. Instructional management.* Orlando, FL: Army Research Laboratory.

Sottilare, R., Graesser, A., Hu, X., & Holden, H. (Eds.). (2013). *Design recommendations for intelligent tutoring systems: Learner modeling* (Vol. 1). Orlando, FL: Army Research Laboratory.

Steenbergen-Hu, S., & Cooper, H. (2013). A meta-analysis of the effectiveness of intelligent tutoring systems on K-12 students' mathematical learning. *Journal of Educational Psychology, 105,* 971–987.

Steenbergen-Hu, S., & Cooper, H. (2014). A meta-analysis of the effectiveness of intelligent tutoring systems on college students' academic learning. *Journal of Educational Psychology, 106,* 331–347.

Tobias, S., & Fletcher, J. D. (2011). *Computer games and instruction.* Charlotte, NC: Information Age.

VanLehn, K. (2006). The behavior of tutoring systems. *International Journal of Artificial Intelligence in Education, 16,* 227–265.

VanLehn, K. (2011). The relative effectiveness of human tutoring, intelligent tutoring systems and other tutoring systems. *Educational Psychologist, 46,* 197–221.

VanLehn, K., Graesser, A. C., Jackson, G. T., Jordan, P., Olney, A., & Rose, C. P. (2007). When are tutorial dialogues more effective than reading? *Cognitive Science, 31,* 3–62.

VanLehn, K., Jordan, P., Rosé, C. P., Bhembe, D., Böttner, M., Gaydos, A., . . . Srivastava, R. (2002). The architecture of Why2-Atlas: A coach for qualitative physics essay writing. In S. A. Cerri, G. Gouarderes, & F. Paraguacu (Eds.), *Intelligent Tutoring Systems: 6th International Conference* (pp. 158–167). Berlin: Springer.

Ward, W., Cole, R., Bolaños, D., Buchenroth-Martin, C., Svirsky, E., & Weston, T. (2013). My science tutor: A conversational multimedia virtual tutor. *Journal of Educational Psychology, 105,* 1115–1125.

Woolf, B. P. (2009). *Building intelligent interactive tutors.* Burlington, MA: Morgan Kaufmann.

Wouters, P., van Nimwegen, C., van Oostendorp, H., & van der Spek, E. D. (2013). A meta-analysis of the cognitive and motivational effects of serious games. *Journal of Educational Psychology, 105,* 249–265.

PART II
Assessment

5

USING CROWDSOURCING AS A FORMATIVE EVALUATION TECHNIQUE FOR GAME ICONS

Ayesha Madni, Gregory K. W. K. Chung,
Eva L. Baker, and Noelle C. Griffin

In the last decade, there has been an increased emphasis on social and emotional learning (SEL) within educational settings. According to the Collaborative for Academic, Social, and Emotional Learning (CASEL), social and emotional learning is the process through which children and adults acquire and successfully apply the knowledge, attitudes, and skills necessary to understand and regulate emotions, set and attain positive goals, feel and show empathy for others, establish and maintain positive relationships, and make responsible decisions (CASEL, 2003; Weissberg & Cascarino, 2013). It is not surprising that this emphasis on SEL couples the increased visibility of bullying incidences across the K-12 grade span (Lim & Hoot, 2015). In particular, peer victimization has become prevalent among elementary school students in recent years (Graham, 2010; Kirves & Sajaniemi, 2012). Research consistently demonstrates the negative short- and long-term behavioral, psychological, and academic outcomes for students as a result of bullying (Graham, 2010; Juvonen & Graham, 2002; Zins & Elias, 2014).

Bullying has been defined as a systematic and repeated aggressive behavior purposefully directed against specific children, including an imbalance of power between the victim and the aggressor (Rigby, Smith, & Pepler, 2004). Among elementary-school-aged children, bullying most often manifests in direct ways including physical and verbal aggression and teasing (Eriksen, Nielsen, & Simonsen, 2014). However, recent research has also demonstrated that elementary-school-aged children engage in exclusion as a form of bullying, and that all forms of bullying are prevalent across genders (Alsaker & Gutzwiller-Helfenfinger, 2012; Pepler & Craig, 2010).

Given the imbalance of power that is pervasive between perpetrator and victim in bullying situations, most children who are bullied tend to engage in nonassertive coping strategies, such as withdrawing, not defending themselves, or crying and letting the bully have his or her way (Alsaker & Gutzwiller-Helfenfinger, 2012; Graham, 2010; Monks et al., 2009). In contrast to physically leaving a conflict situation, which victims do not tend to do, withdrawing involves mentally and emotionally leaving the situation as a form of self-protection by retreating within (Tenenbaum, Varjas, Meyers, & Parris, 2011). Some researchers contend that these types of nonassertive coping strategies on the part of victims might in fact reinforce bullies, causing victimization behaviors to persist (Alsaker & Gutzwiller-Helfenfinger, 2012).

The most important assertive coping skills identified to de-escalate a bullying situation include remaining calm and not aggressing back, saying "stop" assertively, and leaving and seeking help (Monks et al., 2009). According to social cognitive theory, behavioral responses and skills such as resilience (i.e., capacity for positive and successful adaptation despite challenges and/or threatening circumstances) (Fletcher & Sarkar, 2013) are learned socially. Furthermore, children will only demonstrate a new behavior and skill when they feel efficacious about doing so (Bandura, 1997; Monks et al., 2009; Ormrod, 2011). In other words, assertive responses used to de-escalate bullying conflicts can be learned through observation and, especially important, victims will only use them when they feel confident about their ability to implement them.

The evidence on the effectiveness of existing antibullying programs, however, is mixed (Ferguson, San Miguel, Kilburn, & Sanchez, 2007; Smith, Schneider, Smith, & Ananiadou, 2004; Ttofi & Farrington, 2011). This is not surprising because schools often lack the infrastructure, staffing, and resources to effectively implement these programs (CASEL, 2003; Ferguson et al., 2007; Ttofi & Farrington, 2011). In other words, existing antibullying and resilience programs are not always consistently and successfully implemented, thereby compromising the ability to convey pertinent skills to students who need to learn and use them (CASEL, 2003; Monks et al., 2009). Many programs also serve as one-time interventions, and therefore do not reinforce the skills being learned.

Educational video games can aid this problem, being stand-alone interventions that can be implemented across occasions, and where the fidelity of implementation is inherent within the game sequence and design. The role of the teacher in implementing educational video games within the classroom can range from providing students with technical support and setting the context for and/or providing activities that frame the educational video game, to implementing the game as part of instruction or using the game as an example during instruction. Essentially, the role of the teacher is dependent on the instructional purpose and context for which the game was developed. The more hands-on the teacher has to be with the game, the less fidelity of implementation can be determined (Ketelhut & Schifter, 2011; Squire, 2006).

Game-Based Learning

Educational video games have become more popular within the academic setting in recent years. Compared to 10 years ago, there is at present an ever-increasing interest in the academic community to explore the use of games as important learning and assessment tools in K-12 education. In fact, the use of simulations and games in learning and assessment has been expected to increase with 97% of U.S. teens playing some type of digital game on a regular basis (De Wannemacker, Vandercruysse, & Clarebout, 2012; McClarty et al., 2012; Squire, 2011). There is also growing recognition of the applicability of video games in education with the skills and knowledge imparted by a traditional education no longer being seen as adequate preparation for success in life. The next generation of jobs will primarily be characterized by increased technology use, extensive problem solving, and complex communication (Levy & Murnane, 2004; Spector, Merrill, Elen, & Bishop, 2013).

While there is substantial theoretical support for the benefits of video games in learning and education, the empirical support is mixed. Some contend that video games can be detrimental to student learning due to time spent away from other academic activities because of gaming addiction and potential aggressive tendencies (Grüsser, Thalemann, & Griffiths, 2007; Ng & Wierner-Hastings, 2005) and others contend that when moderated and designed to address a specific problem or teach a certain skill, video games have been found to be highly successful teaching and learning tools (Griffiths, 2002; Squire, 2006, 2007; Wouters, van Nimwegen, van Oostendorp, & van der Spek, 2013). Despite these divergent perceptions, a common finding among educators and researchers is that effective games include sound instructional design and pedagogical strategies to appropriately guide students in their learning process (McClarty et al., 2012; Tobias, Fletcher, & Wind, 2014).

Characteristics of sound instructional and pedagogical design include features that engage learners and encourage them to persist, instruction that is individualized and provides a level of challenge, and guidance and immediate feedback (Tobias et al., 2014). Instructional design features generally focus on increasing learner efficiencies in computer-aided instruction (Roytek, 2010), whereas pedagogy often refers to universal principles of learning that apply across practice and instructional modes (Loveless, 2011).

Instructionally Sound Pedagogy

What makes for sound instructional design and pedagogy for game-based learning? Few instructional methods engage learners or induce them to persist on tasks the way games do (Tobias et al., 2014). The reason for this is that games can be individualized to provide a level of challenge, support, and immediate feedback during game play. This would keep students engaged and motivated, and contributes to the development of their self-efficacy. Self-efficacy is a learner's perception of how well he or she believes that he or she is going to do on a particular task and is, therefore, a key contributor to students' overall motivation and to students' implementation of resilience skills in the face of bullying (Bandura, 1997; Tomas, Hesser, & Träff, 2014; Usher & Pajares, 2009).

When students are provided with a level of challenge and support, they tend to have successful mastery experiences. In fact, extensive research supports the finding that self-efficacy is one of the main predictors of student academic performance (Tomas et al., 2014; Usher & Pajares, 2009). Essentially, when students believe that they can succeed at a task, such as computing fractions or getting a bully to leave them alone, they will succeed. This probably further reinforces their beliefs and expectations about future success. In the case of K–3 students and bullying, these students are highly likely to approach a bullying situation with more positive beliefs about their likelihood of success after playing a video game that has guided and supported them to master key antibullying and resilience skills.

Within the context of learning SEL skills, a gaming environment is an ideal place for students to learn appropriate responses given that they can experience and experiment with social interactions and confrontations in a nonthreatening environment (Bachen, Hernández-Ramos, & Raphael, 2012; Hromek & Roffey, 2009). Game-based learning provides a safe environment for learners to make mistakes, receive feedback, and potentially ask for help as part of the learning process. Within an educational video game, the help provided can be targeted, encouraging, purposeful, and anonymous.

However, research evidence supports the fact that students in general do not seek help, and more importantly, that students who are struggling and need help the most seek it the least (Karabenick & Newman, 2013). There are three main reasons for this. One is that these students lack adequate knowledge to seek help. For instance, students might not know whom to seek help from or what questions to ask. Second, students may not want to seek help because it confirms that they might be struggling or failing, and last, students may perceive that seeking help is not going to be useful (Karabenick & Newman, 2013).

In addition to motivational factors, there are also several learning factors that can help explain the benefits that students can gain from effectively designed educational video games. Research studies have demonstrated near and far transfer from games to external tasks when the cognitive demands and cognitive processes across game tasks and external tasks are comparable (McClarty et al., 2012; Mester, 2005; Tobias et al., 2014). Consistent with these findings, cognitive task analysis of game and external tasks is a necessary component of the game development process, especially if transfer to external tasks is the objective (Clark, Feldon, van Merriënboer, Yates, & Early, 2008; Crandall, Klein, & Hoffman, 2006; Schraagen, Chipman, & Shalin, 2000).

There is also growing evidence that students can learn to generalize and transfer learning if they practice in a variety of contexts and across a variety of situations (see Bassok & Holyoak, 1989a, 1989b; Ormrod, 2011). An educational video game provides for an environment where several learning contexts and situations can be created and these can also easily and rapidly change giving the learner a variety of contexts and situations to practice within and learn from.

Educational video games also have the potential to be potent formative assessment tools (Baker, Chung, & Delacruz, 2012; Baker & Delacruz, 2008; Delacruz, Chung, & Baker, 2010). Formative assessment has been defined as the use and interpretation of task performance information with the intent to adapt learning, such as through feedback (Baker, 2006). Formative assessment levels can be developed to be seamless within a game, such that the learners are unaware that they are being assessed. Students' game play performance and process information can be used to improve learning by providing targeted feedback and instructional adaptation (Chung & Baker, 2003a, 2003b; Chung, de Vries, Cheak, Stevens, & Bewley, 2002). In other words, if students are provided with a level that is too difficult, the game can adapt to provide them with an easier level such that they can master the goal, concept, or problem before moving on.

Game Development

Given the importance of educational video games to students' mastering SEL skills, and particularly antibullying and resilience skills, how do we determine if a game is instructionally and pedagogically sound? The key to creating a pedagogically and instructionally sound video game is in the game development process, and particularly in the front-end analysis. The game development process is extensive and contains numerous steps including (1) creating an ontology of the target domain, (2) depicting the underlying concepts and learning objectives in an increasingly complex instructional and pedagogical sequence, (3) determining what features and mechanics best represent the instructional sequence and pedagogical strategies via formative evaluation, and (4) combining the instructional sequence, pedagogical strategies, cognitive demands, and game design features and mechanics in specifications for game tasks or levels (Adams, 2013; Baker, 2003, 2007; Baker, Chung, & Delacruz, 2008; Chung, Delacruz, & Bewley, 2006; Wainess & Koenig, 2010).

Formative Evaluation

Formative evaluation is a systematic collection of information that takes place before or during a project or product implementation with the goal of improving design and performance (Flagg, 2013). Formative evaluation essentially helps the designer of a product, during the early development stages, to increase the likelihood that the final product will serve its intended purpose (Flagg, 2013).

Recent research has also provided evidence for the utility of formative evaluation in strengthening intervention outcomes and implementation (Brown & Kiernan, 2001; Flagg, 2013).

One of the most important steps in the game development process is determining what features and mechanics best represent the instructional and pedagogical sequence which would be essential to student learning. If how students engage with the content is not representative or intuitive in terms of how the key concepts or skills are learned, the students will either not learn anything or develop misconceptions (Ormrod, 2011).

Our game development process therefore involves formatively evaluating whether the intended game mechanics, iconography, graphics, and features make sense to the player and whether they are eliciting the cognitive and metacognitive processes intended (see Baker, Delacruz, Madni, Chung, & Griffin, 2013; Wainess & Koenig, 2010).

A common way of collecting information to fulfill this formative evaluation process involves performing usability studies, think-aloud sessions, and testing with the target population (Adams, 2013; Pinelle, Wong, & Stach, 2008). Think-aloud sessions involve observing and asking questions of the target population as they interact and display their thought process with target mechanics and design features. Think-aloud sessions tend to provide fruitful information, however, they are time, cost, and resource intensive (Adams, 2013; Pinelle et al., 2008). In other words, it is often difficult to have enough time with enough participants to exhaust the feedback possibilities.

Usability sessions involve observing participants as they interact with the target intervention to determine any difficulties with intervention features, such as the game interface (Moreno-Ger, Torrente, Hsieh, & William, 2012; Rubin & Chisnell, 2008). However, usability testing that provides information about game design features and mechanics often takes place after key features and mechanics have already been developed and potentially hardcoded (Moreno-Ger et al., 2012; Rubin & Chisnell, 2008).

Crowdsourcing is emerging as a novel process to obtain feedback (Stolee & Elbaum, 2010; Zhao & Zhu, 2012). The researchers in the current study therefore sought to implement crowdsourcing as a formative evaluation tool to determine the usability of icons representing target antibullying/resilience de-escalating responses and a corresponding escalating incorrect response: "get angry or mad," "keep cool," "stop," and "walk away and alert adult." "Keep cool," "stop," and "walk away and alert adult" are antibullying/resilience responses, whereas "get angry or mad" is an escalating (distractor) response.

The basic idea behind crowdsourcing is to leverage a global community of users with different talents and backgrounds to help perform a task, such as solving a problem, classifying data, refining a product, and similar to formative evaluation, gathering feedback (Parvanta, Roth, & Keller, 2013; Stolee & Elbaum, 2010; Zhao & Zhu, 2012). Recent research in other fields, such as computer science, business, and marketing, has also capitalized on the benefits of crowdsourcing for various research purposes, provided evidence for the utility of using crowdsourcing to collect data, and demonstrated that data obtained through crowdsourced means tend to be valid given the amount of information and responses obtained (Parvanta et al., 2013; Stolee & Elbaum, 2010; Zhao & Zhu, 2012). Given that the purpose of the current research was to elicit feedback on the resilience icons during the development process, we employed crowdsourcing as a convenient, and time-, resource-, and cost-effective means to acquire this information.

The Current Study

The main purpose of the current study was to obtain feedback on and formatively evaluate resilience icons to be utilized as part of an antibullying game. The following research question guided the study: Does the set of resilience icons developed for the antibullying video game convey the meanings intended? Participants were obtained through Mechanical Turk, which is a crowdsourcing web service associated with Amazon (Buhrmester, Kwang, & Gosling, 2011). On Mechanical Turk, participants have the opportunity to self-select tasks that they want to respond to, and researchers can provide some parameters as to who (e.g., master turker or novice) can respond to tasks, how many participants complete tasks, and by when tasks are to be completed. Mechanical Turk participants have to be 18 years of age or older, and they receive compensation for their work. The requester (in this case researcher) specifies Mechanical Turk participant payment (Paolacci & Chandler, 2014; Shapiro, Chandler, & Mueller, 2013). For the current study, the Mechanical Turk participants were paid 10 cents per hit (i.e., "a job" in Amazon Mechanical Turk terminology).

For the current study, the researchers uploaded two separate surveys to Mechanical Turk. The first survey required participants to rate the icons (see Figure 5.1), answering questions such as "how the icon could be improved" and "whether the icon conveyed the intended meaning." The second survey required participants to interpret the icons by providing their thoughts on what the respective icons meant.

Given the social nature of bullying interactions and that children within the target age group might not be able to read, we focused on how icons could be used to represent various behavioral responses that students should exhibit. The notion of using icons to elicit young children's responses has been tested in previous research (Baker, Chung, Delacruz, & Madni, 2013; Baker, Delacruz, et al., 2013). The icons signified both escalating and de-escalating behavioral responses or options that a player could choose from to address various bullying situations. The four icons represented the following responses: "get angry or mad," "keep cool," "stop," and "walk away and alert adult," with "get angry or mad" signifying the escalating response and incorrect option to address bullying and conflict situations. The remaining options represent appropriate responses to

FIGURE 5.1 Images of the icons tested.

de-escalate bullying and conflict situations. These icons are appropriate as they are consistent with literature on resilience and antibullying responses and because the responses indicated by the icons are developmentally appropriate for the specified age range of students (K–3) given that children within this age range can utilize the icons to respond without the need to read or write. Figure 5.1 provides images of the icons tested.

Results

Descriptive statistics were computed for relevant variables and demographic data. Of the 784 participants in the current research, 419 (53.4%) were female and 363 (46.3%) were male. The age of the participants ranged from 18 to 70 with a mean age of 30.23 years (SD = 9.9). Consistent with the literature, a majority of the respondents were either from India or the U.S., with 298 (38%) from the U.S. and 448 (57.1%) from India. The remaining 38 (4.9%) participants included individuals from Canada, China, Egypt, Hungary, Kuwait, Macedonia, Mexico, New Zealand, Pakistan, Peru, the Philippines, Portugal, Romania, Serbia, Tamil Nadu, United Arab Emirates, United Kingdom, and Uruguay (Paolacci & Chandler, 2014).

In terms of educational background, 22 (2.8%) of the participants reported that they had some high school, 55 (7.0%) were high school graduates, 169 (21.6%) had some college but no degree, 52 (6.6%) had an associates degree, 361 (46%) had a bachelors degree, 95 (12.1%) had a masters degree, 19 (2.5%) had another graduate degree (e.g., JD, MD, professional), and 8 (1.0%) reported that they had a doctorate degree.

Quantitative Findings

Of the 784 participants in the study, 400 (51%) completed the first survey where they were tasked to rate the icons, and 384 (49%) completed the Interpret Icons survey. Their time spent on task ranged from 10 to 288 seconds with an average time of 82.96 seconds per task across surveys (SD = 54.9). For Survey 1 specifically, participants' time spent on task ranged from 21 to 288 seconds with a mean time of 108.86 seconds per task (SD = 55.7). For Survey 2, participants' time spent on task ranged from 10 to 256 with a mean time per task of 55.99 seconds (SD = 38.6).

Rate Icons Survey 1

For Survey 1, participants answered one quantitative task in addition to demographic items. This task involved participants indicating whether the respective icons conveyed the meanings intended.

As may be seen in Table 5.1, of the 100 respondents that indicated whether the "get angry or mad" icon conveyed the intended meaning 92 (92%) rated "Yes" and 8 (8%) indicated "No." These findings confirm the usefulness of the "get angry or mad" icon. One hundred participants also rated whether the "walk away and alert adult" icon conveyed the intended meaning. Results demonstrated that the icon did not clearly convey the intended meaning with 51 (51%) rating "Yes" and 49 (49%) of participants indicating "No." These findings indicate that further iterations on the efficacy of this icon have to be completed.

Both of the icons "keep cool" and "stop" were also supported for text confirmation with 93 (93%) participants rating "Yes" and 7 (7%) participants indicating "No" for "stop" and 94 (94%) participants indicating "Yes" and 6 (6%) of the respondents rating "No" for "keep cool." Overall, these findings demonstrate that the icons "get angry or mad," "keep cool," and "stop" convey their respective intended meanings and are interpreted as such, while the "walk away and alert adult" icon needs to be clarified and further tested to convey the meaning intended.

Qualitative Findings

In addition to the demographic and quantitative items in Surveys 1 and 2, participants were required to provide explicit and directive feedback on the icons as well as answer open-ended questions to inform quantitative findings. Results from the qualitative tasks are presented below.

TABLE 5.1 Rate Icons Survey 1 Results: Does the icon convey the meaning intended? (Total n = 400, n per icon = 100)

	"Yes"	"No"
"Get angry or mad"	92%	8%
"Walk away and alert adult"	51%	49%
"Keep cool"	93%	7%
"Stop"	94%	6%

Rate Icons Survey 1

For Survey 1, participants responded to two tasks which included (1) suggesting ways that the icon could be improved to more effectively convey the intended meaning, and (2) answering why they thought the icon did or did not convey the intended meaning.

Did the icons convey the intended meaning?

The qualitative findings for whether the icons conveyed the meanings intended corroborated the quantitative data for the "get angry or mad," "keep cool," and "stop" icons by indicating the correct interpretations. However, respondents consistently stated that the "walk away and alert adult" icon conveyed some variation of walking, but not necessarily walking away, and that the icon did not convey the meaning of seeking help.

How can the icon be improved?

The "get angry or mad," "keep cool," and "stop" icons were all confirmed for utility by the quantitative data. The qualitative data were consistent with the quantitative findings. Specifically, qualitative suggestions for how to improve the "get angry or mad," "keep cool," and "stop" icons focused more on minor desired modifications of facial expressions and characteristics and changes to color schemes as opposed to necessary changes (i.e., changes that would be crucial to ensure understandability of the icon). In terms of modifications to facial expressions and characteristics, approximately 20% of the respondents suggested clarifying the facial expression of the boy in the "get angry or mad" icon to look more angry by for instance raising his eyebrows more, giving him red eyes, making him look more red, and having fumes come out of his ears. For the "keep cool" icon, changes to facial expressions and characteristics involved giving the boy a more serene look, removing his glasses to show his eyes, and giving him a bigger smile. Alternative suggestions included having the boy situated in a calmer context such as relaxing in a chair or providing palm trees in the background.

In terms of color changes, some participants indicated that providing more contrasting colors in the "get angry or mad" icon would help clarify the expression and meaning of the icon by making the image within the icon stand out more. For the "keep cool" icon, some of the respondents indicated that changing the background color to a calmer color, such as yellow, would aid in portraying the intended meaning of the icon. Participants also consistently indicated that the green color background in the "say stop" icon should be changed to a different color such as red or white, given that the color green tends to mean "go."

For the "walk away and alert adult" icon, suggestions for improvement focused primarily on making the need for help more explicit and also clarifying the action of seeking help within the icon. With respect to clarifying the help-seeking aspect of the icon, many of the participants suggested changing the icon to portray the boy in the icon being in trouble or in danger by for instance making his face look more frightened or worried. A majority of the respondents also suggested including some sort of adult figure within the icon to illustrate and convey the meaning that the boy is seeking help or walking toward a help-seeking figure.

Given that the quantitative and qualitative findings in Survey 1 confirmed utility for the "get angry or mad," "keep cool," and "stop" icons, these icons will be directly implemented within the gaming context. For the "walk away and alert adult" icon, the participants' suggestions will be incorporated in later research to include an adult figure within the icon.

Interpret Icons Survey 2

For the Interpret Icons Survey 2, participants provided demographic information in addition to interpreting the icons without knowing the meanings intended and without seeing the corresponding text. Results for the four icons were mostly consistent with Survey 1 in that the "get angry or mad" and "stop" icons were interpreted in line with their intended meanings. More than 95% of the participants consistently interpreted the "get angry or mad" icon as variations of being angry or yelling. With a few exceptions, respondents also consistently interpreted the "stop" icon as stop or a variation thereof. As for the "keep cool" icon, participants provided more varied responses, such as happy, joyful, relaxed, cool, and enjoying life. Similarly, with the "walk away and alert adult" icon, most respondents reported that the icon represented walking or walking in the direction of the arrow. However, none of the participants reported that the icon portrayed the action of seeking help.

Summary and Implications

While the target audience within a crowdsourced environment does not involve young children, the justification behind utilizing a crowdsourced environment involved the number of responses we could receive per icon, that the responses could be supplied from various cultures, and finally that if the participants within the crowdsourced environment did not understand the iconography that we would have to adapt and devise new icons. Similarly, we assumed that if the icons were not understood by the adult participants, that they would not be understandable to the young children, and we would therefore need to reiterate the icons.

Overall, in the cases where the icons were confirmed for utility through the quantitative data, the open-ended answers for how to improve the icon as well as whether the icon conveyed its intended meaning corroborated the quantitative findings. However, participant interpretations of the icons in Survey 2 were not clearly aligned with the findings from Survey 1.

Essentially, for Survey 2, the respondents interpreted the "get angry or mad" and "stop" icons consistently with their intended meanings similar to Survey 1. However, for the "keep cool" icon, participants in Survey 2 provided more varied responses, such as happy, joyful, relaxed, and enjoying life, as compared to ratings for Survey 1. For the "walk away and alert adult" icon, most respondents for Survey 2 reported that the icon represented walking or walking in the direction of the arrow, similar to Survey 1. Moreover, none of the Survey 2 or Survey 1 participants reported that the icon portrayed the action of seeking help.

Taken together, the implications of these findings indicate that, specific to the current effort, the "get angry or mad" and "stop" icons can be directly implemented within the gaming context, while the "keep cool" icon can be introduced within the game with its associated meaning or reworked for clarification. The "walk away and alert adult" icon needs further iterations to convey the help-seeking aspect of the icon and will be re-evaluated for implementation after these iterations. Across efforts, the current findings imply that crowdsourcing can be used as a cost-, time-, and resource-effective formative data gathering tool to obtain feedback and validation data on iconography and related game features.

In summary, the current study focused on formatively evaluating iconography to be utilized as part of an antibullying and resilience video game through a crowdsourced environment. A total of 784 Amazon Mechanical Turk members participated in the study. Both quantitative and qualitative findings confirmed utility for three out of four of the resilience icons to be implemented as part of the game interface. These findings support the use of crowdsourcing as a type of formative evaluation for game design.

Author Note

The work reported herein was supported under the DARPA ENGAGE Program, N00014-12-C-0090, with funding to the National Center for Research on Evaluation, Standards, and Student Testing (CRESST). The findings and opinions expressed here do not necessarily reflect the positions or policies of the Defense Advanced Research Projects Agency, the Office of Naval Research, or the U.S. Department of Defense.

References

Adams, E. (2013). *Fundamentals of game design* (3rd ed.). Indianapolis, IN: New Riders.

Alsaker, F. D., & Gutzwiller-Helfenfinger, E. (2012). Social behavior and peer relationships of victims, bully-victims, and bullies in kindergarten. In S. R. Jimerson, S. M. Swearer, & D. L. Espelage (Eds.), *Handbook of bullying in schools: An international perspective* (pp. 87–99). New York, NY: Routledge.

Bachen, C. M., Hernández-Ramos, P. F., & Raphael, C. (2012). Simulating REAL LIVES: Promoting global empathy and interest in learning through simulation games. *Simulation & Gaming, 43*(4), 437–460.

Baker, E. L. (2003). Multiple measures: Toward tiered systems. *Educational Measurement: Issues and Practice, 22*(2), 13–17.

Baker, E. L. (2006). *Overview: CRESST formative assessment R&D.* Presentation to The William and Flora Hewlett Foundation, Los Angeles.

Baker, E. L. (2007). The end(s) of testing (2007 AERA Presidential Address). *Educational Researcher, 36*, 309–317.

Baker, E. L., Chung, G. K. W. K., & Delacruz, G. C. (2008). Design and validation of technology-based performance assessments. In J. M. Spector, M. D. Merrill, J. J. G. van Merriënboer, & M. P. Driscoll (Eds), *Handbook of research on educational communications and technology* (pp. 595–604). New York, NY: Erlbaum.

Baker, E. L., Chung, G. K. W. K., & Delacruz, G. C. (2012). The best and future uses of assessment in games. In M. C. Mayrath, J. Clarke-Midura, D. H. Robinson, & G. Schraw (Eds.), *Technology-based assessment for 21st century skills: Theoretical and practical implication from modern research* (pp. 229–248). Charlotte, NC: Information Age Publishing.

Baker, E., Chung, G., Delacruz, G., & Madni, A. (2013). *DARPA ENGAGE program review CRESST – TA2.* Presentation at the ENGAGE PI Meeting, Defense Advanced Research Projects Agency, Russell Shilling, Program Manager, Arlington, VA.

Baker, E. L., & Delacruz, G. C. (2008). A framework for the assessment of learning games. In H. F. O'Neil & R. S. Perez (Eds.), *Computer games and team and individual learning* (pp. 21–37). Oxford, UK: Elsevier.

Baker, E. L., Delacruz, G. C., Madni, A., Chung, G. K. W. K., & Griffin, N. (2013). *ENGAGE: Designing games and assessment for young children's physics learning.* Presentation to the Smarter Balanced Assessment Consortium, Los Angeles.

Bandura, A. (1997). *Self-efficacy: The exercise of control.* New York, NY: Freeman.

Bassok, M., & Holyoak, K. J. (1989a). Interdomain transfer between isomorphic topics in algebra and physics. *Journal of Experimental Psychology: Learning, Memory, and Cognition, 15*(1), 153–166.

Bassok, M., & Holyoak, K. J. (1989b). Transfer of domain-specific problem solving procedures. *Journal of Experimental Psychology: Learning, Memory, and Cognition, 16*, 522–533.

Brown, L. J., & Kiernan, N. E. (2001). Assessing the subsequent effect of a formative evaluation on a program. *Evaluation and Program Planning, 24*, 129–143.

Buhrmester, M., Kwang, T., & Gosling, S. D. (2011). Amazon's Mechanical Turk: A new source of inexpensive, yet high-quality, data? *Perspectives on Psychological Science, 6*(1), 4–5.

Chung, G. K. W. K., & Baker, E. L. (2003a). An exploratory study to examine the feasibility of measuring problem-solving processes using a click-through interface. *Journal of Technology, Learning, and Assessment, 2*(2). Available from http://jtla.org

Chung, G. K. W. K., & Baker, E. L. (2003b). Issues in the reliability and validity of automated scoring of constructed responses. In M. D. Shermis & J. E. Burstein (Eds.), *Automated essay grading: A cross-disciplinary approach* (pp. 23–40). Mahwah, NJ: Erlbaum.

Chung, G. K. W. K., Delacruz, G. C., & Bewley, W. L. (2006). *Performance assessment models and tools for complex tasks* (CSE Rep. No. 682). Los Angeles: University of California, National Center for Research on Evaluation, Standards, and Student Testing.

Chung, G. K. W. K., de Vries, L. F., Cheak, A. M., Stevens, R. H., & Bewley, W. L. (2002). Cognitive process validation of an online problem solving assessment. *Computers in Human Behavior, 18*(6), 669–684.

Clark, R. E., Feldon, D., van Merriënboer, J. J., Yates, K., & Early, S. (2008). Cognitive task analysis. *Handbook of research on educational communications and technology, 3,* 577–593.

Collaborative for Academic, Social, and Emotional Learning (CASEL). (2003). *Safe and sound: An educational leader's guide to evidence-based social and emotional learning (SEL) programs.* Chicago, IL: Author.

Crandall, B., Klein, G., & Hoffman, R. R. (2006). *Working minds: A practitioner's guide to cognitive task analysis.* Cambridge, MA: MIT Press.

Delacruz, G. C., Chung, G. K. W. K., & Baker, E. L. (2010). *Validity evidence for games assessment environments* (CRESST Rep. 773). Los Angeles: University of California, National Center for Research on Evaluation, Standards, and Student Testing.

De Wannemacker, S., Vandercruysse, S., & Clarebout, G. (2012). *Serious games: The challenge.* Berlin, Heidelberg: Springer Verlag.

Eriksen, T. L. M., Nielsen, H. S., & Simonsen, M. (2014). Bullying in elementary school. *The Journal of Human Resources, 49*(4), 839–871.

Ferguson, C. J., San Miguel, C., Kilburn, J. C., Jr., & Sanchez, P. (2007). The effectiveness of school-based anti-bullying programs: A meta-analytic review. *Criminal Justice Review, 32*(4), 401–414.

Flagg, B. N. (2013). *Formative evaluation for educational technologies.* New York, NY: Routledge.

Fletcher, D., & Sarkar, M. (2013). Psychological resilience: A review and critique of definitions, concepts, and theory. *European Psychologist, 18*(1), 12–23.

Graham, S. (2010). What educators need to know about bullying behaviors. *Phi Delta Kappan, 92*(1), 66–69.

Griffiths, M. (2002). The educational benefits of videogames. *Education and Health, 20*(3), 47–51.

Grüsser, S. M., Thalemann, R., & Griffiths, M. D. (2007). Excessive computer game playing: Evidence for addiction and aggression? *CyberPsychology & Behavior, 10*(2), 290–292.

Hromek, R., & Roffey, S. (2009). Promoting social and emotional learning with games. *Simulation & Gaming, 40*(5), 626–644.

Juvonen, J., & Graham, S. (2002). Ethnicity, peer harassment and adjustment in middle school: An exploratory study. *Journal of Early Adolescence, 22,* 173–199.

Karabenick, S. A., & Newman, R. S. (2013). *Help-seeking in academic contexts: Goals, groups, and contexts.* New York, NY: Routledge.

Ketelhut, D. J., & Schifter, C. C. (2011). Teachers and game-based learning: Improving understanding of how to increase efficacy of adoption. *Computers & Education, 56*(2), 539–546.

Kirves, L., & Sajaniemi, N. (2012). Bullying in early education settings. *Early Child Development and Care, 182*(3–4), 383–400.

Levy, F., & Murnane, R. J. (2004). *The new division of labor: How computers are creating the next job market.* Princeton, NJ: Princeton University Press.

Lim, S. J. J., & Hoot, J. L. (2015). Bullying in an increasingly diverse school population: A socio-ecological model analysis. *School Psychology International, 36*(3), 268–282.

Loveless, A. (2011). Technology, pedagogy and education: Reflections on the accomplishment of what teachers know, do and believe in a digital age. *Technology, Pedagogy, and Education, 20*(3), 301–316.

McClarty, K. L., Orr, A., Frey, P. M., Dolan, R. P., Vassileva, V., & McVay, A. (2012). *A literature review of gaming in education* (Research report). Retrieved from Pearson website: http://researchnetwork.pearson.com/wp-content/uploads/lit_review_of_gaming_in_education.pdf

Mester, J. P. (2005). *Transfer of learning from a modern multidisciplinary perspective.* Greenwich, CT: Information Age Publishing.

Monks, C. P., Smith, P. K., Naylor, P., Barter, C., Ireland, J., & Coyne, I. (2009). Bullying in different contexts: Commonalities, differences and the role of theory. *Aggression and Violent Behavior, 14,* 146–156.

Moreno-Ger, P., Torrente, J., Hsieh, G. Y., & William, T. (2012). Usability testing for serious games: making informed design decisions with user data. *Human-Computer Interaction, 2012,* 1–14. doi:10.1155/2012/369637

Ng, B. D., & Wierner-Hastings, P. (2005). Addiction to the Internet and online gaming. *CyberPsychology & Behavior, 8*(2), 110–113.

Ormrod, J. E. (2011). *Educational psychology: Developing learners* (7th ed.). Boston, MA: Allyn & Bacon.

Paolacci, G., & Chandler, J. (2014). Inside the turk: Understanding mechanical turk as a participant pool. *Current Directions in Psychological Science, 23*(3), 184–188.

Parvanta, C., Roth, Y., & Keller, H. (2013). Crowdsourcing 101: A few basics to make you the leader of the pack. *Health Promotion Practice, 14*(2), 163–167.

Pepler, D., & Craig, W. (2010). *Understanding and addressing bullying: An international perspective.* Bloomington, IN: AuthorHouse Publishing.

Pinelle, D., Wong, N., & Stach, T. (2008). Heuristic evaluation for games: Usability principles for video game design. *Proceedings of the ACM Conference on Human Factors in Computing Systems (CHI 2008),* 1453–1462.

Rigby, K., Smith, P. K., & Pepler, D. (2004). Working to prevent school bullying: Key issues. In P. K. Smith, D. Pepler, & K. Rigby (Eds.), *Bullying in schools: How successful can interventions be?* (pp. 1–12). New York, NY: Cambridge University Press.

Roytek, M. A. (2010). Enhancing instructional design efficiency: Methodologies employed by instructional designers. *British Journal of Educational Technology, 41*(2), 170–180.

Rubin, J., & Chisnell, D. (2008). *Handbook of usability testing: How to plan, design and conduct effective tests.* Hoboken, NJ: John Wiley & Sons.

Schraagen, M., Chipman, S., & Shalin, V. (Eds.). (2000). *Cognitive task analysis.* Mahwah, NJ: Erlbaum.

Shapiro, D. N., Chandler, J., & Mueller, P. A. (2013). Using Mechanical Turk to study clinical populations. *Clinical Psychological Science,* 1–8.

Smith, J., D., Schneider, B. H., Smith, P. K., & Ananiadou, K. (2004). The effectiveness of whole-school anti-bullying programs: A synthesis of evaluation research. *School Psychology Review, 33*(4), 547–560.

Spector, M. J., Merrill, D. M., Elen, J., & Bishop, M. J. (2013). *Handbook of research on educational communications and technology* (4th ed.). New York, NY: Springer.

Squire, K. D. (2006). From content to context: Videogames as designed experience. *Educational Researcher, 35*(8), 19–29.

Squire, K. D. (2007). Games, learning and society: Building a field. *Educational Technology, 4*(5), 51–54.

Squire, K. D. (2011). *Video games and learning. Teaching and participatory culture in the digital age.* New York, NY: Teachers College Press.

Stolee, K. T., & Elbaum, S. (2010, September). *Exploring the use of crowdsourcing to support empirical studies in software engineering.* Presentation at ESEM, Bolzano-Bozen, Italy.

Tenenbaum, L. S., Varjas, K., Meyers, J., & Parris, L. (2011). Coping strategies and perceived effectiveness in fourth through eighth grade victims of bullying. *School Psychology International, 32*(3), 263–287.

Tobias, S., Fletcher, J. D., & Wind, A. P. (2014). Game-based learning. In J. M. Spector, D. M. Merrill, J. Elen, & M. J. Bishop (Eds.), *Handbook of research on educational communications and technology* (pp. 127–222). New York, NY: Springer Science+Business Media.

Tomas, J., Hesser, H., & Träff, U. (2014). Contrasting two models of academic self-efficacy—Domain-specific versus cross-domain—In children receiving and not receiving special instruction in mathematics. *Scandinavian Journal of Psychology, 55*(5), 440–447.

Ttofi, M. M., & Farrington, D. P. (2011). Effectiveness of school-based programs to reduce bullying: A systematic and meta-analytic review. *Journal of Experimental Criminology, 7*(1), 27–56.

Usher, E. L., & Pajares, F. (2009). Sources of self-efficacy in mathematics: A validation study. *Contemporary Educational Psychology, 34*, 89–101.

Wainess, R., & Koenig, A. D. (2010). *Validation of a methodology for design and development of a game for learning with a multigroup development process.* Presentation at the annual meeting of the American Educational Research Association, Denver, CO.

Weissberg, R. P., & Cascarino, J. (2013). Academic learning + social-emotional learning = national priority. *Phi Delta Kappan, 95*(2), 8–13.

Wouters, P., van Nimwegen, C., van Oostendorp, H., & van der Spek, E. D. (2013). A meta-analysis of the cognitive and motivational effects of serious games. *Journal of Educational Psychology, 105*(2), 249–265.

Zhao, Y., & Zhu, Q. (2012). Evaluation on crowdsourcing research: Current status and future direction. *Information Systems Frontiers, 10*, 1–18.

Zins, J. E., & Elias, M. J. (2014). Social and emotional learning: Promoting the development of all students. *Journal of Educational and Psychological Consultation, 17*(2–3), 233–255.

6

LESSONS LEARNED FROM INTELLIGENT TUTORING RESEARCH FOR SIMULATION

Ray S. Perez, Anna Skinner, and Paul Chatelier

Robelen (2012) indicated that only 16% of American high school seniors are proficient in mathematics and interested in science, technology, engineering, and mathematics (STEM) careers. Even among those who do pursue a college major in the STEM fields, only about half go on to work in a STEM-related career (Robelen, 2012). The United States is falling behind, internationally ranking 25th in mathematics and 17th in science among industrialized nations (Robelen, 2012). Today's approaches to education and training must change if our nation is to be competitive in the dynamic global workforce. Numerous studies have shown that an effective way to teach students is through one-on-one interactions between teachers and students (Bloom, 1984; Kulik & Fletcher, 2015, VanLehn, 2011). One way to achieve one-on-one instruction is through the use of advanced technologies such as intelligent tutoring systems (ITSs) and simulations.

This chapter has six goals: first, to provide a brief history of the development of ITSs; second, to provide an overview of simulations; third, to describe the state of the science in effective instructional strategies for use in intelligent tutoring; fourth, to summarize the state of the science in ITS development; fifth, to provide lessons learned from ITS research to advise the design of more effective simulation-based learning and assessment; and sixth, to describe the research gaps and further research and development required to address these limitations in support of science and technology solutions.

Historical Overview of ITS Development

The development of ITSs began more than 60 years ago; an influential paper at that time was Jamie Carbonell's seminal paper titled, "AI in CAI: An artificial-intelligence approach to computer-assisted instruction" (1970), in which he described a new and more powerful type of computer-assisted instruction, based on the extensive application of artificial intelligence (AI) techniques. The goal of AI research was to develop computer programs that exhibit behavior that is considered intelligent behavior when observed in a human (Feigenbaum, 2003). Much of the research during this period was under the acronym ICAI (intelligent computer-aided instruction); this acronym was later replaced by ITS for intelligent tutoring system (Sleeman & Brown, 1982).

In his paper, Carbonell (1970) described what capabilities such a system would have, providing as an example the SCHOLAR system (Carbonell, 1970). He distinguished ICAI systems from what he called computer assisted instruction (CAI). CAI systems are frame-oriented systems in which the underlying database consists of frames of prespecified pieces of text, questions, and anticipated answers entered in advance by the developers. These systems are not generative (see Uhr, 1969); that is, they do not have the capability to initiate a dialogue between the student and the computer. More importantly they are not capable of providing diagnosis of student errors and remediation of those errors on the fly.

In contrast, ICAI systems are information structure oriented and make use of information networks (e.g., semantic networks) of facts, concepts, and procedures that are capable of generating text, questions, and corresponding answers. These systems are capable of using their information networks to answer student-generated questions; as such, they are capable of conducting a "mixed-initiative" dialogue or conversation (Carbonell, 1970). An important goal of ICAI systems developers was to create a dialogue between the student and the computer in much the same way a human expert tutor would interact with a student, in which questions and answers come from both student and computer. This latter goal of earlier ITSs achieving the capability to provide a mixed-initiative dialogue was accomplished in a limited way.

ITS and CAI communities differed in their use of terms; those differences are reflected in Table 6.1, which compares the use of key terms in ITS and CAI. They differ in the approaches that both ITS and CAI developers used to build their systems. CAI development is based on a systems approach to instructional development, whereas the ITS developer's approach is based on "knowledge engineering," consisting of the extraction and codification of expert knowledge. These differences will be discussed in a later section within the context of important issues to be addressed by ITSs.

Much has changed and much has stayed the same since Carbonell's (1970) seminal paper. The computational power of computers has increased significantly; methods for creating and representing knowledge (i.e., knowledge elicitation) and development of cognitive models (i.e., student and expert) have become more sophisticated; and the "science of learning" has made major advancements in the understanding of how people learn (Bransford, Brown, & Cocking, 1999; Bransford, Brown, Cocking, Donovan, & Pellegrino, 2008; Mayer, 2011; Meltzoff, Kuhl, Movellan, & Sejnowski, 2009; Schraagen, Chipman, & Shute, 2000).

TABLE 6.1 Comparison of Main Terms Used by CAI and ITS Developers

CAI		ITS	
Terms	*Interpretation*	*Terms*	*Interpretation*
Subject matter, tasks, content, knowledge and skills, etc.	External structure of the knowledge	Expertise, problem solving, knowledge, etc.	Expert's internal knowledge state of problem-solving process
Task analysis, content analysis	Methods to analyze and organize knowledge components	Knowledge representation	AI techniques to organize knowledge components into a data structure
Instructional development	Process of systems approach	Knowledge engineering	Extraction and codification of expert's knowledge
Instructional designer	Expert in instructional design and development	Knowledge engineer	Expert in AI
Content base, knowledge base	Subtitles and content elements structured into a database	Expertise module, knowledge base	A database for representing expert's internal knowledge
Subject matter expert	Person who is familiar with the structure and content components of knowledge	Domain expert, problem-solving expert	Person who demonstrates high performance on the given task
Student characteristics, learner variables	Many different variables: descriptive, static, or dynamic nature	Student model, student diagnostic model	Geared to on-task performance information; dynamic and process-oriented nature
Instructional strategy	Rules and procedures for selecting and designing instructional displays and interaction processes; applied to individual- and group-based instruction	Tutorial strategy: heuristic rules	Rules for controlling student–teacher dialogues; applied to one-on-one tutorial settings

Modern-day ITS developers have moved away from the term ICAI to ITS; therefore we will use the term ITS interchangeably with ICAI. Developers of ITSs are still challenged with the difficult technical tasks of constructing individual student models and validating them. Perhaps the most challenging component of an ITS has been the development of the student model. This challenge both relates to the role of individual differences and to assessing on the fly so as to automatically update the student model. The student model changes over the course of the tutoring. It tracks the learner's progress from problem to problem and builds a profile of strengths and weaknesses relative to the domain model (Anderson, Corbett, Koedinger, & Pelletier, 1995). The model is specific to a specific student. Furthermore, developing and validating natural language tutorial dialogues, as well as diagnosis of students' errors and how to remediate them, remain both a science and technology challenge as sometimes errors are unintentional mistakes or reflect a lack of prior knowledge or are misconceptions. Finally, tutoring strategies used for remediation of students' errors are often not driven by learning principles abstracted from the science of learning (i.e., self-explanation and worked examples), notwithstanding the cost and level of effort of developing ITSs (Brown, Burton, & De Kleer, 1982).

For the purpose of this chapter, rather than proposing a definition of an ITS since multiple models and definitions of intelligent tutoring systems have emerged over the last 60 years, we will provide a description of the capabilities that an ideal ITS should have. Based on Carbonell (1970) and more recent research by Kulik and Fletcher (2015), an ITS is a computer-based system that (a) uses models of the subject area, often with expert performance along with underlying concepts requiring a "deeper" understanding, retention, and transfer of the subject matter; (b) provides adaptive models that evolve as the learner acquires sufficient skills and knowledge of the subject area; and (c) applies information from these tutorial models, allowing either the computer tutor or the learner to take the appropriate initiative.

ITSs over the last 60 years have taken various forms and applications. The following list of the various forms of ITSs is not meant to be exhaustive, but provides several representative exemplars. They have included problem-solving monitors, coaches, laboratory instructors, and consultants (Chakraborty, Roy, & Basu, 2010), as well as homework support, virtual laboratories, science simulations, educational games, online resources, and highly interactive web-based courses (Koedinger, Brunskill, Baker, McLaughlin, & Stamper, 2013).

Historical examples, in a variety of applications and domains, include symbolic integration (Kimball, 1982); electronic troubleshooting, the different versions of the SOPHIE systems (Brown et al., 1982); axiomatically-based mathematics, the EXCHECK system (Smith, Graves, Blaine, & Marinov, 1975); interpretation of NMR spectra, the PSM-NMR system (Sleeman & Hendley, 1982); medical diagnosis, the GUIDON system (Clancey, 1983); informal gaming environments such as the West systems (Burton & Brown, 1982); program-plan debugging, the

SPADE systems (Miller, 1982); and a consultancy system for users of MACSYMA, an algebraic manipulation system (Genesereth, 1982). A key evolution in ITS was the development of the Socratic System (Feurzeig, Munter, Swets, & Breen, 1964; Swets & Feurzeig, 1965) in which a computer-based system was built that went beyond drill and practice to a system that had the capability to support a sustained investigative dialogue between the computer and the student. In a typical application, the student is asked to make differential diagnoses based on information (e.g., patient's symptoms) provided by the computer and through a series of interactions with the computer until the student arrives at a correct diagnosis.

Sleeman and Brown (1982) have pointed out a number of shortcomings of these early systems. For example, the instructional material produced in response to a student's query or mistake was often at an inappropriate level of detail, as the system assumed too much or too little student knowledge. The system also assumed particular conceptualizations of the domain, thereby forcing the student's performance into its own conceptual framework. None of these systems could work within the student's model of the domain. The tutoring strategies used by these systems were often not driven by learning principles. Therefore, better theories of instructional design based on theories of learning that are prescriptive were needed. In addition, user interaction was restrictive, limiting the student's responses and thereby limiting the tutor's ability to diagnose the source of the student's error. The shortcomings pointed out by Sleeman and Brown (1982) of the student model not having the capability to provide accurate and appropriate remediation remains a challenge for modern-day ITSs.

Modern-day ITSs generally have four major components: (a) the domain model, (b) the student model, (c) the tutoring model, and (d) the user interface (Anderson, 2007; Anderson, Betts, Ferris, & Fincham, 2013; Anderson et al., 1995; Elson-Cook, 1993; Graesser & D'Mello, 2012; Koedinger, Corbett, & Perfetti, 2012; Psotka, Massey, & Mutter, 1988; Sleeman & Brown, 1982). The student model along with the domain model contains the content/curriculum; the skills, knowledge, and strategies of the subject matter to be tutored; and expert knowledge; as well as the bugs, mal-rules, and misconceptions that students are likely to exhibit while learning the subject matter.

The student model is made up of the cognitive, affective, motivational, and other psychological states that occur during the process of the student's learning. Some ITSs treat the student model as a subcomponent of the domain model, which dynamically changes over the course of the tutoring process (see Anderson et al., 1995, for discussion). It also includes considerations of psychological states outside of the domain model that are considered as parameters to guide tutoring. Some examples of student models include (a) programmed student models (Lumsdaine & Glaser, 1960; Thomas, Davies, Openshaw, & Bird, 1963); (b) overlay models (Atkinson, 1972; Atkinson & Crothers, 1964; Calfee & Atkinson, 1965; Groen & Atkinson, 1966; Pavlik & Anderson, 2008; Smallwood, 1962);

(c) rule-space models based on item response theory (Draney, Pirolli, & Wilson, 1995; Spada & McGraw, 1985; Tatsuoka, 1983); (d) theory-driven knowledge tracing in a cognitive tutor (Anderson, Conrad, & Corbett, 1989); (e) constraint-based modeling (Mitrovic, Ohlsson, & Barrow, 2013; Ohlsson, 1992; Zakharov, Mitrovic, & Ohlsson, 2005); (f) expectation and misconception tailored dialogue (Sottilare, Graesser, Hu, & Holden, 2013); and (g) state and trait models, which assess affective, motivational, and cognitive states/constructs of the learners.

The state and trait models differ from the student models discussed previously because the focus is on learnable skills (e.g., self-regulation). Traits (unlike skills) are stable whereas states (e.g., cognitive) tend to be transient and context-dependent in reaction to stimuli and external conditions. These models afford ITSs the capability to infer traits and states of the learner that could be used by an ITS to make pedagogical decisions. This is a desirable capability due to the roles that both affect and cognition play in the learning process. Recent ITS research has been focused on reliable measurement and detection (Cerri, Clancey, Papadourakis, & Panourgia, 2012; Stone, Skinner, Stikic, & Johnson, 2014) of these traits and states. An example of measurement and detection of cognitive states is discussed in the following sections of this chapter. However, this research is at an immature stage and it is uncertain whether it will serve to increase the overall effectiveness of ITSs.

In this section we describe the various components and their functionality of current ITSs. The early ICAI systems had tutors designed but seldom implemented in any detail and almost never evaluated. The tutor model contains the pedagogical model, sometimes referred to as the instructional model; it uses the domain and student models as inputs and selects tutoring strategies, steps, and sequences of instructional events, driving what the tutor should do next in the interactions between the student and the machine tutor, and is based on the student's actions. This model presumably would use the latest instructional strategies provided by expert human tutors and from the literature on the science of learning (Bourdeau & Grandbastien, 2010; Mayer, 2011). Ideally, the student has the opportunity to take actions, ask questions, and/or request help, and these interactions are all driven by the instructional model (Aleven, McLaren, Roll, & Koedinger, 2006; Rus & Graesser, 2009). This model informs the ITS of what to present first to the student, and then determines what to do next based on whether the student's actions are appropriate as determined by the underlying pedagogical theory.

The user interface is responsible for interpreting the learner's actions through a variety of media (e.g., speech, typing, and mouse clicks) and is capable of providing output in various media formats such as text, diagrams, animations, and agents. In addition to the conventional human–computer interface features, some advanced systems are also able to use natural language interactions, including speech generation and recognition (D'Mello, Graesser, & King, 2010; Graesser & D'Mello, 2012; Graesser, Haiying, & Forsyth, 2014; Johnson & Valente, 2008).

The student model does not operate in isolation. It interacts with the domain, pedagogical, and interface models. Pavlik, Brawner, Olney and Mitrovic (2013) have developed several criteria for evaluating the "usefulness" of a student model, and in many respects it is perhaps the most difficult model to develop, but it is clearly at the center of the ITS's effectiveness. The usefulness criteria proposed by Pavlik et al. (2013) are (a) model fit: student models must fit the data, providing a validity criterion indicating how well the student model can be used to simulate the quantitative and/or qualitative patterns of learning in real students (see Desmarais & Baker, 2012; Schunn & Wallach, 2005, for a discussion); (b) ease of understanding: student modeling methods must be transparent to the developers and users; (c) generalizability: the models must be reusable and flexible in order to be capable of being applied to more than one subject matter area or domain; (d) cost of development: if the development of an effective student model requires excessive time (e.g., person hours and data collection) to determine the parameters of the model it may be too costly for many prospective customers (Pavlik et al., 2013); (e) time scale: this criterion refers to whether the life cycle of the student model was designed to be short term or long term; and (f) learning gains: the intended outcomes provide evidence as to the effectiveness of the pedagogical inferences made about student learning.

Pavlik et al. (2013) have used these criteria to assess seven different student models. Although these six criteria appear useful in assessing a student model, this assessment has not been validated with empirical research. Additionally, trade-offs between these criteria must be considered. For example, the more general a student model is, the less powerful it becomes within a specific domain or application. To obtain estimates of the effect accounted for by these student models one must employ "a value-added approach" (Mayer, 2013) set of experiments. The difficulty of assessing the impact and suitability of the student model stems from the fact that it interacts with the domain, pedagogical, and interface modules and does not operate in isolation. Additional research is needed to establish assessments of how well each of these models addresses specific domains and types of learners.

Overview of Simulations

In this section we describe two types of simulations: instructional simulations and a subset of instructional simulations, namely procedural simulations. However, we begin with a general definition of simulations. Simulators (and models) are abstractions of reality (Moroney & Lilienthal, 2009). Simulations have many different meanings depending on the context and their application. Simulations are the specific application of these models. Models can be mathematical, logical, or based on a cognitive task analysis of the task, domain, or job. Often simulations may deliberately emphasize one part of reality or as in the case of military simulators, one component of a piece of equipment or operational task, called part-task simulators. A specific subset of military simulators includes training devices that provide a physical representation of equipment that has been simplified to enable the acquisition of critical skills for either operations or maintenance. These training devices are designed to represent the functions/behaviors of the actual equipment. In some cases these simulators cost more to produce than the actual equipment.

Generally, there are three reasons for the development of a simulator for training: (a) safety: rehearsal of operational tasks often poses significant risks to the trainee or others, and simulation-based training can provide a safe environment in which mistakes can be made during the learning process; (b) durability: some equipment is much too fragile to use repeatedly for training and could be damaged during training resulting in the equipment taken offline; and (c) affordability: current technology enables the development of simulations that are far cheaper than the actual operational equipment or environment, and can be more easily updated to provide exposure to training scenario variations. The capability to update simulations is critical to schoolhouse training since military equipment is often upgraded to increase operational capabilities where initial training occurs. If designed appropriately, simulators can be moved around and divided into part-task trainers as well as combined into team or multi-mission/use trainers.

According to Jones, Hennessy, and Deutsch (1985), simulators are used for four purposes: (a) training and education; (b) systems and equipment design (e.g., concept and system demonstration), development, test, and evaluation (e.g., operational capability); (c) research on human performance (e.g., effectiveness /troubleshooting); and (d) licensing and certification. However, there are many other applications in which battle or warfare simulations are frequently used to develop more effective tactics and to train warfighters in combat management, special purpose skills, and to evaluate operations systems (Munro, 2014; Munro, Pizzini, & Bewley, 2009).

This chapter will only refer to simulations for training and education involving human interaction with the simulation that permits observation and/or analysis of analogues of real-world situations (e.g., synthetic environments). Simulation in the context of this chapter is the representation of equipment, systems, events, interaction processes, and with the advent of cognitive science, declarative, procedural, and strategic knowledge. The most compelling evidence for the effectiveness of simulators for training is the use of flight simulators. Hays, Jacobs, Prince, and Salas (1992) conducted a meta-analysis of flight simulation research including 247 articles, research reports, and technical reports to train military pilots. Not only did these researchers find that flight simulators were more effective than using actual flight equipment (e.g., jets), they found that full fidelity (e.g., full-motion) did not necessarily improve the effectiveness of the simulator (Metcalfe, Kornell, & Finn, 2009).

Modern simulations used for training generally are categorized as live, virtual, and constructive, as well as combinations of the three (Allard, 2014). Live simulations involve humans and/or equipment in a real environment where time is continuous with trainers and trainees interacting in a mission-focused environment. These types of simulations are considered "human-in-the-loop." Virtual simulations involve simulated human and /or equipment models presented on a computer such as a laptop, desktop, or head-mounted display. Time is typically in discrete steps, allowing trainers and trainees to concentrate on critical tasks. A flight simulator is an example of this type of simulation. Constructive simulations do not involve actual humans or equipment as participants. Rather, the simulation is driven by time and is constrained by a sequence of events. For example, the simulation of the path of a hurricane or earthquake could be constructed through the manipulation of various weather factors such as temperature, pressure, wind currents, and other factors.

Medical Simulations

Over the last two decades, the U.S. Department of Defense has invested in the development of modeling and simulation programs to improve training effectiveness while reducing their reliance on actual costly hardware or live animals and software systems (Friedl & O'Neil, 2013; Perez, 2013). The military medical and health sciences community recently began the systematic use of modeling and simulation for education and training of medical personnel. A key reason for investing in simulation technology is to improve training effectiveness and patient safety (Kunkler, 2006). The design of these simulations has been influenced by the science of learning for skill acquisition and retention (Chung, Gyllenhammer, Baker, & Savitsky, 2013; Kellman, 2013; Perez, 2013), incorporating new methods for identifying critical knowledge, skills, and procedures (Cannon-Bowers, Bowers, Stout, Ricci, & Hildabrand, 2013; Munro & Clark, 2013), new technologies such as virtual reality (Talbot, 2013), objective measures of performance (Mislevy, 2013), and biological fidelity (Talbot, 2013). These issues will be discussed in more detail in the following sections.

In this section we will present a discussion of simulators in general and then focus on instructional simulations. An instructional simulation, according to Mayer (2008), includes a multimedia environment that models a system that is the target of learning for the student, enables students to interact with the simulated system by using rule-based responses, and promotes students' understanding of the target system. In education, simulations are used to support students' learning of scientific and mathematical material (Gredler, 2004; Hettinger & Haas, 2003; Jacobson & Kozma, 2000; Lajoie, 2000; Linn, Davis, & Bell, 2004; Mayer, 2008; Rieber, 2005; Stanney, 2002). The teaching of science and mathematics within an instructional simulation may include domain-specific knowledge such as facts, concepts, procedures, and strategic knowledge. There are many examples of instructional simulations such as the ThinkerTools simulation environment (White, Collins, & Frederiksen, 2011), chemistry simulation (Kozma & Russell, 2005), and physics simulation (Rieber, 2005). Training simulations are used to teach the operation and maintenance of various equipment and medical procedures (Friedl & O'Neil, 2013; Moroney & Lilienthal, 2009). These simulations characterize the operation of dynamic systems to train operators and maintainers not only on how to operate and maintain complex and sophisticated equipment, but on how to have a deeper understanding by forming a mental model of the equipment or system (Perez, Gray, & Reynolds, 2006).

A sophisticated form of simulation used for training and education is virtual reality (VR) simulations. VR is defined as an "interactive experience in which the trainee perceives and engages a synthetic (i.e., simulated via computer) environment by means of a particular set of multisensory human–computer interface devices and interacts with synthetic objects in that environment as if they were real" (Thurman & Russo, 2000, p. 5). These simulations attempt to build a realistic and comprehensive model of the real world to suspend disbelief and cause trainees to experience the feeling of being present in the targeted environment.

An important dimension in simulation-based training is realism, often referred to as fidelity. Early in the evolution of simulations, physical and functional fidelity were considered critical factors, and a common assumption among developers was that the more realistic a simulator was, the higher the probability that the skills and knowledge learned in the simulator would transfer to the real world (e.g., equipment, environment, or task). However, invariably the more realistic a simulator is, the more expensive it is to build (Jones et al., 1985) and research shows that more realism does not always improve the training effectiveness of a simulator (Hays et al., 2012).

A major challenge to designers of VR or any simulation for training is identifying the fidelity requirements for the component technologies (Muller et al., 2006). These fidelity factors are (a) functional fidelity: the ability of the simulator to support the appropriate stimulus response set; (b) psychological fidelity: the degree to which the simulation provides the appropriate performance cues; and (c) physical fidelity: the degree to which the simulation provides multimodal sensory stimulation. The importance of each of these factors is dependent on the types of tasks, skills, and knowledge to be trained.

Fidelity-related design decisions are motivated by the "belief" that the more accurately the VR system stimulates the human sensory system, the higher the probability that the system will provide effective training (Skinner et al., 2010). Thorndike (1906) hypothesized that the transfer of learning is dependent on the presence of identical elements between the initial learning task and the transfer task. An application of Thorndike's theory of transfer is a framework proposed by Stanney and her colleagues (2004). They proposed a multimodal information processing framework based on a working memory (WM) model. The model is based on Baddeley's (1990, 2000) model of working memory where he proposed separate processing capabilities for different sensory modalities and each modality would have a separate working memory component for visual, auditory, tactile, olfactory, and gustatory inputs.

How this framework might be used to determine the multimodal information requirements for a specific training task is proposed by Dean and her colleagues (2008). The method in addition to conducting a cognitive task analysis (CTA) involves the developer conducting a sensory task analysis (STA). The result of the STA is then used to determine how to represent operational cues in the virtual environment and the degree of realism each cue requires. Cue fidelity is critical for medical training simulations (Lou et al., 2014) in which the consequences of an incorrect identification of an internal organ, nerve, blood vessel, or other anatomical structure could be life-threatening.

In addition to fidelity, the research literature has indicated that the underlying pedagogical approach to simulation-based training greatly impacts training effectiveness; for example, unguided simulation-based learning has been shown to be ineffective (Adams, Mayer, MacNamara, Koenig, & Wainess, 2012; DeLeeuw & Mayer, 2011; Mayer, 2004). Thus, researchers have sought to identify instructional strategies that are most effective in guiding simulation-based training and education. The following section provides an overview of research investigating the effectiveness of various instructional strategies, particularly within the context of ITSs, which may be applicable to simulation design and development.

State of the Science in Instructional Strategies

The following provides a review of relevant research literature addressing various instructional strategies that have been shown to be effective in promoting individual learning within the context of one-on-one, small-group, or self-guided instruction, both with and without the use of ITS technologies. We begin with a review of relevant instructional strategies without the use of ITSs in contexts similar to those that could most readily be emulated in an ITS, including worked examples, one-on-one tutoring with an instructor or expert, peer tutoring and collaboration, and self-explanation. In addition to reviewing the effectiveness of the instructional strategies themselves, we further examine mediating variables that may be applicable to ITS-based instruction, such as the effect of various forms of feedback provided to the learner. Furthermore, we provide a review of research aimed at understanding the underlying neural mechanisms of effective tutoring interactions, which may provide insight into optimal methods of achieving similar learning outcomes within ITSs. We then review instructional strategies that have been implemented within ITSs and the demonstrated effects of these approaches to ITS instruction.

Effective Instructional Strategies Without the Use of ITSs

Here we review several instructional strategies that have been empirically validated and have been shown to enhance learning and retention within contexts similar to those that could most readily be emulated in an ITS or simulation-based training environment. Our goal here is to identify gaps in the instantiation and validation of potentially promising ITS and simulation-based instructional strategies, which will be further addressed in the subsequent sections of this chapter. A detailed review of the research literature on instruction is provided by Mayer and Alexander (2011), including individual chapters for instruction based on feedback, examples, self-explanation, peer interactions, cooperative learning, inquiry, discussion, tutoring, visualizations, and computer simulations. Instruction based on computer simulations was covered in detail in the previous section. Here we provide a brief overview of each of the remaining methods of instruction reviewed by Mayer and Alexander, emphasizing those that are most applicable to ITS and simulation design as well as research published within the past three years.

Feedback

A primary element of instruction across learning contexts (i.e., classroom-based, one-on-one tutoring, independent study) involves feedback regarding performance or understanding, whether formal or informal, from an "agent" such as a teacher, parent, peer, book, or the learner's own experience (Hattie, 2009). In a review of 12 meta-analyses assessing feedback in classrooms, Hattie (2009) found an average effect size of .79, placing feedback among the top 10 most influential factors on achievement.

In a recent review, Hattie and Gan (2011) concluded that when and how feedback is received is more important that when and how it is given. This review demonstrated that feedback is most powerful when it makes success criteria transparent to the learner and when it focuses the attention or the learner on the task and learning strategies. Additionally, Hattie and Gan suggest that feedback should be targeted to the level at which the learner is currently functioning or just above, and should challenge the learner to set and monitor learning goals.

Regardless of the form of feedback, the goal is to prompt active information processing based on either active or passive (i.e., intrinsic or extrinsic) instructional events. In addition to passive and active instructional events, Koedinger and Aleven (2007) differentiate interactive instructional events, defining interactivity as not only requiring a response from the learner, but also providing feedback and feedforward cues to the learner's input, providing opportunities for the learner to change a response, elaborate on a response, or proceed to next steps in the problem-solving process. This definition of interactive instructional events includes providing additional feedback or feedforward cues on subsequent responses in an iterative process.

The timing of feedback is critical as well, particularly within the context of errors. For example, Dihoff, Brosvic, and Epstein (2012) demonstrated the effectiveness of combining immediate feedback with the opportunity to answer until correct. However, as summarized by Walton et al. (2014), delayed feedback, also referred to as after action review (AAR), has been shown to be more beneficial than immediate feedback to individual students' learning and retention, and prevents interruption of task flow, particularly in the context of complex or fast-paced learning tasks. Additionally, Carpenter and Vul (2011) found that simply delaying feedback by three seconds, during which only a blank screen was presented, increased retention of face-name pairs. Additional findings have revealed that the learning environment contributes to learning feedback and should be open to errors and disconfirmation, and that feedback should also enable teachers to identify errors in their instruction (Hattie & Gan, 2011).

Worked Examples

Providing learners with a sample problem and solution, also referred to as a worked example, following the explicit introduction of one or more domain principles such as a mathematical theorem or physics laws has been shown to enhance learning and transfer of the subject material, and has been shown to be more effective than completion of a sample problem by the learner (Renkl, 2011). Furthermore, empirical studies have demonstrated that learners should be presented with several examples, rather than a single example, in order to increase understanding and generalizability and application of learned concepts to novel problem sets (Renkl, 2011).

Much research has been dedicated to examining the most effective instructional strategies involving learning by examples, including incorporation of additional effective learning strategies. For example, Schwonke et al. (2007) have provided evidence to indicate that the study and self-explanation of worked examples are more likely to have an effect on conceptual learning than on normal learning. Renkl (2011) provides a set of guidelines, based on the research literature, for incorporating self-explanation, help, and imagery within worked examples, as well as guidelines for the development of example sets that involve easy mapping, meaningful building blocks, learning by errors, model–observer similarity, and interleaving example study with problem solving by gradually fading worked steps.

Self-Explanation

The effectiveness of self-explanation, in which students articulate explanations of the subject matter to themselves, was first demonstrated over 20 years ago by Chi, Bassok, Lewis, Reimann, and Glaser (1989). This instructional strategy has since been studied extensively and has been shown to be effective across multiple studies and subject areas by improving meaningful learning and retention (Fonseca & Chi, 2011). Specifically, self-explanation has been shown to be associated with better learning and understanding of principles and concepts, as well as facilitation of problem solving across age groups, domains, and instructional formats, and has been shown to benefit learners with both high and low prior knowledge (Fonseca & Chi, 2011).

Multiple theories have been suggested to explain why self-explanation enhances learning. For example, VanLehn, Jones, and Chi (1992) proposed a model of the self-explanation effect, suggesting that identification of gaps in knowledge and subsequent filling of those gaps through more in-depth articulations account for much of the self-explanation effect, and that this process involves highlighting relationships between general pieces of domain knowledge. More recently, Calin-Jageman and Horn Ratner (2005) provided evidence to suggest that explanations enhance learning in part by facilitating encoding.

Chi (2009) classifies learning activities as passive, active, constructivist, and interactive, and identifies self-explanation as being constructivist. Chi provides evidence from the research literature that supports the hypothesis that active learning activities produce greater learning outcomes, particularly on measures of deep learning, than passive activities ($d = 0.78$). Additionally, this review found that constructive learning activities produce better outcomes than active, and that interactive learning activities produce better outcomes than constructive. Recently, Mayer (2011) demonstrated that selecting explanations from a list while playing a computer game resulted in better performance on a subsequent transfer test within the game than engaging in typical (generative) self-explanation ($d = 1.20$).

Chi, de Leeuw, Chiu, and LaVancher (1994) also suggested that simply articulating explanations may not be sufficient for learning. They suggested instead that what the students articulate (i.e., the type and quality of articulations) is the critical factor, and that some students are better at generating explanations than others. The assumption is that self-explanations rely on the generation of inference rules and the instantiation of definitions and principles based on the material studied. Effective self-explanations seem to be those that include a generalized conceptual understanding of the material and application of the material learned in instances beyond specific examples provided in the learning material. In this particular study, the authors demonstrated that all students were able to write down the definitions and principles as they were presented in the study materials, but the successful students were also able to apply these definitions and principles to novel examples, indicating that they had generated inference rules. These authors attribute the development of conceptual inference rules to self-articulation. Interestingly, these studies did not account for general or verbal intelligence, which could potentially account for the more effective self-explanations generated by some students.

Peer Interactions

As outlined by Wentzel and Watkins (2011), evidence exists linking learning outcomes to informal peer interactions, peer acceptance, association with peer groups and crowds, friendships, peer interactions in formal learning activities, dyadic learning, and group learning. Specifically, while much of the research involves methodological limitations, peer interactions within the context of both informal and structured learning activities have been shown to be linked to motivation, learning, and academic competencies in school settings. A detailed discussion of the theoretical bases for these phenomena, as well as implications for the implementation of effective peer interaction-based instructional strategies, are offered by Wentzel and Watkins. Additionally, a recent review of the literature demonstrated that peer interactions provide a forum for students to engage in interactive and elaborative feedback discourse while also taking ownership of their learning (Hattie & Gan, 2011).

Cooperative Learning

Peer collaboration or cooperative learning involves instructional methods in which students are organized into small groups in which they work together, helping each other to learn (Slavin, 2011). This form of instruction has also been shown to be an effective active learning technique; empirical studies have demonstrated that students learning in collaborative groups outperformed students that worked alone (e.g., Fawcett & Garton, 2005). Teasley (1995) provided evidence suggesting that peer collaboration provides a social context that supports interpretive cognitive processes and encourages verbalizations that involve reasoning and coherence. Therefore, in addition to benefiting from articulating concepts while learning, there may be added benefits to doing so within a group of other students, rather than to oneself. It is as yet unclear whether similar effects can be obtained within the context of computer-based peer collaboration. Cooperative learning has been shown in empirical studies to not only promote higher achievement, but also greater retention, as compared to individualistic learning experiences (Stevens & Slavin, 1995); however, this instructional strategy has not been effectively implemented with ITSs and may represent an area of future research and development. From a theoretical perspective, the benefits of peer collaboration are thought to stem from increased motivation and social cohesion.

Within the context of structured collaborations involving three or more students, Slavin (1996) concluded that the gains associated with cooperative learning strategies can be attributed to group goals and individual accountability. He argued that group goals provide motivation for individual students to positively contribute to the success of other students and the group as a whole; and that individual accountability is accomplished when the success of the entire group is dependent on the learning and contributions of each and every member of the group, and provides motivation for all students to be actively engaged and to ensure that each student learns the material. Additionally, Slavin (2011) highlights evidence that, in many cases, cooperative learning is informally structured and does not incorporate empirically validated strategies for producing effective outcomes such as group goals and individual accountability.

Inquiry

Inquiry as a form of instruction and learning enhancement dates back to the so-called Socratic method and is widely used across training and educational domains. However, empirical evidence based on controlled experiments is limited. Loyens and Rikers (2011) provide a detailed review of empirical evidence indicating mixed results for inquiry-based instruction across four subsets of learning methods: inquiry-based learning (IBL), problem-based learning (PBL), project-based learning (PjBL), and case-based learning (CBL). While inquiry-based instruction is considered to provide positive learning outcomes overall, particularly for PjBL and CBL, positive effects are only present for some tests and outcomes in the case of IBL and PBL. A detailed discussion of the instantiation and implications within ITSs is provided in the subsequent section of this chapter.

Tutoring

One-on-one peer tutoring has been shown to provide effective interactive learning (Cohen, Kulik, & Kulik, 1982; VanLehn, 2011). Lemke (1990) argues that learning science subject matter in particular requires articulation of concepts and conversing with others that have mastered the subject matter and the language for discussing the subject matter. Peer tutoring involves interaction between two students of differing achievement levels: the tutor and the tutee. A meta-analysis of peer tutoring studies by Cohen et al. (1982) concluded that peer tutoring is beneficial to both tutees and student tutors, increasing understanding, test scores, and attitudes toward the subjects studied within the context of peer tutoring.

A primary question is whether cooperative and peer-tutoring learning strategies provide benefits beyond those that can be attributed to self-explanation. Specifically, can the benefits of interactive learning approaches be attributed solely to the fact that students are required to articulate principles, and thus internalize and conceptualize principles as is required in the context of self-explanation, when demonstrating learning in a group? Conversely, do additional benefits exist related to the interactive and social nature of learning within the context of collaborative and peer-tutoring paradigms? In order to answer this question, a deeper understanding of the potential theoretical bases for self-explanation, peer collaboration, and peer tutoring is needed, as well as a comprehensive summary of literature providing empirical evidence for the benefits of these active learning techniques. As Chi (1996) points out, tutoring involves a series of questions and answers, which result in self-explaining by the tutee, typically in response to a tutor's questions, prompts, or structured scaffolding. This study demonstrated that tutor and tutee co-construction of explanations may be the most beneficial in producing deep learning and in removing misconceptions of the tutee. Therefore, answering tutors' questions may have a more beneficial effect than simply generating explanations to oneself.

Recent research within the domain of neuroscience has begun to explore the underlying neural mechanisms involved in learning during one-on-one interactions. Stephens, Silbert, and Hasson (2010) demonstrated functional magnetic resonance imaging (fMRI)-based neural synchronies between speakers and listeners under varied conditions of story comprehension, providing evidence for detectable spatial and temporal neural coupling in which the listener's brain activity mirrors the speaker's. Furthermore, this research demonstrated that the extent of coupling correlated to the level of story comprehension, with listeners exhibiting predictive anticipatory patterns during high levels of comprehension and cessation of synchronization patterns under conditions of poor comprehension. This synchronization between production and comprehension-based processes may provide insight into the mechanisms by which the brain effectively receives and conveys information.

Stone et al. (2014) examined synchronous electroencephalogram (EEG)- and heart rate variability (HRV)-based psychophysiological monitoring across a tutor and tutee during a spatial reasoning video game, finding small, but significant, correlations in psychophysiological metrics across tutoring dyads that increased with experience and correlated more highly to performance than individual tutee/tutor psychophysiological metrics. While preliminary, these data results imply that synchrony on a psychophysiological level between tutor and tutee impact tutee performance. Further research and development in this area are needed to better understand the underlying neural mechanisms and to determine whether this phenomenon can be extended to human–technology synchrony within the context of ITS computer-based instruction, and whether cognitive state can be modulated by instructional strategies/techniques that the tutor has at hand. Further study and comparison of the underlying neural mechanisms involved in self-explanation, peer tutoring, and peer interaction may provide insight into the neural processes and optimal methods for applying these learning techniques.

In light of this apparent gap in the research literature, further research is needed in which both learning performance and neurophysiological indices would be used to examine differences in learning and brain activations generated during self-explanation, collaborative learning, and peer tutoring. The outcomes of this research could be applied to the development of ITS technologies that include appropriate instructional strategies to tap into the social aspects of learning. This may include increased use of natural language processing to encourage articulation, as well as virtual peers or tutors capable of building rapport and trust with the learner, and motivating the learner to have the desire to perform well in order to please virtual peers and instructors.

ITS-Based Instructional Strategies

Researchers concerned with the use of technology (e.g., computers) in education and training have as their goal to develop computer tutors that are as effective as human tutors (Smith & Sherwood, 1976). Therefore, methods of instruction shown to be effective within the context of human tutoring were the focus of much of the early ITS research and development. For example, Merrill, Reiser, Ranney, and Trafton (1992) investigated and demonstrated commonalities between cognitive tutors and human tutors in terms of interactivity in the context of worked examples. As highlighted by Koedinger and Aleven (2007), another critical component that differentiates the characterization of interactivity of cognitive tutors is that in addition to offering final solutions, cognitive tutors provide solution-specific, step-by-step hints and adaptive problem selection based on nested instructional loops (VanLehn, 2006). A primary benefit of one-on-one tutoring and intelligent tutoring systems is the ability to tailor training style and content to the individual learner and to keep track of the learner's knowledge growth over time. Selection of problems on an individual basis supports student growth and progress (Koedinger & Aleven, 2007). When implemented effectively, this level of customization ensures that problems presented to the learner are of sufficient difficulty and complexity (Ericsson, 2006, 2014) to present a challenge and to require learning to occur while increasing a level of difficulty and complexity that can be mastered by the learner within designated instructional sessions.

This form of so-called "deliberate practice" is consistent with models of expertise acquisition and accelerated learning developed by Anders Ericsson. Ericsson (n.d., 1996, 2004) proposed an expert–performance approach that describes both general skill acquisition and expertise acquisition as an extended series of gradual changes in physiological and cognitive mechanisms mediating performance. The primary mechanism by which this is said to occur is by challenging the physiological systems, including the brain, inducing adaptations over time. Thus, tasks that are initially physically and/or cognitively challenging become easier with practice. In particular, Ericsson specifies that designed, or deliberate, practice is required in order to provide learners with appropriate, typically guided, training tasks. These tasks are ideally beyond the trainee's existing skill level and capabilities initially, but are not beyond a level that can be attained sequentially and within a short time period (typically within a matter of hours) via practice with appropriate feedback.

In addition, Ericsson describes concentration as a critical aspect of the deliberate practice paradigm such that mindless, rote task repetitions and playful engagement do not constitute the form of practice required to achieve expertise. Ericsson further highlights the fact that the concentration required during true deliberate practice inherently limits the amount of practice time that can be engaged in within a given training session. Ericsson (2006) also suggests that expertise acquisition involves the acquisition of increasingly complex mental representations in order to support continued learning and performance improvement, and further specifies that such mental representations must also become increasingly flexible.

Several researchers have put forth the hypotheses that a better understanding of the learner's cognitive and emotional state could support more effective teaching (Baker, Goldstein, & Heffernan, 2011; Craig, Graesser, Sullins, & Gholson, 2004; D'Mello et al., 2005; D'Mello et al., 2008; D'Mello, Picard, & Graesser, 2007). An oft-cited problem involves the effects of stress (i.e., arousal). In order to support automated customization of induced arousal, preliminary research has indicated that real-time neurophysiological measures could be used to assess individual learner cognitive states and drive real-time instructional strategies and content variations. The goal of such real-time user-state-driven ITS modifications would be to assess factors such as cognitive workload and engagement and to tailor problems, feedback, and feedforward information complexity to keep the learner in the "sweet spot" or flow state for optimized learning and retention.

Studies that have assessed emotions and affect during tutoring have identified confusion, frustration, boredom, anxiety, and flow/engagement as the predominant emotions, with delight and surprise occurring less frequently (Baker, D'Mello, Rodrigo, & Graesser, 2010; Craig et al., 2004; D'Mello et al., 2008; D'Mello et al., 2007; Lehman, Matthews, D'Mello, & Person, 2008). Some evidence (D'Mello et al., 2008) has been provided to support correlations of affect to learning performance based on observational analyses and sensor-based analysis of conversational dialogue, posture, and facial features. Specifically, based on observational analyses (Baker et al., 2010), significant learning gains were positively correlated with confusion and flow, and were negatively correlated with boredom. However, limited objective empirical data exist to demonstrate effective coordination of these emotions to learning.

In addition to tailoring learning content and complexity, neurophysiology-based cognitive state information could be used to determine optimal information presentation modalities based on real-time verbal working memory and spatial working memory assessments, adjusting the modality of information presentation as needed to prevent overloading the verbal or spatial cognitive processing systems. Furthermore, such learner cognitive state information could be tracked over time and correlated to performance within and across learning sessions to identify individualized instructional strategies to support rapid knowledge acquisition and long-term retention.

Furthermore, for the past 30 years, developers of ITSs have been driven by the quest for the so-called "two sigma" effect. Benjamin Bloom and his students (1984) found that one-on-one instruction yielded an effect size of two standard deviations over traditional forms of education involving a human tutor interacting with a student. Recently, Kurt VanLehn (2011) found that human tutoring had a positive impact of an effect size of 0.79 and not two standard deviations as previously reported by Bloom. Additionally, Pane, Griffin, McCaffrey, and Karam (2014) conducted a two-year study examining the impact of an algebra tutor on algebra scores for high school students in which no significant effect was found in the first year, and an effect size of only 0.20 was found in the second year.

VanLehn has argued that the two sigma effect has not been replicated nor was it the intent of Bloom's research to demonstrate the effectiveness of one-on-one instruction. Rather it was an attempt to show the effects of using a level of mastery as an instructional strategy (VanLehn, 2013). Additionally, a recent meta-analysis demonstrated that use of ITS was associated with greater achievement in comparison with teacher-led, large-group instruction (g = 0.42), non-ITS computer-based instruction (g = 0.57), and textbooks or workbooks (g = 0.35). Moreover, there was no significant difference between learning from ITS and learning from individualized human tutoring (g = −0.11) or small-group instruction (g = 0.05) (Ma, Adesope, Nesbit, & Liu, 2014).

However, the goal of reaching a two sigma effect remains the gold standard for ITS developers. Perhaps a near-term gold standard for ITS should be g = 0.7 based on the latest meta-analysis results conducted by Kulik and Fletcher (2015) and the recent study by VanLehn (2013). This is still beyond the g = 0.4 that Hattie (2012) suggests as a baseline for educational interventions. Table 6.2 (adapted from VanLehn, 2011) summarizes the findings of a meta-analysis comparing five conditions: no tutoring, human tutoring, answer-based tutoring, step-based tutoring, and substep-based tutoring. The table presents the number of studies included in each calculation, the mean effect size, and the percentage of the comparisons that were reliable at the $p < .05$ level of significance.

TABLE 6.2 Summary of Effect Sizes Adapted from VanLehn (2011) Meta-analysis

Comparison	Number of studies	ES	% Reliable
Answer based vs. No tutoring	165	0.31	40%
Step based vs. No tutoring	28	0.76	68%
Substep based vs. No tutoring	26	0.40	54%
Human vs. No Tutoring	10	0.79	80%
Step based vs. Answer based	2	0.40	50%
Substep based vs. Answer based	6	0.32	33%
Human vs. Answer based	1	−0.04	0%
Substep based vs. Step based	11	0.16	0%
Human vs. Step based	10	0.21	30%
Human vs. Substep based	5	−0.12	0%

VanLehn (2011) has also questioned the hypothesis that the more intelligent tutoring systems behaved like human tutors the more effective the machine tutors would be. He investigated eight behaviors reported in the literature that had been attributed to human tutors and were believed to explain why human tutoring is more effective than machine tutoring. These eight behaviors (instructional strategies) were put in the form of testable hypotheses as follows. Human tutors (a) are able to infer an accurate, detailed model of the student's competence and misunderstanding, which is then used to provide a diagnostic assessment by the tutor to adapt instruction to the needs of the individual student; (b) are better at selecting tasks that are at the right level of complexity and difficulty in order for the student to learn; (c) are able to use sophisticated strategies such as reciprocal teaching (Palinscar & Brown, 1984); (d) enable mixed-initiative interactions so the student can ask questions or change the topic, in contrast with most machine tutors in which student initiative is tightly controlled; (e) have broader global knowledge and deeper knowledge of the domain than machine tutors; (f) are able to increase the motivation of the student to learn; (g) provide feedback to the student in the form of helping the student monitor his or her reasoning and repair any misconceptions he or she may have; and (h) provide scaffolding to the student's reasoning. Scaffolding is defined here as "guided prompting that pushes the student a little further along the same line of thinking, rather than providing the student new information, giving direct feedback on a student's response, or raising a new question or a new issue that is unrelated to the student's reasoning" (Chi, Siler, Yamauchi, Jeong, & Hausmann, 2001, p. 490). VanLehn was only able to find empirical support for the positive effects on learning for the last two tutor behaviors, concluding that unlike the first six hypotheses it seems that a viable explanation for why human tutoring is more effective than machine tutoring is that human tutors use feedback and scaffolding. Moreover, VanLehn (2013) in a more recent paper has examined research on expert human tutors and has observed that these tutors only use feedback and scaffolding.

The lesson to be learned is that modern developers of ITSs may want to focus on ITS components that emulate expert human tutors giving feedback and scaffolding as well as additional instructional strategies that have been shown to be effective in knowledge acquisition and retention across subject matter areas. For example, Mitrovic et al. (2013) demonstrated that students who were interacting with the augmented version of SQL-Tutor that provided positive feedback learned at twice the speed as the students who interacted with the standard, error feedback only version.

State of the Science in ITS Development

This section provides several ITS examples, an overview of the state of the science in ITS effectiveness, and a review of current applications of artificial intelligence (AI) to a new generation of ITSs.

ITS Examples

The following provides examples of three types of ITS technologies: ACT-R Based Tutors, AutoTutor, and SHERLOCK. These examples are not intended to provide a comprehensive review of existing ITSs (for a detailed review, see U.S. Department of Education, Office of Educational Technology, 2013); rather this review is intended to provide an overview of ITS technologies representative of various instructional strategy implementations and targeted tutoring domains (i.e., declarative and procedural knowledge, and mathematics).

ACT-R-Based Tutors

No review of the literature on ITSs could be complete without mentioning the Anderson tutors, also known as cognitive tutors (Anderson et al., 1995). These tutors were designed to teach students to solve problems in LISP, geometry, and algebra. Cognitive tutors are in use at least two days per week by more than 600,000 students a year in 2,600 middle or high schools, and represent one of the most widely used ITS technologies. Cognitive tutors have a 20-year history of research and development and are based on the ACT* theory of learning and problem solving described in *The Architecture of Cognition* (Anderson, 1983). The development of cognitive tutors represents a unique approach to building tutors. They tested the ACT theory by observing whether the ACT* theory designed tutor could optimize learning. Many of the evaluations of cognitive tutors have found evidence of positive learning effects providing support for the ACT* theory. However, as previously noted, in some cases these effects have been shown to be relatively small and have been shown to only produce effects after long-term use (Pane et al., 2014). The development of ACT-R, a unified computational theory of human architecture, provided a sound scientific foundation for the design of training systems.

The underlying architecture of these tutors is driven by the ACT* theory of learning. ACT* theory states that a cognitive skill consists, in large part, of units of goal-related knowledge; and that skill acquisition involves the formulation of thousands of rules that relate to task goals and task state to actions and consequences (Anderson et al., 1995). This theory also makes a distinction between procedural knowledge and declarative knowledge. Procedural knowledge is the ability to use rules to solve a problem whereas declarative knowledge consists of knowing the concepts and rules. The theory refers to the learning process as knowledge compilations, which convert this interpretative problem solving into production rules, and assumes that production rules can only be learned by employing declarative knowledge within the context of problem-solving activities. The last tenet of this theory is strengthening; much like Thorndike's "law of effect" the tenet suggests that both declarative and procedural knowledge acquired strength with practice, successive practice produces smoother and more rapid execution and fewer errors. Later, Anderson, Boyle, Farrell, and Reiser (1987) extracted five principles to guide the design of tutors: (a) represent student competence as a production set; (b) communicate the goal structures underlying the problem solving; (c) provide instruction in the problem-solving context; (d) promote an abstract understanding of the problem-solving knowledge; and (e) minimize working memory load. These tutors make use of two major algorithms: model tracing and knowledge tracing. The model-tracing algorithm evaluates the correctness of each of the student's attempts at solving problems by comparing step by step the student's steps with the possible steps of the cognitive model. The knowledge-tracing algorithm maintains estimates of the probability that the student knows each knowledge component in the cognitive model and is represented by a production rule (Corbett & Anderson, 1994). The knowledge tracer makes use of the information provided by model tracing to determine when the student has provided a correct action or incorrect action.

Anderson and his colleagues initially called their ITSs tutors because they were inspired by the intelligent tutors built in the late 1970s and early 1980s (Sleeman & Brown, 1982; see introduction). The initial design goals were intended to enable the tutor to interact with students much like human expert tutors. However, over the 20 or so years of development, the emulation of human tutors has been de-emphasized. The cognitive tutors have been involved in many evaluations of the LISP, geometry, and algebra tutors. The results of the algebra Cognitive Tutor will be presented here as it is widely used (see Koedinger & Aleven, 2007), and the effects have varied from no significant differences for evaluations that took place in 1987–1988 with the algebra Cognitive Tutor to the most recent wide-scale evaluation (Pane et al., 2014) conducted by the Rand corporation and funded by the U.S. Department of Education, for which small effect sizes were found (i.e., effect size of .22). The Rand study involved seven states and a variety of middle schools and high schools (including 6,800 students in Grades 6–8 and 18,700 students in Grades 9–12). One measure of success of ITSs is the prevalence of their use. According to Carnegie Learning Inc., 600,000 students in more than 2,600 middle and high schools use Carnegie Learning's Cognitive Tutor for algebra. Pane et al. (2014) found the tutor to be more effective than traditional algebra courses. This evaluation matched middle and high school students into pairs randomly assigned to either a traditional algebra curriculum (control) or one that included the algebra Cognitive Tutor (experimental treatment). Positive results in favor of the algebra Cognitive Tutor in the second year of the two-year study were found only for the high schools, but demonstrated that the high school students' performance was superior to the control classes in the second year. Algebra Cognitive Tutor raised their score on average by eight percentile points, for which small effects were found (i.e., effect size of .22).

AutoTutor

AutoTutor is an ITS that helps students learn Algebra 1, Newtonian physics, computer literacy, and critical thinking through the use of advanced tutorial dialogues in natural language. AutoTutor simulates a human tutor by holding a conversation with the learner using natural language processing. The student model of AutoTutor is an example of misconception tailored dialogue (Sottilare et al., 2013).

AutoTutor is theory-driven, and much like ACT-R tutors, AutoTutor's design is driven by explanation-based constructivist theories of learning (Aleven & Koedinger, 2002; Graesser et al., 2014; VanLehn et al., 1992). In addition to being theory-driven it is an ITS that adaptively responds to the learner's actions. It gives immediate feedback to the tutee and guides the tutee on what do next; this guidance reflects what the tutor infers as the learner's state of knowledge. Tutorial strategies used by AutoTutor are empirically based, grounded in research on strategies that are used by expert human tutors. For example, one of the prominent dialogue patterns used by AutoTutor is expectation and misconception tailored (EMT) dialogue, which has been observed to be used by human tutors (Graesser, Hu, & McNamara, 2005; Graesser, Person, & Magliano, 1995; Graesser, VanLehn, Rosé, Jordan, & Harter, 2001).

EMT is based on the observation that human tutors typically have a list of anticipated "good" answers (i.e., expectations) and a list of misconceptions associated with each question or problem, and so does AutoTutor. AutoTutor has at least two goals. The first goal is to coach the student in covering the list of expectations, and the second is to correct the anticipated misconceptions that are detected in the student's interactions with the machine tutor (e.g., talk and actions). AutoTutor simulates the discourse patterns of human tutors and also incorporates a number of ideal tutoring strategies. Another goal of AutoTutor is to provide feedback (positive, neutral, and negative) that adaptively responds to the student; it pumps the learner for additional information (e.g., "what else?"), prompts the learner to fill in missing words, gives hints, fills in missing information with assertions, identifies and corrects inappropriate answers, answers the learner's questions, and summarizes answers (Graesser, Chipman, Haynes, & Olney, 2005). It does this by presenting a series of challenging problems or questions that require verbal explanations and reasoning in an answer. It also engages in a collaborative mixed-initiative dialogue while constructing an answer; this process typically takes approximately 100 conversational turns. AutoTutor provides the content of its turns through an animated conversational agent using natural language with a speech engine and a sensor that is able to identify some facial expressions and rudimentary gestures. For some topics, there are graphical displays, animations of causal mechanisms, or the use of interactive simulations. AutoTutor tracks the cognitive states of the learner by analyzing the content of the dialogue history. AutoTutor dynamically selects the words and statements in each conversational turn in a fashion that is sensitive to what the learner knows. The AutoTutor system also adapts to learners' emotional states in addition to their cognitive states (Graesser et al., 2005). The impact of AutoTutor in facilitating the learning of deep conceptual knowledge has been validated in over a dozen experiments with college students for topics in conceptual physics (Graesser et al., 2014; Graesser, Wiemer-Hastings, Wiemer-Hastings, Kreuz, & the Tutoring Research Group, 1999) and introductory computer literacy (McNamara, O'Reilly, Best, & Ozuru, 2006). Tests of AutoTutor have produced medium and large effect sizes of 0.4 to 1.5, which moves a person from the 50th percentile to the 94th percentile, with a mean of 1.5, depending on the learning measure, the comparison condition, the subject matter, and version of AutoTutor (Graesser et al., 2014).

The most recent version of AutoTutor uses shareable knowledge objects that teach Algebra 1 skills with user-friendly authoring tools. Selection of skills will be (vs. was) based on concept maps and learning progression, and Common Core standards (Graesser & D'Mello, 2012; Graesser et al., 2014). A shareable knowledge objects (SKO) framework declares a composition of services intended to deliver knowledge to a user, with the expected use case being tutoring in natural language. In this context, the SKO framework is not a reimplementation of AutoTutor but a framework for breaking AutoTutor down into minimal components that can be composed to create tutoring modules that may or may not rely on the traditional AutoTutor modules. These minimal components are intended to be used as part of a service-oriented design (Nye, Graesser, & Hu, 2014).

This research integrates AutoTutor, a conversational tutoring system, into ALEKS, a commercial K–12 mathematics learning environment used by hundreds of schools. AutoTutor's technology as applied to ALEKS is intended to enhance ALEKS's procedural practice and worked solutions by adding animated and interactive tutoring agents that help students master math concepts. As in the earlier versions (Graesser & D'Mello, 2012), tutoring is provided by a pair of animated agents (a computer tutor and a computer student) that talk to the student using natural language; the computer student types to the tutor in free text and the tutor speaks back using voice and also provides text. These tutoring sessions focus primarily on math reasoning, analyzing problems and explaining the underlying concepts. It is expected that these dialogues promote higher learning and motivation within the ALEKS system, as they include animated agents who tutor mathematics concepts. The project has as its goal integrating tutoring into a special ALEKS course covering a subset of the ALEKS Algebra 1 course, which is matched to the Common Core.

More recently, a version of AutoTutor was developed for improving literacy skills using trilogues in which the goal is to help adults with low literacy improve their literacy by engaging students in conversation in natural language interacting with two computer agents that use ideal pedagogical strategies (Graesser et al., 2014). These tutors using natural language dialogue yield learning gains comparable to those trained by human tutors, with effect sizes ranging from 0.6 to 2.0 (Graesser & D'Mello, 2012; Graesser et al., 2004; Hu & Graesser, 2004; McNamara et al., 2006). A trilogue is a conversation between a machine tutor and a student in which two agents, one acting as a tutor and the other as a peer, interact with a human student. These agents can take on different roles (Graesser et al., 2014). These tutors simulate the dialogue between tutee and human tutor with high fidelity, finally approaching the capability for machine tutors to have a conversation with a tutee much as envisioned by Jamie Carbonell over 60 years ago; however, these dialogues are scripted.

SHERLOCK

One of the most successful and historically earliest tutors built for a military domain has been SHERLOCK, developed for avionic electronics troubleshooting. SHERLOCK is a tutor that provides a coached practice environment for an avionics electronics troubleshooting task (Lesgold, Lajoie, Bunzo, & Eggan, 1992). This tutor was designed to teach troubleshooting procedures for problems associated with an F-15 manual avionics test station. The curriculum is made up of 34 troubleshooting scenarios that include hints and consists of 20 hours of instruction. However, since it is self-paced, trainee time varies.

One of the most difficult tasks for avionics repairmen is locating and isolating faults in a complex system and then replacing or repairing the faulty part or parts. The results of an evaluation comparing Air Force trainees receiving 20 hours of instruction on SHERLOCK to a control group receiving on-the-job training over the same period of time indicated that the group using the tutor performed significantly better than the group receiving on-the-job training, and their performance was equivalent to experienced technicians having several years of on-the-job experience (Shute, 1991). The average gain score for the SHERLOCK treatment group was equivalent to almost four years of on-the-job experience. These results suggest that the tutor was not only superior in effectiveness but was also able to accelerate the level of expertise of the technicians exposed to the tutor. One explanation for these results is that the developers of the tutor conducted a comprehensive cognitive task analysis.

State of the Science in ITS Effectiveness

In a recent meta-analysis of 50 controlled ITS evaluation studies, Kulik and Fletcher (2015) demonstrated that ITSs raised test scores by 0.63 standard deviations, based on the median effect size (ES) across studies. By comparison to a previous meta-analysis examining computer-aided instruction (CAI) in 165 studies (Kulik & Kulik, 1991), which found an ES of only 0.31, ITS gains were found to be approximately twice as high. Furthermore, by comparison to recent evaluations of human tutoring effectiveness, which have demonstrated an ES of 0.40, ITSs have been shown to exceed the benefits of alternative forms of tutoring.

Kulik and Fletcher's meta-analysis (2015) outcomes indicated that the ES for individual ITS evaluation studies was greater for locally developed as compared to standardized tests, with an average ES of only 0.14 for evaluations using standardized tests, but emphasize that this is consistent with meta-analyses involving both forms of tests and suggest that locally developed tests may provide a more direct application to the targeted instructional programs while standardized tests provide the benefit of being unbiased. Kulik and Fletcher (2015) also examined 16 additional ITS evaluation studies, demonstrating that the fidelity of program implementation impacts evaluation results, with higher quality implementation resulting in stronger gains; and further demonstrating that the type of control group used impacts study outcomes, with conventional control groups generating greater gains (median ES = 0.63) than unconventional control groups (median ES = 0.24) that were taught with materials that were derived from the ITS instructional content.

Current Applications of AI to a New Generation of ITSs

Early researchers have attempted to build ITSs that mimic the behaviors of expert human tutors, and specifically the ability to adapt and tailor instruction to the individual needs of the student. Although to date most intelligent tutors have not been able to accomplish a full two sigma effect, there has been some progress toward this goal (Kulik & Fletcher, 2015). The use of emerging and innovative methods, procedures, and technologies promises that future systems may be able to accomplish the goal of the gold standard of a two sigma effect (Kulik & Fletcher, 2015). Among these promising technologies are virtual humans to be used as an interface for intelligent tutors, game-based learning environments, data mining, and machine learning, as well as new science-based methods and procedures for building student and expert models, and diagnosis and remediation of student errors.

Virtual Humans as an Interface for ITSs

An important goal of ITS developers as stated by Carbonell (1970) was to create between the student and the computer a dialogue in much the same way a human expert tutor would interact with a student where questions and answers come from both student and computer. One of the limitations of early ITSs pointed out by Sleeman and Brown (1982) is that user interactions between the student and computer were restrictive, limiting the student's responses, and thereby limiting the ability of the tutors to provide a mixed-initiative dialogue. Swartout et al. (2013) have presented an argument of how virtual humans provide a new metaphor for students/trainees interacting with a computer, one in which interacting with a computer is much like having a conversation with a real person. Hays et al. (2012) have provided evidence that virtual humans interacting with a human can teach interpersonal skills. Although the dialogue for the avatar is scripted, the authors have presented evidence that this approach is effective in teaching interpersonal skills. This research could address Sleeman and Brown's (1982) criticisms of earlier ITSs.

The use of a virtual human also has the capability to bring social elements that are hard or impossible to elicit using conventional interfaces. The goal would be to build a virtual human that would act as a human-like tutor, having the capability of speech recognition and generation, as well as an inference engine that would be able to respond to the student's questions and provide answers on the fly in a conversation with a student. The initial goal of Swartout and his colleagues at the Institute for Creative Technologies (ICT) was to develop virtual humans that could act as replacements for human role players in training and learning exercises. They cited studies indicating that people respond to virtual humans in much the same way they do to real people (Gratch et al., 2007; Hays et al., 2012; Krämer, Tietz, & Bente, 2003; Reeves & Nass, 1996).

With support from the Office of Naval Research (ONR), ICT has built an immersive environment that uses a virtual human to teach interpersonal skills to Navy junior officers. The INOTS (Immersive Navy Officers Training System) provides the students with a virtual human as a role player in a practice environment that uses various scripted scenarios representing various personnel problems that face junior officers. The INOTS practice environment is used to provide an opportunity for students to practice their newly acquired interpersonal skills to address typical personnel problems. The virtual human plays the role of the sailor who is having a personal problem. The scenarios that students are exposed to vary from advising a sailor who is experiencing financial problems to one who has been in an altercation with another crewmate aboard ship. The virtual human's behavior and how it interacts with students at the present time is scripted and only has the capability to interact in a prescribed way. Studies conducted by ICT have found that students respond to the INOTS virtual human in much the same way as they do to human instructors and that it is just as effective in teaching interpersonal skills (Hays et al., 2012).

However, the long-term goal of this research is to build virtual humans that have the ability to mimic what expert human tutors do to enhance learning such as providing feedback and scaffolding, establishing rapport, building relationships, and providing instruction to the student using mixed-initiative tutorial dialogues. In addition to the virtual human for INOTS, ICT has built virtual humans to act as museum guides (docents) and coaches to provide military service members, veterans, and their significant others with confidential help in exploring and accessing healthcare content and, if needed, to encourage these individuals to seek help from mental health care providers (see Swartout et al., 2013, for details on the formative evaluation of the effectiveness of virtual humans).

Educational Data Mining (EDM)

Recently, research and development has begun to focus on the use of "big data" for evaluating learning systems, as well as for the development and testing of theories that are used to explain learning gains (Scheuer & McLaren, 2012). Data mining, sometimes referred to as data or knowledge discovery, is a subfield of computer science and artificial intelligence (AI), and involves the process of analyzing data from different perspectives and summarizing it into meaningful and actionable information. Koedinger et al. (2013) have suggested that these data-driven techniques could be used to optimize the selection, evaluation, and update functions of intelligent tutors. As of yet, no data have been published that provide evidence that these techniques have improved intelligent tutors; however, these researchers have proposed to use AI techniques such as probabilistic grammar learning, rule induction, Markov decision processes, classification, and integrations of symbolic search and statistical inference for this purpose.

Educational data mining (EDM) could also be used to examine the effects of different instructional interventions or in the case of ITSs to examine the effects of varying instructional strategies for remediation of students' errors and patterns of errors. EDM analytic techniques could also be used to address Sleeman and Brown's critique of earlier ITSs that instructional materials produced by the tutor in response to a student's query or mistake was often not on target, was not at the appropriate level of detail, or the system assumed too much or too little student knowledge. Steps include data acquisition, data preprocessing, data mining, and validation of results.

As noted earlier in this chapter, human tutors differ from today's ITSs in many ways. For example, humans can process natural language, from emotional connections with their students, read facial expressions and body posture, use humor, and perhaps more importantly, they don't just teach but also learn (Moore, 2012). The ability for computers to improve over time is the state of the art for commercial online movie services like Netflix, which for example, recommend new movies to customers based on an analysis of their preferences and the preferences of millions of other customers, and these recommendations improve as customers continue to use the system over time. A machine-based tutor that can learn and improve its teaching as it becomes more familiar with a student is a daunting task. In order to have this capability the system must be able to have four capabilities: (a) systematically manipulate how and when it presents new content and applies new instructional strategies; (b) assess student understanding and use this assessment to provide relevant feedback as part of manipulating the new strategies; (c) provide the appropriate level of scaffolding (e.g., hints and prompts) when the student is "stuck"; and (d) evaluate the impact of the instructional manipulations on student performance and learning. In the next section we identify and describe some promising new emerging technologies that could improve the performance of modern-day tutors.

Lessons Learned from ITSs to Simulations

So what can the developers of simulations learn from those that design and develop intelligent tutoring systems? In other words, can the design of simulators/

simulations be influenced by ITSs? Prior to a discussion of how 60 years of development of ITSs can inform the design of simulations, it is important to point out critical differences between ITSs and simulation-based training. For the most part, modern-day ITSs have primarily, although not all, been designed to teach science, technology, engineering, and math (STEM) learning content. STEM as a domain is stable/static (Koedinger, Anderson, Hadley, & Mark, 1997; VanLehn et al., 2005), whereas many operational training domains involve more complex and dynamic concepts and skills. For example, the U.S. Navy has begun to use simulators to train dynamic tasks, such as shipboard damage control and basic shiphandling maneuvers (Iseli, Koenig, Lee, & Wainess, 2010; Peters, Bratt, & Kirschenbaum, 2011). These tasks are dynamic in that their states change over time (e.g., sea state).

Perhaps the most important lessons learned from ITS research and development that can be used to enhance simulation is the use of cognitive task analysis (CTA). To date, effective ITSs have used CTAs, whereas in traditional simulation training development, the most common approach to describing desired behavior, training needs, training scenarios, and performance metrics has been task analysis (Cannon-Bowers et al., 2013). The principal shortcoming of task analysis is that it only focuses on observable behavior and provides no data on the thought processes involved in performing the target task (Cannon-Bowers et al., 2013). Data on thought processes via CTA are needed to teach complex cognitive skills of the task to be learned. Teaching cognitive skills such as analysis, decision making, and problem solving using task analysis has been problematic (Cannon-Bowers et al., 2013). In medical training for example, Clark and Estes (1996) have shown that by using CTA training needs analyses yield 35% more information than non-CTA based analyses. ITSs are particularly effective for teaching cognitive skills (Kulik & Fletcher, 2015). This is due, in part, to the fact that CTA techniques are primarily used to capture the thought processes, procedural, and declarative knowledge that experts use in performing the target task. Procedural and declarative knowledge make up the expert and domain models of an ITS, which can provide the curriculum/content to be taught and metrics for assessing student performance in a simulator.

With regard to performance metrics Mislevy, Steinberg, Breyer, Almond, and Johnson (1999) have used CTA to develop metrics for assessing performance of dental assistants, in which the test items are designed to discriminate between the behaviors of novices and experts. However, currently, simulator developers lack a pedagogical theory to guide instructional decisions (e.g., sequence of instruction) and what performance metrics to use to assess student progress. Lastly, CTA could be used to create training scenarios. Cannon-Bowers and Bowers (2008) have advocated the use of scenario-based training in simulators as a useful training technique to teach complex skills and abilities. Scenario characteristics include the following: (a) involves mentally processing and connecting the content presented to the question/task; (b) models "real-life" thinking processes that the learner has to be able to perform; (c) presents issue(s) related to the targeted learning outcomes; (d) is sufficiently complete, complex, and focused; (e) presents a situation, problem, or issue; (f) appears to be realistic; (g) has events in a logical order; and (h) has content that is accurate, relevant, and appropriate (adapted from Wong, Ogren, Peters, & Bratt, 2014).

The addition of components from an ITS would enable simulations to be stand-alone training systems; typically, both military and medical simulation in the past have required a human-in-the-loop (Bradley, 2006; McGaghie, Issenberg, Petrusa, & Scalese, 2010). In this case, an instructor provides instruction (e.g., feedback and scaffolding) over the shoulder, while the trainee is using the simulator to learn how to accomplish a task.

When instruction is embedded, as in more recent educational simulations (Cannon-Bowers & Bowers, 2008), pedagogical decisions are primarily driven by preprogrammed scenarios in which the interactions between the simulation and student/trainee are scripted; this means that the designers of simulations must anticipate each instructional decision in advance so that these can be preprogrammed within the training scenarios. They must specify the sequence of instructional events, the granularity of each step, when and which type of feedback is to be provided the trainee, and must anticipate what to do when the trainee provides an incorrect response, which may require providing multiple responses. The system must also take into consideration the trainee's prior knowledge and how to objectively determine whether the trainee has mastered the materials to be learned. In ITSs, all of these pedagogical decisions are made on the fly by the student model interacting with domain, pedagogical, and interface modules (Brown et al., 1982).

These ITS-initiated pedagogical decisions must be guided by theory in order to be effective. Incorporation of a tutor in a simulator would provide an engine for instructional decision making. From the point of view of simulation developers, ITSs generally have been designed to teach static domains (e.g., mathematics and science), although some earlier ITSs such as SOPHIE (Brown et al., 1982) and STEAMER were designed to teach electronic ship skills and troubleshooting skills for the power plant of a ship. Further, traditionally ITSs have not been designed with consideration of fidelity factors such as functional fidelity, psychological fidelity, performance cues, and physical fidelity. Well-designed simulations embedded in an ITS could improve the effectiveness of an ITS due to the simulation's ability to make abstract concepts concrete. An example of the integration of an ITS with a simulator is the Navy's COVE-ITS for teaching advanced ship handling skills (Peters et al., 2011) to naval officers.

Advanced ship handling is a complex skill requiring significant training time and instructor coaching for learners to achieve proficiency. The COVE-ITS uses a natural language interface to provide coaching to the trainee and it utilizes a simulator that has a physics-based model that simulates the dynamics of various ship classes. The ITS component uses a model tracing student mode in which the performance of the trainee is compared to an expert model; when the trainee's performance deviates from that of the expert, the system will provide hints, prompts, and feedback to correct the trainee's behavior. One of the reasons that the developers of COVE-ITS could use a natural language interface is that shiphandling involves a very limited vocabulary that is context bound (Peters et al., 2011). Shiphandling is taught using scripted protocols of how to ask questions, give progress updates, and issue commands/directions.

The tutor monitors students' performance and diagnoses errors made by the student on the fly, which not only provides remediation but also determines the next sequence of instructions without the aid of a human instructor. The tutor has five levels. At Level 0, a novice student observes COVE-ITS on automatic pilot. At Level 1, the system coaches a student though an exercise. At Level 2, the system monitors the student performing in an exercise providing hints, prompts, and feedback when the student's performance is not consistent with the expert model (e.g., the way an expert mariner would perform the exercise). Level 3 is an advanced level in which the student is asked to perform replenishment at sea and the system varies the conditions (e.g., wind and sea state). Level 4, which is currently under development, will be aimed at providing students with advanced exercises with varying conditions (e.g., sea states).

The ultimate goal of the system is to accelerate the development of shiphandling skills to that of a master mariner. Although a training effectiveness study has been performed and found that COVE-ITS-trained students performed just as well as those trained by expert human instructors, the effectiveness of COVE-ITS as a system and the individual components were not assessed separately (Wong et al., 2014).

Research Gaps and Future Directions

Today's ITS developers are still faced with the difficult technical tasks of constructing and validating individual student models and developing effective natural language interfaces. Additionally, tutorial dialogues still remain a challenge, as well as diagnosis of students' errors and how to remediate them. Finally, the cost and level of effort required has been daunting. The way forward for improving the performance of intelligent tutoring systems lies in emerging technologies and new pedagogical theories based on the science of learning: virtual human avatars, data mining, leveraging game-based learning, and a value-added approach.

Virtual Human Avatars as an Interface

An important goal of ICAI systems developers was to create between the student and the computer a dialogue in much the same way that a human expert tutor would interact with a student where questions and answers come from both student and computer (Carbonell, 1970). This goal of earlier ITSs achieving the capability to provide a mixed-initiative dialogue was accomplished in a limited way. A promising technology for meeting this goal is development of a sophisticated intelligent virtual human avatar as interface between the tutor and the student. This interface would have not only the capability of speech recognition and generation but also the capability to recognize the meaning of emotional states and gestures.

Earlier we described the INOT avatar's limited ability to interact with a trainee using speech recognition and generation to teach interpersonal skills. The avatar in this system is scenario driven and the interactions between the avatar and trainee is completely scripted. For example, if the trainee selects a strategy for resolving a personal problem, the avatar is scripted to follow a prespecified set of actions based on the trainee's selected strategy. An ITS could be enhanced by building an intelligent avatar that is driven by the domain, learner, and tutor models and is able to provide a mixed-initiative dialogue with trainees that represents real-world interactions.

Data Mining to Refine the Student Model

Sleeman and Brown (1982) in reviewing earlier ITSs and commenting on their limitations asserted that instructional material produced in response to a student's query or mistake was often at an inappropriate level of detail, as the system assumed too much or too little student knowledge. Recently, there has been a focus on the use of big data for evaluating learning systems and the development and testing of theories that are used to explain learning gains (Scheuer & McLaren, 2012). Koedinger et al. (2013) have suggested that these data-driven techniques could be used to optimize the selection, evaluation, suggestion, and update functions of intelligent tutors.

Thus, further research on the use of data mining and other data analytics could be used to fine-tune the student model (e.g., learner profiles), ensuring that system-generated remediation in response to a student's query or mistake is at the appropriate level of detail and matches the student's level of knowledge. A limitation to this method is that findings are specific to the characteristics of the sample analyzed and only infers from the observed behavioral responses, so we have no idea what students were thinking.

Value-Added Approach to Improve ITS Effectiveness

Kulik and Fletcher (2015) in their recent meta-analysis of research on the effectiveness of intelligent tutoring systems found an average effect size of .69 with outliers achieving a 1.5 sigma. The authors also tell us that it is important to have test alignment, that is the tests that are being used to assess the effectiveness of the ITS must be aligned with the learning objectives that the ITS is designed to teach.

The complexity of the topics to be taught is critical; tutors do not do well teaching topics that only require recognition and recall and they are more appropriate for teaching topics that require decision making and problem solving. Finally, the degree of implementation is important. If tutors are to be effective they must be implemented as designed, and teachers need to be taught how to use the tutors appropriately. What this and other evaluations do not indicate is what components of the tutor account for most of the learning. Typical ITS evaluations are at the system level. An evaluation approach is needed that separately evaluates the individual ITS components; this approach has been coined value-added research, proposed by Mayer (2014). This approach is designed to compare the effectiveness of a base system with that of one that has been enhanced (e.g., more robust student model) and measure the added effectiveness (value) of the more robust student model to assess how effective a tutor is if you remove or disable the student model. Only by including those components of a tutor that add value and increase effectiveness might the cost of a tutor be reduced.

Finally, ITSs provide the ability to not only enhance learning, but to provide insight into learning processes, identifying optimal instructional strategies and providing alternate strategies to the way in which education and training is conducted today.

Author Note

The findings, opinions, and assertions in this chapter are those of the authors and do not constitute an official position or view of the Department of the Navy, or the Department of Defense. This work was partially supported by a grant from the Office of Naval Research (Contract # N00014-14-C-0290).

References

Adams, D. M., Mayer, R. E., MacNamara, A., Koenig, A., & Wainess, R. (2012). Narrative games for learning: Testing the discovery and narrative hypothesis. *Journal of Educational Psychology, 104*, 235–249.

Aleven, V. A., & Koedinger, K. R. (2002). An effective metacognitive strategy: Learning by doing and explaining with a computer-based Cognitive Tutor. *Cognitive Science, 26*(2), 147–179.

Aleven, V., McLaren, B., Roll, I., & Koedinger, K. (2006). Toward meta-cognitive tutoring: A model of help-seeking with a cognitive tutor. *International Journal of Artificial Intelligence in Education, 16*, 101–130.

Allard, T. (2014). ONR training technologies: Delivering to the fleet and force. Retrieved from www.dtic.mil/ndia/2014SET/Allard.pdf

Anderson, J. R. (1983). A spreading activation theory of memory. *Journal of Verbal Learning and Verbal Behavior, 22*(3), 261–295.

Anderson, J. R. (2007). The algebraic brain. In M. A. Gluck, J. R. Anderson, & S. M. Kosslyn (Eds.), *Memory and mind: A festschrift for Gordon H. Bower* (pp. 75–92). New York, NY: Erlbaum.

Anderson, J. R., Betts, S., Ferris, J. L., & Fincham, J. M. (2013). Can neural imaging be used to investigate learning in an educational task? In J. Staszewski (Ed.), *Expertise and skill acquisition: The impact of William G. Chase* (pp. 299–324). New York, NY: Taylor and Francis.

Anderson, J. R., Boyle, C. F., Farrell, R., & Reiser, B. J. (1987). Cognitive principles in the design of computer tutors. In P. Morris (Ed.), *Modeling cognition* (pp. 93–134). New York, NY. Wiley.

Anderson, J. R., Conrad, F. G., & Corbett, A. T. (1989). Skill acquisition and the LISP tutor. *Cognitive Science, 13,* 467–505.

Anderson, J. R., Corbett, A. T., Koedinger, K. R., & Pelletier, R. (1995). Cognitive tutors: Lessons learned. *The Journal of the Learning Sciences, 4*(2), 167–207.

Atkinson, R. C. (1972). Ingredients for a theory of instruction. *American Psychologist, 27,* 921–931.

Atkinson, R. C., & Crothers, E. J. (1964). A comparison of paired-associate learning models having different acquisition and retention axioms. *Journal of Mathematical Psychology, 1,* 285–315.

Baddeley, A. (1990). *Human memory: Theory and practice.* Boston: Allyn & Bacon.

Baddeley, A. (2000). The episodic buffer: A new component of working memory? *Trends in Cognitive Science, 4*(11), 417–423.

Baker, R. S. J. d., D'Mello, S. K., Rodrigo, M. M. T., & Graesser, A. C. (2010). Better to be frustrated than bored: The incidence, persistence, and impact of learners' cognitive-affective states during interactions with three different computer-based learning environments. *International Journal of Human-Computer Studies, 68*(4), 223–241.

Baker, R. S. J. d., Goldstein, A. B., & Heffernan, N. T. (2011). Detecting learning moment-by-moment. *International Journal of Artificial Intelligence in Education, 21*(1-2), 5–25.

Bloom, B. S. (1984). The 2 sigma problem: The search for methods of group instruction as effective as one-to-one tutoring. *Educational Researcher, 13*(6), 4–16.

Bourdeau, J., & Grandbastien, M. (2010). Modeling tutoring knowledge. In R. Nkambou, J. Bourdeau, & R. Mizoguchi (Eds.), *Advances in intelligent tutoring systems* (pp. 123–143). Berlin Heidelberg: Springer.

Bradley, P. (2006). The history of simulation in medical education and possible future directions. *Medical Education, 40*(3), 254–262.

Bransford, J. D., Brown, A. L., & Cocking, R. R. (1999). *How people learn: Brain, mind, experience, and school.* Washington, DC: National Academy Press.

Bransford, J. D., Brown, A. L., Cocking, R. R., Donovan, M. S., & Pellegrino, J. W. (Eds.). (2008). *How people learn: brain, mind, experience, and school* (expanded edition). Washington, DC: National Academy of Science.

Brown, J. S., Burton, R., & De Kleer, J. (1982). Pedagogical, natural language, and knowledge engineering techniques in SOPHIE I, II, and III. In D. Sleeman & J. S. Brown (Eds.), *Intelligent tutoring systems* (pp. 227–282). New York, NY: Academic Press.

Burton, R. R., & Brown, J. S. (1982). An investigation of computer coaching for informal learning activities. In D. Sleeman & J. S. Brown (Eds.), *Intelligent Tutoring Systems* (pp. 79–98). New York, NY: Academic Press.

Calfee, R. C., & Atkinson, R. C. (1965). Paired-associate models and the effects of list length. *Journal of Mathematical Psychology, 2,* 254–265.

Calin-Jageman, R. J., & Horn Ratner, H. (2005). The role of encoding in the self-explanation effect. *Cognition and Instruction, 23*(4), 523–543.

Cannon-Bowers, J. A., & Bowers, C. A. (2008). Synthetic learning environments. *Handbook of research on educational communications and technology, 3*, 317–327.

Cannon-Bowers, J., Bowers, C., Stout, R., Ricci, K., & Hildabrand, A. (2013). Using cognitive task analysis to develop simulation-based training for medical tasks. *Military Medicine, 178*(10S), 15–21.

Carbonell, J. R. (1970). AI in CAI: An artificial-intelligence approach to computer-assisted instruction. *IEEE Transactions on Man-Machine Systems, 11*(4), 190–202.

Carpenter, S. K., & Vul, E. (2011). Delaying feedback by three seconds benefits retention of face-name pairs: The role of active anticipatory processing. *Memory & Cognition, 39*, 1211–1221.

Cerri, S. A., Clancey, W. J., Papadourakis, G., & Panourgia, K. (Eds.). (2012). *Intelligent Tutoring Systems: 11th International Conference, ITS 2012, Chania, Crete, Greece, June 14–18, 2012, Proceedings* (Vol. 7315). Berlin Heidelberg: Springer-Verlag.

Chakraborty, S., Roy, D., & Basu, A. (2010). Development of knowledge based intelligent tutoring system. In P. S. Sajja & R. Akerkar (Eds.), *Advanced knowledge based systems: Model, applications and research* (Vol. 1, pp. 74–100). Retrieved from www.tmrfindia.org/eseries/ebookv1-c5.pdf

Chi, M. T. H. (1996). Constructing self-explanations and scaffolded explanations in tutoring. *Applied Cognitive Psychology, 10*, S33–S49.

Chi, M. T. H. (2009). Active-constructive-interactive: A conceptual framework for differentiating learning activities. *Topics in Cognitive Science, 1*, 73–105.

Chi, M. T. H., Bassok, M., Lewis, M. W., Reimann, P., & Glaser, R. (1989). Self-explanations: How students study and use examples in learning to solve problems. *Cognitive Science, 13*, 145–182.

Chi, M. T. H., de Leeuw, N., Chiu, M.-H., & LaVancher, C. (1994). Eliciting self-explanations improves understanding. *Cognitive Science, 18*, 439–477.

Chi, M. T. H., Siler, S., Yamauchi, T., Jeong, H., & Hausmann, R. (2001). Learning from human tutoring. *Cognitive Science, 25*, 471–534.

Chung, G. K. W. K., Gyllenhammer, R. G., Baker, E. L., & Savitsky, E. (2013). Effects of simulation-based practice on Focused Assessment with Sonography for Trauma (FAST) window identification, acquisition, and diagnosis. *Military Medicine, 178*(10S), 87–97.

Clancey, W. J. (1983). The epistemology of a rule-based system. *Artificial Intelligence, 20*(3), 215–251.

Clark, R. E., & Estes, F. (1996). Cognitive task analysis for training. *International Journal of Educational Research, 25*(5), 403–417.

Cohen, P. A., Kulik, J. A., & Kulik, C.-L. C. (1982). Educational outcomes of tutoring: A meta-analysis of findings. *American Educational Research Journal, 19*(2), 237–248. doi:10.3102/00028312019002237

Corbett, A. T., & Anderson, J. R. (1994). Knowledge tracing: Modeling the acquisition of procedural knowledge. *User Modeling and User-Adapted Interaction, 4*(4), 253–278.

Craig, S. D., Graesser, A. C., Sullins, J., & Gholson, B. (2004). Affect and learning: An exploratory look into the role of affect in learning with AutoTutor. *Journal of Educational Media, 29*(3), 241–250.

Dean, S., Milham, L., Carroll, M., Schaeffer, R., Alker, M., & Buscemi, T. (2008). Challenges of scenario design in a mixed-reality environment. *Proceedings of the Interservice/Industry Training, Simulation, and Education Conference (I/ITSEC) Annual Meeting.*

DeLeeuw, K. E., & Mayer, R. E. (2011). Cognitive consequences of making computer-based learning activities more game-like. *Computers in Human Behavior, 27,* 2011–2016.

Desmarais, M. C., & Baker, R. S. J. d. (2012). A review of recent advances in learner and skill modeling in intelligent learning environments. *User Modeling and User-Adapted Interaction, 22*(1–2), 9–38.

Dihoff, R. E., Brosvic, G. M., & Epstein, M. L. (2012). The role of feedback during academic testing: The delay retention effect revisited. *The Psychological Record, 53*(4), 533–548.

D'Mello, S. K., Craig, S. D., Gholson, B., Franklin, S., Picard, R., & Graesser, A. C. (2005). Integrating affect sensors in an intelligent tutoring system. In *Affective Interactions: The Computer in the Affective Loop Workshop at 2005 International Conference on Intelligent User Interfaces* (pp. 7–13). New York, NY: AMC Press.

D'Mello, S. K., Graesser, A., & King, B. (2010). Toward spoken human–computer tutorial dialogues. *Human–Computer Interaction, 25*(4), 289–323.

D'Mello, S. K., Jackson, G. T., Craig, S. D., Morgan, B., Chipman, P., White, H., & Graesser, A. C. (2008). *AutoTutor detects and responds to learners' affective and cognitive states.* Paper presented at the Workshop on Emotional and Cognitive Issues in ITS held in conjunction with the Ninth International Conference on Intelligent Tutoring Systems, Montreal, Canada.

D'Mello, S. K., Picard, R. W., & Graesser, A. C. (2007). Toward an affect-sensitive AutoTutor. *IEEE Intelligent Systems, 22*(4), 53–61.

Draney, K. L., Pirolli, P., & Wilson, M. (1995). A measurement model for a complex cognitive skill. In P. D. Nichols, S. F. Chipman, & R. L. Brennan (Eds.), *Cognitively diagnostic assessment* (pp. 103–125). Hillsdale, NJ: Erlbaum.

Elson-Cook, M. (1993). Student modeling in intelligent tutoring systems. *Artificial Intelligence Review, 7,* 227–240.

Ericsson, K. A. (n.d.). *Protocol analysis and verbal reports on thinking: An updated and extracted version from Ericsson (2002).* Retrieved from https://psy.fsu.edu/faculty/ericsson/ericsson.proto.thnk.html

Ericsson, K. A. (1996). The acquisition of expert performance: An introduction to some of the issues. In K. A. Ericsson (Ed.), *The road to excellence: The acquisition of expert performance in the arts and sciences, sports, and games* (pp. 1–50). Mahwah, NJ: Erlbaum.

Ericsson, K. A. (2004). Deliberate practice and the acquisition and maintenance of expert performance in medicine and related domains. *Academic Medicine, 79*(10), S70–S81.

Ericsson, K. A. (2006). The influence of experience and deliberate practice on the development of superior expert performance. In K. A. Ericsson, N. Charness, P. J. Feltovich, & R. R. Hoffmann (Eds.), *The Cambridge handbook of expertise and expert performance* (pp. 683–703). New York, NY: Cambridge University Press.

Ericsson, K. A. (2014). Adaptive expertise and cognitive readiness: A perspective from the expert-performance approach. In H. F. O'Neil, R. S. Perez, & E. L. Baker (Eds.), *Teaching and measuring cognitive readiness* (pp. 179–197). New York, NY: Springer.

Fawcett, L. M., & Garton, A. F. (2005). The effect of peer collaboration on children's problem-solving ability. *British Journal of Educational Psychology, 75,* 157–169.

Feigenbaum, E. A. (2003). Some challenges and grand challenges for computational intelligence. *Journal of the ACM, 50*(1), 32–40.

Feurzeig, W., Munter, P. K., Swets, J. A., & Breen, M. N. (1964). Computer aided teaching in medical diagnosis. *Journal of Medical Education, 39,* 746–754.

Fonseca, B. A., & Chi, M. T. H. (2011). Instruction based on self-explanation. In R. E. Mayer & P. A. Alexander (Eds.), *Handbook of research on learning and instruction* (pp. 296–321). New York, NY: Routledge.

Friedl, K. E., & O'Neil, H. F. (2013). Designing and using computer simulations in medical education and training: An introduction. *Military Medicine, 178*(10S), 1–6.

Genesereth, M. R. (1982). The role of plans in intelligent teaching systems. In D. Sleeman & J. S. Brown (Eds.), *Intelligent tutoring systems* (pp. 137–152). New York, NY: Academic Press.

Graesser, A. C., Chipman, P., Haynes, B. C., & Olney, A. (2005). AutoTutor: An intelligent tutoring system with mixed-initiative dialogue. *IEEE Transactions on Education, 48,* 612–618.

Graesser, A. C., & D'Mello, S. (2012). Emotions during the learning of difficult material. In B. Ross (Ed.), *The psychology of learning and motivation* (Vol. 57, pp. 183–226). San Diego, CA: Academic Press.

Graesser, A. C., Haiying, L., & Forsyth, C. (2014). Learning by communicating in natural language with conversational agents. *Current Directions in Psychological Science, 23*(5), 374–380.

Graesser, A. C., Hu, X., & McNamara, D. S. (2005). Computerized learning environments that incorporate research in discourse psychology, cognitive science, and computational linguistics. *Experimental Cognitive Psychology and its Applications: Festschrift in Honor of Lyle Bourne, Walter Kintsch, and Thomas Landauer.* Washington, DC: American Psychological Association.

Graesser, A. C., Lu, S., Jackson, G. T., Mitchell, H. H., Ventura, M., Olney, A., & Louwerse, M. M. (2004). AutoTutor: A tutor with dialogue in natural language. *Behavioral Research Methods, Instruments, and Computers, 36,* 180–192.

Graesser, A. C., Person, N. K., & Magliano, J. P. (1995). Collaborative dialogue patterns in naturalistic one-to-one tutoring. *Applied Cognitive Psychology, 9*(6), 495–522.

Graesser, A. C., VanLehn, K., Rosé, C. P., Jordan, P. W., & Harter, D. (2001). Intelligent tutoring systems with conversational dialogue. *AI Magazine, 22,* 39–51.

Graesser, A. C., Wiemer-Hastings, K., Wiemer-Hastings, P., Kreuz, R., & the Tutoring Research Group. (1999). AutoTutor: A simulation of a human tutor. *Journal of Cognitive Systems Research, 1,* 35–51.

Gratch, J., Wang, N., Okhmatovskaia, A., Lamothe, F., Morales, M., van der Werf, R. J., & Morency, L. P. (2007). Can virtual humans be more engaging than real ones? In *Human-Computer Interaction. HCI Intelligent Multimodal Interaction Environments* (pp. 286–297). Berlin Heidelberg: Springer.

Gredler, M. E. (2004). Games and simulations and their relationships to learning. In D. H. Jonassen (Ed.), *Handbook of research for educational communications and technology* (2nd ed., pp. 571–582). Mahwah, NJ: Erlbaum.

Groen, G. J., & Atkinson, R. C. (1966). Models for optimizing the learning process. *Psychological Bulletin, 66,* 309–320.

Hattie, J. (2009). *Visible learning: A synthesis of over 800 meta-analyses relating to achievement.* London: Routledge.

Hattie, J. (2012). *Visible learning for teachers: Maximizing impact on learning.* New York, NY: Routledge.

Hattie, J., & Gan, M. (2011). Instruction based on feedback. In R. E. Mayer & P. A. Alexander (Eds.), *Handbook of research on learning and instruction* (pp. 249–271). New York, NY: Routledge.

Hays, M. J., Campbell, J. C., Trimmer, M. A., Poore, J. C., Webb, A. K., & King, T. K. (2012). Can role-play with virtual humans teach interpersonal skills? *Proceedings of the Interservice/Industry, Training, Simulation, and Education Conference (I/ITSEC) Annual Meeting.*

Hays, R. T., Jacobs, J. W., Prince, C., & Salas, E. (1992). Flight simulator training effectiveness: A meta-analysis. *Military Psychology, 4*(2) 63–74.

Hettinger, L. J., & Haas, M. W. (Eds.). (2003). *Virtual and adaptive environments: Applications, implications and human performance issues.* Mahwah, NJ: Erlbaum.

Hu, X., & Graesser, A. C. (2004). Human use regulatory affairs advisor (HURAA): Learning about research ethics with intelligent learning modules. *Behavior Research Methods, & Computers, 36,* 241–249.

Iseli, M. R., Koenig, A. D., Lee, J. J., & Wainess, R. (2010, August). Automated assessment of complex task performance in games and simulations. In *Proceedings of the Interservice/Industry Training, Simulation and Education Conference, Orlando, FL.*

Jacobson, M. J., & Kozma, R. B. (Eds.). (2000). *Innovations in science and mathematics education: Advanced designs for technologies of learning.* Mahwah, NJ: Erlbaum.

Johnson, W. L., & Valente, A. (2008). Tactical language and culture training systems: Using artificial intelligence to teach foreign languages and cultures. In M. H. Goker (Ed.), *Proceedings of the 20th National Conference on Innovative Applications of Artificial Intelligence* (Vol. 3, pp. 1632–1639). Palo Alto, CA: AAAI Press.

Jones, E. R., Hennessy, R. T., & Deutsch, S. (1985). *Human factors aspects of simulation.* Washington, DC: National Academy Press.

Kellman, P. J. (2013). Adaptive and perceptual learning technologies in medical education and training. *Military Medicine, 178*(10S), 98–106.

Kimball, R. (1982). A self-improving tutor for symbolic integration. In D. Sleeman & J. S Brown (Eds.), *Intelligent tutoring systems* (pp. 283–308). New York, NY: Academic Press.

Koedinger, K. R., & Aleven, V. (2007). Exploring the assistance dilemma in experiments with cognitive tutors. *Educational Psychology Review, 19*(3), 239–264.

Koedinger, K. R., Anderson, J. R., Hadley, W. H., & Mark, M. A. (1997). Intelligent tutoring goes to school in the big city. *International Journal of Artificial Intelligence in Education, 8,* 30–43.

Koedinger, K. R., Brunskill, E., Baker, R. S. J. d., McLaughlin, E. A., & Stamper, J. (2013). New potentials for data-driven intelligent tutoring system development and optimization. *AI Magazine, 34*(3), 27–41.

Koedinger, K. R., Corbett, A. T., & Perfetti, C. (2012). The knowledge-learning-instruction framework: Bridging the science-practice chasm to enhance robust student learning. *Cognitive Science, 36,* 757–798.

Kozma, R., & Russell, J. (2005). Multimedia learning of chemistry. In R. E. Mayer (Ed.), *Cambridge handbook of multimedia learning* (pp. 409–428). New York, NY: Cambridge University Press.

Krämer, N. C., Tietz, B., & Bente, G. (2003). Effects of embodied interface agents and their gestural activity. In T. Rist, R. S. Aylett, D. Ballin, & J. Rickel (Eds.), *Intelligent Virtual Agents* (pp. 292–300). Berlin Heidelberg: Springer.

Kulik, A., & Fletcher, J. D. (2015). Effectiveness of intelligent tutoring systems: A meta-analytic review. *Review of Educational Research.* Advance online publication. doi:10.3102/0034654315581420

Kulik, C. L. C., & Kulik, J. A. (1991). Effectiveness of computer-based instruction: An updated analysis. *Computers in Human Behavior, 7*(1), 75–94.

Kunkler, K. (2006). The role of medical simulation: An overview. *The International Journal of Medical Robotics and Computer Assisted Surgery, 2*(3), 203–210.

Lajoie, S. P. (Ed.). (2000). *Computers as cognitive tools: No more walls.* Mahwah, NJ: Erlbaum.

Lehman, B. A., Matthews, M., D'Mello, S. K., & Person, N. (2008). What are you feeling? Investigating student affective states during expert human tutoring sessions. In B. Woolf, E. Aimeur, R. Nkambou, & S. Lajoie (Eds.), *Proceedings of the Ninth International Conference on Intelligent Tutoring Systems* (pp. 50–59). Berlin Heidelberg: Springer-Verlag.

Lemke, J. L. (1990). *Talking science: Language, learning and values.* Norwood, NJ: Ablex Publishing.

Lesgold, A., Lajoie, S. P., Bunzo, M., & Eggan, G. (1992). SHERLOCK: A coached practice environment for an electronics troubleshooting job. In J. H. Larkin & R. W. Chabay (Eds.), *Computer-assisted instruction and intelligent tutoring systems: Shared goals and complementary approaches* (pp. 201–238). Hillsdale, NJ: Erlbaum.

Linn, M. C., Davis, E. A., & Bell, P. (2004). Inquiry and technology. In M. C. Linn, E. A. Davis, & P. Bell (Eds.), *Internet environments for science education* (pp. 3–28). Mahwah, NJ: Erlbaum.

Lou, Y., Flinn, J. T., Ganapathy, S., Weyhrauch, P., Niehaus, J., Myers, B., & Cao, C. G. L. (2014). Supporting procedural and perceptual learning in laparoscopic surgery. *Proceedings of the Human Factors and Ergonomics Society Annual Meeting, 58,* 688–692.

Loyens, S. M., & Rikers, R. M. J. P. (2011). Instruction based on inquiry. In R. E. Mayer & P. A. Alexander (Eds.), *Handbook of research on learning and instruction* (pp. 361–381). New York, NY: Routledge.

Lumsdaine, A. A., & Glaser, R. (1960). *Teaching machines and programmed learning: A source book.* Washington, DC: National Education Association, Department of Audiovisual Instruction.

Ma, W., Adesope, O. O., Nesbit, J. C., & Liu, Q. (2014). Intelligent tutoring systems and learning outcomes: A meta-analysis. *Journal of Educational Psychology, 106,* 901–918.

Mayer, R. E. (2004). Should there be a three-strikes rule against pure discovery learning? *American Psychologist, 59*(1), 14.

Mayer, R. E. (2008). Problem-solving assessment in games and simulation environments. In E. L. Baker, J. Dickenson, W. Wulfeck, & H. F. O'Neil (Eds.), *Assessment of problem solving using simulations* (pp. 139–156). New York, NY: Erlbaum.

Mayer, R. E. (2011). *Applying the science of learning.* Upper Saddle River, NJ: Pearson.

Mayer, R. E. (Ed.). (2013). *Teaching and learning computer programming: Multiple research perspectives.* New York, NY: Routledge.

Mayer, R. E. (2014). Cognitive theory of multimedia learning. In R. E. Mayer (Ed.), *The Cambridge handbook of multimedia learning* (2nd ed.). New York, NY: Cambridge University Press.

Mayer, R. E., & Alexander, P. A. (Eds.). (2011). *Handbook of research on learning and instruction.* New York, NY: Routledge.

McGaghie, W. C., Issenberg, S. B., Petrusa, E. R., & Scalese, R. J. (2010). A critical review of simulations-based medical education research: 2003–2009. *Medical Education, 44,* 50–63.

McNamara, D. S., O'Reilly, T., Best, R., & Ozuru, Y. (2006). Improving adolescent students' reading comprehension with iSTART. *Journal of Educational Computing Research, 34,* 147–171.

Meltzoff, A. N., Kuhl, P. K., Movellan, J., & Sejnowski, T. J. (2009). Foundations for a new science of learning. *Science, 325*(5938), 284–288.

Merrill, D. C., Reiser, B. J., Ranney, M., & Trafton, J. G. (1992). Effective tutoring techniques: A comparison of human tutors and intelligent tutoring systems. *The Journal of the Learning Sciences, 2*(3), 277–305.

Metcalfe, J., Kornell, N., & Finn, B. (2009). Delayed versus immediate feedback in children's and adults' vocabulary learning. *Memory and Cognition, 37*(8), 1077–1087.

Miller, M. L. (1982). A structure planning and debugging environment for elementary programming. In D. Sleeman & J. S. Brown (Eds.), *Intelligent tutoring systems* (pp. 283–308). New York, NY: Academic Press.

Mislevy, R. J. (2013). Evidence-centered design for simulation-based assessment. *Military Medicine, 178*(10S), 107–114.

Mislevy, R. J., Steinberg, L. S., Breyer, F. J., Almond, R. G., & Johnson, L. (1999). A cognitive task analysis with implications for designing simulation-based performance assessment. *Computers in Human Behavior, 15,* 335–374.

Mitrovic, A., Ohlsson, S., & Barrow, D. K. (2013). The effect of positive feedback in a constraint-based intelligent tutoring system. *Computers and Education, 60*(1), 264–272.

Moore, A. (2012). *Teaching and learning: Pedagogy, curriculum, and culture.* New York, NY: Routledge.

Moroney, W. F., & Lilienthal, M. G. (2009). Human factors in simulation and training: An overview. In D. A. Vincenzi, J. A. Wise, M. Mouloua, & P. A. Hancock (Eds.), *Human factors in simulation and training* (pp. 3–33). Boca Raton, FL: CRC Press.

Muller, P., Cohn, J., Schmorrow, D., Stripling, R., Stanney, K., Milham, L., & Fowlkes, J. F. (2006). The fidelity matrix: Mapping system fidelity to training outcomes. *Proceedings of the Interservice/Industry, Training, Simulation, and Education Conference (I/ITSEC) Annual Meeting.*

Munro, A. (2014). Software support for teaching and assessing cognitive readiness. In H. F. O'Neil, R. S. Perez, & E. L. Baker (Eds.), *Teaching and measuring cognitive readiness* (pp. 279–299). New York, NY: Springer.

Munro, A., & Clark, R. E. (2013). Cognitive task analysis-based design and authoring software for simulation training. *Military Medicine, 178*(10S), 7–14.

Munro, A., Pizzini, Q. A., & Bewley, W. (2009). Learning anti-submarine warfare in the context of a game-like tactical planner. *Proceedings of the Interservice/Industry, Training, Simulation, and Education Conference (I/ITSEC) Annual Meeting.*

Nye, B. D., Graesser, A. C., & Hu, X. (2014). Multimedia learning with intelligent tutoring systems. In R. E. Mayer (Ed.), *The Cambridge handbook of multimedia learning* (2nd ed., pp. 705–728). Cambridge: Cambridge University Press.

Ohlsson, S. (1992). Constraint-based student modeling. *Journal of Artificial Intelligence in Education, 3,* 429–447.

Palinscar, A. S., & Brown, A. L. (1984). Reciprocal teaching of comprehension-fostering and comprehension-monitoring activities. *Cognition and Instruction, 1*(2), 117–175.

Pane, J. F., Griffin, B. A., McCaffrey, D. F., & Karam, R. (2014). Effectiveness of Cognitive Tutor Algebra I at scale. *Educational Evaluation and Policy Analysis, 36*(2), 127–144.

Pavlik, P. I., & Anderson, J. R. (2008). Using a model to compute the optimal schedule of practice. *Journal of Experimental Psychology: Applied, 14,* 101–117.

Pavlik, P. I., Jr., Brawner, K., Olney, A., & Mitrovic, A. (2013). A review of student models used in intelligent tutoring systems. In R. Sottilare, A. Graesser, X. Hu, & H. Holden

(Eds.), *Design recommendations for intelligent tutoring: Learner modeling* (Vol. 1, pp. 39–68). Orlando, FL: U.S. Army Research Laboratory.

Perez, R. S. (2013). Foreword. *Military Medicine, 178*(10S), iv.

Perez, R. S., Gray, W., & Reynolds, T. (2006). Virtual reality and simulators: Implications for web-based education and training. In H. F. O'Neil & R. S. Perez (Eds.), *Web-based learning: Theory, research, and practice* (pp. 107–132). Mahwah, NJ: Erlbaum.

Peters, S., Bratt, E., & Kirschenbaum, S. (2011). Automated support for learning in simulation: Intelligent tutoring of shiphandling. *Proceedings of the Interservice/Industry, Training, Simulation, and Education Conference (I/ITSEC) Annual Meeting.*

Psotka, J., Massey, L. D., & Mutter, S. A. (Eds.). (1988). *Intelligent tutoring systems: Lessons learned.* Hillsdale, NJ: Erlbaum.

Reeves, B., & Nass, C. (1996). *The media equation: How people treat computers, television, and new media like real people and places.* Stanford, CA: CSLI Publications and Cambridge University Press.

Renkl, A. (2011). Instruction based on examples. In R. E. Mayer & P. A. Alexander (Eds.), *Handbook of research on learning and instruction* (pp. 272–295). New York, NY: Routledge.

Rieber, L. P. (2005). Multimedia learning in games, simulations, and microworlds. In R. E. Mayer (Ed.), *The Cambridge handbook of multimedia learning* (pp. 549–566). New York, NY: Cambridge University Press.

Robelen, E. W. (2012). U.S. math, science achievement exceeds world average. *Education Week, 32.* Retrieved from www.edweek.com/ew/articles/2012/12/11/15timss.h32. html

Rus, V., & Graesser, A. C. (Eds.). (2009). The question generation shared task and evaluation challenge. Available at www.questiongeneration.org

Scheuer, O., & McLaren, B. M. (2012). In N. M. Seel (Ed.), *Encyclopedia of the sciences of learning* (pp. 1075–1079). New York, NY: Springer.

Schraagen, J. M., Chipman, S. F., & Shute, V. J. (2000). State-of-the-art review of cognitive task analysis techniques. In J. M. Schraagen, S. F. Chipman, & V. L. Shalin (Eds.), *Cognitive task analysis* (pp. 467–487). Mahwah, NJ: Erlbaum.

Schunn, C. D., & Wallach, D. (2005). Evaluating goodness-of-fit in comparison of models to data. *Psychologie der Kognition: Reden and vorträge anlässlich der emeritierung von Werner Tack, 115–154.*

Schwonke, R., Wittwer, J., Aleven, V., Salden, R. J. C. M., Krieg, C., & Renkl, A. (2007). Can tutored problem solving benefit from faded worked-out examples? In S. Vosniadou, D. Kayser, & A. Protopapas (Eds.), *Proceedings of EuroCogSci 07. The European Cognitive Science Conference 2007* (pp. 59–64). New York, NY: Erlbaum.

Shute, V. J. (1991). Rose garden promises of intelligent tutoring systems: Blossom or thorn? In NASA, Lyndon B. Johnson Space Center, *Fourth Annual Workshop on Space Operations Applications and Research (SOAR 90)* (pp. 431–438). Retrieved from http://ntrs.nasa. gov/archive/nasa/casi.ntrs.nasa.gov/19910011382.pdf

Skinner, A., Sebrechts, M., Fidopiastis, C. M., Berka, C., Vice, J., & Lathan, C. (2010). Psychophysiological measures of virtual environment training. In P. E. O'Connor & J. V. Cohn (Eds.), *Human performance enhancement in high-risk environments: Insights, developments & future directions from military research* (pp. 129–149). Santa Barbara, CA: Greenwood Publishing Group.

Slavin, R. E. (1996). Research on cooperative learning and achievement: What we know, what we need to know. *Contemporary Educational Psychology, 21*(1), 43–69.

Slavin, R. E. (2011). Instruction based on cooperative learning. In R. E. Mayer & P. A. Alexander (Eds.), *Handbook of research on learning and instruction* (pp. 344–360). New York, NY: Routledge.

Sleeman, D., & Brown, J. S. (Eds.). (1982). *Intelligent tutoring systems.* New York, NY: Academic Press.

Sleeman, D. H., & Hendley, R. J. J. (1982). ACE: A system which analyses complex explanations. In D. Sleeman & J. S. Brown (Eds.), *Intelligent tutoring systems* (pp. 99–118). New York, NY: Academic Press.

Smallwood, R. D. (1962). *A decision structure for teaching machines.* Cambridge, MA: MIT Press.

Smith, R. L., Graves, H., Blaine, L. H., & Marinov, V. G. (1975). Computer-assisted axiomatic mathematics: Mathematics rigor. In O. LeCareme & R. Lewis (Eds.), *Computers in education part 1: IFIP.* Amsterdam: North Holland.

Smith, S. G., & Sherwood, B. A. (1976). Educational uses of the PLATO computer system. *Science, 192*(4237), 344–352.

Sottilare, R. A., Graesser, A. C., Hu, X., & Holden, H. (Eds.). (2013). *Design recommendations for intelligent tutoring: Learner modeling* (Vol. 1). Orlando, FL: U.S. Army Research Laboratory.

Spada, H., & McGraw, B. (1985). The assessment of learning effects with linear logistic test models. In S. E. Embretson (Ed.), *Test design developments in psychology and psychometrics* (pp 169–194). Orlando, FL: Academic Press.

Stanney, K. M. (Ed.). (2002). *Handbook of virtual environments: Design, implementation, and applications.* Mahwah, NJ: Erlbaum.

Stanney, K., Samman, S., Reeves, L., Hale, K., Buff, W., Bowers, C., . . . Lackey, S. (2004). A paradigm shift in interactive computing: Deriving multimodal design principles from behavioral and neurological foundations. *International Journal of Human-Computer Interaction, 17*(2), 229–257.

Stephens, G. J., Silbert, L. J., & Hasson, U. (2010). Speaker-listener neural coupling underlies successful communication. *Proceedings of the National Academy of Sciences, 107*(32), 14425–14430.

Stevens, R. J., & Slavin, R. E. (1995). The cooperative elementary school: Effects on students' achievement, attitudes, and social relations. *American Educational Research Journal, 32*(2), 321–351.

Stone, B., Skinner, A., Stikic, M., & Johnson, R. (2014). Assessing neural synchrony in tutoring dyads. In D. D. Schmorrow & C. M. Fidopiastis (Eds.), *Foundations of augmented cognition: Advancing human performance and decision-making through adaptive systems* (pp. 167–178). Cham, Switzerland: Springer International Publishing.

Swartout, W., Artstein, R., Forbell, E., Foutz, S., Lane, C. H., Lange, B., . . . Traum, D. (2013). Virtual humans for learning. *AI Magazine, 34*(4), 13–30.

Swets, J. A., & Feurzeig, W. (1965). Computer-aided instruction. *Science, 150*(3696), 572–576.

Talbot, T. B. (2013). Balancing physiology, anatomy and immersion: How much biological fidelity is necessary in a medical simulation. *Military Medicine, 178*(10S), 28–36.

Tatsuoka, K. K. (1983). Rule space: An approach for dealing with misconceptions based on item response theory. *Journal of Educational Measurement, 20*, 345–354.

Teasley, S. D. (1995). The role of talk in children's peer collaborations. *Developmental Psychology, 31*, 207–220.

Thomas, C., Davies, I., Openshaw, D., & Bird, J. (1963). *Programmed learning in perspective: A guide to programmed writing*. Chicago: Educational Methods.

Thorndike, E. L. (1906). Principles of learning. New York, NY: A. G. Seiler.

Thurman, R. A., & Russo, T. (2000). Using virtual reality for training. In H. F. O'Neil & D. H. Andrews (Eds.), *Aircrew training: Methods, technologies, and assessments* (pp. 85–104). Mahwah, NJ: Erlbaum.

Uhr, L. (1969). Teaching machines programs that generate problems as a function of interaction with students. In *Proceedings of the 24th ACM National Conference* (pp. 125–134). New York, NY: Association for Computing Machinery.

U.S. Department of Education, Office of Educational Technology. (2013). *Expanding evidence approaches for learning in a digital world*. Washington, DC: Author.

VanLehn, K. (2006). The behavior of tutoring systems. *International Journal of Artificial Intelligence in Education, 16*(3), 227–265.

VanLehn, K. (2011). The relative effectiveness of human tutoring, intelligent tutoring systems, and other tutoring systems. *Educational Psychologist, 46*(4), 197–221.

VanLehn, K. (2013). Model construction as a learning activity: A design space and review. *Interactive Learning Environments, 21*(4), 371–413.

VanLehn, K., Jones, R. M., & Chi, M. T. H. (1992). A model of the self-explanation effect. *Journal of the Learning Sciences, 2*(1), 1–59.

VanLehn, K., Lynch, C., Schulze, K., Shapiro, J. A., Shelby, R., Taylor, L., . . . Wintersgill, M. (2005). The Andes physics tutoring system: Five years of evaluations. In G. McCalla, C. K. Looi, B. Bredeweg, & J. Breuker (Eds.), *Artificial intelligence in education* (pp. 678–685). Amsterdam, Netherlands: IOS Press.

Walton, J., Dorneich, M. C., Gilbert, S., Bonner, D., Winer, E., & Ray, C. (2014). Modality and timing of team feedback: Implications for GIFT. In *Proceedings of the 2nd Annual Generalized Intelligent Framework for Tutoring (GIFT) Users Symposium (GIFTSym2)* (pp. 199–2070).

Wentzel, K. R., & Watkins, D. E. (2011). Instruction based on peer interactions. In R. E. Mayer & P. A. Alexander (Eds.), *Handbook of research on learning and instruction* (pp. 322–343). New York, NY: Routledge.

White, B. Y., Collins, A., & Frederiksen, J. R. (2011). The nature of scientific meta-knowledge. In *Models and Modeling* (pp. 41–76). Netherlands: Springer.

Wong, J. H., Ogren, L., Peters, S., & Bratt, E. O. (2014). Developing and evaluating an intelligent tutoring system for advanced shiphandling. *Proceedings of the Interservice/Industry, Training, Simulation, and Education Conference (I/ITSEC) Annual Meeting*.

Zakharov, K., Mitrovic, A., & Ohlsson, S. (2005). Feedback micro-engineering in EER-Tutor. In C.-K. Looi, G. McCalla, B. Bredeweg, & J. Breuker (Eds.), *Proceedings of the 2005 Conference on Artificial Intelligence in Education: Supporting Learning Through Intelligent and Socially Informed Technology* (pp. 718–725). Amsterdam, The Netherlands: IOS Press.

7

MEASURING LEARNING IN SIMULATIONS AND GAMES

Allen Munro

Introduction

The effects of simulations and games that are intended to promote learning can be measured in a number of conventional ways, such as by administering pre- and post-tests (before and after the interactive experience), and analyzing for improved test performance. When a user scores higher on a test after playing the game or using the simulation than he or she scored on a calibrated pretest, then we say that the user has learned whatever it is that the test measures. Tests can be architected to provide several measures, that is, they can address knowledge in several topic areas related to the game or simulation.

Learning can be measured either during game play (or simulation usage) by observing user actions and/or game outcomes, or after game play using any of a number of techniques, including conventional tests that could also be administered to students learning in conventional contexts such as lectures or group discussions. In modern western educational tradition, assessment is ordinarily carried out after a learning session (or a series of learning sessions, or even as a culminating event in a course). By contrast, in a Socratic dialog, a tutor continuously assesses student responses to determine how to proceed. In many cases, the Socratic tutor is evaluating only one or two small aspects of the student's knowledge at one time, in order to select the best next course of action.

Educational research traditionally has made use of post-treatment measurement of learning to evaluate the effectiveness of a training method. Such comprehensive, summative assessments have many advantages over the individual micro-assessments that a tutor might make to guide one-on-one instruction. Summative assessments can be conducted in a standard, non-individualized way, and they can generate a great deal of data that can be analyzed using the statistical tools that educational researchers have available.

One useful application of post-treatment assessment and analysis has been the study of the effectiveness of particular approaches to learning and instruction. For example, Bernard et al. (2009) conducted a meta-analysis of 74 distance education studies that compared different treatments that encouraged student–student, student–teacher, and/or student–content interactions. Strong interaction experiences were found to correlate with achievement for asynchronous distance education courses, although not for courses with synchronous or face-to-face interactions.

Many studies have been conducted of the effectiveness of media, including interactive simulations and games, in learning environments. A meta-analysis and validation study by Tamim, Bernard, Borokhovski, Abrami, and Schmid (2011) looked at studies that compared a wide variety of uses of computer technology in classrooms with control classrooms that did not use the technology. A significant effect, although low to moderate in magnitude, was found for learning with computer technology, but their analysis suggests that specific factors that affect learning, including "aspects of the goals of instruction, pedagogy, teacher effectiveness, subject matter, age level, fidelity of technology implementation, and possibly other factors" (p. 17) may matter more than the simple fact of having a technology-based intervention. They suggest that future research explore the effects of such factors in a controlled way by utilizing otherwise identical computer-based instruction approaches that differ only in a single such factor of interest.

Levy (2012) points out that assessing in the context of simulation-based tasks provides the prospect for student experiences that are qualitatively different from traditional assessment. He proposes that task-centered assessment make use of three models: a student model of knowledge, a task model (which includes the procedures that a student uses to attempt a task), and an evidence model, which attempts to relate observed student behaviors to elements of the student model. Levy points out that psychometric methods for simulation-based assessments are in their relative infancy in comparison to item response theory methods. Furthermore, questions of validation are problematic: There is reason to expect additional assessment value from simulation task-based assessment as compared with conventional assessment methods. But if different results are produced, it will be difficult to validate simulation-based metrics (except perhaps in some cases, by observing learner performance on tasks in real-world environments).

D'Mello (2013) conducted a meta-analysis of affective outcomes from the use of technology, and Wouters, van Nimwegen, van Oostendorp, and van der Spek (2013) produced a meta-analysis of motivational effects of serious games. D'Mello's analysis revealed that engagement was found to be a frequent outcome; boredom and confusion also occurred in some studies, but much less frequently, and with considerable variance across studies. However, "the source of the affect judgments (self vs. observers) and the authenticity of the learning contexts . . . accounted for greater heterogeneity than the use of advanced learning technologies and training time" (p. 1082). Wouters et al.'s (2013) meta-analysis of cognitive and motivational effects of serious games research showed that the games were more effective than the control treatments for learning, but motivational effects did not reach a level of significance. In sum, these meta-analyses seem to suggest that the positive learning effects of technology (and game-based learning, specifically) are probably not primarily due to increased motivation or more positive affect.

Job-oriented training and education using simulations have a history worthy of note in aviation and in medicine. Hays, Jacobs, Prince, and Salas (1992) conducted a meta-analysis of flight simulator training that found that the use of simulators in combination with jet aircraft training resulted in improvements in learning when compared with jet aircraft training only. (The studies do not appear to have controlled for total training time, but it can at least be concluded that adding simulator training is more effective than not adding simulator training.) Simulator training that supported student-paced progress was more effective than enforced lockstep simulator training. In some studies, student assessments came from subject matter experts who provided subjective evaluations; in other studies, objective measures of student actions during flight testing were recorded.

Simulation-based medical training has been subjected to several meta-analyses. McGaghie, Issenberg, Cohn, Barsuk, and Wayne (2011) found that available studies showed that simulation-based medical education with deliberate practice was superior to traditional medical education in the acquisition of specific skills. (Traditional medical education in procedures makes use of a "see one, do one, teach one" methodology.) Cook et al. (2013) reviewed a larger number of studies, and focused on the specific design features of learning environments. With decreasing effect sizes (all of which were significant at the level of $p = .005$ or better), the following features were found to enhance simulation-based medical education: range of difficulty, interactivity, multiple learning strategies, individualized learning, explicit feedback, and longer practice time.

In general, when the content that is to be learned is a complex cognitive skill, such as the ability to flexibly make appropriate decisions in order to carry out a complex procedure or to address problems in domain of expertise, measuring learning with conventional tests may be inadequate. For example, to know how a user would react to a problematic condition during a procedure, it might not be enough to simply pose a multiple-choice question about how to respond to that condition. ("As you descend to 200 feet above the runway, your wind sheer indicator lights up. Which of these is the most appropriate action to take: A . . . B . . . C . . . or D . . .?" This test item doesn't give a clue whether the user would recognize the wind sheer indicator, or whether he would have chosen a response that is not provided in the question.) The choices presented may include a correct option that the user would not have considered without being prompted. By gathering measures during the use of a simulation or game, we can measure performance in context, which reduces some of these sources of measurement error. It may also reduce or eliminate effects due to test-taking skills, while measuring knowledge and skills in the domain that is to be learned.

One way to measure performance during game play or simulation usage is to have a subject matter expert (SME) closely observe what the user is doing and continuously score elements of that usage, in real time. Two major arguments oppose this approach: First, this is a very expensive approach to measurement, as one SME would be needed for each student; second, lapses of expert attention are likely to occur. An automated measurement system can be costly to develop, but its expense can be amortized over the number of hours of usage of the game or simulation throughout its working life. In addition, an automated observer can be expected to be uniformly attentive and to make measurements without respect to the user's race, sex, ethnicity, religion, sexual preference, or gender identification. Its measures will depend only on performance in context, rather than on such incidentals.

Before considering the details of an approach to measuring performance in simulations and games, it is worth asking under what conditions the use of games and simulations is effective in promoting learning. Although the meta-analyses cited above argue for effects of varying strengths, the work by Cook et al. (2013) shows that specific instructional design features may be important in determining the instructional significance of games and simulations. A number of studies and reviews of studies, such as that by Moreno and Mayer (2007) and by O'Neil, Wainess, and Baker (2005), suggest that game play alone is a less effective approach to learning than other instructional methods. Reviewing these and other studies, Clark, Yates, Early, and Moulton (2010) make the following observation:

> The difficulty with asking people who are learning complex knowledge to discover all or part of the knowledge they are learning is that the discovery process requires a huge amount of unproductive mental effort. Even if a minority of learners succeed and discover what they need to know, the discovery process does not teach them how to discover and the effort required could be invested in more efficient learning from demonstrations and practice exercises. Problem solving during learning is desirable but discovering how to solve a problem in order to learn to solve a problem is not helpful or desirable.
>
> (Clark et al., 2010, p. 271)

What are more effective instructional strategies for learning in complex problem-solving domains? Clark et al. (2010) summarize research results that show that an effective strategy includes at least these learning activities:

1. Motivate learning by explaining the usefulness of what is to be learned.
2. Present and explain requisite new terms, concepts, and processes, relating them to prior knowledge.
3. Demonstrate problem-solving procedures in the domain.
4. Provide opportunities to practice with immediate feedback. (In addition to supporting immediate feedback in some simulation contexts, a less immediate

type of feedback can be supported in after action reviews, or AARs, so long as student session data are recorded and can be replayed.)

Many of these activities, especially the demonstration of problem-solving procedures and working on practice problems with immediate feedback, can be carried out in game and simulation contexts. In fact, providing these learning methods may be much more cost effective in simulations or games than in a corresponding real-life context. For example, demonstrations and practice in the use of cockpit instrumentation and flight controls can be done much less expensively in a simulator than in an airborne modern jetliner. The problem is how to give immediate feedback during practice. It can be done, expensively and sometimes inconsistently, by monitoring performance with SMEs, who must detect opportunities for providing necessary guidance or feedback. If simulations and games can carry out detailed measures of performance at runtime, these measures can be utilized to trigger feedback when it is necessary.

Uses of Evaluation

Ordinarily, when educators are concerned with the measurement of learning results, the purpose is to rank students, or to determine whether students can be certified as having met some standard of competency in a subject. In fact, the studies of measuring learning cited above all focus on these and related uses of evaluations. (In some cases, the purpose is to evaluate the learning effectiveness of a game or simulation treatment, but this can only be achieved by first evaluating how much the learners have acquired.) Such evaluations are typically seen as high stakes, in that they may help to determine promotion at school or at work. In job-training contexts, test-based certifications can have a substantial impact on income, and even on opportunities for employment. Indeed, the standards for educational and psychological testing by the American Educational Research Association, American Psychological Association, and National Council on Measurement in Education (2014) places a significant emphasis on the importance of equity in testing, in part because of the high-stakes nature of summative evaluations. Plake and Wise (2014) describe five major goals of this work, the first of which is "access and fairness for all examinees," which seems particularly important for high-stakes testing.

This chapter is particularly concerned with the uses of evaluation for the purposes of directing or adapting the learning context so as to promote acquisition of the subject matter. It is less concerned with the uses of evaluation for the purposes of providing certification of learning (or, more ambitiously, certification of competence to perform a task).

Measures used to select the next practice problem or to determine what prior knowledge should be referenced when introducing a new topic are not ordinarily seen as high-stakes measures, because they only affect the immediate course of instruction, rather than leaving an accessible persistent performance record. However, if such measures can be used effectively to influence essential elements of learning in a domain, they may have a very high payoff. Consider a surgeon, who through simulator practice becomes familiar with appropriate approaches to unusual conditions in surgery, and who is therefore able to effect a life-saving outcome. Or consider a tactical action officer, who was presented with learning experiences that precisely addressed his or her knowledge deficits during tactics training. Correct decisions in some tactical consequences may save thousands of lives and permit the completion of an essential mission. Although formative evaluations may not be high stakes, in the sense of immediately affecting a learner's career, they may contribute to high-stakes performance.

The TAO Sandbox

My colleagues and I at USC's Center for Cognitive Technology have developed a tactics planning simulation for tactical action officers (TAOs) in the U.S. Navy, called the TAO Sandbox, as described by Munro, Pizzini, and Bewley (2009), Auslander, Molineaux, Aha, Munro, and Pizzini (2009), Munro, Pizzini, and Darling (2013), and Munro, Surmon, et al. (2013). The TAO Sandbox has two modes: an instructor mode that is used for developing tactics problems, and a student mode for working on problem solutions. Actions and events are recorded in problem mode, and these recorded problem sessions can be played back later. (Instructors can replay a student session and provide a review, or AAR, for example.) Students can pause time, and they can control the rate at which simulated time progresses, so that an hours-long exercise in anti-submarine warfare might be played out in just a few minutes. Students have control over the speed and bearing of friendly units, and they can choose to activate and deactivate sensor systems, such as air radar and navigation radar, as well as several types of sonar. The behaviors of simulated neutral and hostile units are determined by a combination of authored and innate behaviors. (Innate behaviors are those that do not have to be explicitly authored. For example, if an author wants a hostile ship to follow a particular multi-leg course, the author must plot the path that the hostile should follow. On the other hand, if that ship has been assigned an attacking posture, it will innately turn toward and fire upon friendly forces whenever the opportunity arises.)

Instructors can use the TAO Sandbox in class to illustrate tactical situations and the outcomes of decisions in any number of scenarios. They can also assign students to work on tactics problems individually or in groups. A recorded student session can be replayed while the student briefs the class on the tactics he used. Advanced students can be given access to instructor mode, so that they can modify problems or create new ones.

We have recently developed new approaches to monitoring performance during problem-solving sessions, which we will describe in this chapter. Two different approaches to assessment in a game or simulation are possible: *assessment by outcome*, and *assessment by procedure*. In assessment by outcome, the learner's end result, such as their answer to a subtraction problem, or in the case of the TAO Sandbox, the survival and/or triumph of the player's friendly forces, is used to assess the learner's knowledge. There are several problems with assessment by outcome: most importantly, suboptimal or even wrong procedures may generate correct results for certain types of problems. Brown and VanLehn (1980) and VanLehn (1990) have shown that the detection of errors in a learner's subtraction algorithms may require the judicious selection of a very wide range of problems that can expose each of the possible "subtraction bugs." Such a thorough approach to analyzing the cognitive task that is being taught makes it possible to use only outcomes to evaluate solutions to problems.

Assessment by procedure takes a different approach to evaluating learner solutions of problems. Rather than considering only the outcomes, it also attempts to evaluate the actions that a learner takes in solving a problem. These actions might include taking actions to access information, performing observable steps, producing intermediate products that will be used in later steps of the problem, and so on. Assessment by procedure might require fewer problem solutions to determine learner competence than assessment by outcome: If two incorrect steps cancel each other out, the outcome might be acceptable, but an observer who notes that the incorrect steps were taken will realize that the learner just got lucky.

In principle, almost every domain of knowledge could be understood well enough to support automated assessment. Obvious exceptions include those fields of knowledge that are on the cutting edge of discovery, where even experts in the field may disagree about what constitutes the correct solutions to problems. Other fields of potential knowledge may have no true experts, because no one has had the opportunity to work on many problems in the domain. Or there may be no true experts to whom an instructional technologist can find access. Surface warfare tactics planning may be one such domain of knowledge. To say that there is substantial disagreement among experts is not the same as saying that everyone's opinion is equal. Experienced practitioners have much that they can teach novices, and they are likely to have substantial areas of agreement. Still, where there is this kind of uncertainty, the difficulty of automated assessment is very high.

In such cases, a hybrid system that supports a combination of automated and human assessment features may prove most useful. An automated system can note—and perhaps point out to the student—actions which are always wrong in the presence of certain problem features. Other student actions that are either likely to be wrong, or that are merely possibly wrong, can be pointed out to a human observer, who can make the call and determine whether remediation is required.

Ontology-Based Measures

Previous research conducted in partnership with the Center for Research on Evaluation, Standards, and Student Testing (CRESST) at UCLA focused on assessing performance in the context of a simulation using a universal approach based on the domain of surface warfare tactics knowledge, rather than on the particulars of specific tactical problems (Munro, Surmon, et al., 2013). We developed an ontology for one significant element of TAO surface warfare planning: anti-submarine warfare (ASW) detect-to-engage. Figure 7.1 shows a simplified graphical representation of the major elements of this ontology. The size of the figure makes its elements unreadable, but the size and complexity of this portion of the representation can be appreciated. The top-most band of concepts relates to the objects that are involved in ASW surface warfare tactics. Units such as ships, helicopters, submarines, and jets; weapons, including missiles, mines, and torpedoes; and virtual objects, such as datums (markers of probable submarine detections), cordons (planned assigned areas, usually sections in concentric circles), range markers, and limiting lines of approach (which mark a particular friendly unit's areas of vulnerability to hostile submarines) are also relevant objects for the ontology.

The bottom band of concepts in this figure are tactical factors that must be considered in making tactical plans in an ASW context, including the geopolitical situation, the type of mission that the planner has been given, and the characteristics of the expected opposition.

Just above the bottom band is a set of properties that relate sets of tactical factors and objects to each other. The largest set of concepts portrayed in this figure lie in between the object nodes at the top and the properties and tactical factors shown in the lower portion of the figure. In order to make the figure

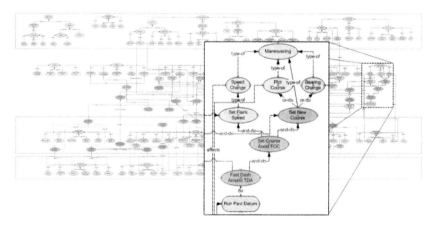

FIGURE 7.1 Diagram of partial ontology for ASW tactics planning (showing size/complexity) with expanded detail.

more readable, many of the lines showing relations among the concepts in this ontology have been omitted.

The detail view (boxed) in Figure 7.1 shows a small subset of the concepts mapped. This section of the ontology map shows a set of concepts related to running a ship past a datum, a potential source of danger from a submarine. If a datum lies ahead, within the limiting lines of a ship, it makes sense to maneuver to run past the datum, skirting the threat area associated with a report of a hostile submarine (see the node in the lower left corner in the detail). This procedure is defined as making a fast dash around the torpedo danger area (TDA). This, in turn, is a multipart action with two components. One (off to the left of the detail) specifies the action of retrieving any towed elements, such as a sonar array. The second, shown here, specifies setting a course to avoid the TDA. This is another compound action, consisting first of increasing speed appropriately. Second, the TAO student needs to set a new course, one that does not put the advance position of the ship within the TDA. The course change can be accomplished in the TAO Sandbox either by plotting a multisegment course, or by simply initiating an appropriate bearing change. Changing speed, plotting a new course, or changing bearing are all types of maneuvering actions.

Every procedure is defined in terms of the actions that it requires and the conditions under which the procedure and its component actions should be undertaken. (Procedures are not scenario-specific; they apply in any scenario that exhibits the conditions for that procedure.) One approach to monitoring student performance is to detect actions and evaluate which, if any, conditions may hold for carrying out a procedure that includes those actions. If conditions hold that should definitely require the procedure, the student can be credited with knowing that the procedure should be carried out and knowing how to perform the steps. If conditions hold that merely permit the procedure, the student can be credited with understanding that the procedure is acceptable if he or she carries out its actions. On the other hand, if a student is observed carrying out the actions of a procedure that is not acceptable under the current conditions, then the student's knowledge of when to perform the procedure can be estimated to be less than would be assumed if the actions had not been taken.

The approach of basing runtime assessments of student actions on a robust ontology has a number of appealing characteristics. It should be possible to build a single rich representation of domain knowledge that can be used to evaluate decisions and actions in any possible exercise in that domain. This would make it possible for instructors to develop many novel problems that could be used to accurately assess student knowledge, without having to develop problem-specific performance metrics, because a domain-universal ontology drives the analysis of performance.

There are also reasons to be concerned about the feasibility of the ontological approach for a rich and complex domain (such as surface warfare planning and tactics). Here is a partial list of such concerns.

- Subject matter experts (SMEs) tend to be very good at determining the criteria for good and poor performance in specific contexts, but are less able to accurately express the evaluation criteria in a universal way that can be applied in all contexts. This makes the process of building accurate ontologies prolonged, labor-intensive, and error-prone. Putative universals are often found to be incompletely expressed (or even simply wrong) as soon as a new context is presented.
- Many tactics problems may involve tens of friendly units and scores of unknown and hostile units, each of which might constitute a threat. Many performance metrics deal with tracking, querying, warning, avoiding, and sensing such potential threats when they approach within prescribed distances. In a simulation that supports time compression, like the TAO Sandbox, a universal approach to measuring these distance-based performance metrics could require checking hundreds or even thousands of potential range crossings every second. This computational burden could be sufficient to interfere with the accurate portrayal of the movements of units and the weapons they launch when the simulation is operating at a high time-multiple.
- Aspects of the geopolitical situation described in a scenario briefing could make it clear that certain units do not have to be treated as potential threats. But universal automated evaluation rules would apply to those units as well as to the actual threats in the problem. As a result, a student's performance could be downgraded by a universal, ontology-based evaluator, when in fact it should not be.

For these and other reasons, it is appropriate to develop a hybrid approach to automated evaluation. Certain universal rules would apply to every problem. For example, it may always be appropriate to shoot down an incoming surface missile, if you have surface-to-air missiles. Other rules would be specific to a given problem. (For example, only the potential threats that will actually come within range of friendly units will be checked for range crossings.)

The rules that are specific to problems should be associated with those problems as data for performing those measures. In the Sandbox, this requirement has been addressed through the addition of *watchers*, entities that observe limit crossings in specific scenarios. Watchers are set up by subject matter experts to watch the distances between specific friendly and threatening units, and to report threshold crossings.

Instructors need to be able to specify range boundaries that must be monitored in order to evaluate the TAO's performance. For example, an instructor could specify that it was "important for DDG-110 to query UNK-8 before it came closer than 35 NM." (That is, the guided missile destroyer designated as DDG-110 should ask the oncoming aircraft designated as UNK-8 before it comes within 35 nautical miles of the destroyer.) Several range types are shown in Figure 7.2, including query range, warning range, the outer and inner CIEA (classification,

FIGURE 7.2 Tactical range rings around a mission essential unit.

identification, and engagement area) bounds, the shine range (an area within which a potential hostile should be illuminated with a targeting radar), and the vital area (an area around a friendly unit that places it within range of the preferred weapons of the hostiles).

In general, allowing potential threats to approach a friendly unit too closely, especially a mission-critical unit (a unit, such as an aircraft carrier, that is essential to the performance of a mission), without taking specified actions may be an indicator that the student is lacking important knowledge or is not exercising required skills. In Figure 7.2, there are two ships at the right. The mission critical unit is the carrier CVN_72; it is at the center of the circular vital area. To the left of the vital area we see a thick ring that is the CIEA. Within that ring is the thin shine range. Farther out from the mission critical area is the warning range—any potential threat should be warned away if it crosses this boundary, heading toward the friendly ships. Still farther out is the query range, where oncoming air threats should be asked their identity and plans. The outermost ring in this figure is the surveillance ring, which marks the area within which unknown units should be actively tracked and monitored.

We first developed a prototype system for adaptive instruction that was demonstrated in the context of a complex Sandbox scenario, which collaborated with a general-purpose rule-based assessment component, the RAC. However, to make the RAC work, it needed to receive specific messages about events from the TAO Sandbox. In the prototype system, we introduced simulation code in the Sandbox that monitored certain situations only in the context of a specific scenario. Rather than introduce more special code to monitor additional situations in the context of the other scenarios, we have instead developed a new facility for creating and editing watchers, entities that authors can add to a problem that monitor threshold violations, such as a contact of interest escaping friendly sensor ranges, or a potential air threat approaching too close to friendly assets without being queried. When the watcher system is fully developed, instructors will be able set up specific watchers to monitor certain situations in specific problem scenarios.

Watcher creation, editing, and deletion are only possible in the instructor mode in the TAO Sandbox. However, the authored watchers will be active during student sessions. When a watcher observes a situation that it was set up to detect, it will inform the RAC of the event. It will also record the event in the session recordings that the Sandbox automatically makes when it runs in problem mode.

Instructors will be able to create new watchers and select current watchers using the command button menu on friendly units. When a new watcher command is issued, a simple watcher editor interface will open in the Sandbox (Figure 7.3).

The watcher editor lets the author or instructor choose which friendly is the base unit for determining the range. It can also specify the type of range that needs to be monitored (query range, radar range, etc.). The *type* information is recorded in the session record and is sent to the RAC, where it may be used to select appropriate adaptations. The relational operator is either < (*less than*), = (*equal to*), or > (*greater than*). When specifying a watcher that should report a contact of interest leaving a friendly ship's radar coverage, the > (greater than) symbol is chosen, because the watcher should report as soon as the distance between the friendly and the COI is greater than the friendly unit's radar range. In contrast, the < (less than) symbol is appropriate when checking whether a threat has closed to a distance that is less than the warning range threshold. The numerical limit is used to specify the threshold distance. The targets list specifies which non-friendly units should be monitored by the rule.

Problem authors can specify the elements of a watcher's configuration using menus and other simple user GUI widgets. In Figure 7.4, the base friendly unit for the watcher is changed.

The limit type pop-up menu lists the range types that can be reported by the watchers. At present, we anticipate that this list will include query, warning, shine, CIEA, vital area, surface radar range, and air radar range (Figure 7.5).

The relational operator menu lets a user choose one of the *less than*, *equals*, or *greater than* comparison operators (Figure 7.6).

Clicking on the limit number will bring up a number entry widget. Users who would rather type a number instead of using the slider can click the number pane in the slider to open a number entry object (Figure 7.7).

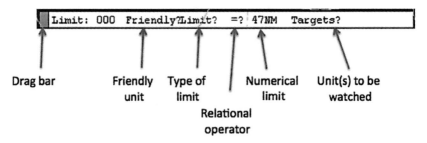

FIGURE 7.3 Watcher editor, used to specify problem-specific reporting rules.

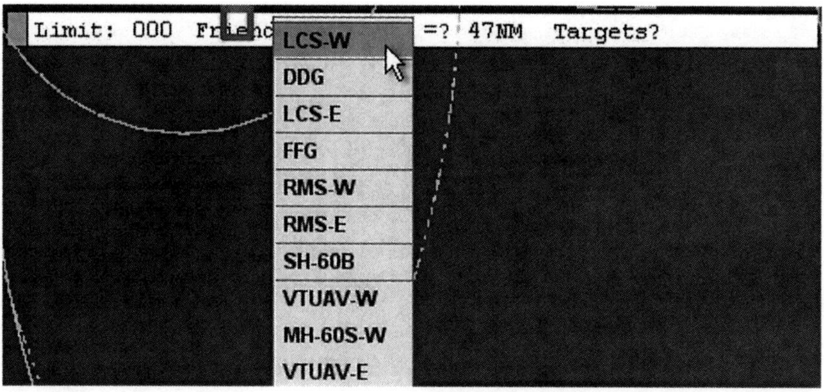

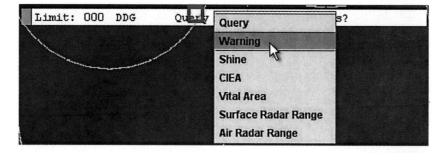

FIGURE 7.4 Selecting which friendly unit the watcher will monitor.

FIGURE 7.5 Choosing the type of limit that the watcher is to check.

FIGURE 7.6 Selecting the *less than* relational operator.

FIGURE 7.7 Entering a watcher's range limit.

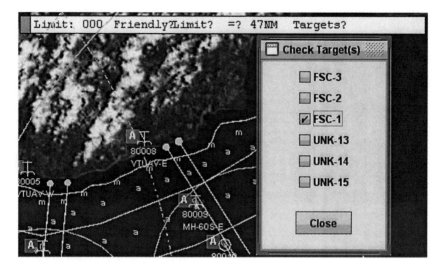

FIGURE 7.8 Choosing the target units that the watcher tracks.

Because the targets field of the watcher editor can have more than one object selected, a checkbox panel interface will be provided to let users specify the targets (Figure 7.8).

Watchers that have multiple targets show the current distance of the closest target, in the case of when the relational operator is *less than*, and they show the distance of the farthest target, when the operator is *greater than*.

Watcher Operations in Problem Mode

Watcher editors are unavailable in problem mode, since the watchers would give away what actions should be taken, rather than allowing the learner to determine what actions to take based on the evolution of the problem. Their effects will be observable only to the extent that they trigger adaptations when they report to RAC rules. However, their reports will play a role in student assessments in the performance reporting system now under development.

When a watcher observes its limit crossing, it will report to the RAC and it will add an observation to the session recording currently being saved to a .rec file. These reports to the RAC include both a generic scoring and additional specific information. For example, if the DDG failed to query the unknown aircraft that approached it, a watcher would send this message to the RAC:

> trigger event Query_Failure realTime 00:01:07 virtualTime 00:09:31 value 0.2 user pco/section_1/Belichick_B session boholisland3 message friendly DDG target UNK-14 limit 22NM distance 19NM

This new message will include in its *message* field all the particulars of which friendly, which target, and what distances were involved in the observation. The RAC, in turn, could make use of these particulars in composing a comment to provide instructional feedback.

Similarly, the hard-coded data recordings that worked only in the Bohol Island scenario will now be replaced with data recordings determined by the specifications of authored watcher objects. In place of the old:

00:01:07 00:09:31 .k.Announce. Failed_to_Query_UnknownAir 0.2

the .rec files will now include observation data that look like this:

00:01:07 00:09:31 .k.Announce. Query_Failure 0.2 DDG UNK-14 19 < 22

which will provide more information about the situation that was observed.

These new approaches to automated measurement will have the potential to trigger RAC rules to bring about interventions and other scenario adaptations.

Triggering Adaptations as a Result of Runtime Measures

Adaptive training requires that some form of assessment occur. Only after determining something about a student's learning needs can a system provide an appropriate intervention or modification to adapt a training environment to the learner's needs. Simulations used for training can observe a student working through a task in the simulation environment and make assessments based on the student's actions. Such performance-based assessment can be used to determine a student's ability to make appropriate decisions to carry out tasks and to perform jobs.

In a performance-based assessment, adaptation occurs in response to student actions or to simulation events that are, at least in part, the outcome of student actions (or inaction) (Figure 7.9).

In this training architecture, the simulation or game reports assessable events. In response to some of these events, the assessment and adaptation component

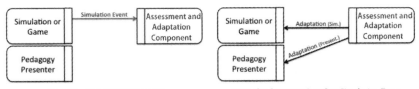

First: Simulation Event Reported   *Second: Adaptation Based on Simulation Event*

FIGURE 7.9 Adaptation architecture.

determines that an adaptation is called for. As in the case for question-based adaptation, adaptations can include presentations, and they can include changes in the simulation, such as the highlighting of objects, the introduction of new elements, or the modification or replacement of a scenario or problem.

We have developed the first version of a new application, the RAC that receives reports about student actions in practice problems and controls the TAO Sandbox for instructional purposes. These components, the Sandbox and the RAC, collaborate by exchanging service requests, data, and confirmations. Other applications can make use of the same set of services to control the Sandbox, directing it to load problems and to present portions of previously recorded problem sessions (Wray & Munro, 2012; Figure 7.10).

The RAC is a reusable application that is intended to work with different simulation-centered training systems. For a given domain, such as "surface warfare tactics in the context of the TAO Sandbox," the RAC loads and interprets a set of rules that specify the instructional adaptations that should occur in that context. With a different set of rules, the RAC could provide adaptive training in a different simulation context, so long as that simulation also adheres to the specified services protocol.

The rule-based adaptive component (RAC) is a supervisory application that works with simulations to provide instructional adaptations in response to users' actions and other events in simulations. The internal structure of the RAC is depicted in Figure 7.11. Simulation events are reported to the RAC, triggering pre-authored rules that refer to those types of events. The triggered rules, depending upon conditions, either do nothing, modify a model of the student's knowledge, or request services of the simulation that constitute an adaptation. (Some rules result both in changes to the student model and in adaptations in the simulation.)

The RAC imports a set of rules that determines its behavior in a simulation context. Each RAC rule has a fairly simple structure, with only a few major components. These are primarily a trigger specification and a list of cases. Both

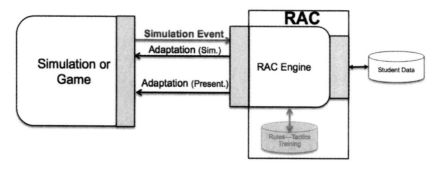

FIGURE 7.10 The RAC and the TAO Sandbox.

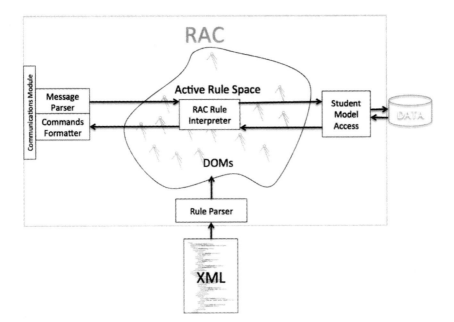

FIGURE 7.11 RAC engine internal structure.

the trigger and each case has an internal structure. Each case has a condition and a set of actions. When a rule is triggered, the RAC engine tests the condition in each case. When a condition is true, it carries the actions specified in the case. Some of these actions may be requests for services from the simulation that adapt it for the current student. Other actions may modify the student model. Student model values can be referenced in conditions, so future rule activations may bring about other adaptive effects due to such changes made to the student model.

A trigger event (such as LoseHostileFromRadar, which occurs when friendly forces lose radar contact with a potential hostile) triggers an authored RAC rule that has a message with a case that includes a condition that the trigger message mentions a possibly hostile fast attack craft (FAC). The action that results is that a chat message-posting service is requested. A composed message is generated that purports to be from the ship that lost contact (perhaps a guided missile frigate or FFG,) to the lead ship requesting permission to attempt to regain contact, for example, "LCS(W) DE FFG, LOST RADAR CTC ON LEAD FAST SURFACE CRAFT. REQUEST PERMISSION TO DEPART PICKET STATION TO MAINTAIN CTC OF TRAILING FSC." The specifics of this message are under the control of the instructor who authors the RAC rule, rather than it having been built into the underlying software.

Universal and Problem-Specific Rules

Instructors and other developers of problem scenarios can create sets of rules that are customized for particular problems. These rules are placed in folders (in the *rules* folder) that have the same name as the problem. When a new problem is started by the Sandbox, it informs the RAC, and the RAC checks to see whether it has a specific set of rules for that problem. If it does, it loads those rules into its rule space, in addition to the universal rules.

Rules are expressed in an XML format. For example, the RAC uses an authored universal rule, which detects when a user has tried to employ a helicopter that is conducting a mine countermeasure operation to instead carry out a visual identification (VID) or an escort. This action typically doesn't make sense, because it would take 90 minutes to retrieve and stow the equipment being used in the search or sweep operation. When the TAO Sandbox detects that a user has done this, it sends a trigger message with the event name "Attempt_To_Use_Helo_Doing_Search" to the RAC.

If the value associated with this event is less than 0.5, the RAC tells the Sandbox to delete any existing comments on the screen and then to present a chat message purporting to be from the mine warfare evaluator. That message reminds the user why the directive to conduct a VID or an escort doesn't make sense in this circumstance. Because this is a universal rule, it will apply in every problem, not just in a particular one.

The chat content that this rule composes is largely fixed, but it contains one variable element, the text that the simulation sent to the RAC with the attribute label *message*. In the case of an Attempt_To_Use_Helo_Doing_Search event, the simulation passes to the RAC the name of the helicopter that was directed to carry out a VID or escort, labeled as the message. This means that a message like this will appear in the simulation communications window:

TAO DE MIWE, SH-60_W WILL BE AVAILABLE IN 90 MINUTES. MUST RECOVER GEAR AND RETURN TO SHIP FOR FUEL AND RECONFIGURATION.

This message makes it clear to the student that the helicopter designated as SH-60_W will not be able to immediately carry out the task requested of it, because it must recover the towed drogue that it is using and return to the ship for refueling and reconfiguration before it can carry out the task.

Conclusions

Detailed performance measures can be made by a game or simulation. Some performance measures can be universal to the game, but others are best specified for application in specific scenarios or problem contexts. Reports of performance measures can be interpreted in real time by a collaborating component that uses rules to determine what adaptations should take place to provide instructional feedback and guide learning.

Summary

Some types of learning can be measured by analyzing task performances in the contexts of simulations or games, rather than by conventional post-treatment assessments. Analyzing performance automatically at runtime offers the potential to provide accurate assessments of who can do the simulated tasks. Such assessments can be utilized by an automated adaptation system to provide instructional feedback or to naturalistically modify the user's task to provide the learning experiences that the individual user needs. A specific approach to measuring detailed elements of performance in a tactics planning simulation, the TAO Sandbox, uses a combination of universal measures and problem-specific measures that can be edited by subject matter experts.

Author Note

The work described here was sponsored by awards from the Office of Naval Research and the Naval Air Warfare Center under contract N61340-12-C-0012, and by the Office of Naval Research and Soar Technology under contract N00014-10-C-052670, as well as by the Office of Naval Research and the Center for Research on Evaluation, Standards, and Student Testing (CRESST) under contracts N00014-08-C-0563 and N00014-09-C-0813.

References

American Educational Research Association, American Psychological Association, & National Council on Measurement in Education. (2014). *Standards for educational and psychological testing*. Washington, DC: Author.

Auslander, B., Molineaux, M., Aha, D.W., Munro, A., & Pizzini, Q. (2009). *Towards research on goal reasoning with the TAO Sandbox* (Technical Note AIC-09-155). Washington, DC: Naval Research Laboratory, Navy Center for Applied Research on Artificial Intelligence.

Bernard, R. M., Abrami, P. C., Borokhovski, E., Wade, C. A., Tamim, R. A., Surkes, M. A., & Bethel, E. C. (2009). A meta-analysis of three types of interaction treatments in distance education. *Review of Educational Research, 79*, 1243–1289.

Brown, J. S., & VanLehn, K. (1980). Repair theory: A generative theory of bugs in procedural skills. *Cognitive Science, 4*, 379–426.

Clark, R. E., Yates, K., Early, S., & Moulton, K. (2010). An analysis of the failure of electronic media and discovery-based learning: Evidence for the performance benefits of guided training methods. In K. H. Silber & R. Foshay (Eds.), *Handbook of improving performance in the workplace, Vol. 1. Instructional design and training delivery* (pp. 263–297). Washington, DC: International Society for Performance Improvement.

Cook, D. A., Hamstra, S. J., Brydges, R., Zendejas, B., Szostek, J. H., Wang, A. T., . . . & Hatala, R. (2013). Comparative effectiveness of instructional design features in simulation-based education: Systematic review and meta-analysis. *Medical Teacher, 35,* 867–898.

D'Mello, S. (2013). A selective meta-analysis on the relative incidence of discrete affective states during learning with technology. *Journal of Educational Psychology,* 105, 1082–1099.

Hays, R. T., Jacobs, J. W., Prince, C., & Salas, E. (1992). Flight simulator training effectiveness: A meta-analysis. *Military Psychology, 4,* 63–74.

Levy, R. (2012). Psychometric advances, opportunities, and challenges for simulation-based assessment. In *Invitational Research Symposium on Technology Enhanced Assessments.* Austin, TX: K-12 Center at ETS.

McGaghie, W. C., Issenberg, S. B., Cohn, E. R., Barsuk, J. H., & Wayne, D. B. (2011). Does simulation-based medical education with deliberate practice yield better results than traditional clinical education? A meta-analytic comparative review of the evidence. *Academic Medicine,* 86, 706–711.

Moreno, R., & Mayer, R. (2007). Interactive multimodal learning environments. *Educational Psychology Review,* 19, 309–326.

Munro, A., Pizzini, Q. A., & Bewley, W. L. (2009). *Learning anti-submarine warfare with a game-like tactical planner.* Paper presented at the Interservice/Industry Training Simulation, and Education Conference (I/ITSEC), Orlando, FL.

Munro, A., Pizzini, Q. A., & Darling, D. (2013). *The TAO Sandbox instructor guide* (Working paper). Redondo Beach, CA: Center for Cognitive Technology, University of Southern California.

Munro, A., Surmon, D., Koenig, A., Iseli, M., Lee, J., & Bewley, W. (2013). Detailed modeling of student knowledge in a simulation context. In V. Duffy (Ed.), *Proceedings of the 2012 applied human factors and ergonomics conference* (Vol. 3, Advances in applied modeling and simulation). Boca Raton, FL: CRC Press, Taylor and Francis.

O'Neil, H. F., Wainess, R., & Baker, E. L. (2005). Classification of learning outcomes: Evidence from the computer games literature. *Curriculum Journal, 16,* 455–474.

Plake, B. S., & Wise, L. L. (2014). What is the role and importance of the revised AERA, APA, NCME Standards for Educational and Psychological Testing? *Educational Measurement: Issues and Practice, 33,* 4–12. doi:10.1111/emip.12045

Tamim, R. M., Bernard, R. M., Borokhovski, E., Abrami, P. C., & Schmid, R. F. (2011). What forty years of research says about the impact of technology on learning: A second-order meta-analysis and validation study. *Review of Educational Research, 81,* 4–28.

VanLehn, K. (1990). *Mind bugs.* Cambridge, MA: MIT Press.

Wouters, P., van Nimwegen, C., van Oostendorp, H., & van der Spek, E. D. (2013). A meta-analysis of the cognitive and motivational effects of serious games. *Journal of Educational Psychology, 105,* 249–265.

Wray, R., & Munro, A. (2012). *Simulation2Instruction: Using simulation in all phases of instruction.* Paper at presented at the Interservice/Industry Training Simulation, and Education Conference (I/ITSEC), Orlando, FL.

8

THE ROLE OF NEUROBIOLOGY IN TEACHING AND ASSESSING GAMES

Ray S. Perez, Jason Ralph, and James Niehaus

Overview

Within two months of its release, the video game Call of Duty: Black Ops (Activision Publishing Inc., 2010) was played for more than 600 million hours worldwide, with sales of over one billion dollars (Albanesius, 2010). U.S. children spent on average 1 hour and 13 minutes playing video games every day in 2009, a 300% increase from 1999 (Rideout, Foehr, & Roberts, 2010). Wide segments of the U.S. population play video games: The average age of game players is 31, with 29% under 18 years old, 32% in the 18–35 year range, and 39% being 36 years or older (Entertainment Software Association, 2014). Video gaming is now pervasive in our society, and some researchers have cited concerns that intensive media use (including watching television, computer use, and video gaming) may be associated with negative health effects, such as obesity, aggressiveness, antisocial behavior, or addiction (e.g., Strasburger, Jordan, & Donnerstein, 2010). However, there is a growing body of evidence that video gaming can have beneficial effects on the organization and function of the brain and learning.

This chapter is divided into two main sections that discuss the role of neurobiology in teaching and assessing games. The first details the use of commercial video games in cognitive research and discusses findings that show evidence of cognitive enhancement due to video game play. The second section is devoted to serious games, video games developed for a non-entertainment purpose such as aiding in educational instruction. Taken together, these two sections provide a summary of the basic research findings that have aided our understanding of human cognition, grounded in the relevant neurobiological structures, and include a discussion of possible applications of future video game research.

Commercial Entertainment Video Game Research

After 30 years of video game research, it is instructive to take a step back and review the most important findings from this research. Here we will document many examples of cognitive skill enhancement and brain activity differences attributable to video game play. Despite these results we have yet to form a consensus regarding the reasons for these differences. What is it about certain types of video games that promote specific changes in brain function? What do these results tell us about the nature of cognition and how it adapts to the environment? The answers to these questions would represent significant advancement in our understanding of the human brain and how it functions. This chapter summarizes what we have learned about video games and the brain and provides guidance for future research needed to resolve remaining questions.

The ability to measure cognitive abilities outside of the psychology lab is one of the key challenges cognitive scientists face. The recent explosion of video games as a widespread pastime (especially for younger adults) has provided an opportunity to measure cognition and training effects in ways that were simply not feasible before. Several lines of research have developed over the past three decades that use video games to measure cognitive functions and the transfer of skill from one domain to another.

The game Space Fortress was developed in the early 1980s specifically for the purpose of measuring cognitive abilities (Mané & Donchin, 1989). Video games have been ubiquitous in the cognitive science literature ever since. Findings from this research have aided in our understanding of many cognitive functions, including but not limited to visual attention, the neuroscience of attention, and learning patterns in the environment. Games have also helped us understand the nature of expertise development on small tasks or domains, which are a particularly important issue as we attempt to develop games that we hope will train people to become experts.

Visual Attention

Research conducted in the past decade has provided evidence of enhanced visual perception and attention among video game players (Boot, Kramer, Simons, Fabiani, & Gratton, 2008; Dye, Green, & Bavelier, 2009; Green & Bavelier, 2003, 2007, 2012). Although there have been cases where replications have failed (Boot et al., 2008), these effects seem to be relatively robust (Dye et al., 2009). Green and Bavelier (2003) found significant differences on a wide array of visual attention tasks when comparing habitual video game players (VGPs) with non-video game players (NVGPs). In a target detection task, VGPs exhibited faster response times, a larger useful field of view, and enhanced distractor filtering abilities.

These results have been confirmed by EEG studies that show differences in neural activity correlated with video game experience in a variety of tasks (Bailey

& West, 2013). To show that these differences were not merely a result of self-selection of VGPs for individuals who already had high visual attention abilities, Green and Bavelier (2003) found that these enhancements were trainable. NVGPs who played video games for as little as 10 hours, 1 hour a day for 10 days, exhibited improved performance on various measures of visual attention.

Interestingly, the differences Green and Bavelier (2003) found are limited to one type of video game: action games in which the player views the game as if he were immersed in a 3D environment (e.g., first-person shooters such as Call of Duty: Black Ops). Most of these games involve making quick decisions (whether to shoot an enemy or avoid shooting a friend). It is clear that the abilities improved in Green's experiments are valuable in these action games. Increased reaction times, distractor processing (i.e., speed of identifying and ignoring non-critical elements of the task), and useful field of view (i.e., the visual area over which information can be extracted with a brief look) all make it easier to make quick decisions in the context of the game. These skills are all useful in many time-dependent high-cognitive load domains, such as sports, emergency aid (including emergency medical technician or EMT, police, and firefighter roles), and military tasks. In contrast, puzzle games like Tetris do not seem to exhibit this training effect (Green & Bavelier, 2003). Therefore, not all video games can be treated equally when considering cognitive effects. Specific aspects of visual presentation and game play, and even emotional aspects of game setting and narrative may significantly impact how game information is processed and what training effects may be discovered.

Neuroscience of Attention

The experiments in the previous section suggest an advantage in selective attentional control for VGPs. This section examines neurological evidence of these effects in relation to our theoretical understanding of the brain's cognitive control pathways (i.e., how the brain modulates the operation of cognitive and emotional subsystems). Neurological evidence can help us learn how action video game play improves these abilities, and can point toward possible applications for video games.

Previous research has localized many control functions to the anterior cingulate cortex (ACC) and the dorsolateral prefrontal cortex (DLPFC) (Cohen et al., 1994; Miller, 2000; Miller & Cohen, 2001). The ACC detects conflict in information processing and alerts the DLPFC of the need to increase attentive control. Todd Braver's dual mechanisms of control (DMC) theory postulates two distinct modes of attentive control (Braver, 2012; Braver, Gray, & Burgess, 2007). Proactive control occurs when task context is held in the DLPFC in preparation for expected events. Reactive control, by contrast, involves the transient activation of the ACC after a conflict-inducing stimulus appears. For instance in the Stroop and Eriksen flanker tasks, incongruent stimuli that prime two competing responses initiate activity in ACC and result in slower response times when compared with congruent stimuli (Botvinick, Braver, Barch, Carter, & Cohen, 2001; Yeung, Bogacz, Holroyd, & Cohen, 2004; Yeung, Ralph, & Nieuwenhuis, 2007).

The two modes of control interact to create what we often refer to as cognitive control. Proactive control increases the activation of responses likely to be needed, reducing ACC activity. Thus a proactive control signature involves sustained activity in the DLPFC and reduced activation of the ACC. Reactive control, on the other hand, features transient activation of the ACC following conflict-inducing stimuli. In order to evaluate the impact of video game play on attention, it is important to determine which control abilities are enhanced. Video game players are better able to deal with unexpected and distracting stimuli, and the evidence to date points to an enhancement of proactive control, but see Bailey, West, and Anderson (2010) for a different view.

Recently, the use of task-switching paradigms has shed some light on the mechanisms of game-related improvements in cognitive abilities (Green, Sugarman, Medford, Klobusicky, & Bavelier, 2012). Task switching involves alternately performing one of two similar tasks. For instance in a common version, participants are asked to determine either if a digit is greater than or less than 5 or if it is even/odd. The measure of interest in these experiments is the difference in response time on trials where the task switches when compared to those when the task repeats. Evidence is solid that VGPs are faster on switch trials. Interestingly, there is no difference in response speed on trials where the task repeats. Thus the improvement in performance is not due to general improvements in response speed, but rather reflects an improved ability to switch between tasks. Green and his colleagues found that this result holds equally for tasks that are mostly cognitive or visual in nature. The effect also holds for vocal or manual responses (Green et al., 2012). These are important findings because they generalize the cognitive improvements beyond the subset of tasks that have obvious connections to the video games themselves. All of the other transfer tasks commonly used to measure improvement are very similar in that they stress visual attention and are all computer based, making them similar to the action video games themselves. Task switching, by contrast, shows improvement in a general cognitive control ability that has implications beyond the realm of video game play.

Task switching results also shed light on the question of proactive versus reactive control. Karle, Watter, and Shedden (2010) found that video game experience selectively benefited task-switching performance in situations where time and information were available that could lead to better preparation for future trials. VGPs did not, however, show an increased ability to resolve proactive interference, which would suggest enhancements in reactive control (Karle et al., 2010). In other words, VGPs are able to use information to prepare for likely task switches, an ability that has applications in the real world where distractions are ubiquitous and maintaining the ability to prepare for upcoming events is of paramount importance. Neural evidence also suggests that video game play enhances proactive mechanisms. Changes in the parietal-frontal control network in VGPs were found using a resting state fMRI procedure (Martínez et al., 2013). Parietal-frontal networks are generally implicated in proactive control functions.

Learning Patterns in the Environment

Recent studies have argued that enhanced selective attention in VGPs is part of an overall improvement in the ability to quickly learn the statistical patterns of the environment (Appelbaum, Cain, Darling, & Mitroff, 2013; Green & Bavelier, 2012) This view fits nicely with the specific cognitive enhancements Green and Bavelier (2003) found. Of particular interest is their finding of increased distractor processing in a flanker task.

Nelli Lavie's attentional load theory (Lavie, 2005; Lavie, Hirst, de Fockert, & Viding, 2004) argues that people with high attentional capacity process extra information, including distractors, in situations of high perceptual load. Lavie's experiments require subjects to identify an N or an X in a circular array including other letters. A flanker letter outside of the circle displays an X or an N, which may be either congruent or incongruent with the target letter in the circular array. Lavie's results suggest that attentional capacity is consumed by the perceptual load caused by the target array, leaving none left over to process the flanking distractor. Thus distractor processing tends to decrease with increasing perceptual load.

Green and Bavelier (2003) found that VGPs performing Lavie's perceptual load task did not exhibit a decrease in distractor processing with increasing perceptual load, suggesting again that VGPs have increased attentional capacity. In the case of Lavie's task, increased capacity caused more interference, but the ability to attend to extra items in a visual scene may allow VGPs to better process and learn the statistical properties of the environment.

The ability to learn the statistical properties of the environment is an important prerequisite for proactive control in the dual mechanisms of control framework (Braver et al., 2007). Effective attentional control relies on the ability to accurately predict the likelihood of specific events occurring in the near future. The ability to extract more information from the environment should lead to enhanced statistical learning. Thus Green and Bavelier have recently hypothesized that the visual enhancements VGPs possess are not an end unto themselves, but aid in a much more important aspect of cognition, the ability to extract information from the environment to guide perceptual learning (Bavelier, Green, Pouget, & Schrater, 2012; Green & Bavelier, 2012).

Action Video Game Impact on Cognitive Skills

Bediou, Adams, Mayer, Green, and Bavelier (in press) present a recent meta-analysis of the effects of commercial action video games on perceptual, attentional, and cognitive skills. They define this genre to include first- and third-person shooters but exclude real-time strategy, role-playing, driving, and fighting video games. Based on 214 comparisons from 52 sources in the literature, this study found that playing action video games improved cognition by more than half a standard deviation on average.

Perception (0.75 standard deviations improvement), top-down attention (0.67 standard deviations improvement), and multi-tasking (0.56 standard deviations improvement) were found to have the highest relationship to action video game playing, and these relationships were found to be causal. That is, action video games produced these cognitive improvements and were not just correlated with these factors. The effects on cognition were found in both cross-sectional studies comparing habitual video game players to non-players or infrequent players as well as intervention experiments where participants were trained from a baseline using 10–50 hours of action video game play. The authors conclude that action video games are potentially powerful tools for enhancing cognition. They note that more work is needed to delineate precisely which features of these games are linked to cognitive improvements and that future work may seek to avoid overly broad genre categorizations.

Discussion on Commercial Entertainment Video Game Research

The past few decades of research using video games have helped to significantly further our understanding of human cognition. In particular, the focus on action video games spearheaded by Green and Bavelier (2003, 2007, 2012) has moved us forward. This research program has begun a migration out of the psychology lab and into the real world. It is almost surely not a coincidence that the games found to elicit changes in cognitive abilities are also the games that are rated as most engaging.

The immersive quality of these action video games cannot be overlooked when we consider the connection between the brain and the environment. In total, this research has provided evidence that the brain is particularly adept at gathering and using information in the environment. The evidence from working memory training suggests that people build cognitive strategies that match the precise nature of the task environment. Thus the more the task environment resembles the world, the more useful that information will become. The brain uses all the information at its disposal to make predictions about what is likely to happen and cognitive control is the brain's way of reconciling those predictions with reality. Video game play may provide people with practice in gathering and using information to make better predictions. As Green points out (Green et al., 2012), the basic cognitive improvements in selective attention and visual processing may be byproducts of this core ability.

Serious Games Research

This section is devoted to serious games that are designed expressly to provide educational content and instruction. Early examples of popular serious games are

Where in the World is Carmen Sandiego? (Broderbund Software, 1985) and The Oregon Trail (Broderbund Software, 1974), which were designed to teach geography and life on the American frontier. These serious game developers hoped to capitalize on the entertainment value of games to teach content during game play and advance the goals of education.

We will begin this discussion by addressing the following: (a) serious games definitions, (b) the role of theory in serious games, (c) the use of narrative in games, (d) motivation in serious games, and (e) design features of games.

Serious Games Definitions

In the literature on games there have been several definitions of serious games and the related term simulation games. Simulation games are games where "instruction is delivered via personal computer that immerses trainees in a decision-making exercise in an artificial environment in order to learn the consequences of their decisions" (Sitzmann, 2011, p. 490). These games have been characterized by Malone (1981) as being intrinsically motivating. The term serious game can be used to refer to simulation games designed to address complicated and thought-provoking issues, such as in military combat and training first responders. There has been some debate in categorizing games in these categories. Sitzmann (2011) has argued that these distinctions are not helpful. She combines both types of games and refers to them as computer-based simulation games (Tennyson & Jorczak, 2008) with the following characteristics: They are entertaining, interactive, rule governed, goal focused, and competitive and they also stimulate the player's imagination (Driskell & Dwyer, 1984; Gredler, 1996; Tobias & Fletcher, 2007; Vogel et al., 2006). The term serious game has also been applied to (a) training simulations that use video game technology (e.g., a game engine), but do not have any game-like qualities (e.g., competition or score) and (b) any sort of game (e.g., a card game) used for purposes other than entertainment, such as training, informing, or persuasion. This chapter uses the term serious game to refer to video games that are designed expressly to provide educational content and instruction, also including game-like training simulations. We present these findings with the aforementioned caveat that game factors such as play style and interaction have direct ramifications for player cognitive effects and that each effect must be considered together with the game that invoked that effect.

The Role of Theory in Serious Games

A central issue in developing serious games is to identify what design features make video games effective in motivating play and holding attention. If these design principles are identified, they may be applied to the design of new serious games, leading to increased learning without sacrificing these benefits. Malone

(1981) has emphasized the importance of intrinsic motivation and play-type activities for enhancing deep learning. Intrinsically motivated gamers appear to exert more effort to learn the material, enjoy learning more, and are likely to apply the material learned outside of the game environment, that is, to transfer.

Garris, Ahlers, and Driskell (2002) proposed an input–process–outcome model that, like Malone, focuses on motivational characteristics of simulation games. They argued that game playing is a cyclical relationship including user judgments, user behavior, and system feedback. These interactions are the source of engagement. They are fed by the instructional content and game characteristics, and the game-playing cycle produces the learning outcomes. These interactions create a "flow" state that represents an optimal performance condition where the player is oblivious to their surroundings (Csikszentmihalyi, 1990). Then, to enhance transfer to real-world tasks, Garris et al. recommend that after each game-playing session, trainees attend a debriefing session in which the game and its application are discussed, connecting tacit learning to explicit learning.

Tennyson and Jorczak (2008) focus on the cognitive aspects of game play that affect learning. They propose the interactive cognitive complexity theory, suggesting that simulation games are more effective than other instructional methods because they simultaneously engage both affective and cognitive processes. This theory is an information processing model proposing that learning is the result of an interaction between internal and external variables of the game player's cognitive (e.g., memory, knowledge bases, and executive control) and affective (e.g., motivation and attitudes) systems. It is interesting to note that Bavelier et al. (2012) have proposed that first-person shooter games such as Call of Duty: Black Ops increase perceptual skills because they enhance executive control. Tennyson and Jorczak (2008) propose that because simulation games engage both affective and cognitive structures they should be more effective than other instructional methods that only target one of these systems.

The current theoretical understanding has much room for improvement to aid in the design and creation of serious games. First, these theories are difficult to test, given that terms such as flow do not easily lend themselves to operational definitions that would enable researchers to develop objective and reliable measures. Second, game designers need guidance to find a match between game style and instructional objectives to be taught. For example, are games such as Angry Birds (Rovio Entertainment, 2009) appropriately used to teach the fundamental concepts of geometry? Is a 3D and virtual game environment more effective for learning triage than a 2D photorealistic game environment? What elements of game play most influence learning outcomes, and how do they interact with target domains? This latter question begets the inquiry of how much simulation fidelity is appropriate for teaching specific instructional objectives. This issue is of particular relevance to game developers since improved fidelity usually comes at increased cost.

Fidelity is a multidimensional construct and not simply a high/low choice. Alexander, Brunyé, Sidman, and Weil (2005) define fidelity in terms of (a) physical fidelity, the degree to which the experience "looks, sounds, and feels like the operational environment" (p. 4), (b) functional fidelity, the degree to which the simulation behaves like the operational environment, and (c) psychological fidelity, the degree to which the simulation evokes the feeling of being in the operational environment—a similar notion to the concepts of presence or transportation (Gerrig, 1993). Among these factors, initial evidence supports a positive correlation between fidelity and learning transfer (Alexander et al., 2005). For example, the physical fidelity aspect of haptic sensation (e.g., tactile force feedback) in laparoscopic skill simulators or F16 landing simulations increase learning effectiveness and improve autonomic response correlation with real tasks. However, the authors also note that improved fidelity along any of these dimensions must be closely aligned with the education or training goals; this finding is supported by later simulation studies (Curtis, DiazGranados, & Feldman, 2012). Improving fidelity across a serious game bears significant cost and does not guarantee improved learning outcomes, possibly even creating detrimental effects as trainees are forced to incorporate more information that may be irrelevant to the task, as described in early research on transfer (Thorndike, 1906). Unfortunately, the research on connections between dimensions of fidelity and learning outcomes is still emerging, and current studies do not yet provide strong indication on levels or types of fidelity required for specific domains or tasks.

Are some domains better suited to applying games as an instructional method? Serious games have been used to teach different domains, ranging from subjects that are part of school curriculum (e.g., biology, mathematics, physics; White, 1984), to job-oriented domains (e.g., job knowledge and skills), to more basic cognitive processing (e.g., executive control). Some of these domains may be more appropriate for teaching with computer games than others. For example, Wouters, van Nimwegen, van Oostendorp, and van der Spek's (2013) meta-analysis found a large effect size for language: $d = .66$. They reason that games that afford a rich multimodal environment have characteristics, graphics, and dynamic visualization that may facilitate better linguistic encoding of meaning and interpretation of words. This finding is explained by application of dual coding theory proposed by Clark and Paivio (1991). This theory suggests that subject matter presented in two modalities—visual and auditory—appears to be beneficial for teaching a language.

Are games more effective for children or adults? Wouters et al. (2013) found that for most age groups with the exception of adults, learning with serious games was more effective than conventional instruction. This finding was contrary to the findings by Vogel et al. (2006) who did not find differences between children and adults. However, Wouters et al. (2013) provided a caveat that it may be premature to draw a conclusion from their findings because the adult age group was made up of only two comparisons.

The Use of Narratives in Games

Wouters et al. (2013) found that serious games with a narrative are no more effective than serious games without a narrative when compared with conventional instruction. This result suggests that including a narrative in the design of a serious game does not improve its ability to facilitate learning. Furthermore, Adams, Mayer, MacNamara, Koenig, and Wainess (2012) and Novak, Johnson, Tenenbaum, and Shute (2014) found that adding a storyline to a game likewise did not make the game more effective. This finding is not only surprising but also counterintuitive, because it is believed that a factor in the success of commercial games is the plot or storyline (Prensky, 2001) that provides a context for the game. Stories have been demonstrated when compared to expository text to yield better recall and generate more inferences (Graesser, Olde, & Klettke, 2002; Mayer, Griffith, Naftaly, & Rothman, 2008). An explanation for this negative finding is that the addition of a narrative may detract from learning by subjecting the learner to cognitive overload (Adams et al., 2012).

Narrative is a commonly used structure to promote audience engagement across mediums, and it is therefore curious that these effects were not readily discovered in serious games. This finding may be the result of methodological limitations. Long-term motivational factors of narrative engagement may not be duplicated in shorter, controlled experiments focused on learning outcomes from a prescribed dose of gaming. Narrative topic or quality was not controlled for in many of these studies. However, emerging work in serious games centered on narrative has shown significant learning effects for narrative engagement and motivation (Rowe, 2013), suggesting that careful and iterative design of narrative and game play interaction may lead to future gains.

Motivation

One of the most appealing reasons for using serious games to teach instructional objectives has been the observation that commercial games are highly motivating (Garris et al., 2002; Malone, 1981), entertaining, and engaging (cf. Rideout et al., 2010). These terms are not single constructs, but they describe a host of empirically-tested factors influencing desire to play or achieve at the core task. However, the results of Wouters et al.'s (2013) meta-analysis failed to find support for the hypotheses that these factors directly influence learning. This finding may, again, be the result of methodological limitations, as long-term motivation to interact with the game is difficult to study in controlled environments. Within short studies, games that are more engaging may have more content devoted to the enjoyment of the play experience and less devoted to the actual learning task. For example, memorizing a list of spelling words may be the most efficient method to learn to spell those words, and a game using those spelling words may take more time to complete. However, trainers and educators must consider both the task and the necessary types of motivation for the learners to apply themselves to the learning. In support of this hypothesis, Habgood and Ainsworth (2011) found that when the instructional content is integrated with the game play mechanisms, these games were found to be more effective at teaching than games that did not integrate these features.

Design Features of Games

A key question in the game literature for both commercial and serious games has been, what are the key design features that account for learning? Not much empirical research has been conducted to date to identify those design features either in commercial games or in serious games. However, Sitzmann (2011) and Wouters et al. (2013) have identified in computer-based simulation games moderator variables that are hypothesized to enhance learning and motivation. These are entertainment value of the game, the instructional domain, the age of the player, the level of fidelity, whether the game was played as an individual or in a group, whether the majority of the instruction in the simulation game was active or passive, and the use of narrative. Game characteristics considered by Kapp (2012) include the following:

- Story or plot (i.e., narrative, although this has found limited support in recent meta-analyses).
- Game play used to attain mastery of learning objectives.
- Characters that are realistic enough for the learner to relate to and learn from.
- Competition, either between the learner and the game simulator or between other learners.
- Recognition and rewards based on the achievement levels attained during game play.
- Increasing levels of complexity to extend skill development and embed the learned skills.
- Challenges that build skill mastery and relevancy to the learner's job performance.
- Continual individualized feedback to reinforce correct behavior and remediate incorrect behavior.

Some of these characteristics overlap with those investigated by Sitzmann (2011) and Wouters et al. (2013). Sitzmann (2011) found a differential effect for whether the majority of the game was active or passive. Active learning is defined as reviewing materials with a human or computer tutor, participating in a discussion, or completing an assignment. Passive learning is defined as listening to a lecture, reading a textbook, or watching a video.

Strong claims have been made of the potential benefits of these types of computer games to learning, while the literature of the effectiveness of these games remains ambiguous. For example, O'Neil and Perez (2008, p.ix) noted, "While effectiveness of game environments can be documented in terms of intensity and longevity of engagement . . . as well as the commercial success of the games, there is much less solid empirical information about what learning outcomes are systematically achieved." Since 2008, there has been mounting evidence from research that serious games can enhance learning. Mayer (2011) categorizes game research into three categories: a value-added approach, which addresses how specific game features foster learning and motivation; a cognitive consequences approach, which examines what people learn from serious games; and a media comparison.

In the recent past, two meta-analytic studies on serious games have been conducted, one by Sitzmann (2011) and more recently one by Wouters et al. (2013). Both Sitzmann (2011) and Wouters et al. (2013) focused on Mayer's media comparison approach where they investigated whether people learn better from a core game versus the core game with one feature added. The rationale for the latest meta-analysis by Wouters et al. (2013) was based on the observation that previous studies on the effectiveness of games lacked scientific rigor, and that the meta-analysis by Sitzmann only looked at studies with adults on job knowledge and skills. With respect to design features it is still not clear which instructional and contextual factors and design features have an impact on the effectiveness of serious games.

Overall, these meta-analyses of the cognitive and motivational effects of serious games found that serious games produced superior performance, that is, they were 61% more effective than computer-based instruction, and that serious game players retained more than computer-based trainees, 64.06% retention in serious game players compared to 58.71% in computer-based trainees (Sitzmann, 2011). They also found that performance was even better when the serious game was supplemented by additional instruction (57.93% unsupplemented to 65.91% supplemented) (Wouters et al., 2013). Game-based education is equally effective for teaching both declarative knowledge (e.g., facts, principles, and concepts) and procedural knowledge (e.g., steps in a procedure), and the effectiveness of the games increased with multiple practice sessions, with an overall effect of 70.54% (Sitzmann, 2011; Wouters et al., 2013). They concluded that learners in serious games learned more as compared to those learners taught with conventional instruction methods, when the games were augmented with other instructional methods, when multiple training sessions were involved, and when game players worked in groups (Sitzmann, 2011; Wouters et al., 2013).

Sitzmann's (2011) goal was to review the literature on the instructional effectiveness of computer-based simulation games for teaching work-related knowledge and skills. Prior to Sitzmann (2011) and Wouters et al. (2013), studies on the effectiveness of serious games combined studies of adults and children and they included not only studies of work-related knowledge and skills but also academic subjects (e.g., geography and life on the American frontier). Finally, games are effective across demographic variables (Vogel et al., 2006).

The Navy has developed a game-based trainer to teach critical survival skills (e.g., how to fight a fire, control a flood in a compartment, and how to perform treatment and evacuation of mass causalities aboard a ship) to incoming Navy recruits. The damage control trainer (DCT) teaches decision-making, communication, and navigation skills and situation awareness. The DCT group was compared to a control group on a transfer task. Those recruits who played the DCT prior to the transfer task had 67% better situation awareness, had 80% improved communications, made 38% more correct decisions, and finished their tasks in 50% less time than the control group (Hussain, Bowers, & Blasko-Drabik, 2014).

Evidence for Commercial Serious Game-Based Training

The evidence for current commercial serious game-based training is mixed. Great hope was created by Jaeggi, Buschkuehl, Jonides, and Perrig (2008) in which training on an adaptive n-back task yielded improvements in fluid intelligence. Jaeggi et al.'s adaptive n-back task has been cited as justification for claims of cognitive enhancement in game-based training systems such as Lumosity and Cogmed. These results have recently been called into question (Redick et al., 2013), as numerous design flaws in the studies have been noted. The recent Melby-Lervåg and Hulme (2013) meta-analysis of working memory training concludes that evidence shows that training using game-based methods can lead to transfer to related tasks, but no improvement in general abilities has been found and the effects of training often dissipate with time.

Commercial game-based training systems may be taking advantage of a common misconception we have regarding our cognitive abilities. Many believe that improvement at one task is indicative of an increase in our cognitive capacity. However, much like the statistical learning discussed by Green and Bavelier (2012), people tend to learn the specifics of the training task and incrementally improve performance, and, unfortunately, transfer might not occur for tasks that are even slightly different. For instance, one might think that training on the game Tetris (Pajitnov & Pokhilko, 1984) would lead to improvements in the ability to mentally rotate objects. The evidence shows that this is in fact the case, but only for the objects actually used in the game. Mental rotation is not improved for other shapes (Sims & Mayer, 2002).

Another example is that of the n-back task, in which players are presented a sequence of stimuli and attempt to indicate when the current item matches one that is some number, n, previous. For example, a 4-back task with numbers might consist of the string "1 8 4 8 7 7 1 7 4 5 4" presented serially, one at a time, from left to right. The third 7 in the sequence should be indicated by the player, since a 7 was shown four items back. Increasing n increases the difficulty of the task. The n-back has been the focus of working memory training for some time (Jaeggi et al., 2008; Jaeggi, Buschkuehl, Perrig, & Meier, 2010; Redick et al., 2013). Many of the basic claims made by video game training systems such as Lumosity rely on a view that training the n-back improves working memory capacity. It may be that n-back training results in strategic specialization which improves performance on the n-back and n-back-like tasks, but provides no expansion of basic memory ability. Further research is needed.

Conclusions on Serious Games Research

In this chapter, we defined serious games as games designed expressly to provide educational content and instruction. We identified the role of theory in simulation games, including the input–process–outcome model, cognitive aspects of game play, and the findings on game fidelity. We examined the relations between domains, audiences, and suitability for serious games. We reviewed how narrative and motivational aspects of serious games have yet to be strongly linked to effectiveness, despite many anecdotal reports. Finally, we reviewed some evidence that serious games produce superior performance and increased retention over computer-based instruction. Overall, these findings are mixed, and it appears that in many cases, the key dimensions of serious games have yet to be identified or systematically studied to determine their bearing on effectiveness.

Conclusions and Future Research in Games

Based on emerging results reviewed in this chapter, the neurobiology of games presents a promising research frontier. The community must learn from past failures and build on successes with sound research principles. We need better understanding of core game mechanisms (e.g., style of play) and player strategies (e.g., gaming the game) affecting learning outcomes. Not all games are created equal when it comes to fostering learning and brain plasticity—some game mechanisms may be more effective than others for specific kinds of skills, which suggests that we need a research effort to identify those game dynamics that are most effective to induce learning and brain plasticity. This research could benefit from Mayer's value-added approach (2011) addressing how specific game features foster learning and motivation.

Developers need increased attention to individual differences in game design. Individual players of games may have varying ways to play a game and that may be influenced by prior experience or individual differences (e.g., neurophysiological). Game designers may want to leverage these differences. There must be greater focus on social and emotional skills. As noted by Tennyson and Jorczak (2008), games may not only impact the cognitive system but also the affective system. We need to know more about how these games impact the affective system and how they foster learning and brain plasticity.

Developers need improved game validation methodologies and benchmarks. To support recent claims of the effectiveness of commercial games for enhancing cognitive ability, systems such as Lumosity and Cogmed need objective demonstrations of their efficacy, which call for larger multisite studies that allow independent evaluation of game and intervention efficacy. Additionally, not much research has been conducted to determine the assessment of learning progress and outcomes in a game context. For example, the designer and users of a game may want to measure objectively and reliably students' game performance moment by moment, which may only include a single measurement. So the issue is, how do you measure student performance objectively and reliably when you may have only one data point?

Finally, for practical deployment, developers need sustainable and scalable publishing models for education and training, including methodology for translation research not only to document the beneficial effect of serious and commercial games but also to translate these results into commercially viable products.

Author Note

Any opinions, findings, and conclusions or recommendations expressed in this material are those of the authors and do not necessarily reflect the views of the Office of Naval Research. This material is based upon work supported by The United States Navy under Contract No. N00014-11-C-0426.

References

Activision Publishing, Inc. (2010). Call of Duty: Black Ops [Video game software]. Santa Monica, CA.

Adams, D. M., Mayer, R. E., MacNamara, A., Koenig, A., & Wainess, R. (2012). Narrative games for learning: Testing the discovery and narrative hypothesis. *Journal of Educational Psychology, 104,* 235–249.

Albanesius, C. (2010, December 27). "Call of Duty: Black Ops" gamers log 600M hours of play time. PCMag.com. Retrieved from www.pcmag.com/article2/0,2817,2374762,00.asp

Alexander, A. L., Brunyé, T., Sidman, J., & Weil, S. A. (2005, November). From gaming to training: A review of studies on fidelity, immersion, presence, and buy-in and their effects on transfer in PC-based simulations and games. *DARWARS Training Impact Group, 5,* 1–14. Retrieved from www.aptima.com/publications/2005_Alexander_Brunye_Sidman_Weil.pdf

Appelbaum, L. G., Cain, M. S., Darling, E. F., & Mitroff, S. R. (2013). Action video game playing is associated with improved visual sensitivity, but not alterations in visual sensory memory. *Attention, Perception and Psychophysics, 75*(6), 1161–1167.

Bailey, K., & West, R. (2013). The effects of an action video game on visual and affective information processing. *Brain Research, 1504,* 35–46. doi:10.1016/j.brainres.2013.02.019

Bailey, K., West, R., & Anderson, C. A. (2010). A negative association between video game experience and proactive cognitive control. *Psychophysiology, 47,* 34–42. doi:10.1111/j.1469-8986.2009.00925.x

Bavelier, D., Green, C. S., Pouget, A., & Schrater, P. (2012). Brain plasticity through the life span: Learning to learn and action video games. *Annual Review of Neuroscience, 35,* 391–416.

Bediou, B., Adams, D. M., Mayer, R. E., Green, C. S., & Bavelier, D. (in press). Meta-analysis of action video game impact on perceptual, attentional, and cognitive skills. *Psychological Bulletin.*

Boot, W. R., Kramer, A. F., Simons, D. J., Fabiani, M., & Gratton, G. (2008). The effects of video game playing on attention, memory, and executive control. *Acta Psychologica, 129,* 387–398.

Botvinick, M. M., Braver, T. S., Barch, D. M., Carter, C. S., & Cohen, J. D. (2001). Conflict monitoring and cognitive control. *Psychological Review, 108,* 624–652. doi:10.1037//0033-295X.I08.3.624

Braver, T. S. (2012). The variable nature of cognitive control: A dual mechanisms framework. *Trends in Cognitive Sciences, 16*(2), 106–113. doi:10.1016/j.tics.2011.12.010

Braver, T. S., Gray, J. R., & Burgess, G. C. (2007). Explaining the many varieties of working memory variation: Dual mechanisms of cognitive control. In A. R. A. Conway, C. Jarrold, M. J. Kane, A. Miyake, & J. N. Towse (Eds.), *Variation in working memory* (pp. 76–106). New York, NY: Oxford University Press.

Broderbund Software. (1974). The Oregon Trail [Video game software]. Eugene, OR: Author.

Broderbund Software. (1985). Where in the World Is Carmen Sandiego? [Video game software]. Eugene, OR: Author.

Clark, J. M., & Paivio, A. (1991). Dual coding theory and education. *Educational Psychology Review, 3,* 149–210.

Cohen, J. D., Forman, S. D., Braver, T. S., Casey, B. J., Servan-Schreiber, D., & Noll, D. C. (1994). Activation of the prefrontal cortex in a nonspatial working memory task with functional MRI. *Human Brain Mapping, 1,* 293–304.

Csikszentmihalyi, M. (1990). *Flow: The psychology of optimal experience.* New York, NY: Harper Perennial.

Curtis, M. T., DiazGranados, D., & Feldman, M. (2012). Judicious use of simulation technology in continuing medical education. *Journal of Continuing Education in the Health Professions, 32*(4), 255–260.

Driskell, J. E., & Dwyer, D. J. (1984). Microcomputer videogame based training. *Educational Technology, 24*(2), 11–17.

Dye, M. W. G., Green, C. S., & Bavelier, D. (2009). The development of attention skills in action video game players. *Neuropsychologia, 47,* 1780–1789.

Entertainment Software Association. (2014). *Essential facts about the computer and video game industry.* Retrieved from www.theesa.com/wp-content/uploads/2014/10/ESA_EF_2014.pdf

Garris, R., Ahlers, R., & Driskell, J. E. (2002). Games, motivation, and learning: A research and practice model. *Simulation and Gaming, 33*(4), 441–467.

Gerrig, R. J. (1993). *Experiencing narrative worlds: On the psychological activities of reading.* New Haven, CT: Yale University Press.

Graesser, A. C., Olde, B., & Klettke, B. (2002). How does the mind construct and represent stories. In M. C. Green, J. J. Strange, & T. C. Brock (Eds.), *Narrative impact: Social and cognitive foundations* (pp. 231–263). Mahwah, NJ: Erlbaum.

Gredler, M. E. (1996). Educational games and simulations: A technology in search of a (research) paradigm. In D. H. Jonassen (Ed.), *Handbook of research for educational communications and technology* (pp. 521–539). New York, NY: Macmillan.

Green, C. S., & Bavelier, D. (2003). Action video game modifies visual selective attention. *Nature, 423,* 534–537.

Green, C. S., & Bavelier, D. (2007). Action-video-game experience alters the spatial resolution of vision. *Psychological Science, 18*(1), 88–94. doi: 10.1111/j.1467-9280.2007. 01853.x

Green, C. S., & Bavelier, D. (2012). Learning, attentional control, and action video games. *Current Biology, 22*(6), R197–R206. doi:10.1016/j.cub.2012.02.012

Green, C. S., Sugarman, M. A., Medford, K., Klobusicky, E., & Bavelier, D. (2012). The effect of action video game experience on task-switching. *Computers in Human Behavior, 28,* 984–994. doi:10.1016/j.chb.2011.12.020

Habgood, M. J., & Ainsworth, S. E. (2011). Motivating children to learn effectively: Exploring the value of intrinsic integration in educational games. *Journal of the Learning Sciences, 20*(2), 169–206.

Hussain, T. S., Bowers, C., & Blasko-Drabik, H. (2014). Impact of individual game-based training on team cognitive readiness. In H. F. O'Neil, R. S. Perez, & E. L. Baker (Eds.), *Teaching and measuring cognitive readiness* (pp. 325–353). New York, NY: Springer.

Jaeggi, S. M., Buschkuehl, M., Jonides, J., & Perrig, W. J. (2008). Improving fluid intelligence with training on working memory. *Proceedings of the National Academy of Sciences of the United States of America, 105*(19), 6829–6833. doi:10.1073/pnas.0801 268105

Jaeggi, S. M., Buschkuehl, M., Perrig, W. J., & Meier, B. (2010). The concurrent validity of the N-back task as a working memory measure. *Memory, 18*(4), 394–412.

Kapp, K. M. (2012). *The gamification of learning and instruction: Game-based methods and strategies for training and education.* San Francisco: John Wiley & Sons.

Karle, J. W., Watter, S., & Shedden, J. M. (2010). Task switching in video game players: Benefits of selective attention but not resistance to proactive interference. *Acta Psychologica, 134,* 70–78. doi:10.1016/j.actpsy.2009.12.007

Lavie, N. (2005). Distracted and confused? Selective attention under load. *Trends in Cognitive Sciences, 9*(2), 75–82.

Lavie, N., Hirst, A., de Fockert, J. W., & Viding, E. (2004). Load theory of selective attention and cognitive control. *Journal of Experimental Psychology: General, 133*(3), 339–354.

Malone, T. W. (1981). What makes things fun to learn? A study of intrinsically motivating computer games. *Pipeline, 6*(2), 50.

Mané, A., & Donchin, E. (1989). The Space Fortress game. *Acta Psychologica, 71,* 17–22.

Martínez, K., Solana, A. B., Burgaleta, M., Hernández-Tamames, J. A., Álvarez-Linera, J., Román, F. J., . . . Colom, R. (2013). Changes in resting-state functionally connected parietofrontal networks after videogame practice. *Human Brain Mapping, 34,* 3143–3157.

Mayer, R. E. (2011). Multimedia learning and games. In S. Tobias & J. D. Fletcher (Eds.), *Computer games and instruction* (pp. 281–305). Amsterdam: Elsevier.

Mayer, R. E., Griffith, E., Naftaly, I., & Rothman, D. (2008). Increased interestingness of extraneous details leads to decreased learning. *Journal of Experimental Psychology: Applied, 14,* 329–339.

Melby-Lervåg, M., & Hulme, C. (2013). Is working memory training effective? A meta-analytic review. *Developmental Psychology, 49*(2), 270–291.

Miller, E. K. (2000). The prefrontal cortex and cognitive control. *Nature Reviews Neuroscience 1*, 59–65. doi:10.1038/35036228

Miller, E. K., & Cohen, J. D. (2001). An integrative theory of prefrontal cortex function. *Annual Review of Neuroscience, 24*, 167–202. doi:10.1146/annurev.neuro.24.1.167

Novak, E., Johnson, T. E., Tenenbaum, G., & Shute, V. J. (2014). Effects of an instructional gaming characteristic on learning effectiveness, efficiency, and engagement: Using a storyline for teaching basic statistical skills. *Interactive Learning Environments*, 1–16.

O'Neil, H. F., & Perez, R. S. (Eds.). (2008). *Computer games and team and individual learning.* Oxford, UK: Elsevier.

Pajitnov, A., & Pokhilko, V. (1984). Tetris Multiple Platforms [Video game software]. Moscow, Russia.

Prensky, M. (2001). Digital natives, digital immigrants part 1. *On the Horizon, 9*(5), 1–6.

Redick, T. S., Shipstead, Z., Harrison, T. L., Hicks, K. L., Fried, D. E., Hambrick, D. Z., . . . Engle, R. W. (2013). No evidence of intelligence improvement after working memory training: A randomized, placebo-controlled study. *Journal of Experimental Psychology: General, 142*(2), 359–379.

Rideout, V. J., Foehr, U. G., & Roberts, D. F. (2010). *Generation M2: Media in the lives of 8- to 18-year-olds.* Menlo Park, CA: Henry J. Kaiser Family Foundation.

Rovio Entertainment. (2009). Angry Birds iOS [Video game software]. Espoo, Finland.

Rowe, J. P. (2013). *Narrative-centered tutorial planning with concurrent Markov decision processes* (Unpublished doctoral dissertation). North Carolina State University, Raleigh, NC.

Sims, V. K., & Mayer, R. E. (2002). Domain specificity of spatial expertise: The case of video game players. *Applied Cognitive Psychology, 16*(1), 97–115.

Sitzmann, T. (2011). A meta-analytic examination of the instructional effectiveness of computer-based simulation games. *Personnel Psychology, 64*(2), 489–528.

Strasburger, V. C., Jordan, A. B., & Donnerstein, E. (2010). Health effects of media on children and adolescents. *Pediatrics, 125*(4), 756–767.

Tennyson, R. D., & Jorczak, R. L. (2008). A conceptual framework for the empirical study of instructional games. In H. F. O'Neil & R. S. Perez (Eds.), *Computer games and team and individual learning* (pp. 3–20). Amsterdam: Elsevier.

Thorndike, E. L. (1906). *Principles of teaching.* New York, NY: A. G. Seller.

Tobias, S., & Fletcher, J. D. (2007). What research has to say about designing computer games for learning. *Educational Technology, 47*(5), 20–29.

Vogel, J. J., Vogel, D. S., Cannon-Bowers, J., Bowers, C. A., Muse, K., & Wright, M. (2006). Computer gaming and interactive simulations for learning: A meta-analysis. *Journal of Educational Computing Research, 34*, 229–243.

White, B. Y. (1984). Designing computer games to help physics students understand Newton's laws of motion. *Cognition and Instruction, 1*(1), 69–108.

Wouters, P., van Nimwegen, C., van Oostendorp, H., & van der Spek, E. D. (2013). A meta-analysis of the cognitive and motivational effects of serious games. *Journal of Educational Psychology, 105*(2), 249–265.

Yeung, N., Bogacz, R., Holroyd, C. B., & Cohen, J. D. (2004). Detection of synchronized oscillations in the electroencephalogram: An evaluation of methods. *Psychophysiology, 41*, 822–832. doi:10.1111/j.1469-8986.2004.00239.x

Yeung, N., Ralph, J., & Nieuwenhuis, S. (2007). Drink alcohol and dim the lights: The impact of cognitive deficits on medial frontal cortex function. *Cognitive, Affective, & Behavioral Neuroscience, 7*(4), 347–355.

PART III

Cognitive/Motivational Issues

9

THE ROLE OF METACOGNITION IN STEM GAMES AND SIMULATIONS

Richard E. Mayer

Introduction

Purpose

The purpose of this chapter is to review the literature on the role of metacognitive strategies in games and simulations and to suggest a research agenda. The focus is on metacognitive strategies that improve how people learn. The chapter begins with a definition of metacognition, rationale for the educational importance of metacognitive strategies, and rationale for the potential of educational games and simulations as a venue for incorporating and teaching metacognitive strategies. Then the chapter reviews research on identifying and measuring metacognitive strategies for learning, research on teaching of metacognitive strategies in computer-based environments, and research on promoting metacognition in games and simulations. The chapter concludes by suggesting an agenda for research on the role of metacognitive strategies in educational games and simulations.

What Is Metacognition?

Metacognition refers to awareness and control of one's own cognitive processing (Mayer, 2001, 2008). When metacognition is applied to a learning situation, it depends on three kinds of knowledge as summarized in Table 9.1—metacognitive beliefs, metacognitive strategies, and cognitive strategies.

As shown in the first two lines of Table 9.1, it is useful to distinguish between metacognitive strategies and metacognitive beliefs. Metacognitive beliefs for learning refers to people's beliefs of how they process information, their own strengths and weaknesses in processing information, their current level of

TABLE 9.1 Three Kinds of Knowledge Involved in Metacognition

Type	Definition	Example
Metacognitive beliefs	Beliefs about how one learns, one's strengths and weaknesses as a learner, and the demands of learning tasks	Believing you need to work hard to understand complicated lessons
Metacognitive strategies	Methods for selecting, monitoring, managing, and evaluating cognitive strategies during learning	Knowing when to outline and assessing how well outlining is helping you learn
Cognitive strategies	General methods for how to do something	Outline a passage

proficiency, and the demands of various tasks. Examples of metacognitive beliefs for learning tasks include thinking, "I learn better from graphics than from words" or "I can learn math if I work hard enough" or "I need to take notes when I read textbooks." Metacognitive beliefs are related to epistemological beliefs, that is, beliefs about the nature of knowledge and how learning works (Hofer & Pintrich, 2002) and self-efficacy beliefs, that is, beliefs about one's capacity to perform a task (Schunk, 1991).

Metacognitive strategies for learning refers to people's strategies for planning, monitoring, managing, and evaluating their cognitive activity during learning. Planning involves selecting appropriate cognitive strategies and allocating sufficient resources for applying them. Monitoring involves gauging how well one comprehends the material and detecting any need for adjustments. Managing refers to coordinating appropriate cognitive strategies during learning. Evaluating refers to assessing the overall process and product of learning. Examples of metacognitive strategies for learning tasks include thinking, "I did not understand the sentence I just read so I better read it again" or "That material is not important for my purposes so I will ignore it." Metacognitive strategies are related to self-regulation, that is, the learner's ability to take responsibility for his or her own learning, including planning, goal setting, self-monitoring, and self-assessment (Cannon-Bowers & Bowers, 2010; Winne, 2010).

The focus of this review is on the second aspect of metacognition, namely, metacognitive strategies for cognitive processing during learning. In the context of a typical learning task, such as learning from a multimedia lesson, metacognitive strategies include determining what is important, judging how well one understands the material, identifying anything that needs to be clarified, recognizing how the material relates to one's prior knowledge, monitoring one's progress toward a learning goal, monitoring the effectiveness of the learning strategy one is using, and determining whether one should use a different learning strategy. In the context of performing a problem-solving task, such as finding information about a medical problem on the Internet, metacognitive strategies include gathering relevant information, judging the value of information, and integrating information.

As shown in the last two lines of Table 9.1, it is useful to distinguish between two kinds of strategies—*cognitive strategies* for how to do something and *metacognitive strategies* for how to choose and manage cognitive strategies. In short, cognitive strategies focus on knowing what to do (such as outlining a passage or rereading a confusing sentence) and metacognitive strategies focus on determining when to do it and on judging how well it is working (Anderson et al., 2001; Mayer, 2001). Instruction and training generally focus on facts, concepts, and procedures, which are useful for performing routine tasks; however, when the goal is to help people become more effective learners and problem solvers, the instructional focus needs to be broadened to include cognitive and metacognitive strategies. In short, people may learn appropriate facts, concepts, and procedures but not know when and how to use them in learning and performing. The missing elements in their knowledge are cognitive and metacognitive strategies for learning.

Drawing from research in cognitive science, Mayer (2008) distinguishes among five kinds of knowledge: *facts*—factual knowledge describing elements in the world; *concepts*—models, categories, schemas, or principles; *procedures*—a step-by-step process; *strategies*—a general method; and *beliefs*—thoughts about learning. This taxonomy maps nicely onto the more traditional analysis of learning outcomes into *knowledge* (which corresponds to facts and concepts), *skills* (which corresponds to procedures and strategies), and *attitudes* (which corresponds to beliefs). It also maps onto Anderson et al.'s (2001) revision of Bloom's taxonomy, which proposes four types of knowledge: *factual knowledge* (corresponding to facts), *conceptual knowledge* (corresponding to concepts), *procedural knowledge* (corresponding to procedures), and *metacognitive knowledge* (corresponding to strategies and beliefs). In this chapter, the focus is on an aspect of this last kind of knowledge— metacognitive strategies.

Rationale for a Focus on Metacognitive Strategies

Metacognitive strategies are essential for a student to become a self-regulated learner, that is, a learner who takes responsibility for their own learning (Winne, 2010). However, many students lack well-developed metacognitive skills, perhaps because metacognitive strategies are not a central focus of school curricula. For example, in a report published by the U.S. Institute of Education Sciences, Pashler et al. (2007) recognized the central role of metacognition in learning:

> Psychological research has documented the fact that accurately assessing one's degree of learning is not something that comes easily to our species, and fostering this ability is a useful, albeit neglected, component of education.
> (p. 1)

In short, the rationale for teaching of metacognitive strategies is that they represent a crucial set of skills that are underemphasized in many curricula.

We expect people to be able to learn, but we rarely provide them with sufficient guidance in how to be an effective learner. We expect people to be able to apply what they have learned, but we rarely provide them with sufficient guidance on how to be an effective problem solver. In short, metacognitive strategies for learning and problem solving are part of the hidden curriculum—knowledge we want students to learn but often do not teach them. This observation helped spur an interest in teaching of learning and problem-solving strategies that reached prominence in the 1980s (Mayer & Wittrock, 2006; O'Neil, 1978; Pressley & Levin, 1983; Pressley & Woloshyn, 1995; Weinstein & Mayer, 1985). The next step in this work is to broaden the array of 21st century skills to include metacognitive strategies—that is strategies for selecting, managing, monitoring, and evaluating cognitive strategies (Pellegrino & Hilton, 2012).

Rationale for a Focus on Games and Simulations

What is the best way to help people develop the kinds of cognitive and metacognitive strategies they need to be effective learners and problem solvers? One promising approach is to leverage the motivating features of educational games and simulations as a venue for incorporating and teaching of cognitive and metacognitive strategies (Honey & Hilton, 2011; Mayer, 2014; O'Neil & Perez, 2008; Tobias & Fletcher, 2011). Educational researchers have recognized the motivational properties of computer-based video games: "Video games used for entertainment seem inherently motivating to game players" (Tennyson & Jorczak, 2008, p. 3). Based on the popularity of commercially available games, proponents argue that games and simulations are motivating so learners are more likely to choose to learn with them and to persist longer in learning with them as compared to conventional media (Gee, 2003; Pensky, 2001). Games offer an informal learning environment that may be more appealing to learners who have not been successful in formal learning environments, and games can be used to supplement and extend formal learning by using time that would otherwise not be allocated to learning activity (Johnson & Mayer, 2010; Mayer & Johnson, 2010).

Although many strong claims have been made for the potential educational benefits of computer games, these claims are often not accompanied by convincing evidence from rigorous scientific research (Hayes, 2005; Honey & Hilton, 2011; Mayer, 2011b, 2014; O'Neil & Perez, 2008; Tobias & Fletcher, 2011). Some critics question whether games can be used effectively to promote learning or whether they are worth the extra cost (Clark, Yates, Early, & Moulton, 2010). To guide the design of educationally effective computer games and simulations, it would be useful to have adequate research evidence concerning which game features promote learning for which kinds of learners under which conditions for which kinds of learning objectives (Mayer & Johnson, 2010; Shen & O'Neil, 2008; Tennyson & Jorczak, 2008). For example, O'Neil and Perez (2008, p. ix) noted, "While the effectiveness of game environments can be documented in terms of intensity and longevity of engagement . . . as well as the commercial success of games, there is much less solid empirical information about what learning outcomes are systematically achieved." In another recent review of game research, Hannafin and Vermillion (2008, p. 215) observed, "Games are very motivating and have tremendous potential in education, but despite a rapidly growing research base, there is yet insufficient evidence to draw definitive conclusions." Similarly, in another review of game research, Young et al. (2012, p. 61) concluded, "Many educationally interesting games exist, yet evidence for their impact on student achievement is slim."

The history of research on the instructional effectiveness of games is somewhat disappointing. In spite of a history of scholarly writing on the educational potential of game playing dating back to Abt's (1970) classic book, *Serious Games*, as well as a small but growing research base on more recent computer games (Gredler, 2001; Hayes, 2005; Mayer, 2014; O'Neil & Perez, 2008; Raessens & Goldstein, 2005; Rieber, 2005; Tobias & Fletcher, 2011; Vorderer & Bryant, 2006), there remains a strong need for evidence-based principles for the design of educational games and simulations. Perez (2008, pp. 302–303) succinctly summarized the existing research literature on the science of game design: "There is a lack of a pedagogical base to guide game design." In short, O'Neil and Perez (2008, p. ix) concluded that "there is almost no guidance for game designers and developers on how to design games that facilitate learning."

In short, educational games and simulations offer an enticing but unproven venue for teaching of educationally relevant material, including cognitive and metacognitive strategies. Although a few studies have examined the role of metacognition in game-based training (Orvis, Horn, & Belanich, 2009), there is a need for research that focuses on the effectiveness of games for teaching and prompting metacognitive learning strategies in learners.

Research Review

This section reviews the small but growing base of empirical research and theory on metacognitive strategies in computer-based environments (Azevedo & Aleven, 2013; Greene & Azevedo, 2010), while recognizing the larger literature on metacognition in a variety of settings (Baumeister & Vohs, 2004; Boekaerts, Pintrich, & Zeidner, 2000; Hacker, Dunlosky, & Graesser, 2009; Hartman, 2001; Waters & Schneider, 2010). First, this section reviews research on identifying and measuring metacognitive strategies for learning; second, it reviews research on teaching or prompting metacognitive strategies for learning; and third, it reviews research on designing games and simulations that promote metacognition.

Identifying and Measuring Metacognitive Strategies for Learning

A first step is to identify potentially important metacognitive strategies and techniques for measuring them. Overall, researchers have focused mainly on metacognition for academic learning and have developed three kinds of approaches to measuring metacognitive strategies: self-report surveys, thinking aloud protocols, and online activity during learning (Schraw, 2010).

The most common technique for measuring metacognition is self-report inventories. Table 9.2 presents three commonly recognized types of metacognitive judgments that learners can make concerning their learning (adapted from Graesser, D'Mello, & Person, 2009; Schneider, 2010; Schraw, 2009). Metacognitive survey items may be presented as statements to be rated or as items on a checklist. When they are presented in the form of a prediction of how well the learner expects to do on a test, such as asking whether or not the learner would be able to solve a given problem, they are a subtype of judgment of learning (JOL) or feeling of knowing (FOK) that can be called *calibration of performance* items. Schraw (2009) has noted these kinds of calibration judgments can be made before testing (proscriptive), during testing (concurrent), or after testing (retrospective).

Another widely used approach on metacognition surveys involves questions about strategy use during learning, such as those contained in the Motivated Strategies for Learning Questionnaire (MSLQ) developed by Pintrich and De Groot (1990). On the MSLQ, students are asked to rate on a 7-point scale ranging from 1 (*not at all true of me*) to 7 (*very true of me*) for questions such as, "I ask myself questions to make sure I know the material I have been studying" or "When I'm reading I stop once in a while to go over what I have read." Items on self-

TABLE 9.2 Measuring How Well Learners Assess Their Learning

Type of judgment	When	Description
Ease of learning (EOL)	Judging how hard it will be to learn some material (before learning)	"How hard will it be to learn the terms in this table?"
Judgments of learning (JOL)	Recognizing how well one learned or predicting how well one will perform (during or after learning)	"How many of the terms in this table will you be able to define?"
Feeling of knowing (FOK)	Recognizing trouble in learning or predicting trouble in performing (during or after learning)	"Which terms will you not be able to define?"

regulation and strategy use constitute self-regulated learning strategies and account for two of the five scales on the test. Importantly, self-reported use of these self-regulated learning strategies were found to correlate with academic performance (Pintrich & De Groot, 1990).

In his pioneering analysis of metacognitive learning strategies, Schoenfeld (1987) proposed cognitive processing such as planning, checking, monitoring, selecting, revising, and evaluating. Research shows that students' self-reported use of these kinds of metacognitive strategies is positively related to successful learning outcomes (Koedinger, Aleven, Roll, & Baker, 2009; Pintrich, 2004).

Tobias and Everson (2009) distinguished among four types of metacognitive processes:

- *monitoring knowledge*—judging what one has learned and what one needs to learn;
- *selecting strategies*—using strategies intended to promote learning;
- *evaluating learning*—judging how well one is learning; and
- *planning*—developing and monitoring a plan for learning.

In particular, they developed the knowledge monitoring assessment (KMA) to assess how well students could distinguish between what they know and what they do not know (or which problems they have learned to solve and which problems they have not learned to solve). After instruction in mathematics, students were shown a series of math problems and asked to predict whether or not they could solve them. Pintrich, Wolters, and Baxter's (2000) review of metacognitive assessment instruments found that KMA had high predictive validity, and Tobias and Everson (2009) reviewed additional evidence. Winne and Muis (2011) examined statistical metrics that best express judgment accuracy.

A second commonly used measurement technique is thinking aloud protocols. Table 9.3 lists the names and examples of metacognitive statements frequently made by students trained in self-regulated learning as they learned from a hypermedia lesson on the circulatory system, as adapted from a pioneering study by Azevedo and Cromley (2004). Students were asked to think aloud during a 45-minute online learning episode, and the resulting statements were coded into categories such as shown in the table. The 14 metacognitive statements listed in the table represent an important starting point for identifying potential meta-cognitive strategies for learning that could be taught in game-like environments.

In a review, Azevedo, Moos, Johnson, and Chauncey (2010) reported that most concurrent thinking aloud comments involve learning strategies (77% of comments) such as previewing, rereading, summarizing, and note-taking, whereas spontaneous comments about planning (5% of comments) and monitoring (16%) are less common. When monitoring does occur, the most common comments concern feeling of knowing or judgment of learning.

TABLE 9.3 Metacognitive Strategies for Learning (adapted from Azevedo & Cromley, 2004)

Metacognitive component	Example
Planning	
Developing a plan	"First I'll look around to see the structure of the environment, and then I'll go to specific sections . . ."
Activating prior knowledge	". . . I vaguely remember learning about the role of blood in high school."
Monitoring	
Recognizing successful comprehension	". . . I'm starting to get it . . ."
Recognizing unsuccessful comprehension	"I don't know this stuff . . ."
Posing a question	"What do I know from this?"
Monitoring progress	"Those were our goals, we accomplished them."
Using Strategies	
Taking notes	"I'm going to write that under heart."
Summarizing	"This says that white blood cells are involved in destroying foreign bodies."
Drawing	"I'm trying to imitate the diagram as best as possible."
Reading notes	[Looks at notes.] "Carry blood away. Arteries—away."
Making inferences	[Looks at diagram.] "So the blood . . . goes from the atrium to the ventricle . . ."
Managing Task Demands	
Managing time	"I'm skipping over that section because 45 minutes is too short to get into all the details."
Seeking help	"Do you want me to give you a more detailed answer?"
Enjoying	
Expressing interest	"This stuff is interesting."

In another review, Winne and Nesbit (2009) listed several major challenges to successful metacognition (for which I have created labels), including:

- *judging learning*—"learners are poor judges of what they know" (p. 262);
- *using strategies*—"learners are unschooled about tools for studying effectively" (p. 263);

- *having productive beliefs*—"learners' belief systems can impede productive self-regulated learning" (p. 263);
- *benefiting from errors*—"learners may not be able to benefit from errors" (p. 265); and
- *seeking help*—"learners don't often seek help usefully" (p. 265).

Winne (2010) noted that thinking aloud protocols—both concurrent (i.e., during learning) and retrospective (i.e., after learning)—may be able to provide information not available in self-report inventories. However, thinking aloud protocols are more difficult to collect and may be so intrusive that they affect the learning process. Furthermore, they are not scored in real time and thus cannot influence timely formative assessment.

A third way to measuring a learner's metacognitive processing during learning is to examine log files of a learner's interactions with an online instructional system. Winne and Nesbit (2009, p. 266) noted: "Software that logs learners' interactions as they use the software's features in learning has become common." This approach has been used successfully with intelligent tutoring systems to examine how students seek and use help information or how students detect and correct errors (Aleven, Roll, McLaren, & Koedinger, 2010; Koedinger et al., 2009). In examining online logs of computer-based tutoring and transcripts of human-to-human tutoring, Graesser et al. (2009, p. 365) reported that students typically ask metacognitive questions that attempt to confirm or verify their knowledge (e.g., "Isn't this Newton's second law?"), request definitions of terms (e.g., "What is a Newton?"), or ask how to perform a procedure (e.g., "How do you get this square root?").

Teaching or Prompting Metacognitive Strategies for Learning

The previous section shows that significant progress is being made in identifying and measuring metacognitive processes that are related to academic performance, particularly on reading comprehension tasks. An important next step is to develop instructional programs that help students learn effective metacognitive skills and to design instructional environments that prime appropriate metacognitive processing in learners during learning.

In a landmark experimental study, Azevedo and Cromley (2004) asked students to learn about the human circulatory system in a computer-based hypermedia environment. Some students (control group) received no pretraining whereas other students (trained group) received 30 minutes of metacognitive training before the learning task, focusing on the processing needed for planning, monitoring, using strategies, and judging task difficulty and demands. The trained group demonstrated better metacognitive processing during learning and greater learning gains.

In another experimental study, human tutors used a script to provide prompts for metacognitive processing as students learned about the human circulatory system in a hypermedia environment (Azevedo, Moos, Greene, Winters, & Cromley, 2008). The prompts focused on using learning strategies such as summarizing, coordinating information sources, rereading, hypothesizing, control of context, judgment of learning, drawing, using mnemonic devices, taking notes, and reading notes; and on metacognitive monitoring such as activating prior knowledge, setting goals, and time and effort planning. Students who received prompts from human tutors showed more effective metacognitive processing during learning, achieved higher post-test scores, and developed a more sophisticated mental model of the human circulatory system than did students who were not given prompts. In additional studies, including adaptive scaffolding of metacognitive processing during learning of science topics in a hypermedia environment resulted in improvements in metacognitive processing during learning and greater gains in learning outcomes (Azevedo, Cromley, & Seibert, 2004; Azevedo, Cromley, Winters, Moos, & Greene, 2005).

In addition to human tutors, intelligent tutoring systems have been developed to teach metacognitive processes, such as MetaTutor, iSTART, SEEK, iDRIVE, and AutoTutor (Graesser & McNamara, 2010). MetaTutor is an intelligent tutoring system that teaches students to use 13 learning strategies in the context of hypermedia-based learning about how the human body works (Azevedo et al., 2010). On-screen agents help guide the phases of planning (such as setting goals), monitoring (such as judgments of learning, feeling of knowing, content evaluation, monitoring the effectiveness of strategies, and monitoring progress toward goals) and applying learning strategies (such as identifying relevant information, taking notes, drawing tables or figures, rereading, elaborating, making inferences, and coordinating information sources). iStart trains readers to engage in self-explanation, including monitoring comprehension, paraphrasing, making bridging inferences, making predictions, and elaborating (McNamara, O'Reilly, Rowe, Boonthum, & Levinstein, 2007). SEEK encourages students to engage in metacognitive processing as they search web pages on plate tectonics, by asking students to rate and describe the reliability and usefulness of information on a site (Halpern, 2002). In iDRIVE learners observe online agents discuss how to learn a scientific topic by asking deep questions (Gholson & Craig, 2006). Rather than providing direct instruction or examples of how to learn in a computer-based environment, AutoTutor engages the learner in a dialog about an academic topic that is intended to stimulate deep thinking and thereby promote metacognitive processes in the learner (Graesser, Penumasta, Ventura, Cai, & Hu, 2007). Intelligent tutoring systems that are sensitive to the learner's metacognition have been shown to be effective in improving school achievement (Pane, Griffin, McCaffrey, & Karam, 2014). What is now needed is a research base of rigorous controlled experiments documenting which features of these tutors are effective in promoting learning.

A promising initial effort to establish a research base on what works with computer tutors for metacognition is summarized by Koedinger et al. (2009). They report strong evidence that cognitive tutors can be successful in prompting learners to engage in self-explanation and error self-correction, and that student learning outcomes in computer-based environments improve as a result. They also report less success in improving learning outcomes with online tutors that prompt learners to not game the system or to seek help when needed.

Fostering Metacognitive Strategies With STEM Computer Games and Simulations

Based on recent reviews by Mayer (2014; in press), this chapter examines six principles for the design of metacognitive aids to learning with games and simulations: self-explanation principle and reflection principle, which are intended as aids for monitoring comprehension during learning; feedback principle and guided practice principle, which are intended as aids for managing cognitive processing during learning; and realism and personalization principles, which are intended as aids for designing pedagogical agents that give metacognitive advice. These six principles are summarized in Table 9.4.

Self-Explanation Principle

The self-explanation principle is that people learn better from games and simulations when they are asked to select an explanation for their moves (Mayer, in press). This principle is based on the idea that the act of self-explaining causes students to engage in the metacognitive processes of evaluating and repairing their knowledge. Although much of the research base for self-explanation comes from research with paper-based lessons (Fonseca & Chi, 2011) or multimedia lessons

TABLE 9.4 Six Principles for Fostering Metacognitive Strategies With STEM Computer Games and Simulations

Principle	Implementation
Self-explanation	Ask learners to select an explanation for their moves in a game.
Reflection	Ask learners to relate their game experience to underlying principles of the game.
Feedback	Provide explanative feedback for correct moves in a game.
Guided practice	Provide advice during game play.
Realism	Pedagogical agents do not need to be perceptually realistic, unless realism is part of the instructional objective.
Personalization	Pedagogical agents should use conversational or polite wording.

(Roy & Chi, 2005), complementary research documents the effectiveness of self-explanation prompts in computer-based science games (Johnson & Mayer, 2010; Mayer & Johnson, 2010; Moreno & Mayer, 2005; van der Meij & de Jong, 2011) and computer-based mathematics games (O'Neil et al., 2014).

For example, in the Circuit Game college students play a 10-level computer game about how electrical circuits work, in which they must solve circuit problems either with or without being asked to explain each move by selecting an explanation from a menu. On an embedded transfer test in the game's final level, the self-explanation group performed better on solving new circuit problems than did the control group (Johnson & Mayer, 2010; Mayer & Johnson, 2010). Importantly, the effects of self-explanation prompts were strongest when students were asked to select an explanation from an on-screen menu rather than to type the explanation into a textbox, perhaps because typing was too disruptive to game flow (Johnson & Mayer, 2010).

In the Design-a-Plant simulation game, high school and college students learn about environmental science by traveling to a distant planet that has specified environmental conditions (such as heavy rainfall and winds) and being asked by an on-screen character named Herman-the-Bug to choose the roots, stem, and leaves of a plant that could survive there. Students performed better on a transfer test if they were asked to generate explanations for their correct choices during the game (Moreno & Mayer, 2005).

Similarly, high school students who played a frog-leaping game intended to teach logical reasoning performed better on a problem-solving transfer test if they had received specific prompts during the game to explain their moves and monitor their progress (Lee & Chen, 2009). Self-explanation prompts also resulted in improved performance on a computer-based simulation intended to teach physics (van der Meij & de Jong, 2011). In a computer simulation game intended to teach fraction arithmetic, elementary school students learned more efficiently when they answered focused self-explanation prompts (O'Neil et al., 2014). Overall, there is promising initial evidence that adding self-explanation prompts to STEM computer games and simulations can improve learning.

Reflection Principle

The reflection principle is that people learn better from games and simulations when they are prompted before the game to reflect on underlying principles during game play (Mayer, in press). The prompts are intended to encourage the learner to reflect on the principles that underlie the game. The reflection principle is based on prompts given before the game whereas the self-explanation principle is based on prompts given during the game. The reflection principle is an extension of work showing the benefits of reflection activities with multimedia presentations (Moreno & Mayer, 2010).

For example, Fiorella and Mayer (2012) asked college students to play the Circuit Game. In one experiment, the reflection group was given a printed list of general principles about electrical circuits before the game and was asked to verify each one while playing, and in another experiment the reflection group was given a printed list containing the beginning of each principle before the game and was asked to select words to complete each principle while playing the game. In both experiments, the reflection group outperformed the control group, which received no reflection sheets, on a problem-solving transfer test.

Additional support comes from a study by White and Frederiksen (1998) in which students learned better from a physics simulation game if they were asked to define the underlying principles of the game after completing the game. Overall, there is encouraging initial evidence for the idea that games can be more effective when students are asked to engage in reflection activities.

Feedback Principle

The feedback principle is that people learn better from games and simulations when they are given explanations for correct moves. Research on the benefits of explanative feedback—an explanation of why an answer is correct—has a long history in educational psychology as one of the most powerful instructional techniques (Hattie & Gan, 2011). The rationale is that feedback prompts learners to reassess and modify their thinking.

In the Circuit Game, described in a previous section, students performed better on a problem-solving post-test if they received an on-screen explanation of the correct solution for each problem they attempted (Mayer & Johnson, 2010). In the Design-a-Plant Game, described in a previous section, students performed better on a transfer test if they received explanative feedback from Herman-the-Bug showing how the appropriate roots, stem, and leaves allow the plant to grow in the planet's environment (Moreno, 2004; Moreno & Mayer, 2005). In a computer-based simulation called the Bunny Game, elementary school students learned to add and subtract signed numbers better if they received explanative feedback after each answer in which they saw an on-screen bunny move along a number line (Moreno & Mayer, 1999). Rieber, Tzeng, and Tribble (2004) found that students who learned about the laws of motion with a computer-based simulation performed better on a post-test if they received graphical feedback that explained the motion of objects in the simulation. Overall, there is some encouraging initial support for including explanative feedback in computer games and simulations.

Guided Practice Principle

A related principle for managing cognitive processing during learning is the guided practice principle: People learn better from games and simulations when they are given metacognitive guidance during game play (Mayer, in press). This principle is based on the idea that novices need guidance in discovery learning environments, such as exploring a new game or simulation. The issue of how much guidance to provide during discovery learning has a long and contentious history (de Jong, 2005; Kirschner, Sweller, & Clark, 2006; Mayer, 2004), but preliminary research suggests that students learn better when metacognitive guidance is provided during learning in the form of giving advice or relevant information.

For example, Leutner (1993) asked students to play a farming simulation game either with or without occasional online advice from a character in the game. Students who received the advice performed much better on a post-test about the principles of erosion as compared to students who did not receive advice. Similarly, Biswas, Leelawong, Schwartz, Vye, and The Teachable Agents Group at Vanderbilt (2005) asked students to learn about river ecosystems through interacting with a simulation game called Betty's Brain. Students who received advice from an on-screen agent and relevant information from Betty performed better on a transfer test than those who were free to learn on their own. Neulight, Kafai, Kao, Foley, and Galas (2007) found that students who played a simulation game about infectious diseases improved their conceptual understanding more if they also received direct instruction related to infectious disease. In contrast, middle school students played a math game based on an aunt and uncle's remodeling business either with or without occasional advice from an on-screen character, but in this case the advice group performed about the same as the no advice group on a math post-test in the context of a different game (Van Eck & Dempsey, 2003). Overall, metacognitive advice appears to be a potentially useful addition to computer games and simulations, at least in some situations.

Realism Principle

Sometimes advice, feedback, and guidance are provided by an on-screen pedagogical agent within the game or simulation. The realism principle is that people do not learn better from pedagogical agents who give metacognitive advice in games and simulations when realism is increased (Mayer, in press). That is, pedagogical agents who provide metacognitive advice are not necessarily more effective when they are rendered with perceptual detail. Realism (or a sense of presence) in a game or simulation is not expected to aid learning if a high level of perceptual detail is not needed for learning the academic content. This principle is consistent with research on the role of realism for illustrations in multimedia presentations (Clark & Mayer, 2011).

For example, students did not learn better in the Design-a-Plant Game when it was rendered in virtual reality with a head-mounted display rather than on a desktop computer (Moreno and Mayer, 2002). In some cases, students learn just as well from games and simulations when the agent's image is not even on the screen (Mayer, Dow, & Mayer, 2003; Moreno, Mayer, Spires, & Lester, 2001).

Although realism does not help when it is not relevant to the instructional goal, realism may be useful for simulations that correspond to the to-be-learned task such as piloting an aircraft or performing surgery (Clark & Mayer, 2011; Hayes & Singer, 1989; Honey & Hilton, 2011).

Personalization Principle

The personalization principle is that people learn better from games and simulations when a pedagogical agent uses polite or conversational wording to give metacognitive advice (Mayer, in press). Consistent with research on multimedia learning (Mayer, 2005, 2009), personalization in games and simulations is intended to prime learners to try harder to make sense of their learning experience.

One line of research shows that students perform better on a transfer test if they play the Design-A-Plant Game with an on-screen agent who uses conversational wording rather than formal wording (Moreno & Mayer, 2000, 2004). Another line of research shows that students learn better in an industrial engineering simulation game called Virtual Factory when the on-screen agent uses polite wording to give advice and feedback (Wang et al., 2008). Overall, there is some support for using conversational wording in providing metacognitive advice.

Although there is not yet a substantial base of research on teaching metacognitive strategies with games (Orvis et al., 2009), there is some promising evidence that students can improve spatial cognition skills by playing computer-based action games or puzzle games that require repeated performance of the target skills (Feng, Spence, & Pratt, 2007; Green & Bavelier, 2003, 2006, 2007; Mayer, 2011b, 2014; Sims & Mayer, 2002) and that students can improve their performance skills by interacting with simulations of the task environment that include sufficient guidance (de Jong, 2005). These two promising lines of video game research suggest that teaching of metacognitive skills may be best achieved when the learner has repeated opportunities to engage in the to-be-learned strategies within an authentic task environment and when appropriate guidance is provided.

Toward a Research Agenda

This section outlines three genres of games research and three types of research questions involved in developing a research agenda for examining how to design effective games and simulations involving metacognitive strategies.

Three Genres of Game Research

As shown in Table 9.5, Mayer (2011b, 2014) and Mayer and Johnson (2010) have distinguished three genres of game research: value-added research, cognitive consequences research, and media comparison research. Although each genre can

TABLE 9.5 Three Genres of Game Research

Genre	Definition	Example
Value added	Determining which features of a game or simulation affect learning	Do people learn better when self-explanation prompts are added to a game or simulation?
Cognitive consequences	Determining the effects of playing an off-the-shelf game or simulation	Do people improve in creative thinking after playing a creativity game repeatedly?
Media comparison	Determining whether people learn better from playing a game or simulation rather than from conventional media	Do people learn metacognitive strategies better from playing a game or viewing a PowerPoint presentation?

contribute to the research base, the value-added research warrants particular attention because it has the most relevance for instructional designers. The goal of value-added research is a collection of design principles specifying which features improve learning of cognitive and metacognitive strategies in game and simulation environments, as well as boundary conditions such as whether the feature works better for certain kinds of learners.

Three Types of Research Questions

As shown in Table 9.6, in carrying out value-added research, researchers can ask three kinds of questions: what works, when does it work, and how does it work (Mayer, 2011a). Given the preliminary nature of the field, a reasonable research approach is to build an evidence base concerning the first question—that is, determining which instructional features are effective in promoting learning metacognitive strategies with games and simulations. The consensus among educational researchers is that the research method should be appropriate for answering the research question (Shavelson & Towne, 2002). When the goal of research is to determine what works—that is, the effectiveness of an instructional method—the most appropriate research method is an experimental comparison (Phye, Robinson, & Levin, 2005; Schneider, Carnoy, Kilpatrick, Schmidt, & Shavelson, 2007; Shavelson & Towne, 2002). For example, Schneider et al. (2007, p. 5) note "the randomized field trial is the best design for making causal inferences about the effectiveness of educational programs and practices." The major criteria for experimental comparisons are *experimental control* (i.e., experimental and control groups receive identical treatment except for one feature), *random assignment* (i.e., learners are randomly assigned to groups), and *appropriate measures* (i.e., for each group the mean, standard deviation, and sample size are reported for a relevant measure of learning) (Mayer, 2011a).

TABLE 9.6 Three Types of Game Research Questions

Question	Example	Research method
What works?	Do people learn better when self-explanation prompts are added to game?	Experimental comparison
When does it work?	Does adding self-explanation prompts work better for low-knowledge learners?	Factorial experimental comparison
How does it work?	How does adding self-explanation prompts affect cognitive processing during learning?	Observation, interview, or questionnaire

As an evidence base develops it is also useful to determine the boundary conditions for instructional effects, as indicated by the second question about when a feature has an instructional effect. In this situation, a factorial experimental design is appropriate in which the control and treatment conditions are given to two or more kinds of learners (such as low-knowledge versus high-knowledge learners). The goal is to determine whether the effects of the instructional feature are stronger for one kind of learner than another, for example.

Finally, as indicated in the third question, it is useful to collect converging evidence concerning the mechanisms that cause instructional effects, such as differences in cognitive processing during learning. To answer this question, observational studies are helpful such as analyzing performance using activity logs of every learner keystroke, analyzing performance on embedded tests, asking for self-reports of cognitive processing either during learning or after learning, or using online physical measures such as eye tracking, blood biometrics, or brain activity.

Overall, the time appears to be ripe for research on games and simulations as tools for teaching metacognitive strategies. To the extent that this chapter stimulates that research, it can be considered a success.

Author Note

Preparation of this chapter was supported by Grant N000141110225 from the Office of Naval Research.

References

Abt, C. C. (1970). *Serious games*. New York, NY: Viking.

Aleven, V., Roll, I., McLaren, B. M., & Koedinger, K. R. (2010). Automated, unobtrusive, action-by-action assessment of self-regulation during learning with an intelligent tutoring system. *Educational Psychologist, 45*, 224–233.

Anderson, L. W., Krathwohl, D. R., Airasian, P. W., Cruikshank, K. A., Mayer, R. E., Pintrich, P. R., . . . Wittrock, M. C. (2001). *A taxonomy for learning, teaching, and assessing.* New York, NY: Longman.

Azevedo, R., & Aleven, V. (Eds.). (2013). *International handbook of metacognition and learning technologies.* Berlin: Springer Science.

Azevedo, R., & Cromley, J. G. (2004). Does training on self-regulated learning facilitate students' learning with hypermedia? *Journal of Educational Psychology, 96,* 523–535.

Azevedo, R., Cromley, J. G., & Seibert, D. (2004). Does adaptive scaffolding facilitate students' ability to regulate their learning with hypermedia? *Contemporary Educational Psychology, 29,* 344–370.

Azevedo, R., Cromley, J. G., Winters, F. I., Moos, D. C., & Greene, J. A. (2005). Adaptive human scaffolding facilitates adolescents' self-regulated learning with hypermedia. *Instructional Science, 33,* 381–412.

Azevedo, R., Moos, D. C., Greene, J. A., Winters, F. I., & Cromley, J. G. (2008). Why is externally-facilitated regulated learning more effective than self-regulated learning with hypermedia? *Educational Technology Research & Development, 56,* 45–72.

Azevedo, R., Moos, D. C., Johnson, A. M., & Chauncey, A. D. (2010). Measuring cognitive and metacognitive regulatory processes during hypermedia learning: Issues and challenges. *Educational Psychologist, 45,* 210–223.

Baumeister, R. F., & Vohs, K. D. (Eds.). (2004). *Handbook of self-regulation.* New York, NY: Guilford.

Biswas, G., Leelawong, K., Schwartz, D., Vye, N., & The Teachable Agents Group at Vanderbilt. (2005). Learning by teaching: A new agent paradigm for educational software. *Applied Artificial Intelligence, 19,* 363–392.

Boekaerts, M., Pintrich, P. R., & Zeidner, M. (Eds.). (2000). *Handbook of self-regulation.* San Diego, CA: Academic Press.

Cannon-Bowers, J., & Bowers, C. (2010). Synthetic learning environments: On developing a science of simulation, games, and virtual worlds for training. In S. W. J. Kozlowski & E. Salas (Eds.), *Learning, training, and development in organizations* (pp. 229–262). New York, NY: Routledge.

Clark, R. C., & Mayer, R. E. (2011). *E-learning and the science of instruction.* San Francisco: Pfeiffer.

Clark, R. E., Yates, K., Early, S., & Moulton, K. (2010). An analysis of the failure of electronic media and discovery-based learning. In K. H. Silber & W. R. Foshay (Eds.), *Handbook of improving performance in the workplace* (pp. 263–297). San Francisco: Pfeiffer.

de Jong, T. (2005). The guided discovery principle in multimedia learning. In R. E. Mayer (Ed.), *The Cambridge handbook of multimedia learning* (pp. 215–228). New York, NY: Cambridge University Press.

Feng, J., Spence, I., & Pratt, J. (2007). Playing an action video game reduces gender differences in spatial cognition. *Psychological Science, 18*(10), 850–855.

Fiorella, L., & Mayer, R. E. (2012). Paper-based aids for learning with a computer-based game. *Journal of Educational Psychology, 104,* 1074–1082.

Fonseca, B. A., & Chi, M. T. H. (2011). Instruction based on self-explanation. In R. E. Mayer & P. A. Alexander (Eds.), *Handbook of research on learning and instruction* (pp. 296–321). New York, NY: Routledge.

Gee, J. P. (2003). *What video games have to teach us about learning and literacy.* New York, NY: Palgrave.

Gholson, B., & Craig, S. D. (2006). Promoting constructive activities that support learning during computer-based instruction. *Educational Psychology Review, 18,* 119–139.

Graesser, A., & McNamara, D. (2010). Self-regulated learning in learning environments with pedagogical agents that interact in natural language. *Educational Psychologist, 45,* 234–244.

Graesser, A. C., D'Mello, S., & Person, N. (2009). Meta-knowledge in tutoring. In D. J. Hacker, J. Dunlosky, & A. C. Graesser (Eds.), *Handbook of metacognition in education* (pp. 361–382). New York, NY: Routledge.

Graesser, A. C., Penumasta, P., Ventura, M., Cai, Z., & Hu, X. (2007). Using LSA in MetaTutor: Learning through mixed initiative dialogue in natural language. In T. Landauer, D. McNamara, S. Dennis, & W. Kintsch (Eds.), *Handbook of latent semantic analysis* (pp. 243–262). Mahwah. NJ: Erlbaum.

Gredler, M. E. (2001). Educational games and simulations: A technology in search of a (research) paradigm. In D. Jonassen (Ed.), *Handbook of research for educational communication and technology* (pp. 521–540). Mahwah, NJ: Erlbaum.

Green, C. S., & Bavelier, D. (2003). Action video game modifies visual selective attention. *Nature, 423,* 534–537.

Green, C. S., & Bavelier, D. (2006). Effect of action video games on the spatial distribution of visuospatial attention. *Journal of Experimental Psychology, 32,* 1465–1478.

Green, C. S., & Bavelier, D. (2007). Action-video-game experience alters the spatial resolution of vision. *Psychological Science, 18,* 88–94.

Greene, J. A., & Azevedo, R. (2010). The measurement of learners' self regulated cognitive and metacognitive processes while using computer-based learning environments. *Educational Psychologist, 45,* 203–209.

Hacker, D. J., Dunlosky, J., & Graesser, A. C. (Eds.). (2009). *Handbook of metacognition in education.* New York, NY: Routledge.

Halpern, D. F. (2002). *An introduction to critical thinking* (4th ed.). Mahwah, NJ: Erlbaum.

Hannafin, R. D., & Vermillion, J. R. (2008). Technology in the classroom. In T. L. Good (Ed.), *21st century education: A reference handbook* (Vol. 2, pp. 209–218). Thousand Oaks, CA: Sage.

Hartman, H. J. (Ed.). (2001). *Metacognition in learning and instruction.* Dordrecht, The Netherlands: Kluwer.

Hattie, J., & Gan, M. (2011). Instruction based on feedback. In R. E. Mayer & P. A. Alexander (Eds.), *Handbook of research on learning and instruction* (pp. 249–271). New York, NY: Routledge.

Hayes, R. T. (2005). *The effectiveness of instructional games: A literature review and discussion* (Technical Report 2005-004). Orlando, FL: Naval Air Warfare Center Training Systems Division.

Hayes, R. T., & Singer, M. J. (1989). *Simulation fidelity in training system design.* New York, NY: Springer-Verlag.

Hofer, B. K., & Pintrich, P. R. (Eds.). (2002). *Personal epistemology.* Mahwah, NJ: Erlbaum.

Honey, M. A., & Hilton, M. L. (Eds.). (2011). *Learning science through computer games and simulations.* Washington, DC: National Academies Press.

Johnson, C. I., & Mayer, R. E. (2010). Adding the self-explanation principle to multimedia learning in a computer-based game-like environment. *Computers in Human Behavior, 26,* 1246–1252.

Kirschner, P., Sweller, J., & Clark, R. E. (2006). Why minimal guidance during instruction does not work: An analysis of the failure of constructivist, discovery, problem-based, experiential, and inquiry-based teaching. *Educational Psychologist, 41,* 75–86.

Koedinger, K., Aleven, V., Roll, I., & Baker, R. (2009). In vivo experiments on whether supporting metacognition in intelligent tutoring systems yields robust learning. In D. J. Hacker, J. Dunlosky, & A. C. Graesser (Eds.), *Handbook of metacognition in education* (pp. 383–412). New York, NY: Routledge.

Lee, C., & Chen, M. (2009). A computer game as a context for non-routine mathematical problem solving: The effects of type of question prompt and level of prior knowledge. *Computers & Education, 52,* 530–542.

Leutner, D. (1993). Guided discovery learning with computer-based simulation games: Effects of adaptive and non-adaptive instructional support. *Learning and Instruction, 3,* 113–132.

Mayer, R. E. (in press). Metacognition strategies. In H. F. O'Neil (Ed.), *What works in games and simulations?* Charlotte, NC: Information Age Publishing.

Mayer, R. E. (2001). Cognitive, metacognitive, and motivational aspects of problem solving. In H. J. Hartman (Ed.), *Metacognition in learning and instruction* (pp. 87–102). Dordrecht, The Netherlands: Kluwer.

Mayer, R. E. (2004). Should there be a three strikes rule against discovery learning? The case for guided methods of instruction. *American Psychologist, 59,* 14–19.

Mayer, R. E. (Ed.). (2005). *The Cambridge handbook of multimedia learning.* New York, NY: Cambridge University Press.

Mayer, R. E. (2008). *Learning and instruction* (2nd ed.). Upper Saddle River, NJ: Pearson Merrill Prentice Hall.

Mayer, R. E. (2009). *Multimedia learning* (2nd ed.). New York, NY: Cambridge University Press.

Mayer, R. E. (2011a). *Applying the science of learning.* Upper Saddle River, NJ: Pearson.

Mayer, R. E. (2011b). Multimedia learning and games. In S. Tobias & J. D. Fletcher (Eds.), *Can computer games be used for instruction?* (pp. 281–306). Greenwich, CT: Information Age Publishing.

Mayer, R. E. (2014). *Computer games for learning: An evidence-based approach.* Cambridge, MA: MIT Press.

Mayer, R. E., Dow, G. T., & Mayer, S. (2003). Multimedia learning in an interactive self-explaining environment: What works in the design of agent-based microworlds? *Journal of Educational Psychology, 95,* 806–813.

Mayer, R. E., & Johnson, C. I. (2010). Adding instructional features that promote learning in a game-like environment. *Journal of Educational Computing Research, 42,* 241–265.

Mayer, R. E., & Wittrock, M. C. (2006). Problem solving. In P. Alexander, P. Winne, & G. Phye (Eds.), *Handbook of educational psychology* (pp. 287–303). Mahwah, NJ: Erlbaum.

McNamara, D. S., O'Reilly, T., Rowe, M., Boonthum, C., & Levinstein, I. B. (2007). iSTART: A web-based tutor that teaches self-explanation and metacognitive reading strategies. In D. S. McNamara (Ed.), *Reading comprehension strategies: Theories, interventions, and technologies* (pp. 397–420). Mahwah, NJ: Erlbaum.

Moreno, R. (2004). Decreasing cognitive load for novice students: Effects of explanatory versus corrective feedback on discovery-based multimedia. *Instructional Science, 32,* 99–113.

Moreno, R., & Mayer, R. E. (1999). Multimedia-supported metaphors for meaning making in mathematics. *Cognition and Instruction, 17,* 215–248.

Moreno, R., & Mayer, R. E. (2000). Engaging students in active learning: The case for personalized multimedia messages. *Journal of Educational Psychology, 92,* 724–733.

Moreno, R., & Mayer, R. E. (2002). Learning science in virtual reality environments: Role of methods and media. *Journal of Educational Psychology, 94,* 598–610.

Moreno, R., & Mayer, R. E. (2004). Personalized messages that promote science learning in virtual environments. *Journal of Educational Psychology, 96,* 165–173.

Moreno, R., & Mayer, R. E. (2005). Role of guidance, reflection, and interactivity in an agent-based multimedia game. *Journal of Educational Psychology, 97,* 117–128.

Moreno, R., & Mayer, R. E. (2010). Techniques that increase generative processing in multimedia learning: Open questions for cognitive load research. In J. L. Plass, R. Moreno, & R. Brunken (Eds.), *Cognitive load theory* (pp. 153–177). New York, NY: Cambridge University Press.

Moreno, R., Mayer, R. E., Spires, H. A., & Lester, J. C. (2001). The case for social agency in computer-based teaching: Do students learn more deeply when they interact with animated pedagogical agents? *Cognition and Instruction, 19,* 177–213.

Neulight, N., Kafai, Y. B., Kao, L., Foley, B., & Galas, C. (2007). Children's participation in a virtual epidemic in the science classroom: Making connections to natural infectious diseases. *Journal of Science Education and Technology, 16,* 47–58.

O'Neil, H. F. (Ed.). (1978). *Learning strategies.* New York, NY: Academic Press.

O'Neil, H. F., & Perez, R. S. (Eds.). (2008). *Computer games and team and individual learning.* Amsterdam: Elsevier.

O'Neil, H. F., Chung, G. K. W. K., Kerr, D., Vendlinski, T. P., Buschang, R. E., & Mayer, R. E. (2014). Adding self-explanation prompts to an educational computer game. *Computers in Human Behavior, 30,* 23–28.

Orvis, K. A., Horn, D. B., & Belanich, J. (2009). An examination of the role of individual differences play in videogame-based learning. *Military Psychology, 21,* 461–481.

Pane, J. F., Griffin, B. A., McCaffrey, D. F., & Karam, R. (2014). Effectiveness of Cognitive Tutor Algebra I at scale. *Educational Evaluation and Policy Analysis, 36,* 127–144.

Pashler, H., Bain, P. M., Bottage, A., Graesser, A., Koedinger, K., McDaniel, M., & Metcalfe, J. (2007). *Organizing instruction and study to improve student learning* (NCER Report 2007–2004). Washington, DC: Institute of Education Sciences.

Pellegrino, J. W., & Hilton, M. L. (Eds.). (2012). *Education for work and life.* Washington, DC: National Academies Press.

Pensky, M. (2001). *Digital game-based learning.* New York, NY: McGraw-Hill.

Perez, R. S. (2008). Summary and discussion. In H. F. O'Neil & R. S. Perez (Eds.), *Computer games and team and individual learning* (pp. 287–306). Amsterdam: Elsevier.

Phye, G. D., Robinson, D. H., & Levin, J. (Eds.). (2005). *Empirical methods for evaluating educational interventions.* San Diego, CA: Elsevier Academic Press.

Pintrich, P. R. (2004). A conceptual framework for assessing motivation and self-regulated learning in college students. *Educational Psychology Review, 16,* 385–407.

Pintrich, P. R., & De Groot, E. (1990). Motivated and self-regulated learning components of classroom academic performance. *Journal of Educational Psychology, 82,* 33–40.

Pintrich, P. R., Wolters, C. A., & Baxter, G. P. (2000). Assessing metacognition and self-regulated learning. In G. Schraw & J. P. Impara (Eds.), *Issues in the measurement of metacognition* (pp. 43–98). Lincoln, NE: Boros.

Pressley, M., & Levin, J. R. (Eds.). (1983). *Cognitive strategy instruction.* New York, NY: Springer-Verlag.

Pressley, M., & Woloshyn, V. (1995). *Cognitive strategy instruction* (2nd ed.). Cambridge, MA: Brookline Books.

Raessens, J., & Goldstein, J. (Eds.). (2005). *Handbook of computer game studies*. Cambridge, MA: MIT Press.

Rieber, L. P. (2005). Multimedia learning in games, simulations, and microworlds. In R. E. Mayer (Ed.), *The Cambridge handbook of multimedia learning* (pp. 549–568). New York, NY: Cambridge University Press.

Rieber, L. P., Tzeng, S., & Tribble, K. (2004). Discovery learning, representation, and explanation within computer-based simulation: Finding the right mix. *Learning and Instruction, 14*, 307–323.

Roy, M., & Chi, M. T. H. (2005). The self-explanation principle in multimedia learning. In R. E. Mayer (Ed.), *The Cambridge handbook of multimedia learning* (pp. 271–286). New York, NY: Cambridge University Press.

Schneider, B., Carnoy, M., Kilpatrick, J., Schmidt, W. H., & Shavelson, R. J. (2007). *Estimating causal effects*. Washington, DC: American Educational Research Association.

Schneider, W. (2010). Metacognition and memory development in childhood and adolescence. In H. S. Waters & W. Schneider (Eds.), *Metacognition, strategy use, & instruction* (pp. 54–81). New York, NY: Guilford.

Schoenfeld, A. H. (1987). What's all this fuss about metacognition? In A. H. Schoenfeld (Ed.), *Cognitive science and mathematics education* (pp. 189–213). Hillsdale, NJ: Erlbaum.

Schraw, G. (2009). Measuring metacognitive judgments. In D. J. Hacker, J. Dunlosky, & A. C. Graesser (Eds.), *Handbook of metacognition in education* (pp. 415–429). New York, NY: Routledge.

Schraw, G. (2010). Measuring self-regulation in computer-based learning environments. *Educational Psychologist, 45*, 258–266.

Schunk, D. (1991). Self-efficacy and academic motivation. *Educational Psychologist, 26*, 207–231.

Shavelson, R. J., & Towne, L. (Eds.). (2002). *Scientific research in education*. Washington, DC: National Academy Press.

Shen, C.-Y., & O'Neil, H. F. (2008). Role of worked examples to stimulate learning in a game. In H. F. O'Neil & R. S. Perez (Eds.), *Computer games and team and individual learning* (pp. 185–204). Amsterdam: Elsevier.

Sims, V. K., & Mayer, R. E. (2002). Domain specificity of spatial expertise: The case of video game players. *Applied Cognitive Psychology, 16*, 97–115.

Tennyson, R. D., & Jorczak, R. L. (2008). A conceptual framework for the empirical study of instructional games. In H. F. O'Neil & R. S. Perez (Eds.), *Computer games and team and individual learning* (pp. 3–20). Amsterdam: Elsevier.

Tobias, S., & Everson, H. T. (2009). The importance of knowing what you know: A knowledge monitoring framework for studying metacognition in education. In D. J. Hacker, J. Dunlosky, & A. C. Graesser (Eds.), *Handbook of metacognition in education* (pp. 107–127). New York, NY: Routledge.

Tobias, S., & Fletcher, D. (Eds.). (2011). *Computer games and instruction*. Greenwich, CT: Information Age Publishing.

van der Meij, J., & de Jong, T. (2011). The effects of directive self-explanation prompts to support active processing in a simulation-based learning environment. *Journal of Computer Assisted Instruction, 27*, 411–423.

Van Eck, R., & Dempsey, J. (2003). The effect of competition and contextualized advisement on the transfer of mathematics skills in a computer-based instructional simulation game. *Educational Technology Research and Development, 50*, 23–41.

Vorderer, P., & Bryant, J. (Eds.). (2006). *Playing video games: Motives, responses, and consequences.* Mahwah, NJ: Erlbaum.

Wang, N., Johnson, W. L., Mayer, R. E., Rizzo, P., Shaw, E., & Collins, H. (2008). The politeness effect: Pedagogical agents and learning outcomes. *International Journal of Human Computer Studies, 66,* 96–112.

Waters, H. S., & Schneider, W. (Eds.). (2010). *Metacognition, strategy use, and instruction.* New York, NY: Guilford Press.

Weinstein, C. E., & Mayer, R. E. (1985). The teaching of learning strategies. In M. Wittrock (Ed.), *Handbook of research on teaching* (pp. 315–327). New York, NY: Macmillan.

White, B. Y., & Frederiksen, J. R. (1998). Inquiry, modeling, and metacognition: Asking science accessible to all students. *Cognition and Instruction, 16,* 3–118.

Winne, P. H. (2010). Improving measurements of self-regulated learning. *Educational Psychologist, 45,* 267–276.

Winne, P. H., & Muis, K. R. (2011). Statistical estimates of learners' judgments about knowledge in calibration of achievement. *Metacognition and Learning, 6,* 179–193.

Winne, P. H., & Nesbit, J. C. (2009). Supporting self-regulated learning with cognitive tools. In D. J. Hacker, J. Dunlosky, & A. C. Graesser (Eds.), *Handbook of metacognition in education* (pp. 259–277). New York, NY: Routledge.

Young, M. F., Slota, S., Cutter, A. B., Jalette, G., Mullin, G., Lai, B., Simeoni, Z., . . . Yukhymenko, M. (2012). Our princess is in another castle: A review of trends in serious gaming for education. *Review of Educational Research, 82,* 61–89.

10

THE ROLE OF MOTIVATION, AFFECT, AND ENGAGEMENT IN SIMULATION/GAME ENVIRONMENTS

A Proposed Model

Robert Rueda, Harold F. O'Neil, and Elena Son

The use of technology to promote learning goals is now a well-established educational practice. However, a continuing problem has been understanding the underlying processes that govern the effectiveness of technology-enhanced learning environments. While this situation has improved, there are still many aspects that have not been entirely understood. Most often simulations involve targeted training components designed to achieve specific learning goals. Mayer (2011a) divided game and simulation research into three categories: a value-added approach, which questions how specific game features foster learning and motivation; a cognitive consequences approach, which investigates what people learn from serious games; and a media comparison approach, which investigates whether people learn better from serious games than from conventional media.

Not surprisingly, the cognitive aspects of learning within these three areas of research have been relatively more studied (Mayer, 2005; also see O'Neil, Baker, & Perez, this volume; O'Neil, Wainess, & Baker, 2005, for a review; Wouters, van Nimwegen, van Oostendorp, & van der Spek, 2013) than the motivational aspects, which are the focus of this chapter. This is not to say that motivation has been ignored (see, for example, Huang, Huang, & Tschopp, 2010; Wouters et al., 2013). However, the deep connections between cognition, learning, and motivation that contemporary educational psychology emphasizes (Anderman & Dawson, 2011) suggest that more attention needs to be focused on the motivational aspects of these special types of learning environments (cf. Zusho, Anthony, Hashimoto, & Robertson, 2014).

This chapter proposes a model which could form the basis for further work in this area. While the question "Are games more motivating?" (Wouters et al.,

2013) has received substantial attention, the question addressed here is, "What are the motivational processes during the simulation experience from the perspective of the learner?" In order to address this issue, we provide a brief overview of motivation theories as the foundation for the chapter, and discuss what is known about motivational aspects of simulations. Finally, building on existing work in this area, we propose a model which links motivational variables with engagement and which can provide a foundation for testable hypotheses and implications for design purposes.

Distinguishing Gaming Environments

It is important to recognize that there are a range of computer-mediated environments that fall under the general label of games and simulations. One issue with reviews of research on games and simulations is the lack of consistency of terminology. The three most commonly used terms in the literature are game, simulation, and simulation game, yet there is variation in the education and training literature on how these terms are defined (Amory, 2002; Crookall, 2010; Garris, Ahlers, & Driskell, 2002; Gredler, 1996; Rieber, 2005; Tobias & Fletcher, 2011). While some of these authors have argued for distinguishing these types of learning environments, Sitzmann (2011) questioned the usefulness of distinguishing educational tools as simulations or simulation games.

While there is still not complete consensus in the literature on the definition of games and simulations, for expediency we follow Sitzmann's (2011) suggestion to blur the distinction between the labels of simulations and serious games, and use the terms serious games and simulations interchangeably to refer to those environments whose focus is learning and training and increasing skill level across one or more domains.

We would argue for considering games, including recreational games, and simulations as being two endpoints on a continuum that may share some common characteristics. For example, what are called serious simulations may have pleasurable or entertaining features, and recreational games may lead to increased learning. Thus, it can be argued that it is more important to characterize the features of a specific learning environment rather than general categories of learning environments in general. In this chapter we use the term simulations, and focus on those simulations that have a clear goal of increasing proficiency or imparting skills on academic or work-related content. With this consideration regarding the distinction among these environments in mind, we now turn to a look at motivation.

Motivational Considerations

Much of the early work on motivation in the mid-20th century, reflecting the behaviorist orientation at the time, focused primarily on motivation as stable drives related to innate needs. For example, motivation to pursue a food reward could be induced in rats by increasing hunger through food deprivation. Motivation in past decades, especially in popular conceptions, has been seen as a stable, generalized, inherent trait, such that an individual was seen to be "motivated" or not. In contrast, a unifying theme of contemporary views of motivation focuses on a learner's domain-specific beliefs or interpretations of various aspects of a specific learning situation, task, or domain (Wentzel & Wigfield, 2009). While motivation applies to all facets of human behavior, the focus here is on motivational considerations related to learning tasks and contexts, often called achievement motivation (Alderman, 2004). More specifically, as noted earlier, the prime concern is with one specific type of learning context, simulation and gaming environments.

Expectancies and Values

It is important to realize that there is no overarching theory of motivation, but rather there are various subtheories that focus on various components. They are loosely linked, however, in the sense that they are most closely tied to a social cognitive perspective (see Bandura, 1986), and they focus on a learner's beliefs, values, and goals. Motivation has been defined as "the process whereby goal-directed activity is instigated and sustained" (Schunk, Pintrich, & Meece, 2008, p. 4). In a comprehensive review which linked various components of motivation, Pintrich (2003) focused on four components with significant research support. These include a learner's *expectancies* and *values*. Expectancies (will I succeed or not?) are based on self-efficacy beliefs (am I capable of being successful?) and attributional beliefs (what are the reasons that I succeeded or failed?). In turn, values are based on interest and goal orientation (do I want to perform better than everyone else, or do I want to achieve mastery?). As Pintrich noted, these variables form an expectancy-value model in which motivation is based on the interaction of these domain-specific beliefs. Values have been shown to be most influential in starting an activity, while expectancies have been shown most influential in persisting at an activity (National Research Council and the Institute of Medicine, 2004).

Expectancy-value theory conceptualizes intrinsic interest (the subjective interest in the content of a task) as one of four dimensions of task value (Wigfield & Cambria, 2010a; Wigfield & Eccles, 2002). The other three task values include attainment value or importance (the importance of doing well on a task), utility value (usefulness of a task in terms of future goals), and cost value (perceived negative aspects of engaging in a task) (Wigfield & Cambria, 2010b). There are other somewhat related perspectives on interest as well. Schunk, Meece, and Pintrich (2013) and others (Ainley, Hidi, & Berndorff, 2002) distinguish among state-like as opposed to trait-like aspects of interest. Personal interest is seen as a relatively stable, enduring disposition, while situational interest is seen as interest in a specific task or activity. There is still some disagreement in the literature about specific aspects of interest, for example, the specific contributions of different types of interest to performance (Lepper, Master, & Yow, 2008; Renninger, Pachrach, & Posey, 2008). However, interest is frequently cited as an important aspect of both games and simulations (e.g., Bachen, Hernández-Ramos, & Raphael, 2012).

Since motivational beliefs are not externally visible, how can we tell when someone is motivated? Motivation researchers typically use three behavioral and/or cognitive indicators that are linked to the motivational beliefs just described: active choice, persistence, and effort (Schunk et al., 2013). That is, the choices a person makes regarding starting a task or not, their persistence in carrying out that task, and the amount of effort they invest are assumed to be a function of interaction of the motivational beliefs just described. A review of the voluminous research on each of these motivational variables is beyond the scope of this chapter, but comprehensive reviews are available in Karabenick and Urdan (2012), Schunk et al. (2013), and Wentzel and Wigfield (2009).

A summary of generalized motivational principles was provided in a synthesis by Pintrich (2003) and included the following:

- Adaptive self-efficacy and competence beliefs motivate students.
- Adaptive attributions and control beliefs motivate students.
- Higher levels of interest and intrinsic motivation motivate students.
- Higher levels of value motivate students.
- Goals motivate and direct students.

While much of the work in these motivational areas has focused on motivation in classroom and academic contexts, simulation environments are now overwhelmingly seen as an important extension of traditional educational and assessment tools and approaches, and thus the motivational dimensions of such environments are important to study. Moreover, an important assumption of this review is that motivational principles (not specific beliefs) are developmentally consistent. That is, while specific motivational beliefs may vary widely, the principles do not differentially apply to young students or adult learners. That is, the specifics of individual motivational factors (content, duration, intensity, etc.) will vary developmentally and even culturally but the motivational principles themselves will not. For example, what is interesting to a fourth-grade student will not likely interest an adult, although the degree of interest is still presumed to mediate choice of activities. Likewise, taking the GRE for an adult student or taking a spelling test in elementary school may be very different tasks, but the amount of effort and persistence in each case is presumed to be related to expectancies concerned with one's own abilities and successful completion of the activity.

Researchers have investigated various motivational variables within the gaming and simulations contexts, such as attribution (Fisher, Marshall, & Nanayakkara, 2009; Tzeng & Chen, 2012), goal orientations (Bell & Kozlowski, 2008), and self-efficacy (Andrade et al., 2012; Seijts & Latham, 2011). As one example, in a recent study, Tzeng and Chen (2012) investigated the effects of praise (ability or effort) on children's computer game performance, self-efficacy, choice of game difficulty level, self-serving attribution, and appreciation for game design. Participants who received either ability or effort praise had greater self-efficacy compared to the no-praise group in the addition game. Furthermore, individuals with a high level of ability attribution felt more efficacious than participants with either a high level of effort attribution or a low level of internal attribution. Participants with high ability attribution also selected easier game difficulty levels compared to both high effort attribution and low internal attribution individuals.

Motivation Versus Engagement

In the motivation literature, active choice, persistence, and effort are commonly used behavioral and cognitive indicators of the influences of underlying motivational processes. Specifically, active choice refers to selecting a task when an individual is free to choose. Persistence is defined as the time one spends on a task despite challenges. Effort refers to how hard an individual works on a task (Pintrich, 2003; Schunk et al., 2013). In that respect, they mediate the effects of motivational processes on specific achievement outcomes both in and out of gaming contexts. Work that has focused on these three indicators is often found in the literature on *engagement* (Azevedo, 2015; Fredricks, Blumenfeld, & Paris, 2004; Greene, 2015; Lawson & Lawson, 2013; Sinatra, Heddy, & Lombardi, 2015). The importance of the concept in contemporary research and theory on learning and instruction is highlighted in a recent comprehensive handbook (Christenson, Reschly, & Wylie, 2012). The prevailing conception of engagement is represented in a framework consisting of multiple dimensions or indicators, as outlined in Fredricks et al. (2004) and others (Furrer & Skinner, 2003; Jimerson, Campos, & Greif, 2003; Skinner, Furrer, Marchand, & Kindermann, 2008). Fredricks et al. (2004) proposed that engagement is a multidimensional construct including behavioral engagement (actively performing learning activities), cognitive engagement (using cognitive strategies to foster deep learning), and affective engagement (expressing enjoyment about learning).

Furrer and Skinner (2003) and Skinner et al. (2008) included both behavioral (e.g., working hard and trying) and affective dimensions (e.g., enjoyment of learning, involvement, and interest) in their definition of engagement as "active, goal-directed, flexible, constructive, persistent, focused interactions with the social and physical environments" (Furrer & Skinner, 2003, p. 149). Other researchers have focused less on the affective aspects of engagement in favor of behavioral and cognitive aspects such as concentration, effort, use of cognitive and metacognitive strategies such as planning and monitoring, and persistence during the initiation and execution of a cognitive task (Cox & Guthrie, 2001; Furrer & Skinner, 2003; Guthrie & Wigfield, 2000; Kirsch et al., 2002).

An important strand of the work relating engagement to achievement has been done in the area of reading. Studies on reading engagement have demonstrated significant relations between affective engagement and behavioral engagement in reading (i.e., reading amount and breadth and strategic reading) (Guthrie, 2008; Wang & Guthrie, 2004). In a recent study, for example, investigators found that motivation, including intrinsic motivation, self-efficacy, perceived difficulty, value, and devalue, as well as prosocial and antisocial goals, had a direct and indirect influence, through engagement—operationalized as dedication and avoidance—on informational text comprehension in classrooms with traditional reading/language arts instruction (Guthrie, Klauda, & Ho, 2013). For students participating in an intervention (Concept-Oriented Reading Instruction; Guthrie et al., 2013), which provided supports for motivation, engagement, and cognitive strategies in reading, all motivation variables mentioned earlier predicted engagement; however, engagement did not predict informal text comprehension.

In addition to these studies on reading, other recent research has suggested that the impact of motivational beliefs on achievement outcomes is mediated by engagement (e.g., Lee, Lee, & Bong, 2014). Patrick, Ryan, and Kaplan (2007), for example, showed that personal motivational beliefs (mastery goals, academic and social efficacy) were related to engagement in the classroom, such as self-regulation—a type of cognitive engagement—and task-related interaction—a type of behavioral engagement.

While engagement is clearly seen as an important variable in the learning and motivational literature, there is a wide variety of approaches (Christenson et al., 2012; Eccles & Wang, 2012). Some researchers have begun to challenge the assumption of linear relationships among motivation, engagement, and achievement, and have also proposed considering engagement in a broader framework that moves beyond the individual to a more expansive ecological perspective (Lawson & Lawson, 2013). While there is not consensus on the optimal approach to engagement as a construct, its importance in mediating learning outcomes has wider support.

Cognitive Engagement and Self-Regulated Learning

In a simulation environment, it is likely that what might be termed the cognitive aspects of engagement might be most critical in mediating learning outcomes. An important aspect of engagement in this context is the use of cognitive strategies, including self-regulated learning strategies (Zimmerman, 2013). There is evidence that suggests that learners who self-monitor their learning progress and engagement with tasks generate internal feedback. This internal feedback works to assess possible gaps in performance, and the result may lead to improved learning outcomes (Azevedo & Cromley, 2004). Learners who are able to select effective learning strategies appropriate to a given task or activity are able to regulate their learning as well as acquire and maintain new skills.

One of the central aspects of self-regulated learning is students' ability to select, combine, and coordinate learning activities (Zimmerman & Schunk, 2013). The cognitive aspects of effective self-regulated learning are elaboration (such as generative note-taking) and organizational strategies (such as creating outlines or concept maps) and control strategies (such as setting goals or monitoring progress). Additionally, effective learning requires adaptive motivational beliefs such as those reviewed earlier, including self-efficacy, interest, goal orientation, attributions, and other variables, which in turn affect effort and persistence in learning. There is a significant body of research findings that support the connection between motivational variables, learning strategies, self-regulatory behavior, and academic achievement (Lee et al., 2014; Marsh, Hau, Artelt, Baumert, & Peschar, 2006; Ning & Downing, 2010; Rotgans & Schmidt, 2012; Rueda et al., 2010; Schunk & Zimmerman, 2008).

While the work on engagement distinguishes between motivational beliefs and engagement, one issue is that behavioral and cognitive indicators are sometimes mixed with affective factors (enjoyment and other emotions) or even other motivational variables (interest). However, recent extensions of motivational theory and work in the area of emotions have suggested that these are separate dimensions (Linnenbrink-Garcia & Pekrun, 2011a). The next section briefly discusses recent work (Linnenbrink-Garcia & Pekrun, 2011b) which has tried to distinguish these aspects, in particular achievement-oriented emotions, in a more integrated framework.

Motivation and Emotions

Pekrun, Elliot, and Maier (2009) defined emotions as "multiple component processes that comprise specific affective, cognitive, physiological, and behavioral elements" (p. 116). For example, in the case of anxiety, they note that this might include nervous feelings, worries, increased activation, and anxious facial expression. They distinguish these emotions from mood, which are of lower intensity and are not tied to a specific referent in the environment. At a more general level, both emotions and moods are sometimes combined under the wider construct of affect. Pekrun et al. (2009) note that there has been inconsistency and confusion in the literature regarding the differentiation of these distinct constructs.

In an academic context, achievement emotions are those that relate to "competence-relevant activities or outcomes" (Pekrun et al., 2009, p. 116), such as in a simulation. There has been a significant amount of work on emotions related to achievement in educational contexts, but much of the work has been characterized by (a) a lack of connectedness among various emotional constructs and (b) a focus on emotions related to achievement outcomes as opposed to emotions related to precipitating events. As one example, there is extensive work on test anxiety (Zeidner, 2007), but it has typically been looked at in isolation and in the context of the relationships between anxiety and related emotional constructs.

Emotional variables may be especially important but understudied aspects of simulations and games. A recent meta-analysis (D'Mello, 2013) of the relative frequency of emotions across several different types of gaming environments (intelligent tutoring systems, serious games, simulation environments, and simple computer interfaces) found that engagement/flow was frequently found, in contrast to more negative emotions such as contempt, anger, disgust, sadness, anxiety, delight, fear, and surprise. There was more variability for boredom, confusion, curiosity, happiness, and frustration, and the effects were mediated by the type of measurement (self-reported emotional states vs. an external observer) and whether the context was in a classroom or a laboratory. A second meta-analysis (Wouters et al., 2013) indicated that serious games do not lead to increases in motivation.

Pekrun, Frenzel, Goetz, and Perry (2007) have noted that work on emotions, in addition to being inconsistent on terminology, has tended to focus on *outcome emotions* which are related to achievement outcomes (joy at a high score on an exam after it has been completed) as opposed to *activity emotions* related to precipitating activities which produce those outcomes (anger about failing an unfair assignment). These authors proposed an integrated model—the control-value theory of achievement emotions—which both considers the dual dimensions of achievement motivations (control and values) and which ties together a range of achievement emotions into an integrated framework.

The model takes into consideration whether the focus of the motivational appraisals is prospective, retrospective, or focused on the emotions that take place during an activity. It also takes into account the emotional *valence* (positive vs. negative) and *activation* potential (activating vs. deactivating) of the various categories of achievement emotions (see Table 10.1). More importantly, building on expectancy-value theories of motivation (Wigfield, Tonks, & Klauda, 2009), this framework also connects these emotional constructs to important motivational variables and engagement (Goetz, Frenzel, Pekrun, & Hall, 2006; Linnenbrink-Garcia & Pekrun, 2011a; Pekrun, 2000, 2006; Pekrun, Elliot, & Maier, 2006; Pekrun, Goetz, Titz, & Perry, 2002; Pekrun & Linnenbrink-Garcia, 2012).

A central focus of this theoretical framework is the arousal of achievement-related emotions, specifically a learner's appraisals of the *control of* and *value for* achievement activities and their past and future outcomes. At the heart of the theory is the notion that individuals experience specific achievement emotions depending on the degree of control they feel and on the subjective importance of the activity or task. According to the theory, these control and value appraisals are the proximal determinants of specific emotions, which are then related to various learning and achievement outcomes.

TABLE 10.1 A Three-Dimensional Taxonomy of Achievement Emotions

	Positive[a]		Negative[b]	
Object focus	Activating	Deactivating	Activating	Deactivating
Activity focus	Enjoyment	Relaxation	Anger Frustration	Boredom
Outcome focus	Joy Hope Pride Gratitude	Contentment Relief	Anxiety Shame Anger	Sadness Disappointment Hopelessness

Note: Adapted from Pekrun et al. (2007).

[a]Positive, pleasant emotion. [b]Negative, unpleasant emotion.

Recent work has connected emotional variables with a variety of motivational variables, including goal orientations. For example, a recent study by Pekrun et al. (2009) proposed and tested a model linking achievement goals and achievement emotions to academic performance. The study recruited undergraduate students to examine the relationships among goals and emotions and their predictive power for exam performance in an introductory-level psychology course. Achievement goals were found to predict discrete achievement emotions, and these in turn were found to predict performance outcomes. The results suggested that mastery goals were predictive of activity-focused emotions (enjoyment, boredom, anger), performance approach goals were found to predict positive outcome-focused emotions (hope, pride), and performance avoidance goals were found to predict negative outcome-focused emotions (anxiety, hopelessness, shame).

The advantage of Pekrun's (2007; Pekrun & Linnenbrink Garcia, 2012) framework for the current purposes is that it specifies testable relationships among environmental (task-relevant) factors, such as cognitive demands, autonomy support, goal structures and expectations, and feedback loops which then relate to motivational judgements or "appraisals." The model specifies that these motivational appraisals in turn have an impact on achievement emotions, which finally mediate learning-relevant cognitive engagement variables (use of learning strategies, self-regulation of learning) and learning outcomes. In addition, there are clear intervention implications that differ by the locus of the difficulty (the environment, the individual's appraisals, the individual's emotions, or the individual's use of cognitive resources, such as learning strategies and self-regulation of learning).

While the control-value model was not developed specifically with simulation environments in mind, it is reasonable to propose that it is generalizable especially because emotions are one key aspect of simulation gaming (Hofstede, de Caluwé, & Peters, 2010). It also offers the advantage of providing a comprehensive theoretical framework which integrates key motivational, emotional, and engagement variables. Moreover, there is both qualitative and quantitative empirical support for many of the hypothesized relationships including in gaming environments (Bell & Kozlowski, 2008; Tao, Cheng, & Sun, 2009). For example, Bell and Kozlowski (2008) included motivational, cognitive, and emotional variables into their structural equation model to examine the effects of designs elements, such as error framing (e.g., errors are good vs. errors are bad) on computer-based simulation performance. State *performance-approach* orientation was positively related to self-efficacy, whereas state *performance-avoid* orientation and state anxiety were negatively related to self-efficacy. Mastery orientation was positively related to metacognitive activity, which in turn was positively associated with self-efficacy and intrinsic motivation. In turn, self-efficacy and intrinsic motivation were positively related to transfer and knowledge, respectively. In a related study, Pekrun, Goetz, and Perry (2005) found positive correlations between enjoyment, hope, and pride with control, outcome, and overall success expectations. They also found that anxiety, shame, and hopelessness were negatively related, as would be expected.

It is clear that cognitive, motivational, and emotional factors are important in considering the design and impact of simulations, which are increasingly seen as an important extension of traditional educational and assessment tools and approaches. The next section considers these issues in the context of simulation environments. The focus is on developing a conceptual model which relates specific motivational variables to aspects of engagement, emotions, and learning-related cognitive factors with the aim of achieving learning goals in simulation-related tasks. We will summarize the research that examines motivation in simulation environments, and then discuss and relate it to the conceptual model that can be used to design testable studies.

Motivational Considerations in Simulation Environments

Two assumptions often permeate discussions of computer learning environments—that they are more effective than nontechnology-based learning, and that they are inherently more motivating. With respect to the first assumption, the results are mixed. Earlier studies have provided evidence, for example that students develop expert behaviors, such as knowledge development, pattern recognition, problem solving, qualitative thinking, and principled decision making as their individual expertise with simulations increase (Jacobson & Archodidou, 2000; VanDeventer & White, 2002).

However, after a review of a large number of studies on learning from simulations, de Jong and van Joolingen (1998) concluded that there was no clear and unequivocal outcome in favor of simulations, and in fact some students have difficulty using these types of learning environments (Azevedo, Guthrie, & Seibert, 2004; Garris et al., 2002; Leemkuil, de Jong, de Hoog, & Christoph, 2003;

O'Neil & Fisher, 2004). However, more recent literature in the medical area indicated large effect sizes for medical simulations (Cook, 2012; McKinney, Cook, Wood, & Hatala, 2012; Tamim, Bernard, Borokhovski, Abrami, & Schmid, 2011). Specifically, using a second order meta-analysis, the impact of technology on learning was a small effect size (.33) (Tamim et al., 2011).

More recent analyses have provided somewhat mixed results as well, including in terms of motivational outcomes. Wouters et al. (2013), for example, found in a meta-analysis of the cognitive and motivational aspects of simulations that compared to traditional instruction, simulations were found to be more effective in terms of learning and retention but not in terms of motivation. In another meta-analysis, Sitzmann (2011) found that simulations were more effective relative to comparison groups in post-training self-efficacy, declarative knowledge, procedural knowledge, and retention although the effects were reduced when the comparison groups experienced active engagement during training. Vogel et al. (2006) in a third meta-analysis found that simulations yielded more positive cognitive gains than traditional teaching methods, but these effects were most pronounced when the learner controlled the sequence of the program compared to when the program controlled the sequence.

Many of the explanations for these inconsistent results have focused on cognitive factors (Azevedo, Cromley, Winters, Moos, & Greene, 2005) and have suggested that computer-based environments by themselves may not produce strong instructional effects without intentional design of instructional learning principles. For example, Gee (2003) reviewed evidence suggesting that well-designed computer environments incorporate many long-established learning principles, such as providing time on task and practice, fostering transfer by providing multiple opportunities to apply earlier learning to later problems, and adjusting scaffolding as needed. There is some evidence that students from a variety of backgrounds make significant learning gains after playing well-designed simulations (Cook et al., 2013; Mitchell & Savill-Smith, 2004). In contrast, simulation environments that rely on discovery, problem-based, experiential, and inquiry-based techniques do not work instructionally (Kirschner, Sweller, & Clark, 2006; O'Neil & Fisher, 2004) and a likely cause is ineffective instructional design (Leemkuil et al., 2003).

In addition to instructional factors, however, motivational issues may help explain some of the uneven findings because it has been reported that motivation is an important factor in simulation performance variance in a variety of contexts (Burguillo, 2010; Ebner & Holzinger, 2007; Harris & Reid, 2005; Papastergiou, 2009). Some researchers have examined motivational outcomes, including self-efficacy (Creutzfeldt, Hedman, & Felländer-Tsai, 2012), intrinsic and extrinsic motivation (Liu, Cheng, & Huang, 2011), and interest (Bachen et al., 2012) in engaging in simulations. For example, students learning computational problem-solving skills through a simulation showed greater intrinsic motivation and lower extrinsic motivation compared to students learning these skills via traditional instruction (Liu et al., 2011).

In the early literature, it was often assumed that simulations were motivating just because they were technology-based or represented a change from traditional face-to-face learning environments. Since there are indications that the picture may be more complex (Sitzmann, 2011; Vogel et al., 2006; Wouters et al., 2013), consideration of motivational variables merits additional systematic attention in both research and in simulation design. In considering motivation in simulation environments, there are two aspects which are explored here. One aspect focuses on the motivational attributes of simulation environments, and the other on individual motivational characteristics. These two areas are explored in the following sections.

Motivational Features of Simulation Environments

Although we have used the term *simulation* throughout, a comprehensive and influential discussion of the motivational characteristics of games from Garris et al. (2002) is relevant to the discussion. While Garris et al. focused on what was termed game environments, their framework is relevant to the current discussion. Garris et al. proposed a three-part (input–process–outcome) comprehensive model that attempts to connect game characteristics with learner motivation. In the model, the inputs included instructional content and game characteristics. These two inputs feed into the game cycle, which includes user judgments, user behavior, and system feedback. During the game cycle, these three elements occur in a cyclical and repeating fashion, depending upon the number of game cycles engaged in by the user. At the outcome stage, which is linked to the game cycle, learning outcomes are realized.

One of the key elements of the Garris et al. (2002) model is the notion of "game cycles" which represents the cyclical nature of most games and simulations. As others have noted (Astleitner & Wiesner, 2004; Huang et al., 2010), simulations represent iterative learning processes, which may be represented in the form of mastering a particular skill and moving to the next level of challenge or learning. Motivation in this context is a function of complex and interactive processes among all the simulation instructional elements and the individual. Thus motivation can differ at different stages of the simulation experience. Just as an individual's initial state of knowledge and learning might be expected to change in the course of a simulation, motivational and emotional states might be expected to change as well as a function of time playing, changing levels of expertise, familiarity, and so on.

While Garris et al. (2002) focused on games, it was earlier noted that the distinctions between simulations and recreational games may not be as rigid as often thought and may depend more on the learner's goals than the label. However, in those situations where the learner is intentionally setting out to learn academic or work-related content, O'Neil et al. (2005) and other authors have noted that some of the important dimensions in simulations with an intentional focus on learning academic or work-related content might be goals, elements of competition and playfulness, use of privileges and penalties, and use of a linear goal structure. Many simulations with this type of emphasis have a goal of discovering causal relationships in a nonlinear fashion, are designed for specific skill mastery, and have well-defined achievable goals with predictable outcomes. Thus, from the learner's perspective, in this type of environment, the player's motivation to engage is likely to be based on the desire to learn more about a situation or domain, and is more likely to be required and nonvoluntary.

In those situations where the primary goal is recreational, it is reasonable to hypothesize that the most critical features for simulation games would be rules, goals, authenticity, and challenge. With respect to rules and goals, it can be speculated that clear goals and rules would result in higher levels of motivation and engagement. Malone and Lepper (1987) note that individuals desire an optimal level of challenge, one which presents activities that are neither too easy nor too difficult to perform. While goals should be clearly specified, it is possible to introduce a higher degree of challenge by introducing the possibility of multiple goals, or multiple solutions to achieve a goal, and some degree of uncertainty with respect to obtaining that goal. As Garris et al. (2002) suggest, it would be ideal to employ progressive difficulty levels, multiple goals, and a certain amount of informational ambiguity to ensure an uncertain outcome. Performance feedback and score keeping allow the individual to track progress toward desired goals.

Authenticity is another critical dimension that can vary depending on the goal. For example when the learner's primary goal is recreation, simulations may be most effective when they emulate *fantasy* conditions, and where the goal is to learn academic or work-related content and/or skills, simulations may be most effective when they resemble real-world conditions (Wu, Lee, Chang, & Liang, 2013). For example, learning how to operate a motor vehicle in an automobile driving simulation apparatus may be most motivating to learners when it is most like authentic driving conditions. In contrast, a racecar simulation may be most motivating when it allows one to suspend real-world driving conditions and reduces the need to consider real-world restraints (speed, obstacles, traffic laws, consequences of crashing, etc.). This is not to say that simulations with an academic or work-related focus are devoid of fantasy elements, nor that those with a recreational focus are devoid of authentic elements. However, for the learning goal of mastering academic and/or work-related content, a key variable would be the degree of authenticity to real-world problem-solving and decision-making contexts and environments.

One additional important factor is the role of feedback. Research on learning suggests that the most effective feedback is explanatory as opposed to being just corrective (Krause, Stark, & Mandl, 2009; Shute, 2008). Simulations designed to offer explanations or additional information, for example, might help facilitate elaboration, correction of misconceptions, and filling of knowledge gaps. Feedback can be seen as a simulation characteristic which would operate interactively with an individual's performance during a simulation learning cycle. As learning researchers have shown, feedback is an environmental variable that influences individual self-efficacy (Chan & Lam, 2010) and control expectations (Pekrun, 2009). For example, it has been shown that individuals react to feedback, including progress feedback, by maintaining successful strategies and modifying unsuccessful ones (Hattie & Gan, 2011). Moreover, there is evidence that feedback that provides information about an individual's mastery of learning strategies (Hendry, Bromberger, & Armstrong, 2011) and that links the mastery of strategies to outcome success both contribute positively to self-efficacy (Pekrun, 2009).

In sum, in terms of input characteristics, clear goals and rules, authenticity, and optimal level of challenge can be hypothesized to be critical elements of simulations that would be expected to impact motivational variables, while effective feedback would be a critical feature during a specific learning cycle.

Individual Motivation in Simulations

Current views of motivation suggest that self-efficacy, attributions, control beliefs, interest, intrinsic motivation, value, and goal orientation are key motivation constructs related to achievement outcomes (Schunk et al., 2013). In the model proposed by Garris et al. (2002) and other recent attempts (Przybylski, Rigby, & Ryan, 2010), which are specific to gaming environments, various motivational factors are included, but they do not take into account learner goals and possible mediators of outcomes, such as emotional factors as possible variables despite the importance of emotional aspects of games described by investigators such as D'Mello (2013), and Granic, Lobel, and Engels (2014). Where emotional factors have been considered, they have been examined apart from motivation and engagement (D'Mello, 2013) except in a few cases (Bell & Kozlowski, 2008).

In order to build on efforts to consider motivation in investigating simulation environments, it seems desirable to include a wide range of variables that more recent motivational frameworks have shown to influence achievement outcomes, such as expectancy-value theory (Eccles, 2007; Wigfield & Eccles, 2000) or more recent elaborations, such as the control-value framework described earlier (Pekrun, 2007; Pekrun et al., 2007; Pekrun et al., 2009; Pekrun & Linnenbrink-Garcia, 2012).

One advantage of a control-value approach is that it links key motivational variables to achievement emotions, indicators of engagement, and later learning/ training outcomes. The control-value approach encompasses goal orientations (mastery, performance approach, and performance avoidance) as well as specific motivational variables including value (intrinsic and extrinsic) and control (outcome expectancies and attributions) dimensions. In addition, the approach includes relevant achievement-related emotions, such as enjoyment and relaxation as positive activity-focused emotions; as well as anger, frustration, and boredom as negative activity-focused emotions. Furthermore, control-value theory includes joy, hope, pride, gratitude, contentment, and relief as positive outcome-focused emotions, as well as anxiety, shame, anger, sadness, disappointment, and hopelessness as negative outcome-focused emotions. As indicated earlier, activity-focused emotions are centered on a learner's control and value appraisals of a given task or activity, while outcome-focused emotions are centered on the outcomes of the task or activity. As the earlier part of this chapter suggested, motivational variables and emotional variables are assumed to be predictive of engagement variables which then are related to learning or training outcomes.

While the control-value approach was not developed with a simulation environment in mind, it is reasonable to hypothesize that simulations represent a special case of, rather than a distinct case of, specialized learning environments. It would be reasonable to propose that these variables would operate to mediate learning outcomes in simulation situations in ways consistent with what the research has suggested in other learning contexts.

Connecting Simulation/Game Features to Motivation, Emotional Factors, and Engagement: A Proposed Control-Value Approach and Model

The simulation characteristics mentioned earlier (goals, rules, authenticity, challenge, and feedback during a simulation cycle) are important background variables that need to be considered in trying to account for learning outcomes in simulation exercises. However, an important cognitive variable that merits consideration is prior knowledge.

Prior Knowledge

The role of prior knowledge in learning is one of the most robust findings in the learning literature (Mayer & Alexander, 2011). Prior knowledge has been shown to be related to learning in a host of domains including science learning (Duschl & Hamilton, 2011), reading comprehension (Fox & Alexander, 2011), and many other domains. The extensive research in this area indicates that when learners have more extensive declarative and procedural knowledge in a given domain, they are better able to learn information in that domain (Mayer, 2011b). This type of knowledge is based on a learner's experience over time, and thus can be something that a participant in a simulation would bring to the experience as opposed to new knowledge created during the simulation experience.

A Proposed Model

Taking into account the preceding information on simulation/game characteristics, individual background characteristics, motivational variables, emotional indicators, engagement factors, and outcomes, it is possible to propose a conceptual model which unites these features. The proposed model is found in Figure 10.1. The model is organized around four stages, including inputs, pre-simulation/game appraisals, simulation/game cycle, and simulation/game outcomes. The inputs are divided into two types, one related to the context, and one pertaining to the learner. The simulation/game context assumed to be important includes goals and rules, authenticity to real-world problems or work-related contexts, and level of challenge. The key learner background variable is task-relevant prior knowledge.

The pre-simulation/game appraisals block includes initial interest, goal orientations, and self-efficacy. Following contemporary goal orientation research (Maehr & Zusho, 2009) and drawing from control-value theory (Pekrun & Linnenbrink-Garcia, 2012), goal orientations are divided into three categories: mastery, performance approach, and performance avoidance. The next simulation/game block is made up of one or more cycles during the course of a simulation/game. In this cycle emotions influence engagement, which subsequently impacts performance. In turn, performance influences feedback, which impacts attributions, self-efficacy, and interest during the simulation/game cycle. Each performance cycle is composed of engagement and feedback. The emotion variables in the model refer to achievement-related emotions, including activity-focused emotions (enjoyment, boredom, and anger), positive outcome-focused emotions (hope and pride), and negative outcome-focused emotions (anxiety, hopelessness, and shame). The motivational variables during the simulation/game cycle are attribution, self-efficacy, and interest (intrinsic or situational interest and extrinsic interest).

The final simulation/game outcomes block includes learning and motivation outcomes. Learning outcomes are based on the specific content of the simulation

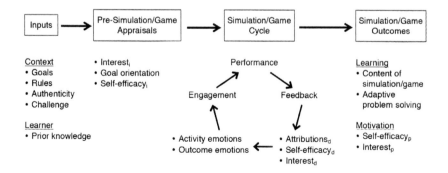

Note. $_i$ = initial. $_d$ = during simulation/game cycle. $_p$ = post-simulation/game cycle.

FIGURE 10.1 A proposed model of motivational, emotional, and engagement aspects of simulation/game environments.

as well as more general adaptive problem solving. The motivation outcomes are post-simulation/game cycle self-efficacy and interest. The specific relationships proposed among the variables are consistent with the research that has been discussed, although no comprehensive study has been conducted to date which has tested all aspects of the relationships proposed with such a broad array of variables.

It should be noted that the model proposed here is organized in a linear fashion. This is primarily for convenience and conceptual clarity, with the full recognition that simulation experiences are dynamic systems and that learners' experiences change over time. The intent here is to provide a comprehensive model that integrates a number of factors, which are typically not considered in unison, into one conceptual framework as a guide to future research.

Conclusion

The literature on learning outcomes related to simulations/games is not entirely clear as noted earlier. There is some evidence that learners do develop specific skills and that simulations and games can be useful in promoting understanding in conceptually difficult domains such as math and science (de Jong, 2011). But there is evidence that not all are equal, and that design issues are a critical consideration, including those design features that impact motivation. Moreover, there are considerations related to cost, delivery, time constraints, evaluation, and extent of guidance in simulations. While there are many opportunities offered by simulation training environments, there is a need to systematically evaluate and design them with powerful learning and motivational features embedded. The current inconsistent nature of the research on simulations may be due to the lack of sound instructional design as well as inconsistencies in terminology and constructs. It is hoped that our proposed model will provide a beginning framework to move this work forward.

Author Note

The work reported herein was supported by grant number N000141110089 (DCAPS) as well as N00014-14-C-0146 (ENGAGE) from the Office of Naval Research and the Defense Advanced Research Projects Agency to the National Center for Research on Evaluation, Standards, and Student Testing (CRESST). The findings and opinions in this work are those of the authors and do not necessarily reflect the positions or policies of the Office of Naval Research or the Defense Advanced Research Projects Agency.

References

Ainley, M., Hidi, S., & Berndorff, D. (2002). Interest, learning, and the psychological processes that mediate their relationship. *Journal of Educational Psychology, 94*, 545–561.

Alderman, M. K. (2004). *Motivation for achievement* (2nd ed.). Mahwah, NJ: Lawrence Erlbaum.

Amory, A. (2002). Building an educational adventure game: Theory, design, and lessons. *Journal of Interactive Learning Research, 12*, 249–263.

Anderman, E. M., & Dawson, H. (2011). Learning with motivation. In R. E. Mayer & P. A. Alexander (Eds.), *Handbook of research on learning and instruction* (pp. 219–242). New York, NY: Routledge.

Andrade, A. D., Cifuentes, P., Mitzer, M. J., Roos, B. A., Ramanakumar, A., & Ruiz, J. G. (2012). Simulating geriatric home safety assessments in a three-dimensional virtual world. *Gerontology & Geriatrics Education, 33*, 233–252.

Astleitner, H., & Wiesner, C. (2004). An integrated model of multimedia learning and motivation. *Journal of Educational Multimedia and Hypermedia, 13*(1), 3–21.

Azevedo, R. (2015). Defining and measuring engagement and learning in science: Conceptual, theoretical, methodological, and analytical issues. *Educational Psychologist, 50*(1), 84–94.

Azevedo, R., & Cromley, J. G. (2004). Does training on self-regulated learning facilitate students' learning with hypermedia? *Journal of Educational Psychology, 96*(3), 523–535.

Azevedo, R., Cromley, J. G., Winters, F. I., Moos, D. C., & Greene, J. A. (2005). Adaptive human scaffolding facilitates adolescents' self-regulated learning with hypermedia. *Instructional Science, 33*, 381–412.

Azevedo, R., Guthrie, J. T., & Seibert, D. (2004). The role of self-regulated learning in fostering students' conceptual understanding of complex systems with hypermedia. *Journal of Educational Computing Research, 30*, 87–111.

Bachen, C. M., Hernández-Ramos, P. R., & Raphael, C. (2012). Simulating REAL LIVES: Promoting global empathy and interest in learning through simulation games. *Simulation & Gaming, 43*(4), 437–460.

Bandura, A. (1986). *Social foundations of thought and action: A social cognitive theory.* Englewood Cliffs, NJ: Prentice-Hall.

Bell, B. S., & Kozlowski, S. W. J. (2008). Active learning: Effects of core training design elements on self-regulatory processes, learning, and adaptability. *Journal of Applied Psychology, 93*(2), 296–316.

Burguillo, J. C. (2010). Using game theory and competition-based learning to stimulate student motivation and performance. *Computers & Education, 55*(2), 566–575.

Chan, J. C. Y., & Lam, S. (2010). Effects of different evaluative feedback on students' self-efficacy in learning. *Instructional Science, 38*(1), 37–58.

Christenson, S. L., Reschly, A. L., & Wylie, C. (Eds.). (2012). *Handbook of research on student engagement.* New York, NY: Springer.

Cook, D. A. (2012). If you teach them, they will learn: Why medical education needs comparative effectiveness research. *Advances in Health Sciences Education, 17*, 305–310.

Cook, D. A., Hamstra, S. J., Brydges, R., Zendejas, B., Szostek, J. H., Wang, A. T., . . . Hatala, R. (2013). Comparative effectiveness of instructional design features in simulation-based education: Systematic review and meta-analysis. *Medical Teacher, 35*, e867–e898.

Cox, K., & Guthrie, J. T. (2001). Motivational and cognitive contributions to students' amount of reading. *Contemporary Educational Psychology, 26*(1), 116–131.

Creutzfeldt, J., Hedman, L., & Felländer-Tsai, L. (2012). Effects of pre-training using serious game technology on CPR performance—An exploratory quasi-experimental transfer study. *Scandinavian Journal of Trauma, Resuscitation and Emergency Medicine, 20*(1), 1–9.

Crookall, D. (2010). Serious games, debriefing, and simulation/gaming as a discipline. *Simulation & Gaming, 41*(6), 898–920.

de Jong, T. (2011). Instruction based on computer simulations. In R. E. Mayer & P. A. Alexander (Eds.), *Handbook of research on learning and instruction* (pp. 446–466). New York, NY: Routledge.

de Jong, T., & van Joolingen, W. R. (1998). Scientific discovery learning with computer simulations of conceptual domains. *Review of Educational Research, 68*, 179–202.

D'Mello, S. (2013). A selective meta-analysis on the relative incidence of discrete affective states during learning with technology. *Journal of Educational Psychology, 105*(4), 1082–1099. doi: 10.1037/a0032674

Duschl, R., & Hamilton, R. (2011). Learning science. In R. E. Mayer & P. A. Alexander (Eds.), *Handbook of research on learning and instruction* (pp. 78–107). New York, NY: Routledge.

Ebner, M., & Holzinger, A. (2007). Successful implementation of user-centered game based learning in higher education: an example from civil engineering. *Computers & Education, 49*(3), 873–890.

Eccles, J. S. (2007). Families, schools, and developing achievement-related motivations and engagement. In J. E. Grusec & P. D. Hastings (Eds.), *Handbook of socialization* (pp. 665–691). New York, NY: The Guilford Press.

Eccles, J. S., & Wang, M. (2012). So what is student engagement anyway? In S. L. Christenson, A. L. Reschly, & C. Wylie (Eds.), *Handbook of research on student engagement* (pp. 133–147). New York, NY: Springer.

Fisher, K. R., Marshall, P. J., & Nanayakkara, A. R. (2009). Motivational orientation, error monitoring, and academic performance in middle childhood: A behavioral and electrophysiological investigation. *Mind, Brain, and Education, 3*(1), 56–63.

Fox, E., & Alexander, P. A. (2011). Learning to read. In R. E. Mayer & P. A. Alexander (Eds.), *Handbook of learning and instruction* (pp. 7–31). New York, NY: Routledge.

Fredricks, J., Blumenfeld, P., & Paris, A. (2004). School engagement: Potential of the concept, state of the evidence. *Review of Educational Research, 74*(1), 59–109.

Furrer, C., & Skinner, E. (2003). Sense of relatedness as a factor in children's academic engagement and performance. *Journal of Educational Psychology, 95*(1), 148–162.

Garris, R., Ahlers, R., & Driskell, J. E. (2002). Games, motivation, and learning: A research and practice model. *Simulation and Gaming, 33*(4), 441–467.

Gee, J. P. (2003). *What video games have to teach us about learning and literacy.* New York, NY: Palgrave Macmillan.

Goetz, T., Frenzel, A., Pekrun, R., & Hall, N. C. (2006). Emotional intelligence in the context of learning and achievement. In R. Schulze & R. D. Roberts (Eds.), *Emotional intelligence: An international handbook* (pp. 233–253). Cambridge, MA: Hogrefe & Huber Publishers.

Granic, I., Lobel, A., & Engels, R. C. M. E. (2014). The benefits of playing video games. *American Psychologist, 69*(1), 66–78.

Gredler, M. E. (1996). Educational games and simulations: A technology in search of a (research) paradigm. In D. H. Jonassen (Ed.), *Handbook of research on educational communications and technology* (pp. 521–539). New York, NY: Macmillan.

Greene, B. A. (2015). Measuring cognitive engagement with self-report scales: Reflections from over 20 years of research. *Educational Psychologist, 50*(1), 14–30.

Guthrie, J. T. (Ed.). (2008). *Engaging adolescents in reading.* Thousand Oaks, CA: Corwin Press.

Guthrie, J. T., Klauda, S. L., & Ho, A. (2013). Modeling the relationships among reading instruction, motivation, engagement, and achievement for adolescents. *Reading Research Quarterly, 48*(1), 9–26.

Guthrie, J. T., & Wigfield, A. (2000). Engagement and motivation in reading. In M. L. Kamil, P. B. Mosenthal, P. D. Pearson, & R. Barr (Eds.), *Handbook of reading research* (Vol. 3, pp. 403–422). New York, NY: Longman.

Harris, K., & Reid, D. (2005). The influence of virtual reality play on children's motivation. *Canadian Journal of Occupational Therapy, 72*(1), 21–30.

Hattie, J., & Gan, M. (2011). Instruction based on feedback. In R. E. Mayer & P. A. Alexander (Eds.), *Handbook of research on learning and instruction* (pp. 249–271). New York, NY: Routledge.

Hendry, G. D., Bromberger, N., & Armstrong, S. (2011). Constructive guidance and feedback for learning: The usefulness of exemplars, marking sheets and different types of feedback in a first year law subject. *Assessment and Evaluation in Higher Education, 36*(1), 1–11.

Hofstede, G. J., de Caluwé, L., & Peters, V. (2010). Why simulation games work—In search of the active substance: A synthesis. *Simulation & Gaming, 41*(6), 824–843.

Huang, W., Huang, W., & Tschopp, J. (2010). Sustaining iterative game playing processes in DGBL: The relationship between motivational processing and outcome processing. *Computers & Education, 55*, 789–797.

Jacobson, M. J., & Archodidou, A. (2000). The design of hypermedia tools for learning: Fostering conceptual change and transfer of complex scientific knowledge. *Journal of the Learning Sciences, 9*(2), 145–199.

Jimerson, S. R., Campos, E., & Greif, J. L. (2003). Toward an understanding of definitions and measures of school engagement and related terms. *California School Psychologist, 8*, 7–27.

Karabenick, S., & Urdan, T. (Eds.). (2012). *Advances in motivation and achievement* (Vol. 16). Bingley, UK: Emerald Group.

Kirsch, I., de Jong, J., LaFontaine, D., McQueen, J., Mendelovits, J., & Monseur, C. (2002). *Reading for change: Performance and engagement across countries.* Paris: OECD.

Kirschner, P. A., Sweller, J., & Clark, R. (2006). Why minimal guidance during instruction does not work: An analysis of the failure of constructivist, discovery, problem-based, experiential, and inquiry-based teaching. *Educational Psychologist, 41*, 75–86.

Krause, U., Stark, R., & Mandl, H. (2009). The effects of cooperative learning and feedback on e-learning in statistics. *Learning and Instruction, 19*(2), 158–170.

Lawson, M. A., & Lawson, H. A. (2013). New conceptual frameworks for student engagement: Research, policy, and practice. *Review of Educational Research, 83*(3), 432–479.

Lee, W., Lee, M., & Bong, M. (2014). Testing interest and self-efficacy as predictors of academic self-regulation and achievement. *Contemporary Educational Psychology, 39*, 86–99.

Leemkuil, H., de Jong, T., de Hoog, R., & Christoph, N. (2003). KM Quest: A collaborative internet-based simulation game, *Simulation & Gaming, 34*, 89–111.

Lepper, M. R., Master, A., & Yow, W. Q. (2008). Intrinsic motivation in education. In M. L. Maehr, S. A. Karabenich, & T. C. Urdan (Eds.), *Advances in motivation and achievement: Vol. 15. Social psychological perspectives* (pp. 521–555). Bingley, UK: Emerald Group Publishing Limited.

Liu, C., Cheng, Y., & Huang, C. (2011). The effect of simulation games on the learning of computational problem solving. *Computers & Education, 57*, 1907–1918.

Linnenbrink-Garcia, L., & Pekrun, R. (2011a). Students' emotions and academic engagement: Introduction to the special issue. *Contemporary Educational Psychology, 36(1)*, 1–3.

Linnenbrink-Garcia, L., & Pekrun, R. (Eds.). (2011b). Students' emotions and academic engagement: Special Issue. *Contemporary Educational Psychology, 36(1)*.

Maehr, M. L., & Zusho, A. (2009). Achievement goal theory: The past, present, and future. In K. R. Wentzel & A. Wigfield (Eds.), *Handbook of motivation at school* (pp. 77–104). New York, NY: Routledge/Taylor & Francis Group.

Malone, T. W., & Lepper, M. R. (1987). Making learning fun: A taxonomy of intrinsic motivations for learning. In R. E. Snow & M. J. Farr (Eds.), *Aptitude, learning, and instruction: Vol. 3. Conative and affective process analyses* (pp. 223–253). Hillsdale, NJ: Lawrence Erlbaum.

Marsh, H. W., Hau, K., Artelt, C., Baumert, J., & Peschar, J. L. (2006). OECD's brief self-report measure of educational psychology's most useful affective constructs: Cross-cultural, psychometric comparisons across 25 countries. *International Journal of Testing, 6(4)*, 311–360.

Mayer, R. E. (2005). Cognitive theory of multimedia learning. In R. E. Mayer (Ed.), *The Cambridge handbook of multimedia learning* (pp. 31–48). New York, NY: Cambridge University Press.

Mayer, R. E. (2011a). *Multimedia learning*. New York, NY: Cambridge University Press.

Mayer, R. E. (2011b). *Applying the science of learning*. Boston, MA: Pearson.

Mayer, R. E., & Alexander, P. A. (2011). Introduction to research on learning. In R. E. Mayer & P. A. Alexander (Eds.), *Handbook of research on learning and instruction* (pp. 3–6). New York, NY: Routledge.

McKinney, J., Cook, D. A., Wood, D., & Hatala, R. (2012). Simulation-based training for cardiac auscultation skills: Systematic review and meta-analysis. *Journal of General Internal Medicine, 28*, 283–291.

Mitchell, A., & Savill-Smith, C. (2004). *The use of computer and video games for learning: A review of literature*. London: Learning and Skills Development Agency.

National Research Council and the Institute of Medicine. (2004). *Engaging schools: Fostering high school students' motivation to learn* (Committee on Increasing High School Students' Engagement and Motivation to Learn). Washington, DC: National Academies Press.

Ning, H. K., & Downing, K. (2010). The reciprocal relationship between motivation and self-regulation: A longitudinal study on academic performance. *Learning and Individual Differences, 20(6)*, 682–686.

O'Neil, H. F., & Fisher, Y.-C. (2004). A technology to support leader development: Computer games. In D. V. Day, S. J. Zaccaro, & S. M. Halpin (Eds.), *Leader development for transforming organizations* (pp. 99–121). Mahwah, NJ: Lawrence Erlbaum Associates.

O'Neil, H. F., Wainess, R., & Baker, E. L. (2005). Classification of learning outcomes: Evidence from the computer games literature. *The Curriculum Journal, 16(4)*, 455–474.

Papastergiou, M. (2009). Digital game-based learning in high school computer science education: Impact on educational effectiveness and student motivation. *Computers & Education, 52(1)*, 1–12.

Patrick, H., Ryan, A. M., & Kaplan, A. (2007). Early adolescents' perceptions of the classroom social environment, motivational beliefs, and engagement. *Journal of Educational Psychology, 99(1)*, 83–98.

Pekrun, R. (2000). The control-value theory of achievement emotions. In J. Heckhausen (Ed.), *Motivational psychology of human development* (pp. 143–164). Oxford, UK: Elsevier Science.

Pekrun, R. (2006). The control-value theory of achievement emotions: Assumptions, corollaries, and implications for educational research and practice. *Educational Psychology Review, 18*, 315–341. doi: 10.1007/s10648-006-9029-9

Pekrun, R. (2007). The control-value theory of achievement emotions: An integrative approach to emotions in education. In R. Schulze & R. D. Roberts (Eds.), *Emotional intelligence: An international handbook* (pp. 13–36). Cambridge, MA: Hogrefe & Huber Publishers.

Pekrun, R. (2009). Emotions at school. In K. R. Wentzel & A. Wigfield (Eds.), *Handbook of motivation at school* (pp. 575–604). New York, NY: Routledge.

Pekrun, R., Elliot, A. I., & Maier, M. A. (2006). Achievement goals and discrete achievement emotions: A theoretical model and prospective test. *Journal of Educational Psychology, 98*, 583–597.

Pekrun, R., Elliot, A. I., & Maier, M. A. (2009). Achievement goals and achievement emotions: Testing a model of their joint relations with academic performance. *Journal of Educational Psychology, 101*, 115–135.

Pekrun, R., Frenzel, A., Goetz, T., & Perry, R. P. (2007). The control-value theory of achievement emotions: An integrative approach to emotions in education. In P.A. Schutz & R. Pekrun (Eds.), *Emotion in education* (pp. 13–36). San Diego, CA: Academic Press.

Pekrun, R., Goetz, T., & Perry, R. P. (2005). *Achievement Emotions Questionnaire (AEQ). User's manual.* Munich, Germany: Department of Psychology, University of Munich.

Pekrun, R., Goetz, T., Titz, W., & Perry, R. P. (2002). Academic emotions in students' self-regulated learning and achievement: A program of quantitative and qualitative research. *Educational Psychologist, 37*, 91–106.

Pekrun, R., & Linnenbrink-Garcia, L. (2012). Academic emotions and student engagement. In S. L. Christenson, A. L. Reschly, & C. Wylie (Eds.), *Handbook of research on student engagement* (pp. 259–282). New York, NY: Springer.

Pintrich, P. R. (2003). A motivational science perspective on the role of student motivation in learning and teaching contexts. *Journal of Educational Psychology, 95*(4), 667–686.

Przybylski, A. K., Rigby, C. S., & Ryan, R. M. (2010). A motivational model of video game engagement. *Review of General Psychology, 14*(2), 154–166.

Renninger, K. A., Pachrach, J. E., & Posey, S. K. E. (2008). Learner interest and achievement motivation. In M. L. Maehr, S. A. Karabenich, & T. C. Urdan (Eds.), *Advances in motivation and achievement: Vol. 15. Social psychological perspectives* (pp. 461–491). Bingley, UK: Emerald Group Publishing Limited.

Rieber, L. P. (2005). Multimedia learning in games, simulations, and microworlds. In R. E. Mayer (Ed.), *The Cambridge handbook of multimedia learning* (pp. 549–567). New York, NY: Cambridge University Press.

Rotgans, J. I., & Schmidt, H. G. (2012). The intricate relationship between motivation and achievement: Examining the mediating role of self-regulated learning and achievement-related classroom behaviors. *International Journal of Teaching and Learning in Higher Education, 24*(2), 197–208.

Rueda, R., Lim, H. J., O'Neil, H., Baker, E., Griffin, N., Brockman, S., & Sirotnik, B. (2010). Ethnic differences in students' approaches to learning: Self-regulatory cognitive and motivational predictors of academic achievement for Latino/a and White college students. In M. S. Khine & I. M. Saleh (Eds.), *New science of learning: Cognition, computers, and collaboration in education* (pp. 133–162). New York, NY: Springer.

Schunk, D. H., Meece, J. R., & Pintrich, P. R. (2013). *Motivation in education: Theory, research, and applications.* Upper Saddle River, NJ: Pearson.

Schunk, D. H., Pintrich, P. R., & Meece, J. L. (2008). *Motivation in education: Theory, research, and applications*. Upper Saddle River, NJ: Pearson/Merrill Prentice Hall.

Schunk, D. H., & Zimmerman, B. J. (2008). *Motivation and self-regulated learning: Theory, research, and applications*. New York, NY: Taylor & Francis.

Seijts, G. H., & Latham, G. P. (2011). The effect of commitment to a learning goal, self-efficacy, and the interaction between learning goal difficulty and commitment on performance in a business simulation. *Human Performance, 24*, 189–204.

Shute, J. V. (2008). Focus on formative feedback. *Review of Educational Research, 78*(1), 153–189.

Sinatra, G. M., Heddy, B. C., & Lombardi, D. (2015). The challenges of defining and measuring student engagement in science. *Educational Psychologist, 50*(1), 1–13.

Sitzmann, T. (2011). A meta-analytic examination of the instructional effectiveness of computer-based simulation games. *Personnel Psychology, 64*, 489–528.

Skinner, E., Furrer, C., Marchand, G., & Kindermann, T. (2008). Engagement and disaffectation in the classroom: Part of a larger motivational dynamic? *Journal of Educational Psychology, 100*(4), 765–781.

Tamim, R. M., Bernard, R. M., Borokhovski, E., Abrami, P. C., & Schmid, R. F. (2011). What forty years of research says about the impact of technology on learning: A second-order meta-analysis and validation study. *Review of Educational Research, 81*(1), 4–28.

Tao, Y., Cheng, C., & Sun, S. (2009). What influences college students to continue using business simulation games? The Taiwan experience. *Computers & Education, 53*, 929–939. doi: 10.1016/j.compedu.2009.05.009

Tobias, S., & Fletcher, J. D. (2011). *Computer games and instruction*. Charlotte, NC: Information Age.

Tzeng, J., & Chen, C. (2012). Computer praise, attributional orientations, and games: A re-examination of the CASA theory relative to children. *Computers in Human Behavior, 28*, 2420–2430.

VanDeventer, S. S., & White, J. A. (2002). Expert behavior in children's video game play. *Simulation and Gaming, 33*(1), 28–48.

Vogel, J. J., Vogel, D. S., Cannon-Bowers, J., Bowers, C. A., Muse, K., & Wright, M. (2006). Computer gaming and interactive simulations for learning: A meta-analysis. *Journal of Educational Computing Research, 34*(3), 229–243.

Wang, J., & Guthrie, J. T. (2004). Modeling the effects of intrinsic motivation, extrinsic motivation, amount of reading, and past reading achievement on text comprehension between U.S. and Chinese students. *Reading Research Quarterly, 39*(2), 162–186.

Wentzel, K. R., & Wigfield, A. (Eds.). (2009). *Handbook of motivation at school*. New York, NY: Taylor and Francis.

Wigfield, A., & Cambria, J. (2010a). Expectancy value theory: Retrospective and prospective. In S. Karabenick & T. C. Urdan (Eds.), *Advances in motivation and achievement, Vol. 16A. The decade ahead: Theoretical perspectives on motivation and achievement* (pp. 35–70). Bingley, UK: Emerald Publishing Group Ltd.

Wigfield, A., & Cambria, J. (2010b). Students' achievement values, goal orientations, and interest: Definitions, development, and relations to achievement outcomes. *Developmental Review, 30*, 1–35.

Wigfield, A., & Eccles, J. S. (2000). Expectancy Value Theory of motivation. *Contemporary Educational Psychology, 25*, 68–81. doi: 10.1006/ceps.1999.1015.

Wigfield, A., & Eccles, J. S. (2002). The development of competence beliefs, expectancies for success, and achievement values from childhood through adolescence. In

A. Wigfield & J. S. Eccles (Eds.), *Development of achievement motivation* (pp. 91–120). San Diego, CA: Academic Press.

Wigfield, A., Tonks, S., & Klauda, S. L. (2009). Expectancy–value theory. In K. R. Wentzel & A. Wigfield (Eds.), *Handbook of motivation at school* (pp. 55–76). Mahwah, NJ: Lawrence Erlbaum Associates.

Wouters, P., van Nimwegen, C., van Oostendorp, H., & van der Spek, E. (2013). A meta-analysis of the cognitive and motivational effects of serious games. *Journal of Educational Psychology, 105*(2), 249–265.

Wu, H., Lee, S. W., Chang, H., & Liang, J. (2013). Current status, opportunities and challenges of augmented reality in education. *Computers & Education, 62,* 41–49.

Zeidner, M. (2007). Test anxiety in educational contexts: Concepts, findings, future directions. In P. A. Schutz & R. Pekrun (Eds.), *Emotion in education* (pp. 159–177). San Diego, CA: Elsevier.

Zimmerman, B. J. (2013). Theories of self-regulated learning and academic achievement: An overview and analysis. In B. J. Zimmerman & D. H. Schunk (Eds.), *Self-regulated learning and academic achievement: Theoretical perspectives* (2nd ed., pp. 1–37). New York, NY: Routledge.

Zimmerman, B. J., & Schunk, D. H. (Eds.). (2013). *Self-regulated learning and academic achievement: Theoretical perspectives.* New York, NY: Routledge.

Zusho, A., Anthony, J. S., Hashimoto, N., & Robertson, G. (2014). Do video games provide motivation to learn? In F. C. Blumberg & F. Blumberg (Eds.), *Learning by playing: Video gaming in education* (pp. 69–86). New York, NY: Oxford University Press.

11

CAN GAMES FACILITATE ACCESS TO COLLEGE?

Zoë B. Corwin, Robert W. Danielson,
Gisele Ragusa, and William G. Tierney

Bringing College Access Practices to Scale

Ensuring postsecondary opportunities for all students remains a persistent challenge. Over the past decade a variety of college resource websites have been developed to provide students with information about postsecondary institutions and financial aid. Most recently, diverse college resource mobile applications and games have gained popularity as tools to help students navigate the complicated process of learning about and applying to college (College Summit, 2013; Corwin, Frome, & Groark, 2014). Yet little is known about this rapidly evolving "e-space" for college learning, in particular with regards to the experiences of first generation and/or low-income students (Corwin, Tierney, Fullerton, & Ragusa, 2014; Get Schooled Foundation, 2013). This makes it increasingly difficult for educators and college support staff in high schools to determine which application or other resources best meet the needs of their diverse students.

This chapter describes multidimensional research designed to examine the impact of two college access focused games (one card and one digital) on low-income high school students' access to college. Research questions sought to understand the effects of game play on players' college knowledge and college-going efficacy. Data were obtained using mixed methods at three urban high schools with low-income students. The study's quantitative findings indicate positive effects of game play on cultivating students' college-going efficacy and college knowledge. Interview data add a nuanced perspective on the effects of game play on college plans.

The Importance of College Access

Obtaining a college education is critical to ensuring the economic and social well-being of America's youth—especially those from low-income backgrounds. It is well understood that over a lifetime a college graduate is likely to earn $1.2 million more than a high school graduate. During the recent recession, jobs were scarce for everyone, and the unemployment rate for high school graduates was nearly double that of college graduates, underscoring the importance of providing equitable access to college for all high school students (Tierney, Ragusa, Corwin, & Fullerton, 2013). Research has indicated that as a consequence of earning significantly more over their lifetime, college graduates adopt a healthier lifestyle and become more civically engaged than their counterparts who have attained lower levels of education (Mazumder, 2003).

While the literature has long indicated that academic preparation and achievement are important predictors of college enrollment for students from low-income backgrounds (Adelman, 1999; Perna, 2005; Reid & Moore, 2008), more recent studies suggest that ensuring access to college and subsequent college success is more complex. As three examples, scholars have turned attention to the role of emotional intelligence on predicting college success (Sparkman, Maulding, & Roberts, 2012), the impact of self-efficacy on college GPA and persistence rates for first-generation students (Vuong, Brown-Welty, & Tracz, 2010), and the extent to which college-going climate at the high school level influences students' college outcomes (Roderick, Coca, & Nagaoka, 2011). Other studies highlight the complexity of choosing a college and determining a good fit. De los Santos and de los Santos (2006) illustrated that many Latino students chose to enroll in two-year colleges despite eligibility for four-year universities due to institutional proximity to parents' households, low-cost tuition, and flexibility in schedule so that the students could maintain employment while attending college. The phenomenon of undermatching, where academically qualified low-income students underestimate the caliber of the college or university they believe they can attend and enroll in less selective institutions, continues to garner attention in academic and policy circles (Bastedo & Flaster, 2014; Roderick et al., 2011; Roderick, Nagaoka, Coca, & Moeller, 2008; Smith, Pender, & Howell, 2013). Researchers have also shown that misperceptions about college affordability can deter students from considering applying to college (Baum & Schwartz, 2012; Cowan, 2011; McDonough & Calderone, 2006; Perna, 2006, 2010); even completing the simplified Free Application for Federal Student Aid (FAFSA) is a significant challenge for students with limited experiences with finances, particularly for those who are yet to have a bank account (Bettinger, Long, Oreopoulos, & Sanbonmatsu, 2009; 2012).

Unfortunately, many students do not receive appropriate support as they prepare for college. Due to budget shortfalls, many high schools have cut their college counselor positions leaving students with fewer school-based support providers to guide them through the steps of completing college applications and once accepted, deciding which college to attend (Bruce & Bridgeland, 2012; McKillip, Rawls, & Barry, 2012; Savitz-Romer & Liu, 2014). Traditional college outreach practices, while well-intentioned, have been only modestly effective in increasing college going for first generation and/or low-income students (Tierney, Corwin, Fullerton, & Ragusa, 2014). Effective college access programs and strategies exist; however, they are not easily brought to scale due to limited funding (Tierney et al., 2013). With high numbers of high school students spending time using digital media, capitalizing on social media and digital games for college access and support presents a potential tool to engage students in college preparation processes in novel and relevant ways (DeAndrea, Ellison, LaRose, Steinfield, & Fiore, 2012).

The Context and Focus of the Study's College Access Games

A critical hurdle in ensuring access to college lies in the application process itself. While significant numbers of low-income students hold high college aspirations and have met college admissions requirements, many qualified students slip through the college outreach grasp during the college application process. Such students have done well in high school, but lack the support—at home and/or at school—to successfully complete and submit college applications (Bruce & Bridgeland, 2012; McKillip et al., 2012; Perna, 2014; Savitz-Romer & Liu, 2014). The college access games that we developed and tested were designed to meet the particular needs of these students. Recognizing that a majority of teenagers were avid users of social media and games (Lenhart et al., 2008), the research team launched collaborations with local high school students and their teachers to create a suite of games to engage students in learning about the college application process. These games provide interventions that meet the unique needs of low income, first-generation high school students and capitalize on their interest in social media and collaborative game play. Results of the pilot studies on two of these game interventions are described in this chapter.

To develop the college access games, the team engaged in an iterative process of game conceptualization, design, and testing (Corwin, Tierney, Swensen, Bouchard, Fullerton, & Ragusa, 2012; Fullerton, 2014). When conceptualizing the games, the research team drew insight from student and practitioner focus groups and subsequently identified important central themes that were incorporated into the games: achieving balance between academics and extracurricular activities, managing time, and keeping track of application deadlines. These were all themes that pertain to valuable college knowledge and social capital related to college success (Conley, 2005, 2012), but are seldom of focus in traditional high school classrooms or college resource websites.

The first game, called Application Crunch, is a card game for three to four players intended to stimulate discussion about the college application process, encourage students to critically consider all the steps of applying to college, and illustrate the importance of meeting college application deadlines. It was originally designed as a paper prototype to inform development of an online game, however it gained popularity during the testing process and was then printed and used as a part of the research process. With this game, each player takes on the role of a high school student and college applicant. Players juggle time among academics, extracurricular activities, employment, and service while competing for college applications and scholarships. To win Application Crunch, players must be accepted to college, save enough money to pay for tuition and other college expenses, and build the kind of character who can succeed in their chosen school.

As previously described, Application Crunch served as a prototype for a second game, called Mission: Admission, a web-based college access game situated in the social networking platform Facebook where a player role plays a college applicant. This game is played in real time over the course of a week. In other words, when it's 4:00 p.m. on a Monday in the real world, it's 4:00 p.m. on a Monday in the Mission: Admission game. Players create an avatar that navigates a high school campus. They have to determine where to spend their avatar's limited game "energy" while putting together competitive college applications. Players study a calendar of deadlines with application requirements and decide where they will apply and how they will cover the costs of college. Game-based energy accrues over time and players learn to check back in regularly and shepherd their avatar through college-access-related, deadline-driven activities. To be successful in the Mission: Admission game, the player must meet all application deadlines, submit robust applications, and be able to afford the college of his or her choice. Players can ask questions of friends in their real Facebook networks and obtain hints for how to play by clicking on the virtual college counselor within the game's virtual college center. The Mission: Admission game was developed in conjunction with high school students and is therefore whimsical in tone yet complex in game mechanics, involving strategy to play as opposed to simply clicking through the game. Successful game strategies for this game involve effective time management, acute awareness of college application deadlines, strategic requests of recommendation letters, obtaining leadership roles in extracurricular or service activities, and earning high academic achievement. Each of these strategies is critical to college access, and ultimately for college admission, and reflect strategies that require practice for learners with limited college-related experiences.

Research Approach

The rationale behind designing the college access games was that when strategies are practiced in the context of the game, players have an opportunity to make mistakes in a safe space without actual consequences (Gee, 2007a, 2007b). They then have the opportunity to adjust and practice strategies and subsequently gain mastery in navigating the college application process in advance of their real-life college applications. The games thus provide safe and low-stakes opportunities to practice skills and strategies necessary to successfully achieve college access. Beyond designing and testing the games multiple times during the development process, we needed to holistically assess the impact of the two games in a larger research context. As such, we relied on a multipronged mixed methods approach to respond to three important research questions:

1. What are the effects of game play on student learning?
2. How does game play influence players' college-going self-efficacy?
3. How does the social context of game play affect students' experiences with the game?

The game-based research occurred in schools serving Title I students in Los Angeles. We measured the impact of students' understanding of college and financial aid application practices, in addition to their self-efficacy in applying for, getting into, and enrolling in college. Key decisions that we focused on were application process strategies and the choices that players made in preparing for college applications and college choice. In addition, we collected data on students' use of technology and social media, in particular with regards to college.

Our assessment metrics consisted of: (1) pre- and post-test questionnaires designed to measure changes in players' college-going self-efficacy and college knowledge; (2) longitudinal interviews designed to better understand context of game play and obtain qualitative insight into the effects of game play on college aspirations and plans; (3) classroom observations intended to document student engagement and usability; and (4) teacher interviews designed to determine how games might be best implemented within classrooms. Each of the components of the questionnaires was tested for validity and reliability using well-established statistical procedures and item response theory (Wilson, 2011).

We used an iterative, multidimensional analytical schema to assess the impact of the games. Figure 11.1 provides the illustration of the analytical schema that informed the assessment of the games' impacts. The schema is informed by learning theory and college access research. It illustrates the interconnectedness between theoretical constructs, game-based constructs, student factors associated with college readiness, and what is addressed in our games both in terms of learning and affective factors. It portrays the research design outlined above but is expanded to include factors influencing college access and readiness and measures of additional long-term outcomes conducive to evaluating effects of game play well beyond the game play session. The study results outlined below serve as the foundation for a larger study including long-term components (reflected in the schema, Figure 11.1).

Two Specific Game-Based Studies

Study 1: Application Crunch (the Card Game)

The Application Crunch game was originally designed as a card game prototype for future electronic games. We engaged in an exploratory study using this game

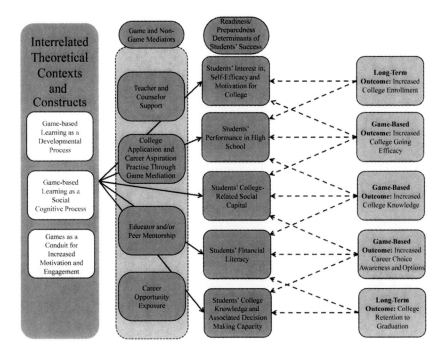

FIGURE 11.1 Game-based analytical schema (accounting for non game factors).

with a modest sample size and results are reported as a study pilot that is a precursor of a larger intervention study.

Data Sources, Instrumentation, and Analyses

For this study, data were collected from 236 students (treatment: $n = 65$; quasi-control: $n = 171$) from three high schools. The students' ages ranged from 15–18 and students were in Grades 9 through 12 with the majority in Grades 11 (68.8%) and 12 (22.6%). The majority of the students in this study were of Latino descent (92.3%) with small percentages of the students of African American, Asian, White, or mixed ethnicities. In terms of gender, 51.4% of the student participants were female. Nearly all of the participating students (97%) received free or reduced price lunches (a widely accepted federal poverty indicator).

As described above, both qualitative and quantitative analyses were conducted for this research effort. In terms of qualitative data, we observed a subset of students ($n = 65$) during play sessions with the Application Crunch card game and collected extensive field notes. These field notes were coded using a combination of structural, descriptive, and theoretical (pertaining to college access literature and game theory) coding techniques and then thematically analyzed (Saldaña,

2009). In terms of the quantitative data collected for the pilot, descriptive statistics and *t* tests were used to understand the trends in the data.

Quantitative Findings: Card Game

For these analyses we chose to focus on three specific research questions: (a) Are the instruments we created reliable? (b) Does playing the card game increase college knowledge and college-going self-efficacy? and (c) Is the effect of playing Application Crunch different for males and females? Given the iterative nature of the project, these analyses focus on exploring how students interacted with the game so that both the game experience as well as the instruments used to measure the experience can be modified in the future. Additionally, due to the large number of students absent for the pretest phase, only post-test data were used for these analyses.

Regarding the first question (Are the instruments we created reliable?), we submitted two of our researcher-created instruments (a 20-item college-going knowledge measure and a 15-item, 4-point Likert scale measuring college-going self-efficacy where 1= low efficacy) to reliability analyses. The initial results were promising—both measures indicated good reliability (Cronbach's alpha for knowledge = .786 and self-efficacy = .877). However, the item-by-item analysis of the knowledge measure indicated that some items were not performing well. Specifically, seven items had a mean of 0.5 or less—indicating that less than half of the students could answer the question correctly. Removing these seven items increased the Cronbach's alpha to .807 and raised the average score from approximately 10 correct answers (out of 20, approximately 50%) to an average of eight correct answers (out of 13, approximately 62%). We opted to retain this 13-item measurement of college knowledge for our remaining analyses.

Regarding our second question (Does playing the card game increase college-going knowledge and college-going self-efficacy?), post-test scores for each of these two scales were examined via independent samples *t* tests. Results indicate that individuals who played the card game at least once (approximately one third of the sample) scored significantly higher on both measures of college-going knowledge, $t(152) = 2.773$), and college-going self-efficacy, $t(148) = 2.819$, all analyses conducted at the $p < .05$ level. Specifically, students who played Application Crunch scored an average of 70.3% on the knowledge measure ($SD = 22\%$) and reported an average self-efficacy score of 3.02 ($SD = .50$). By contrast, students who did not play Application Crunch scored an average of 58% on the knowledge measure ($SD = 28\%$) and an average self-efficacy score of 2.77 ($SD = .51$).

Finally, we examine our last research question (Is the effect of playing Application Crunch different for males and females?) by performing the same statistical analyses above on only those students who played Application Crunch. Results indicate that, statistically, the effect of the game was similar for both males and females. Specifically, we found no significant differences between college-going knowledge, $t(50) = 0.739$, ns., and college-going self-efficacy, $t(53) = 1.957$, $p = .056$, by gender. However, it is interesting to note that in both cases the average score for females was slightly larger (knowledge, 72.6% vs. 68.1%; self-efficacy, 3.15 vs. 2.89) and in the second analysis approached significance.

    As an aggregate, the findings from these analyses indicate our measures were reliable, that playing Application Crunch promoted college-going knowledge and college-going self-efficacy, and that these findings were similar for males and females. As mentioned earlier, the process of game creation and measurement creation are both iterative, and as such, these analyses indicate some areas of improvement. First, our measure of college-going knowledge had a number of items which students routinely missed (one item was answered correctly by only 12% of students). It could be that some of these items were simply too difficult for students, or that the content of these questions did not come up during the regular course of play. This should be examined more thoroughly in the next iterations. Second, we find it interesting that females who played Application Crunch almost outscored males on our measure of self-efficacy ($p = 0.056$). While females and males played in similar numbers (25 and 27, respectively), there may have been some aspect of the game that resonated more with females, making them feel more efficacious. Alternatively, it could be the style in which the game is played, or perhaps whom the players are playing with. To determine the answers to these questions, follow-up studies using other techniques including interviews, observations, and perhaps think-aloud protocols could be employed to further our understanding of how we can improve Application Crunch.

Qualitative Findings: Card Game

In addition to the closed set questions on the questionnaire, we administered an open-ended questionnaire to a subset of 50 students after they had played Application Crunch. Participant responses to the two selected questions below illustrate how the game contributed to their general college knowledge and college application strategies. The open-ended questions "What did you learn playing the game?" and "How will you play differently the next time?" provided players with an opportunity to reflect on their game experience without structured responses prompted by the researchers. Students were not limited to filling in one answer. Their verbatim responses are paraphrased and grouped thematically in Table 11.1. Responses are aligned with the learning objectives of the Application Crunch game.

    The table illustrates that there are definite parallels between the players' game strategies and their general reported college knowledge gained from the Application Crunch game. This suggests that game play and its associated strategic focus may lead to generalized college knowledge, which is a primary intent of the game.

TABLE 11.1 Evidence of College Knowledge and Strategic Game Play

Categorized responses for question "What did you learn playing the game?": Reported evidence of college knowledge	Frequency (%)
Extracurricular activities and service make applications competitive	12 (12.8)
Importance of time management/keeping track of deadlines	11 (11.7)
Diverse types of financial aid available	11 (11.7)
Different requirements for different schools	10 (10.6)
College costs	8 (8.5)
Diverse types of colleges	7 (7.4)
FAFSA is critical	6 (6.4)
Save money	5 (5.3)
Apply early	3 (3.2)
Ensure completeness and accuracy of college application	3 (3.2)
What to do on first day of college/roommate questions	3 (3.2)
Importance of applying for all financial aid	2 (2.1)
Diverse types of degrees	2 (2.1)
Life skills are important	2 (2.1)
It is helpful to have a job	2 (2.1)
Start preparing early	2 (2.1)
Take advantage of all opportunities	1 (1.1)
It is difficult to apply to college	1 (1.1)
Make informed decisions	1 (1.1)
Strive to be the top in your classes	1 (1.1)
Take the SAT	1 (1.1)
Total: College Knowledge	94 (100)

Categorized responses for question "How will you play differently the next time?": Strategic game play (specific to Application Crunch)	Frequency (%)
Make smart decisions/strategize/stay organized	15 (23.4)
Apply to a wide range of schools	14 (21.9)
Manage time/pay attention to deadlines	13 (20.3)
Earn money/apply to scholarships	10 (15.6)
Stay focused	3 (4.7)
Engage in community service	3 (4.7)
Look for more letters of recommendation	1 (1.6)
Answer questions well	1 (1.6)
Make sure application is correct	1 (1.6)
Choose a different character	1 (1.6)
Be prepared	1 (1.6)
"Earn" personal stories	1 (1.6)
Total: Strategic Game Play	64 (100)

Study 2: Mission: Admission (the Facebook Game)

Research from the exploratory study of the Application Crunch card game informed the design, development, and testing of the second game, the online intervention Mission: Admission. This second game is built into the Facebook platform and takes place in real time. In other words, if it is 3 p.m. on a Friday, it is 3 p.m. on a Friday in the game. Players select an avatar and guide the avatar through a week of preparing for and applying to college. The player has a fixed amount of energy to spend on studying, doing extracurricular activities, and applying to college and for financial aid. Within the game, students can ask questions of their real-life Facebook friends and of a virtual college counselor. Successful game play depends on a player's ability to manage deadlines, balance activities, understand the college application process, and follow through on plans. The tone of the game is upbeat and snarky. The findings below derive from an exploratory study. Data were collected at three urban high schools serving a high majority of low-income students. Students played the game one to five times in a three-week period.

Data Sources, Instrumentation, and Analyses

A total of 489 students participated in this study. The majority (85.3%) of the sample identified as Latino, and boys and girls were split roughly evenly, with approximately 51% of the sample identifying as male and 49% as female. Nearly all (92%) of the respondents reported that their family owned a computer, and 88% of respondents indicated that they had Internet access at home. Roughly 63% of participants owned a smartphone. A large majority of the respondents in the sample (82%) indicated that they had a Facebook account, yet just more than a third (36%) said they used Twitter.

Out of 489 participants, 123 students played the game (25.2%). Looking only at the respondents who played, 8.9% played the game once, 13.8% played the game twice, 7.3% played the game three times, 33.3% played the game four times, and 36.6% played the game five times. We observed a subset of students in three classrooms as they played the game. We also conducted a series of longitudinal interviews with a group of 50 students at three times during the school year (prior to college application deadlines, during financial aid application season, and when students were determining where to enroll in college).

Data collection for the Mission: Admission game study followed a similar research design to the Application Crunch card game and included socio-demographic information; technology access information; the previously described college-going efficacy scale; and college knowledge concept inventory with subscales that measured knowledge about college application processes, admissions processes, college choice, and college financial literacy; observations; longitudinal interviews; and interviews with teachers and counselors. The data set entailed

489 matched pre- and post-tests from quasi-control and intervention groups, interviews with 50 students, and observations of game play with 97 students.

Due to the nature of the online game platform (embedded in Facebook), the intervention group was introduced to the online game at school and was provided several structured opportunities to play the game at school over the course of three weeks. Students could also continue game play at home, thus accounting for broad variances in the number of times students played the game.

Quantitative Results: Online Game

Given the promising results from the card game, the game design team attempted to recreate the experience in a more accessible way to many students—as a free, online application that was linked to the user's Facebook account. In analyzing the effects of the online game, we focused on three research questions similar to those discussed earlier related to the card game: (a) Were the instruments reliable? (b) Did playing the game increase college knowledge and college-going self-efficacy? and (c) Did males and females interact with the game differently? Because of the iterative nature of the project, these analyses were conducted to explore how students interacted with the game with the express purpose of using this understanding to further modify the game.

Regarding the first question (Were the instruments reliable?), we submitted four researcher-created instruments (a college-going self-efficacy scale, a college social influences scale, an Internet survey designed to better understand the demographics of the student population, and a college-going knowledge scale) to reliability analyses. The results were very promising—the college-going self-efficacy, social influences, and Internet demographic scales all achieved very high reliability scores (Cronbach's alpha = .905, .808, and .863, respectively.) The college-going knowledge measure was found to be less reliable (Cronbach's alpha = .339), indicating that the alignment between the content in the game and the content measured by the scale should be reexamined. Nevertheless, we decided to include the measure of college-going knowledge in the following analyses because we also analyzed this theme through qualitative data, and caution the reader to be conservative when interpreting the results.

Regarding the second question (Does playing the game increase college knowledge and college going self-efficacy?), post-test scores for each of the four scales were examined via independent samples t tests. Results indicate that individuals who played the game at least one time (roughly 25% of the total sample) scored significantly higher on all four scales, self-efficacy, $t(451) = 3.14$, social influences, $t(464) = 2.265$, Internet use, $t(417) = 4.11$, and knowledge, $t(487) = 4.08$; all analyses conducted at the $p < .05$ level. More specifically, students who played the game at least once scored roughly one half standard deviation higher on all scales (except for social influences, where they scored roughly .2 standard deviations higher).

While these findings are in line with what we expected, they also highlight two significant areas for improving the research instruments. First, as discussed before, the reliability of the college knowledge measure was rather low—this analysis revealed that the average score on the measure was roughly 50% (SD = 17%). So, while students who played the game did better than their peers, very few students did well on this measure. This finding further suggests that we should reexamine the correspondence of the test content with the game content.

The relatively smaller difference on college social influences indicates the second area for improvement. While players indicated significantly higher scores on college-going social influences, the difference was smaller than the other findings. This is somewhat concerning to us as the game was created to specifically leverage social media to increase social influences, which would in turn influence college-going efficacy and knowledge. These findings could be further explored using think-aloud protocols and follow-up focus group interviews. It may be the case that the change in social influences is not immediately seen; but rather may take weeks to manifest. This, too, could be explored with the next iteration of the game. In either case, it is promising that the game produced results that were congruent with our hypotheses.

Finally, we examined the last research question, do males and females interact with the game differently? Our study finds that for the most part, males and females interacted with the game in a very similar fashion. Specifically, we found no significant differences between males and females who played the game in terms of college-going self-efficacy, $t(106)$ = 1.15, n.s., social influences, $t(117)$ = .644, n.s., knowledge, $t(121)$ = .649, n.s., and their use of the Internet, $t(111)$ = 1.11, n.s. However, two interesting findings emerged. First, when looking at all students, females were nearly twice as likely to play the game at least once— 31% of females played at least one game compared with only 15% of males, $t(478)$ = 4.03, $p < .05$. Furthermore, females who played the game played at significantly higher rates than males; on average, females completed 4.0 games (SD = 1.23) while males completed only 3.4 games (SD = 1.42), $t(121)$ = 2.30, $p < .05$.

As an aggregate, study findings indicate that playing Mission: Admission promoted college-going self-efficacy, college-going social influences, and college knowledge. Our findings also indicate that these effects are not different for male or female players. However, due to the iterative nature of the project, results indicate a number of areas for further research. First, the college knowledge measure could be substantively improved. These analyses indicate that the measure was not very reliable, which may be due to the difficulty of the measure (roughly 84% of students scoring at or below 75%) or poor alignment between the measure and the content in the game. Second, while college-going social influences were greater for students who played the game, this result was not as large as some of the other measures (like self-efficacy). Finally, while no gender differences were observed for the outcome measures, females reported playing Mission: Admission at significantly higher rates and more frequently. Follow-up studies, including think-aloud protocols, focus group interviews, and expanding the time-scale of data collection, may allow us to determine how we can further improve Mission: Admission.

Qualitative Findings: Online Game

The qualitative findings from the study offer a nuanced view of how the game affected students' perceptions of the college application process and growth of college concepts. Thematic analyses of observations and interviews suggest that playing Mission: Admission had a positive impact on students' college preparation process in several ways.

The games increased college knowledge. Players learned new college vocabulary and used the vocabulary during game play. Vocabulary usage was more pronounced when students played the game two or more times. As one example, when students played the game one time, approximately half missed applying to the Free Application for Federal Student Aid (FAFSA) deadline. As the game session progressed, they consequently learned that it would be challenging to afford college without applying to FAFSA. When they played a second time, their understanding of the term "FAFSA" had increased dramatically, resulting in higher rates of in-game FAFSA application. Eleventh-grade students overlooked the FAFSA deadline more frequently than seniors during the first round of game play. Once students learned the term and concept, they often advised friends to apply to the game's FAFSA deadline. In a different but related study of Mission: Admission server-level data conducted by colleagues from USC's School of Cinematic Arts, analysis of students' behaviors during game play corroborated this observation. As Figure 11.2 shows, back-end server-level data revealed that while approximately 54% of players applied to FAFSA during the first game played, approximately 72% of players who played four times applied to FAFSA and approximately 92% of players who played eight times applied to the game's FAFSA deadline.

Qualitative data revealed that the game helped students expand their awareness about college admission and financial aid processes. Students expressed that they had learned the differences among college types (e.g., two year, four year, private, etc.), the different requirements by postsecondary type, and that the financial aid and college admissions processes were not mutually exclusive. When asked if he learned anything playing Mission: Admission, one student replied:

> Yeah. I learned a lot, like recommendations. I didn't know about FAFSA or. . . I didn't know about [requesting letters of] recommendation or the things you have to do, just to make you look better for colleges to accept you. Then colleges, I didn't know there were city colleges or modern colleges or country colleges. . . I guess it made me think more about what I want to do.

Percent Players Applied to In-Game FAFSA by Games Played

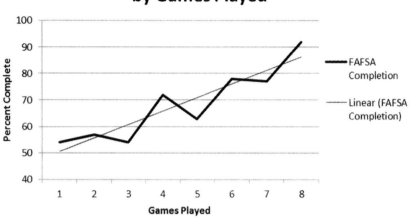

FIGURE 11.2 Back-end data illustrating Mission: Admission frequency of FAFSA application.

Students drew multiple parallels between their real-world lives and their fictional game characters. For example, if an avatar was accepted at a selective private university—a student player might name a specific university or college that fit into that category such as "USC" or "Stanford."

Another student's explanation of what she had learned from the game included socio-emotional lessons:

> Cause you just learn the process of, not just of applying to college, but just how a student would kind of go through that. Cause you have energy levels and stuff, so it's kind of the way that you go through it. Not just academically and the actual applying stuff, but also personally how you're gonna feel, which is you're gonna lose energy and you have to meet that timeline.

These findings indicate that students' college knowledge associated with the application process was limited prior to playing the game. The students reported having learned specific knowledge from the game in their post-game interviews.

The games cultivated college application strategies

All students who were formally interviewed or informally questioned after game play were able to articulate how they would adjust their play for subsequent game sessions. The most common themes they articulated were: the importance of paying attention to deadlines, balancing academics and extracurricular activities, planning ahead when requesting letters of recommendation, and applying for financial aid while applying to college. In one student's explanation of his strategy development, he points out how his approach to the game changed over time:

> It's like a trial and error thing. You see what best suits you, like specifically like just going to academics and just like clicking away [to level up in academics]. My first strategy was just to get a level five on specific items, but once I noticed that colleges have specific requirements, I first—the first thing I do now, once I get into the game, is basically click on the calendar, see what colleges I could apply to, to a specific interest that the [avatar] character has, apply to FAFSA on the first day [of game play] so I'll never forget it. Or I'll star [on the game calendar] the specific events that I want to go into when I don't have enough energy points so I won't ever forget about them.

After sharing their strategies for success in subsequent play (e.g., "I would pay better attention to deadlines" or "I'm going to make sure to apply to a wide range of schools"), the vast majority of students were also able to draw connections between game strategies and how the game related to real-life college applications. Moving forward, we are focusing research attention at the server level on how players' strategies develop over the course of game play.

Games facilitated college-related dialogue between peers and adults

The game play facilitated peer-to-peer collaboration. Students who played Mission: Admission appeared to care about each other's success during game play. While observing game play, researchers noted a trend of students starting to play alone, but then leaning over to view peers' screens as game play progressed. Class volume during game play included laughter and playful taunting. Many students verbally shared their strategies while playing by explaining their game decisions during game play to their neighbors. As students advanced their understanding of game strategies, they more frequently helped each other to compile strong college applications for their avatars and navigate game play.

Observational data also illustrated multiple instances of game-instigated student-to-adult interactions. When students were provided with a question generated through the game mechanism, they either responded via the game's social networking feature or discussed the question within a peer group. If they could not figure out the answer to a question, they sought the expertise of an adult in the room. One student's response when asked if he talked to anyone at school about college illustrates the value in structuring opportunities for students to interact with adults around college issues:

To be honest, I'm not only shy, but I just feel like I wouldn't know the right questions to ask. I wouldn't even begin to know how to approach the teacher and ask them, "Oh, can you help me with this?" I think that's actually what's holding me back 'cause other than that, I don't mind speaking up or anything at school.

Because the game generates questions for students, it serves as a catalyst for conversations about college. It is worth noting that the question component and subsequent peer-to-peer and/or student-to-adult interactions were even more pronounced in—and an overwhelmingly popular feature of—the card game. Teachers in interviews stated this component of the game was particularly useful.

The games were engaging for students

In interviews, a large majority of players stated that they would play the game again and would invite their peers and/or younger siblings to play. In one class where students had played the game, after two weeks of game play, the teacher posed the question through Edmodo (an online classroom social network), "Are you enjoying playing the game?" Of the students, 86% responded "yes!" 7% replied "not so much," and 7% said they were no longer playing.

Teachers welcomed a fun opportunity to introduce college guidance activities into the curriculum and facilitate dialogue around the college application process. One teacher explained that through game play, students learned the value of requesting letters of recommendation with ample time and that when she assigned students to request a letter in real life, the class who had played the game did so in a timely fashion (in comparison to other classes who lagged behind). When first playing the game, that same teacher gave students the option of using the in-game tutorial or bypassing the tutorial. Most students opted to follow the tutorial. Consequently, students learned how to play the game quickly and the teacher did not need to intervene. The teacher kept track of players' progress in the game by following badges earned through the game's badge function. As students garnered more badges, they engaged in friendly competition over who could accumulate the most badges. The teacher used the badge count as a way to encourage game play.

It is important to note that students' positive attitudes toward the game pertained mostly to play within school environments. Even students who enjoyed playing the game in class tended not to play at home. When asked why this might be the case, one student explained,

I guess it's just on them. Cause—our society isn't—wasn't taught to play games like that. Like they'll probably get bored easily. They will probably rather play games that they think are fun.

We were not surprised by this finding due to the great variety and popularity of non-educational games students play in their free time.

The social context of game play mattered

Several student interview participants played as juniors and again as seniors. A senior student reflected on the value of playing the game as a junior: "If you play as a junior, this game teaches how your life is going to be next year, how realistic things are going to be, and if you're not up for the responsibility then you're going to fall behind . . . so that game teaches you a sense of meeting deadlines, learning to remember things, so it's really useful." Another student distinguished the differences playing the game as a junior and as a senior, "[Playing as a senior is] a bit more, it's more like what we're going through. So it's a bit more personal now, I guess you can say." After being asked what the game was like to play as a senior, another student commented:

> Realistic in a sense just because—I mean it's one thing to miss a deadline in the game, because it's a game, you know? But it makes me realize if I miss this deadline in real life then—this isn't a game, you're not getting a second chance for that deadline. You know, so it makes me realize . . . like when I missed that [game] deadline, I was like, "Oh man, that's not good, not good."

Another senior summed up his experience: "Well, now that I'm actually in the process of applying, I can see how it connects with what I'm actually doing. As compared to when I was a junior, it was kind of just new information." These findings emphasize that context—including temporal context—affects how students experience the content of a game and overall game experience.

Discussion and General Implications

Research on the card game was instrumental in informing the development of the online game and related research protocols. Specifically, iterative playtesting of the card game with the target audience gave researchers and game designers the opportunity to test out game mechanics, verify which game themes and narrative to include in the online version, and confirm the value of role playing for this topic. In response to initial study findings, including feedback from students and teachers, the design team developed and refined the online game so that it cultivated intended learning objectives.

Findings from research using both college access games are promising. We saw, through quantitative and qualitative analyses, increases in college-going efficacy after game play and improvements in college knowledge. Game play was engaging to students, cultivated college application strategies, and worked well as a college guidance tool for practitioners.

It is important to note, however, that while we can show that game play positively affected college-going self-efficacy, we cannot make causal claims that playing the game influenced college application behaviors or plans. In interviews with a select group of students, several explained how lessons learned through game play factored into their college application behaviors. Yet several of those students experienced a mismatch in where they had hoped they would attend and where they enrolled. Some of the mismatch occurred because students were not accepted to the college of their choice. In other cases, students opted not to attend a particular college because they did not feel like they received enough financial aid or they opted to attend colleges closer to home. We probed into how students were accessing information and support in guiding those decisions and found online resources did not play a prevalent role as college choice tools; individualized personal support played a more significant role. The nuances in how social media and technology affect the decisions students make about college choice clearly merit further exploration.

Results from the game intervention studies indicate the potential of innovative tools to engage students in learning about college. We were able to document that the game play fulfilled its intended college-related learning objectives. The games increased high school students' college-going efficacy and expanded their college knowledge. Such tools, however, are not used in a vacuum. To say that the games were unequivocally effective without examining the actual college behaviors of students and social context of game play would not present a full picture of the intervention. Further research is needed to unpack the role of the game and/or other online interventions in supporting students in converting college and career aspirations into actual college plans and attendance. We believe that the schema presented in Figure 11.1, including analysis of long-term outcomes, provides a viable framework for a larger study.

Lessons Learned

We learned through the research that both of the games provided an essential safe space for the learners (Whitton, 2012) to make life-related mistakes that did not have career-related consequences. Players of the games were able to try out ideas as they navigated the college application process without a life-changing consequence. If they missed a deadline on a college application in the game, they learned about its consequence in a safe environment and self-corrected (particularly in subsequent game play rounds) without suffering costs in real life. Or, if they failed to apply to the FAFSA deadline in the game and were unable to afford the college of their choice, they made sure to apply to FAFSA the second time they played. These safe errors in decisions not only provided space for life decision adjustments without dire costs, they facilitated students' learning in meaningful ways that were connected to reality and therefore were applicable to choice making in everyday life.

We also learned that to demonstrate long-term impacts from games for college, connections to other resources associated with college access are important. One challenge to game play is that when it ends, it ends. By this we mean that connections to extension-type resources are limited by the game situation unless these connections are made deliberate via curricular expansion or other such activities that broaden learning to real life. Resource expansion is essential to achieving broad impact from games, as this helps to ground knowledge gained from game play into other situations, thus enabling generalization.

One of the most important and perhaps less empirical findings from our game research is that games should be fun and engaging. We learned that games are social and that players seek out the social fabric in game play. We found that the students who played were engaged both with the game and with one another during play. We noted interaction across students during game play, cheers during game-related triumphs, and smiles throughout game–student interactions. While one might think that fun is not necessary for learning to occur, Schunk (2011) found it to be a mediator to learning and particularly if it is to be generalized to other situations. Given that we intended for the learning from the games to be generalizable from game to real application to college, this was a critical finding in our research. As such, building in player-to-player interaction is an important consideration for future game development.

Author Note

The authors would like to acknowledge Genevieve Conley and Dennis Wixon for assistance with data analysis pertaining to the Mission: Admission game (see Figure 11.2). We are grateful to the USC Office of the Provost, TG, the Rosalinde and Arthur Gilbert Foundation, the Bill & Melinda Gates Foundation, and the Institute for Education Sciences (R305A110288) for supporting the project referred to in this chapter. The text does not reflect the views of these organizations.

References

Adelman, C. (1999). *Answers in the tool box: Academic intensity, attendance patterns, and Bachelor's degree attainment*. Washington, DC: U.S. Department of Education.

Bastedo, M. N., & Flaster, A. (2014). Conceptual and methodological problems in research on college undermatch. *Educational Researcher, 43*, 93–99. doi:10.3102/0013189X14523039

Baum, S., & Schwartz, S. (2012). *Is college affordable? In search of a meaningful definition* (Issue Brief). Washington, DC: Institute for Higher Education Policy.

Bettinger, E. P., Long, B. T., Oreopoulos, P., & Sanbonmatsu, L. (2009). *The role of simplification and information in college decisions: Results from the H&R Block FAFSA experiment* (No. w15361). Cambridge, MA: National Bureau of Economic Research.

Bettinger, E. P., Long, B. T., Oreopoulos, P., & Sanbonmatsu, L. (2012). The role of application assistance and information in college decisions: Results from the H&R Block FAFSA experiment. *The Quarterly Journal of Economics, 127*(3), 1205–1242.

Bruce, M., & Bridgeland, J. (2012). *2012 National survey of school counselors: True north—Charting the course to college and career readiness.* New York, NY: College Board Advocacy & Policy Center National Office for School Counselor Advocacy.

College Summit. (2013). *The college summit app map.* Washington, DC: Author. Retrieved from http://collegeappmap.org/pdf/

Conley, D. T. (2005). *College knowledge.* San Francisco, CA: Jossey-Bass.

Conley, D. T. (2012). *A definition of college and career readiness.* Eugene, OR: Educational Policy Improvement Center. Retrieved from www.epiconline.org/publications

Corwin, Z. B., Frome, K., & Groark, M. (2014). *Technological innovations for college access.* Los Angeles: Pullias Center for Higher Education.

Corwin, Z. B., Tierney, W. G., Fullerton, T., & Ragusa, G. (2014). Introduction: Why games and social media? In W. G. Tierney, Z. B. Corwin, T. Fullerton, & G. Ragusa (Eds.), *Postsecondary play: The role of games and social media in higher education* (pp. 1–20). Baltimore, MD: John Hopkins.

Corwin, Z. B., Tierney, W. G., Swensen, E., Bouchard, S., Fullerton, T., & Ragusa, G. (2012). *Gaming the system: Fostering college knowledge through play.* Los Angeles: Pullias Center for Higher Education.

Cowan, B. W. (2011). Forward-thinking teens: The effects of college costs on adolescent risky behavior. *Economics of Education Review, 30*(5), 813–825.

de los Santos, A. G., Jr., & de los Santos, G. E. (2006). Latina/os and community colleges: A pathway to graduate studies? In J. Castellanos, A. M. Gloria, & M. Kamimura (Eds.), *The Latina/o pathway to the Ph.D.* (pp. 37–53). Sterling, VA: Stylus.

DeAndrea, D. C., Ellison, N. B., LaRose, R., Steinfield, C., & Fiore, A. (2012). Serious social media: On the use of social media for improving students' adjustment to college. *The Internet and Higher Education, 15*(1), 15–23.

Fullerton, T. (2014). What games do well: Mastering concepts in play. In W. G. Tierney, Z. B. Corwin, T. Fullerton, & G. Ragusa (Eds.), *Postsecondary play: The role of games and social media in higher education* (pp. 125–145). Baltimore, MD: John Hopkins.

Gee, J. P. (2007a). *What video games have to teach us about learning and literacy* (2nd ed.). New York, NY: Palgrave/Macmillan.

Gee, J. P. (2007b). *Good video games and good learning: Collected essays on video games, learning, and literacy.* New York, NY: Peter Lang.

Get Schooled Foundation. (2013). *How is technology addressing the college access challenge? A review of the landscape, opportunities and gaps.* Seattle, WA: Author.

Lenhart, A., Kahne, J., Middaugh, E., Macgill, A. R., Evans, C., & Vitak, J. (2008). *Teens, video games, and civics: Teens' gaming experiences are diverse and include significant social interaction and civic engagement.* Washington, DC: Pew Internet & American Life Project.

Mazumder, B. (2003). Family resources and college enrollment. *Economic Perspectives, 27*(4), 30–41.

McDonough, P. M., & Calderone, S. (2006). The meaning of money: Perceptual differences between college counselors and low-income families about college costs and financial aid. *The American Behavioral Scientist, 49*(12), 1703–1718.

McKillip, M. E., Rawls, A., & Barry, C. (2012). Improving college access: A review of research on the role of high school counselors. *Professional School Counseling, 16*(1), 49–58.

Perna, L. W. (2005). The key to college access: Rigorous academic preparation. In W. G. Tierney, Z. B. Corwin, & J. E. Colyar (Eds.), *Preparing for college: Nine elements of effective outreach* (pp. 113–134). Albany, NY: SUNY Press.

Perna, L. W. (2006). Understanding the relationship between information about college prices and financial aid and students' college-related behaviors. *American Behavioral Scientist, 49*(2), 1620–1635.

Perna, L. W. (2010). Toward a more complete understanding of the role of financial aid in promoting college enrollment: The importance of context. In *Higher education: Handbook of theory and research* (pp. 129–179). Netherlands: Springer.

Perna, L. W. (2014). The need to increase college enrollment and completion. In W. G. Tierney, Z. B. Corwin, T. Fullerton, & G. Ragusa (Eds.), *Postsecondary play: The role of games and social media in higher education* (pp. 45–70). Baltimore: MD: Johns Hopkins University Press.

Reid, M. J., & Moore, J. L. (2008). College readiness and academic preparation for postsecondary education: Oral histories of first-generation urban college students. *Urban Education, 43*, 240–261.

Roderick, M., Coca, V., & Nagaoka, J. (2011). Potholes on the road to college: High school effects in shaping urban students' participation in college application, four-year college enrollment, and college match. *Sociology of Education, 84*(3), 178–211.

Roderick, M., Nagaoka, J., Coca, V., & Moeller, E. (2008). *From high school to the future: Potholes on the road to college.* Chicago, IL: Consortium on Chicago School Research at University of Chicago.

Saldaña, J. (2009). *The coding manual for qualitative researchers.* Thousand Oaks, CA: Sage.

Savitz-Romer, M., & Liu, P. (2014). *Counseling and college completion: The road ahead. A summary report from the strengthening school counseling and college advising convening.* Cambridge, MA: Harvard Graduate School of Education.

Schunk, D. H. (2011). *Learning theories: An education perspective* (6th ed.). Upper Saddle River, NJ: Prentice Hall.

Smith, J., Pender, M., & Howell, J. (2013). The full extent of student-college academic undermatch. *Economics of Education Review, 32*, 247–261.

Sparkman, L. A., Maulding, W. S., & Roberts, J. G. (2012). Non-cognitive predictors of student success in college. *College Student Journal, 46*(3), 642–652.

Tierney, W. G., Corwin, Z. B., Fullerton, T., & Ragusa, G. (Eds.). (2014). *Postsecondary play: The role of games and social media in higher education.* Baltimore, MD: Johns Hopkins Press.

Tierney, W. G., Ragusa, G., Corwin, Z. B., & Fullerton, T. (2013). *Ready or not, here we play: The impact of Collegeology games on college readiness, access and student success.* Los Angeles: Pullias Center for Higher Education.

Vuong, M., Brown-Welty, S., & Tracz, S. (2010). The effects of self-efficacy on academic success of first-generation college sophomore students. *Journal of College Student Development, 51*(1), 50–64.

Whitton, N. (2012). The place of game-based learning in an age of austerity. *Electronic Journal of e-Learning, 10*(2), 249–256.

Wilson, M. R. (2011). *Constructing measures.* New Jersey: Lawrence Erlbaum.

PART IV

Psychometric Issues

12

INFERENCE IN GAME-BASED ASSESSMENT

Kristen E. DiCerbo, Robert J. Mislevy, and John T. Behrens

Introduction

While there has been interest in games as learning environments for more than a decade (e.g., Gee, 2003), recently researchers have sought to use games as assessment tools (Behrens, Frezzo, Mislevy, Kroopnick, & Wise, 2006; Shute, 2011). Games and assessments share a number of attributes that make them logical partners, including a process model or activity cycle that includes activity presentation, evidence scoring, evidence accumulation, and selection of the next activity to maximize a particular function (motivation, engagement, or information, for example; Behrens et al, 2006). The instrumentation of games allows for the collection of fine-grained interaction information, holding the promise of gathering evidence of both final products and the process of arriving at them.

Recent efforts in game-based assessment have taken differing approaches to defining the context of the game. For example, the Virtual Performance Assessments project (Clarke-Midura, Code, Dede, Mayrath, & Zap, 2011) clearly positioned their activities as assessments with a primary goal of using immersive virtual environments to assess scientific inquiry. Alternately, the Nephrotex project (Chesler, Arastoopour, D'Angelo, Bagley, & Shaffer, 2012) was designed primarily as a method of providing engineering students with an authentic practical experience in which to see the application of the knowledge and skills they were learning to the professional norms of engineering practice. However, along with that, the research team developed a method of epistemic network analysis allowing them to use in-game interactions to assess elements of skills, knowledge, identity, values, and epistemology of engineering. Finally, Newton's Playground (Shute, Ventura, & Kim, 2013) was designed as an unobtrusive or "stealth" assessment, in which the game player's experience was primarily one of fun and flow (Nakamura & Csikszentmihalyi, 2002) while the evidence gathering was woven invisibly into the game experience. In each of these examples, extensive work was done evaluating how to best use data from game play to make inferences about what students know and can do. However, the context and experience of the players were quite different.

The space of potential contexts and purposes for game-based assessment may also be described as "use cases" (Mislevy et al., 2014). In software design, a use case is a description of a given scenario, including the people, actions, goals, and processes, in which the software will be used. Table 12.1 lays out a continuum of scenarios in which game-based assessment may be used based on Mislevy et al. (2014), and also enumerates characteristics of each type relevant to making inferences. Understanding the context of use also helps us understand the claims to be made from the assessment and the reach of the inference desired. For example, when gathering information to inform game activity, inference is only meant to apply to the game. When a game is used in formative assessment by learners and teachers, the user has moderate to high levels of information about how the game fits in with what they have been studying, and the language skills and background knowledge the game might require; this information is used in conjunction with results from individualized game play to guide individual students' learning. When data are gathered as an end-of-course assessment, this information is also available to the teacher, but the inferences about ability made from game play are meant to transfer to the application of those skills in other classroom activities, and likely outside the school environment; hence a bit higher

TABLE 12.1 Features of Use Cases for Assessment

Use case	Amount of information known about learner	Degree of standardization required	Emphasis on learning	Distance of inference
Information for internal game purposes	Low	Low	High	Very close
Formative assessment: Information for learners	Moderate to high	Low	High	Close
Formative assessment: Information for teachers	Moderate to high	Low to moderate	High	Close
Information for designers	Low	Low	Moderate	Close
End-of-course assessment	Moderate to high	Moderate to high	Low	Moderate
Large-scale accountability assessment/educational surveys	Low	High	Low	Far

degree of standardization is useful in order to extrapolate further from the game context. In each of these cases, although a game may be the method of activity, the principles of assessment still apply. Familiar concepts like validity and reliability are still important, but their application will depend on the particular use case under consideration and the associated inference to be made.

Games are often touted for their ability to offer an authentic experience and model the complexity of the real world (Behrens et al., 2006). However, the extent to which inferences made from game-based assessment apply to other contexts is still unclear. Does the evidence gained from players' actions, accumulated over a period of game play, indicate how well they will use and apply skills outside of the game environment? This is essentially a question of generalizability and transfer. A recurring observation in experimental studies of transfer is that it is quite rare and difficult to achieve (Detterman & Sternberg, 1993; Goldstone & Day, 2012; Larsen-Freeman, 2013). In addition, studies of the generalizability of performance assessments in the 1990s yielded generally poor results (Shavelson, Baxter, & Gao, 1993; Shavelson, Ruiz-Primo, & Wiley, 1999). How can we best conceptualize these issues in game-based assessment and what approaches should we take to investigate them?

There are two separate but related aspects to this discussion: (a) the cognitive or socio-cognitive process of transfer and (b) the statistical inference of generalizability, or variance across contexts. The literature base for the first aspect centers around the psychological processes of the learner and aspects of a learning context that do or do not facilitate the activation of similar patterns of cognitive resources in dissimilar situations (e.g., Bransford & Schwartz, 1999; Saxe, 1988). The literature base around the second aspect is concerned with understanding the amount of variance introduced into scores by context-specific elements of an assessment (and thereby estimating how much of the score is context-specific versus generalizable, e.g., Brennan, 2011). This chapter will explore both of these lenses while examining the challenge of making inferences in highly contextualized environments. It begins with a discussion of claims and evidence and then a review of challenges to inference particular to game-based assessment. We conclude with suggestions of approaches to understand and make use of the rich context of games in an assessment framework.

Threaded Example

For illustrative purposes, references will be made throughout the paper to the Jackson City scenario in SimCityEDU (www.simcityedu.org), developed by GlassLab. GlassLab, a collaboration between the Institute of Play, Electronic Arts, ETS, and Pearson, works to develop a variety of assessment and learning games. SimCityEDU, based on the popular SimCity commercial game, offers players various challenges in which they are asked to solve problems facing a city, generally requiring them to balance elements of environmental impact, infrastructure needs, and employment. The game scenarios are designed to assess systems thinking. Often named on lists of 21st century skills, systems thinking is also a cross-cutting concept in the Next Generation Science Standards (NGSS; NGSS Lead States, 2013). Essentially, it is the understanding of how various components of a system influence each other. It encompasses concepts such as feedback, adaptation, and emergent behavior. Proponents believe that by viewing pieces of a problem as part of a larger whole, the full impact of potential problem solutions will be more likely considered. They argue that most of the difficult problems in today's society are complex connections of related causes and effects, so learners need to be able to understand and consider this complexity in systems.

Following a review of existing conceptualizations of systems thinking (particularly Shute, 2011, and Cheng, Ructtinger, Fujii, & Mislevy, 2010), a learning progression for the construct was developed as part of the student model for the game (see Table 12.2). Learning progressions are empirically grounded and testable hypotheses about how a learner's understanding and skills develop over time (Corcoran, Mosher, & Rogat, 2009). They are particularly useful in describing the gap between a starting point of instruction and a desired endpoint.

In the Jackson City scenario, the player enters the city and is told that residents seem unhappy and are leaving the city. Interaction with the Sim characters reveals that they are having trouble with air pollution. Players can explore data maps that show which buildings are polluting the air, how power is dispersed in the city, and how various areas are zoned. Players discover that coal plants are the biggest cause of pollution in the city. However, coal plants also provide much of the power in the city. Power impacts both resident happiness and jobs (unpowered businesses close down).

In the game, players can bulldoze buildings, place new power structures (wind, solar, or coal generated), build new roads to expand their city, and zone and

TABLE 12.2 Systems Thinking Learning Progression From SimCityEDU

Level	Description
1. Acausal	The player is not reasoning systematically about causes and effects
2. Univariate	The player tends to focus on a single causal relationship in the system
3a. Early Multivariate	The player has considered multiple effects resulting from a single cause
3b. Multivariate	The player has considered multiple causes in relation to their multiple effects
4. Emergent Patterns	The player attends to and intervenes on emergent patterns of causality that arise over time

dezone residential, commercial, and industrial areas in order to achieve their goals. They can monitor the effects of their actions on pollution and jobs with the on-screen thermometers. The players' actions are captured and provide evidence for their level of systems thinking. For example, a player at Level 2, characterized by univariate thinking, is likely to focus solely on the relationship between the coal plants and pollution and will move forward with bulldozing coal plants. A player at Level 3a may recognize the multiple effects of coal plants, both causing pollution and providing power. In this case, the player would be observed placing alternative energy options and bulldozing coal plants, but perhaps ignoring the city's unemployment problem. This is not to say we believe a given student is "at" some particular level, even at a given point in time and with regard to a given system. A progression-level characterization of a person's systems thinking and actions can vary with the contexts and contents of situations. We will see that how much performance varies, in what ways, and with what sensitivity to systems and contexts, is a central concern for inference about such broadly defined skills. A player at Level 3b would address the pollution and power tradeoffs and would also create new commercial zones to increase jobs available in the city. These individual observations of actions and sequences are extracted from log files and provide evidence in a Bayesian network (BN). The BN is trained to provide probability estimates that individuals at each level of the systems thinking would be observed engaging in each activity, activity grouping, or sequence. Then, as a player progresses through the game, their actions are recorded and the probabilities of their achievement of each level of systems thinking updated.

The hypotheses about the relationships between actions in the game and levels of the learning progression must of course be tested. In the case of SimCityEDU, this initially involved several cycles of cognitive labs during which learners were asked to think aloud while playing the game. This allowed researchers to relate code statements as indicative of various levels of systems thinking and relate that to game play. In addition, quantitative techniques can potentially be deployed, relating game events to measures of systems thinking external to the game. However, valid, reliable measures of systems thinking are not common, and limited the feasibility of this technique.

Claims and Evidence

The process of assessment can be described as a simple chain: observation of a performance leads to a claim about what the learner can do which leads to use of that claim. The assessment activity provides the observations of what a learner does while the inferential machinery of measurement provides a characterization of capabilities and attributes (claims) and this is then used to understand future behavior and likelihoods however distal or proximal.

To accomplish this, a long train of computational methods can be brought to bear to link observations to an ultimate score or probability class. In the end, however, the interpretation of outputs from the computational machinery always falls back to linking the observation ("what they did") to the score or other characterization which serves as a claim. The assessment problem is thereby always based on questions regarding the meaning of the observations as they relate to the characterization of the attributes. This understanding itself rests on our concept of what a task is and in what ways we construe some activities to be evidence for some attributes.

The Language of Claims

It has been often suggested that the goal of educational assessment is the characterization of students' knowledge, skills, and abilities (KSAs; Mislevy, Steinberg & Almond, 2002) or more broadly, knowledge, skills, and attributes (Behrens & DiCerbo, 2014a). Consider a math question asking students to interpret a histogram. It might consist of a display with the number of households by age bands and a question of the form "How many households are 54 years old or younger?" To accomplish this task, one must know the mechanics of interpreting the graphic so as to identify the bars relevant to the task, as well as have the skills necessary to identify the amounts represented by the relevant bars, and be able to sum them as needed. Tasks of this form are typically labeled as providing evidence for or supporting claims about (1) finding values in graphical displays, (2) interpretation of bar charts, (3) interpretation of data displays, or (4) understanding data. In evolving common educational parlance we can exchange "labeled as providing evidence for X" with "aligned to the standard called X."

Claims 1–4 increase in abstraction and become increasingly generalized in their scope. Quality performance on the bar chart task provides positive evidence for each of these claims in different levels of specificity. The task is constant, but the degree of abstraction with which we can characterize it varies. This is an asymmetric relationship. This task can by itself provide evidence for a number of increasingly broad and abstract claims, yet comprehensive support for more abstract claims will require a range of additional data in order to "fill in" evidence for the breadth.

In highly diagnostic situations the linkage between the observation and claim is very close. In such a case we may say the inferential distance is small to reflect the fact that the evidentiary warrants required and the amount of background assumptions required are small. This is helpful for situations in which either specific observational information is sought (can they add 2 + 2?), but when more generalized claims are made, more pieces of evidence need to be brought to bear. This can be accomplished by integrating numerous pieces of discrete information as has been accomplished in what Behrens and DiCerbo (2014b) call the item paradigm or by integrating observations over a broader range of inputs from logs or other stream-based evidence identification systems. While discrete scoring events occurring on discrete tasks were required in the earlier technological epoch which

DiCerbo and Behrens (2012) call the "digital desert," broader, more integrated tasks are often able to provide appropriate evidence for broader, more generalized claims by building evidence models from numerous features of the performance. This is what we see in the game-based assessments. Rather than decompose activity into numerous discrete pieces and then "adding them back up" through psychometric synthesis, in game-based inference observations are made across a broader pattern of log-based event evidence from integrated activity. This provides both new challenges and new opportunities for assessment.

Affordances of Games That Impact Inference

In addition to the promising affordances of games that make them good candidates for gathering assessment evidence, there are also particular aspects of games that provide challenges to making inferences based on game play activity (Zapata-Rivera & Bauer, 2012). Each of these features makes a game more appealing, but also adds difficulty to the prospect of extracting meaningful evidence. When designing game-based assessments, assessment designers may find themselves struggling with the amount of choice in a game, the amount of data produced, game genres and associated game mechanics, types of performances, and the role of context.

Choice

Games typically provide players with meaningful choices about their path through the game. They are designed such that players perceive options, and that the option chosen has consequences and often cannot be undone. These components contribute to the emotional reactions that draw players into a game (Morrison, 2013). This corresponds to the education literature that relates student feelings of self-determination to mastery goals and positive achievement outcomes (Ciani, Sheldon, Hilpert, & Easter, 2011; Deci, Vallerand, Pelletier, & Ryan, 1991). However, in assessment, the focus is usually on gathering very specific information, and choice can impede the ability to observe players in activities that will elicit evidence that is needed to make strong inferences about particular, targeted aspects of proficiency. For example, in SimCityEDU there are four scenarios, the first two of which provide scaffolding to introduce players to game play. The second scenario is designed to teach players how zoning in the city works. However, players do not have to play all of the scenarios; the lockstep requirement was removed after players in play testing strongly objected to it. Unfortunately, if they do not play the second scenario, we do not have evidence of whether they understand the zoning function. If instead they play Jackson City, it is difficult to know whether a lack of commercial zoning is because they do not have the systems thinking abilities to think about the jobs variable along with pollution or because they do not know how to zone in the game. In Stephen

Toulmin's (1958) terminology for arguments, such sources of difficulty unrelated to the construct of interest introduce alternative explanations for poor performance. Messick (1989) calls them sources of construct-irrelevant variance in his classic chapter on validity.

There are at least four ways of minimizing the effect of choice on inference. First, in the example above, prerequisite skills can be inserted as gates within a challenge. Zoning a particular area might be required within the Jackson City scenario. Second, choice can be offered in places where essential assessment evidence is not being gathered. Third, players can be given the illusion of meaningful choice when in fact the choice does not have a significant impact on play. For example, in many games players are given options of customizing their avatars with everything from skin, hair, and eye color to clothing and items. However, it is not clear that even this generally "meaningless" activity does not have impact on play, as it may encourage personal identification with the character (Kafai, Fields, & Cook, 2007). Finally, activities can be designed such that the same thing can be observed in multiple situations.

An example of this last approach appears in the Hydrive simulation-based coached practice system for learning to troubleshoot the hydraulic systems of the F15 aircraft (Gitomer, Steinberg, & Mislevy, 1995). The designers were interested in whether learners engaged in a technique called "space splitting" in which using particular diagnostic tests greatly decreases the portion of the problem space where the fault may be located. However, depending on how learners approached the problem, they might arrive at situations in which space splitting was appropriate at differing places and times in their work. Therefore, it is impossible to set a rule looking for space splitting at a set time or place. Rather, an agent was designed to examine the task following each learner action and determine whether space splitting was a viable response. If so, it then "listened" to see whether or not the learner engaged the technique in his next sequence of moves. In other words, the task was dynamically monitored for opportunities to observe the behavior of interest.

Volume and Type of Data

Games can produce large volumes of data. Compare the potential data capture from a multiple-choice question, which allows capture of the response selected as represented in a single alphanumeric character, to that of a game, which allows recording of detail down to locations and timestamps of individual mouse clicks. The sheer amount of data is usually cited as a benefit for assessment (DiCerbo & Behrens, 2012). However, it also presents a challenge to discover what is important in this "ocean" of data. To make strong inferences, meaningful evidence needs to be extracted from the plethora of information in a log file. In many cases, the constructs being assessed with games are less well defined than traditional achievement skills, and the hypotheses about what constitutes evidence of these constructs are under development.

Not only do games provide more data, but the performances given by the learners are very different than traditional assessment performances. While most traditional assessments involve selecting a response or producing a brief numeric or language-based response, in games the performance may involve a broad range of open-form performances such as configuring a computer network (Frezzo, DiCerbo, Behrens, & Chen, 2013), diagnosing a patient (Clauser, Margolis, Clyman, & Ross, 1997), or rescuing a friend from a vampire (DiCerbo, 2014). A log of actions from these performances is considered a work product from which evidence must be extracted (Shute, Ventura, Bauer, & Zapata-Rivera, 2009). While the activities in these experiences are informed by theory in order to evoke performances that provide certain classes of evidence, in many cases working theories lack the detail needed to link specific behavior observations with specific inferences about latent attributes. It is often the case that there are unanticipated patterns of activity in the logs that could serve as evidence, if detected (Behrens, Mislevy, DiCerbo & Levy, 2012). This is certainly the case in Jackson City and the assessment of systems thinking. Designers had initial hypotheses about the evidentiary value of activities related to removing and replacing energy sources in the city, as described above; however, it was not apparent what other patterns of game play might be indicative of systems thinking proficiency.

One way to address the need to generate hypotheses is through the use of exploratory data analysis (EDA; Behrens, 1997; Behrens, DiCerbo, Yel, & Levy, 2012; Tukey, 1977). EDA is a conceptual framework with a core set of ideas and values aimed at providing insight into data as it is presented to the working researcher, and to encourage understanding probabilistic and nonprobabilistic models in a way that guards against erroneous conclusions. EDA relies heavily on the use of graphics to uncover patterns in data with the goal of developing a detailed and accurate mental model of data, which can then lead to hypothesis construction. In Jackson City, the use of these techniques in early play testing data revealed a group of players who appeared to be using the zoning strategy of "dezone everything." This group on average dezoned more industrial, commercial, and residential portions of the city than all other players. A hypothesis was developed that these students were more likely to be in the lowest level of systems thinking, not considering the direct effects of their game actions. There was clearly not an a priori hypothesis that players would engage in this pattern of behavior during design, but systematic exploration of the data suggested an attempt to confirm this dezoning and systems thinking relationship in independent data was warranted.

Tukey (e.g., 1986) did not consider methodology as a bifurcation between exploratory and confirmatory, but considered quantitative methods to be applied in stages of exploratory, rough confirmatory, and confirmatory data analyses. In this view, EDA is aimed at the initial goals of hypothesis generation and pattern detection following the detective analogy. It is therefore differentiated from the (correctly) maligned practice of snooping through data to find the data and model that will most likely lead to significant results. Rather, EDA generates hypotheses that are later confirmed with separate data.

Genres and Game Mechanics

Although games are often referred to as one monolithic category, in fact there are different genres of games just as there are different genres of books. Just as some people prefer mysteries over science fiction, some people will prefer single player simulation games like SimCityEDU over massively multiplayer online role playing games like World of Warcraft (http://us.blizzard.com/en-us/games/wow/) or puzzle games like Candy Crush (www.royalgames.com/games/puzzle-games/candy-crush/). These games have differing methods of motivation and reinforcement, and different game mechanics (the constellation of actions used to advance the game). In Minecraft (https://minecraft.net/), for example, a major mechanic is placing blocks, while in World of Warcraft it is completing quests. Individuals motivated by completing difficult tasks, earning points and in-game money, and enhancing reputation will likely be more engaged with quest-type games, while those motivated by exploration and creation will be engaged with "sandbox" games. Given that a premise of game-based assessment is that tasks that are more motivating will yield more valid assessment results (Liu, Bridgeman, & Adler, 2012; Schmit & Ryan, 1992; Sundre & Wise, 2003), the likelihood that different games will be differentially motivating to players should concern those making inferences from the results.

Contextualization, Generalizability, and Validity

The Paradox of Context in Game-Based Assessment

The engagement that games can evoke is an attractive feature for learning and at least some use cases (Gee, 2007; Shaffer, 2007). Engagement is often defined in three dimensions: behavioral (effort, participation), affective (interest, attitude), and cognitive (self-regulation) (Appleton, Christenson, & Furlong, 2008). In games, engagement is related to flow, or the state of fully energized focus on a task (Csikszentmihalyi, 1990). This is achieved in part by specificity and depth; designers create situations with enough context to pull players in, to make decisions and feel their effects, and to apply ideas in actions that matter emotionally (so that abstract relationships and higher-level concepts take form in connections players can see). These are conditions that research has shown promote learning (Bransford, Brown, & Cocking, 2000; Lave & Wenger, 1991). Yet the same contextualization taps into longstanding debates on transfer in psychology. The issues hold important consequences for inference in game-based assessment in the guises of generalizability and validity. In turn, developments from psychology hold insights for game-based assessment designers to improve their functioning as both environments for learning and vehicles for assessment.

The central issue in discussions of transfer is that of people's reasoning in situations that can appear quite different on their face, yet exhibit similar structures under the surface. These similar structures can be conceptual structures such as mathematical relationships, physics models, and systems relationships like negative feedback, or activity structures such as model revision, troubleshooting strategies, and generating conceptualizations that encompass multiple perspectives. Contextualized experience develops capabilities for such reasoning, but is initially closely tied to the particulars of the situations and contents. Studying just the abstracted versions, even though broadly applicable and potentially powerful, can produce instead isolated knowledge that fails to activate in relevant situations (Bransford & Schwartz, 1999; Perkins & Salomon, 1989; Schalk, Saalbach, & Stern, 2011). For example, Saxe (1988) found that children selling candy in the streets of Brazil carried out sophisticated mathematical reasoning with ratios, marginal profits, and adjustments for inflation as embedded in a social system, yet struggled with identical problems expressed symbolically. Their peers in schools were more fluent with the symbol-system manipulations and stereotyped problems, but floundered in identical candy-selling situations.

The situation of transfer is even more ambiguous, and less encouraging, for at least some of the proficiencies known currently as 21st century skills (Binkley et al., 2012)—skills such as creativity, problem solving, communication, and collaboration. The issue is that these are umbrella terms used to discuss important capabilities, but of rather different kinds in different domains. Displaying good problem solving to repair aircraft hydraulic systems may have little to do with problem solving when carpet laying, managing employees in a shoe store, or finding lost sheep. In any domain, nevertheless, most observers would agree that the kinds of capabilities being referred to are important. And most would also agree that it is worthwhile to provide experiences that help students develop such capabilities in context, in games, and in any number of other educational and everyday settings. Examples in game-based assessment include persistence (DiCerbo, 2014; Ventura, Shute, & Zhao, 2012) and creativity (Shute et al., 2009). As with systems thinking in SimCityEdu, abstracted conceptual frameworks for these kinds of skills can guide game design and feedback for their appearance in context. Again there are empirical validity questions for the quality of inference from evidence in context. Inference beyond a given context calls for a skeptical stance. There is evidence that 21st century skills are not unitary, either cross-content or cross-context. Learners may in fact develop capabilities that are describable by the terms we use for 21st century skills, but we should not expect to be able to measure them as well-defined, unitary, and universally applicable traits with either drop-in-from-the-sky assessments or assessments that are particular to specific situations and content areas.

This is precisely the inferential challenge for a game like SimCityEdu. The learning progression for systems thinking shown in Table 12.2 was very helpful to the designers for building challenges that required increasingly higher levels of thinking in the game context—that is, the particular systems, in the particular SimCity-like environment. It was helpful too to characterize players' performance, again in the game context. And a crucial facet of validating inference in SimCityEdu is exactly at this level: Do the inferences based on students' actions in this environment suitably capture their thinking, so that inferences through the measurement model are valid summaries of their thinking? Does feedback based on these evaluations help further their learning in this environment?

Affirmative answers to these questions do not in themselves tell us much about how the students might fare in systems thinking, as examined through the same learning-progression lens, in other contexts, or about other systems. Variations among students' performances with respect to levels of learning progressions can show striking variability in different contexts and different content areas (Sikorski & Hammer, 2010). Despite the usefulness of learning progressions at the level of generality of Table 12.2 in designing instruction and framing local inferences, we should not take contextualized evidence uncritically as evidence of singular higher-level proficiencies. Rather, there must be empirical investigation of the extent to which the evidence relates to the proficiencies outside the game context. From the perspective of assessment, we must examine the generalizability of inferences from the game context, to determine the evidentiary value of the observations for other contexts. From the perspective of validity, the very same contextualization that strengthens inference within those contexts and contents also constitutes construct-irrelevant variance for inferences that extend to other contexts and contents. From the perspective of design, we must turn to the literature on learning for guidance on how to maximize the portability of what students can learn in games, and the range of what assessors can learn from students' performance in games.

Perspectives

Students are more likely to be able to recognize structures and processes at higher levels, and use them to organize their thinking and their actions, when they have worked reflectively with them in multiple contexts. Kintsch and Greeno (1985) work through examples of arithmetic word problems from a connectionist, situative, psychological perspective. With sufficient experience, a person develops resources to activate appropriate abstract arithmetic schemas in a given real-world situation with certain triggering features. To use an apt term from Fauconnier and Turner (2002), the person constructs a "cognitive blend" of the real-world situation and the abstract schema to reason through.

The "classic" transfer literature oftentimes appears contradictory in terms of whether or not we are likely to see the types of transfer we desire (Schwartz,

Bransford, & Sears, 2005; Schwartz, Chase, & Bransford, 2012). The narrowest definition of transfer is the repetition of a learned skill in a new situation (Detterman & Sternberg, 1993). However, others have argued that if a skill is truly learned, the learner should be able to flexibly use the skill depending on the demands of the situation, not just repeat the skill blindly (Schwartz et al., 2005). Even with this somewhat expanded definition, however, the traditional transfer literature focuses on "transferring out" from one learned task to another sequestered problem-solving task (Schwartz et al., 2005). Transfer is seen as a single event in which a unitary piece of knowledge or skill either does or does not get applied in a new situation, and research focuses around questions of whether and under what conditions transfer is likely to take place (Barnett & Ceci, 2002).

Hammer, Elby, Scherr, and Redish (2005) argue that knowledge and reasoning abilities are composed of many fine-grained mental resources that may or may not be activated at a given time; they are not intact units. Therefore, rather than focusing on the transfer of a unitary skill, Hammer et al. focus on patterns of activating resources. Of course, resources activate in sets, and a set that activates together frequently may come to be seen as a unit. This observation of sets may give rise to the unitary view of transfer. However, observation and research of learners in context reveal occasions when some, but not all, resources act together. In this case, their research focuses on epistemological frames (for example, a classroom lecture or a physics homework problem) that cue activations of particular resources and mechanisms by which educators can create sets of resource activations.

Finally, there is the position that we should not be focusing on whether knowledge in one situation "transfers out" to other situations, but whether students' knowledge "transfers in" to help students learn more effectively in a new situation. This is the notion of "preparation for future learning" (PFL; Arena, 2012; Bransford & Schwartz, 1999). From the PFL perspective, the critical question is not whether students transfer knowledge or activate resources in the new situation, but whether they are able to acquire new knowledge and skills more efficiently after a given learning experience. In light of the preceding discussion, an inference of particular interest in the case of SimCityEDU might be the claim that yes, even though the particulars of given models or content are necessary to employ some higher-level capability such as systems thinking, experience in a contextualized game facilitates learning to do systems thinking in the next context where it applies.

The conversation above comes largely from the learning community and concerns the psychological process of transfer. However, the issue of student performance across contexts also has a history in the assessment community in discussions of generalizability theory (G theory; Cronbach, Gleser, Nanda, & Rajaratnam, 1972). G theory grew out of the desire to better understand the causes of error in test scores. It defines facets, or elements of an assessment performance that can vary from administration to administration. For example, variance across scores could be the result of rater effects (on person-scored items), item effects, occasion effects, or interactions between types of effects. Analyses are conducted to determine the contribution of the different sources of measurement "error," or the effect of the specific context on the "true score." The fact that we know little about the strength of inference from a studied context to a context about which we have no information is an instance of the "hidden facet" problem described by Cronbach and his colleagues.

Proponents of G theory would argue we should run generalizability studies that enable the estimation of variance due to context effects. Relatedly, it would be possible to design a series of studies to measure the effects of game dynamics and design features. Systematically varying features and examining the impact on outcomes on a case-by-case basis could be quite time-consuming. However, digital environments, constructed properly, can be set up for A/B testing in which different configurations of a game are randomly presented to different players. The large numbers of players who can be given access to games allow for quick investigations of various features and dynamics. Information from these assessments could not only provide data to support inferences but would enable a better understanding how these contextual variables might be used intentionally to enhance learning in games.

Based on this brief review, there are a number of lenses through which to view the primary question of how to interpret inferences made from highly contextualized activity. Even in traditional assessment, there are many assumptions built in about aspects of an item that "don't make a difference." For example, in math word problems, we assume the color of the objects or whether we use apples or bananas will not affect the difficulty. But we know from ethnographic research such as Saxe's (1988) previously mentioned candy-seller study that the impact can be profound. Even if we could identify all the possible dimensions that could potentially impact difficulty, it is not clear how many we should model. Given that games are so much more contextualized than traditional assessment items, the list of features of a scenario that may affect difficulty of the activity appears to be infinite.

Do Tasks Exist?

In addition to understanding the interpretive challenges in the language of claims that serve as outputs in the assessment process, we need to consider the language of tasks and observations that serve as inputs as well. Consider the highly constrained histogram task discussed above. It can be thought of as benefiting from a simple and clean presentation which is unencumbered by complex reading passages that could inject construct-irrelevant variance related to reading comprehension, or elaborate multistep task demands that could inject variance related to short-term memory capacity or visual strategy experience, and so on. These other possible variations suggest, however, that we think carefully about what it means for this task to be "a task" and what way it is "a task" both in reference to different claims it may support as well as what the fundamental aspects of the task are that make it the task we think it is, as operationalized by the labels we would associate with it for evidence-accumulating procedures (e.g., finding values, interpreting bar charts).

Fundamental to the notion of transfer of inference from one task to another is the question of when an activity represents a task associated with a specific claim and when it does not. Because the claims related to assessments are difficult to connect conceptually, we discuss three hidden simplification heuristics commonly used to constrain evidentiary interpretation: averaging over, assuming out, and remaining silent on boundary conditions.

To illustrate these ideas, let us consider the claim that a learner "has good penmanship" and the corresponding task of creating a handwriting sample that ensures all letters in the alphabet will be written. Regardless of the scope of the performance, there will need to be some "averaging over." Consider for instance, whether good penmanship means good on each letter, or good on most letters with weakness allowed on some, or perhaps all meet some minimum but a certain number need to be above another threshold. Regardless of the exact specification, the point to keep in mind is that the claim is a linguistic tool and the meaning will be imprecise though it will necessarily have to carry the weight of the inferential design over variations. Indeed, this is part of the fundamental nature of psychometrics in which the claims are considered the basis for interpreting unobservable latent traits that have probabilistic mappings into specific observations (Mislevy, Behrens, DiCerbo & Levy, 2012).

Another way that variation is addressed is that certain conditions are "assumed away" as not relevant to the social meaning of the task. For example, to claim good penmanship, it is likely that we assume the performance of interest occurs on a school desk or library table but conditions such as writing while riding on a car, skydiving, or floating in outer space are assumed away with assent to standard practice. Accordingly, there is a field or ring of social expectation that exists around activities without having to justify the myriad construct-irrelevant conditions. This allows the easy communication of information without having to negotiate the near-infinite regress to statements of what is and is not common knowledge or common assumption.

Third, and perhaps most common, task designers are often silent on the boundary conditions. If outer space is assumed away, where is the boundary for relevance? Lower case letters only, mixed, upper and lower, pencil only, pencil and pen, before writing for 30 minutes, after writing for 30 minutes, and so on? In many educational testing situations, the boundary conditions are very tight and generalization beyond those tight interpretations are deemed construct-irrelevant. In turn, the face validity of well designed "clean" tasks is thought to provide the necessary conditioning information.

Returning to our histogram example, we can likewise consider how the three hidden simplification heuristics may operate. The task can be considered as consisting of a histogram, a required operation on it, and the communication of the conclusion of the operation. In this context there are not numerous pieces of information that must be averaged over (e.g., numerous letters written) but rather numerous design features and their potential variations. When we look at the histogram, we may consider it an average or prototypical histogram insofar as it averages the possibility of performance on a wider or narrower histogram, taller or shorter, or colored somewhat differently. Indeed the graphical patterns are myriad. Likewise, we consider the vertical axis an average of possible vertical axes which can be averaged over with no loss as we are attempting to arrive at an estimation of proficiency across numerous categories. If they are considered as possible minimal sources of variation, we average over them in the thought experiments. If we consider them irrelevant, we "assume them out."

The empirical reality, however, is more complex. Consider the results of an experiment using the histogram. Recall that the respondent was asked to compute how many members of the household were below a given age. The task requires addition of the heights of all of the columns below 65. In the experimental manipulation of the question, the number of bars and the initial number aligned with tick marks on the y-axis were varied randomly across participants. Across several thousand responses we can see the probability correct varies as a function of these simple properties of the number of relevant bars and the starting place of the tick marks. Counting and summing fewer bars lead to a higher probability of success and would generally be taken to reflect a higher level of ability as the underlying surface of responding was not understood. While all these versions of the task (or are they different tasks?) provide support for the claims related to interpreting histograms specifically and data displays in general, they do so in unanticipated and differential ways.

This example illustrates how even when a task is scored as right and wrong and captured by a single bit of information, the task is actually a sample from a domain of possible tasks that generate different variations in evidence for the supposed claims. This view suggests that in most contexts of task design and analysis, tasks do not exist as islands of observations, but can be thought of as points in a design surface with a corresponding response surface of outcome probabilities that can relate task attributes to outcome attributes. In practice however, task design space is averaged over and recast as a single item representing an observation generalized to a claim.

The hidden simplification heuristics described above are required for predigital environments where only single points of experience can be created and response scoring needs to be simplified (e.g., a test question). In rich digital environments that DiCerbo and Behrens (2012) characterize as comprising the "digital ocean," however, numerous opportunities for data collection and complex pattern recognition can occur. In these contexts not only can tasks vary over time and features, in fact games can be designed to specifically capture and respond to the information of the outcome response surface (Stamper et al., 2012). As a digital system, it can collect data rapidly and evolve quickly in turn. A promising approach would be to combine the advantages of template-based design from ECD with the variation modeling discussed here. This would allow both a theoretical framework to approach the tasks as well as an empirical approach to evaluating and revising them.

A Way Forward

Given the concerns and constraints described to this point, will we be able to use game play evidence to make inferences about knowledge, skills, and attributes outside the game? The following conceptualizations, singly and together, hold promise as approaches to allow appropriate inference and interpretation of results outside of the game environment.

First, we can note some strategies from the literature on transfer and more recent but compatible research from a situative perspective on learning that appear to hold for game-based learning as well (Hammer et al., 2005). Using these ideas in design offers the best chances of strengthening inference beyond the specific contexts and contents of a game-based assessment: (a) Use multiple situations that differ on the surface to draw out underlying patterns; (b) Call learners' attention to the patterns; (c) Use the more abstract language and representations from the domain as they apply to particulars of situations; (d) Have students engage in reflection at the level of the abstracted tools, as they apply to specifics in multiple situations that differ on the surface.

These strategies help build construct-relevant thinking into students' activities in and around a game—using a term from Messick (1989), to reduce threats to validity from construct underrepresentation. In addition, we can look more closely at the design process to focus on use case, increase the quality of evidence we can evoke, and deal with threats from construct-irrelevant variance.

Assessment Use Cases

As introduced earlier, there are a variety of use cases for assessment. Table 12.1 outlines some of these and characteristics of them that might influence design decisions. For example, in large-scale accountability applications, there is a low emphasis on learning and a desire to make inferences far from the context of game play. In formative assessment designed to provide feedback to the learners there is a high emphasis on learning, and inferences can remain close to the context of the game. If cases of differential item functioning were found due to a context variable in a game (in which an activity was found to be substantially more difficult for one group under study than another), that would not be acceptable in the large-scale accountability application. However, it might even be desirable in a formative assessment application if that context variable could be used to assist in learning for one of the groups, as long as similar learning opportunities were ultimately provided for all players. Similarly, in more formative scenarios the teacher and learner have a substantial amount of information about the learner's skill profile while none of this information is brought to bear in large-scale accountability assessments. Strategies such as the one described above in which mastered skills are used to anchor the assessment of unknown skills are not easily employed without the prior knowledge of player skills.

Evidence-Centered Game Design

Evidence-centered game design (ECgD; Mislevy et al., 2014) is a fusion of ECD with the agile design process of software design that is common in the entertainment game industry. ECgD seeks to address both assessment considerations and game considerations from the beginning of the design process by (a) defining competencies from a non game perspective, (b) integrating the externally defined competency with game competency, (c) creating formative feedback essential to game play, and (d) simultaneously iterating game design and assessment design (Mislevy, Behrens, DiCerbo, Frezzo, & West, 2012). A key component of the first two steps is that the traditional ECD domain analysis identifies practices of the expected competencies. For example, finding related components in a system is a practice of systems thinking (Shute & Ventura, 2013).

With this information about implementations characteristic of the domain, the game designer can then design contexts and mechanics around these practices. In Jackson City, designers used the game data maps as a mechanic that allows players to uncover relationships among components. In addition, features like being able to turn off a coal plant before bulldozing it allows players to test relationships without taking irreversible action. Simultaneously, assessment designers can consider the types of evidence that may emerge from the practice. In the case of Jackson City, they might look for evidence of a "change and observe" sequence in which one variable is manipulated and then the player does something to observe the effect of the manipulation on one or more other variables.

By beginning with the identification of *characteristic* features of domain situations and affordances in domain analysis, and building game situations and mechanics around them from the start, designers are building the typical, usual representations into the core of the game. Using higher-level concepts and representations in game and feedback, in as engaging and natural a way as possible, sets the stage for the recognition of these higher-level concepts by players. In addition, these common representations and practices can be documented for creation of other scenarios.

Designing in Construct-Irrelevant Variance

Rather than focusing on building one context or game scenario, creating multiple narratives and designs may help players recognize occasions for the application of knowledge across contexts. In assessment design, it is common to seek to eliminate as many sources of construct-irrelevant variance as possible (Haladyna & Downing, 2004). However, as discussed above, many of the contextual features that make games interesting and engaging are likely sources of construct-irrelevant variance. Rather than removing them, which could seriously degrade the game experience, designers should consider instead creating a number of markedly different contexts in which the targeted practices can be employed. These changes might involve simply putting a different skin and narrative on the same activity. For example, the same basic math activity could be accomplished in the context of the deep sea, space, or the mountains. It might also involve larger changes to game mechanics or even genres. Rather than eliminating potential sources of construct-irrelevant variance from scenarios at the risk of decreasing players' engagement, the designer includes such features but varies them so their influence does not accumulate. (Half a century ago, in the context of factor analysis, Humphreys, 1962, recognized this strategy for both increasing validity and recognizing certain threats to validity; Cronbach, 1989.)

The use of design templates can facilitate this creation of multiple contexts (Riconscente, Mislevy, & Hamel, 2005). Templates can both enumerate the immutable elements of an activity related to a given competency and the features that can be varied with the expected results. As a simple example, a template for activities aimed at players uncovering relationships among components might indicate characteristic features of a system with multiple components while variable features might be the number of cause-and-effect relationships and the direction (positive or negative) of those relationships. In addition, features such as the means by which tests of relationships are done could be specified as variable. Such an approach would provide a principled framework for designing learning situations and providing contextualized feedback, and at the same time developing formally equivalent situations to assess transfer of learning in a traditional sense or preparation for future learning in the Bransford and Schwartz (1999) sense (Hammer et al., 2005).

In conjunction with this design strategy are companion strategies for a *use approach* of game-based and outer contextualized learning and assessment experiences, and an *assessment approach* for properly handling the data that emerge. The use approach is a generalization of the instructional strategy that Robinson (2010) describes for second language acquisition, to provide complex learning experiences for students without overwhelming them: Use learning experiences that are complex and realistic, but matched to learners so that they are already familiar with many of their aspects and can focus on novel targeted aspects. The same idea can be applied to assessment (Hansen & Mislevy, 2006): A task can draw upon resources from multiple areas, but if the assessor already knows that students are capable with respect to certain aspects, they are not apt to be significant sources of difficulty. Only the targeted aspects are. These aspects are determined not just by what the task is in itself, but also on the known relationships between what the task demands and the examinees can already do. The targeted aspects of proficiency are the object of measurement. They are what the proficiency variables in psychometric models must address. Just what variables are needed in a model and what they mean will depend critically on the context and purpose of the assessment. Their interpretations with respect to, for example, systems thinking describe students' capabilities under favorable conditions, rather than in a sample of conditions from a broad universe.

This is a "conditional" rather than "marginal" inference—less typical in familiar assessments, but one that is useful when dealing with contextualized learning (Mislevy et al., 2013). Examples of conditional inference include doctoral dissertations and the Advanced Placement Studio Art portfolio assessments; demonstrating some higher level proficiency is accomplished by in-depth work in particular context and content, to demonstrate that accomplishment in selected instances that meet prespecified criteria. In a similar vein, completing a marathon—any marathon—is evidence of a certain level of capability in running, despite variation in the difficulty of courses. In practice, assessment is often interpreted as marginal, when in fact it is assuming away and silent on the boundary conditions. By being clear about the conditional inference of an assessment, we are making explicit the context of the assessment and our expectation of inference.

Modeling Variance

Finally, the ability to gather fine-grained information about learner–computer interaction in digital games provides us with the ability to model contextual variance. Above we described an experiment with the histogram task in which the number of bars and starting point on the y-axis were manipulated. As a result, we were able to estimate the difficulty values of each combination of these variables in the task. Knowing the difficulty values of the combinations allowed us to estimate proficiency of the learners conditional on which combination of values they received. With thousands of learners playing a game, it is possible to build variation into the game in ways that allow us to statistically model the effects of that variation.

Above we talked about design templates, but in the assessment world there has been promising recent work on activity templates (Behrens, 2013). These are the specifications that allow for the automatic generation of a task within certain parameters as learners are engaging with them. For example, in the histogram example, the activity template provides the range of values for the number of bars (perhaps 4 to 10) and starting point on the axis. The software then generates the activity "on the fly" for each learner on each occasion of the task. From an assessment perspective, this allows for implementation of various combinations of the variable elements specified in the design templates. From a game perspective, this allows for replayability with new experiences for the player. Over thousands of trials, the difficulty of various combinations of the varied elements can be modeled. Clearly, this type of analysis relies on large numbers of players and observations, but represents the promise of the digital era.

In a game environment, rather than needing to decompose and structure all aspects of the tasks for simplified scoring, the environment allows for claims that are more broad and integrative. While still using evidentiary machinery to integrate across observations, the integrative claims suggest search for patterns in activity across streams of action in contrast or in addition to the summarization of many discrete tasks. This approach benefits from the possibility of creating rich naturalistic opportunities but increases the burden for more integrative evidence specification and development of that specification using exploratory methods. It also requires new mechanisms for tagging and managing game-based activities in a post-item world.

Discussion

The question of where and when inferences from game-based assessment can be extended is not easily answered. A first step is to be thoughtful about design. The use cases foreseen for the game will tell us how far stakeholders would like inferences to extend. As learning and assessment are more entwined in particular use cases, we can determine how their interplay might emphasize one or the other at a given point in a learning experience.

One area not yet discussed is what might be considered very near transfer, or transfer from one part of a game to another. Commercial off-the-shelf games are generally designed to place players in challenges right at the cusp of their ability, where play is not so frustrating they quit but is adequately challenging. In order to do this, an estimate of skill is needed, in this case it is skill at game play. Educational games can similarly be designed such that early information about knowledge, skills, and abilities can be used on the fly to adjust the events and demands of game play. In order for this to work, the domain-specific skills in one game area or level must transfer to another. This ability allows for the creation of adaptivity in games based not just on game play skill, but content area constructs as well.

The actual design of tasks will benefit from explicit indications of which features can and should be manipulated. The best leverage we have may be to provide learners with representations and concepts in ways they are most likely to bring them to bear in their lives. However, it may take research to know which representations those are, and we should expect occasionally counterintuitive results. For example, in studying troubleshooting skills Newell (1969) introduced the terms strong methods and weak methods to define problem-solving procedures, the first of which require well-organized domain-specific knowledge and the latter of which are more time-consuming but general heuristics. Newell and Simon (1972) found that it was actually the "weaker" methods that transferred across domains because "strong" methods worked by exploiting understandings of particular systems. The same principle is likely to apply to creativity, communication, and systems thinking. We are likely to find greater transfer of methods that do not rely heavily on domain-specific content (Perkins & Salomon, 1989; Tricot & Sweller, 2014). However, if our desired inference is limited to a specific domain, assessment of strong methods makes sense.

Expectations regarding the intended use of inference from game-based assessment must be communicated to the end users. Given that any assessment itself occurs in a socio-cultural context, the human elements of interpretation must be considered alongside the statistical elements of evidence about generalizability and transfer. We need to communicate effectively about which situations we expect an inference will apply and which situations it is not designed to apply. However, the mechanisms by which to do this are not yet clear. Research suggests that communication of ideas such as measurement error to general audiences is difficult (Zwick, Zapata-Rivera, & Hagerty, 2014). In the face of rising optimism about the promise of game-based assessment, expectations for the capabilities of extracting inference from game play must be grounded by the realities of working in a context-rich environment, and matched in design and inference to the purpose they are intended for. There is much to be gained, but it will take careful thought and principled work to achieve.

References

Appleton, J. J., Christenson, S. L., & Furlong, M. J. (2008). Student engagement with school: Critical conceptual and methodological issues of the construct. *Psychology in the Schools, 45*, 369–386.

Arena, D. A. (2012). *Commercial video games as preparation for future learning* (Unpublished doctoral dissertation). Stanford University, Palo Alto, CA.

Barnett, S. M., & Ceci, S. J. (2002). When and where do we apply what we learn? A taxonomy for far transfer. *Psychological Bulletin, 128*, 612–637.

Behrens, J. T. (1997). Principles and procedures of exploratory data analysis. *Psychological Methods, 2*(2), 131–160.

Behrens, J. T. (2013). *Templates as socio-cognitive exemplars: Transfer and generalization as foundational design goals.* Paper presented at the meeting of the National Council for Educational Measurement, San Francisco, CA.

Behrens, J. T. & DiCerbo, K. E. (2014a). Harnessing the currents of the digital ocean. In J. A. Larusson & B. White (Eds.), *Learning analytics: From research to practice* (pp. 39–60). New York, NY: Springer.

Behrens, J. T. & DiCerbo, K. E. (2014b). Technological implications for assessment ecosystems: Opportunities for digital technology to advance assessment. *Teachers College Record, 116*, 1–22.

Behrens, J. T., DiCerbo, K. E., Yel, N., & Levy, R. (2012). Exploratory data analysis. In I. B. Weiner, J. A. Schinka, & W. F. Velicer (Eds.), *Handbook of psychology: Research methods in psychology* (2nd ed., pp. 34–70). New York, NY: Wiley.

Behrens, J. T., Frezzo, D., Mislevy, R., Kroopnick, M., & Wise, D. (2006). Structural, functional and semiotic symmetries in simulation-based games and assessments. In E. Baker, J. Dickieson, W. Wulfeck, & H. F. O'Neil (Eds.), *Assessment of problem solving using simulations* (pp. 59–80). New York, NY: Erlbaum.

Behrens, J. T., Mislevy, R. J., DiCerbo, K. E., & Levy, R. (2012). Evidence centered design for learning and assessment in the digital world. In M. Mayrath, J. Clarke-Midura, D. H. Robinson, & G. Schraw (Eds.). *Technology-based assessments for 21st century skills: Theoretical and practical implications from modern research* (pp. 13–54). Charlotte, NC: Information Age Publishing.

Binkley, M., Erstad, O., Herman, J., Raizen, S., Ripley, M., Miller-Ricci, M., & Rumble, M. (2012). Defining twenty-first century skills. In P. Griffin, E. Care, & B. McGaw (Eds.), *Assessment and teaching of 21st century skills* (pp. 17–66). Netherlands: Springer.

Bransford, J. D., Brown, A. L., & Cocking, R. R. (2000). *How people learn: Brain, mind, experience, and school* (expanded ed.). Washington, DC: National Academy Press.

Bransford, J. D., & Schwartz, D. L. (1999). Rethinking transfer: A simple proposal with multiple implications. *Review of Research in Education, 24,* 61–100.

Brennan, R. L. (2011). *Using generalizability theory to address reliability issues for PARCC assessments: A White Paper.* Iowa City, IA: Center for Advanced Studies in Measurement and Assessment (CASMA), University of Iowa.

Cheng, B., Ructtinger, L., Fujii, R., & Mislevy, R. J. (2010). *Assessing systems thinking and complexity in science.* Menlo Park, CA: SRI International.

Chesler, N. C., Arastoopour, G., D'Angelo, C. M., Bagley, E. A., & Shaffer, D. W. (2012). Design of a professional practice simulator for educating and motivating first-year engineering students. *Advances in Engineering Education, 3.* Retrieved from http://edgaps. org/gaps/wp-content/uploads/aee-vol03-issue03-01.pdf

Ciani, K. D., Sheldon, K. M., Hilpert, J. C., Easter, M. A. (2011). Antecedents and trajectories of achievement goals: A self-determination theory perspective. *British Journal of Educational Psychology, 81,* 223–243.

Clarke-Midura, J., Code, J., Dede, C., Mayrath, M., & Zap, N. (2011). Thinking outside the bubble: Virtual performance assessments for measuring complex learning. In M. C. Mayrath, J. Clarke-Midura, D. H. Robinson, & G. Schraw (Eds.), *Technology-based assessments for 21st century skills: Theoretical and practical implications from modern research* (pp. 125–147). Charlotte, NC: Information Age.

Clauser, B. E., Margolis, M. J., Clyman, S. G., & Ross, L. P. (1997). Development of automated scoring algorithms for complex performance assessments: A comparison of two approaches. *Journal of Educational Measurement, 34*(2), 141–161.

Corcoran, T., Mosher, F. A., & Rogat, A. (2009). *Learning progressions in science: An evidence-based approach to reform* (No. CPRE Research Report #RR-63). Philadelphia, PA: Consortium for Policy Research in Education.

Cronbach, L. J. (1989). Construct validation after thirty years. In R. L. Linn (Ed.), *Intelligence: Measurement, theory, and public policy: Proceedings of a symposium in honor of Lloyd G. Humphreys* (pp. 147–171). Urbana, IL: University of Illinois.

Cronbach, L. J., Gleser, G. C., Nanda, H., & Rajaratnam. N. (1972). *The dependability of behavioral measurements: Theory of generalizability for scores and profiles.* New York, NY: John Wiley & Sons.

Csikszentmihalyi, M. (1990). *Flow: The psychology of optimal experience*. New York, NY: HarperCollins.

Deci, E. L., Vallerand, R. J., Pelletier, L. G., & Ryan, R. M. (1991). Motivation and education: The self-determination perspective. *Educational Psychologist, 26*(3–4), 325–346.

Detterman, D. K., & Sternberg, R. J. (1993). *Transfer on trial: Intelligence, cognition, and instruction*. New York, NY: Ablex Publishing. Retrieved from http://psycnet.apa.org/psycinfo/1993-98301-000

DiCerbo, K. E. (2014). Game-based assessment of persistence. *Journal of Educational Technology & Society, 17*, 17–28.

DiCerbo, K. E., & Behrens, J. (2012). Implications of the digital ocean on current and future assessment. In R. Lissitz & H. Jiao (Eds.), *Computers and their impact on state assessment: Recent history and predictions for the future* (pp. 273–306). Charlotte, NC: Information Age.

Fauconnier, G., & Turner, M. (2002). *The way we think: Conceptual blending and the mind's hidden complexities*. New York, NY: Basic Books.

Frezzo, D. C., DiCerbo, K. E., Behrens, J. T., & Chen, M. (2013). An extensible microworld for learning in the computer networking professions. *Information Sciences, 264*, 91–103.

Gee, J. P. (2003). What video games have to teach us about learning and literacy. *Computers in Entertainment (CIE), 1*(1), 1–4.

Gee, J. P. (2007). *What video games have to teach us about learning and literacy* (2nd ed.). New York, NY: Palgrave.

Gitomer, D. H., Steinberg, L. S., & Mislevy, R. J. (1995). Diagnostic assessment of troubleshooting skill in an intelligent tutoring system. In P. Nichols, S. Chipman, & R. L. Brennan (Eds.), *Cognitively diagnostic assessment* (pp. 73–101). Hillsdale, NJ: Lawrence Erlbaum Associates.

Goldstone, R. L., & Day, S. B. (2012). Introduction to "New Conceptualizations of Transfer of Learning." *Educational Psychologist, 47*, 149–152.

Haladyna, T. M., & Downing, S. M. (2004). Construct-irrelevant variance in high-stakes testing. *Educational Measurement: Issues and Practice, 23*(1), 17–27. doi:10.1111/j.1745-3992.2004.tb00149.x

Hammer, D., Elby, A., Scherr, R. E., & Redish, E. F. (2005). Resources, framing, and transfer. In J. Mestre (Ed.), *Transfer of learning from a modern multidisciplinary perspective* (pp. 89–120). Greenwich, CT: Information Age Publishing.

Hansen, E. G., & Mislevy, R. J. (2006). Accessibility of computer-based testing for individuals with disabilities and English language learners within a validity framework. In M. Hricko (Ed.), *Online assessment and measurement: Foundations and challenges* (pp. 212–259). Hershey, PA: Information Science Publishing.

Humphreys, L. G. (1962). The organization of human abilities. *American Psychologist, 17*(7), 475.

Kafai, Y. B., Fields, D.A., & Cook, M. S. (2007). Your second selves: Resources, agency and constraints in avatar design in a tween virtual world. In Akira Baba (Ed.), *Situated Play: Proceedings of the Third International Conference of the Digital Games Research Association (DiGRA)* (pp. 31–39). Tokyo, Japan: The University of Tokyo.

Kintsch, W., & Greeno, J. G. (1985). Understanding and solving word arithmetic problems. *Psychological Review, 92*(1), 109.

Larsen-Freeman, D. (2013). Transfer of learning transformed. *Language Learning, 63*, 107–129.

Lave, J., & Wenger, E. (1991). *Situated learning: Legitimate peripheral participation.* Cambridge: Cambridge University Press.

Liu, O. L., Bridgeman, B., & Adler, R. (2012). Measuring learning outcomes in higher education: Motivation matters. *Educational Researcher, 41*, 352–362.

Messick, S. (1989). Validity. In R. L. Linn (Ed.), *Educational measurement* (3rd ed., pp. 13–103). New York, NY: American Council on Education/Macmillan.

Mislevy, R. J., Behrens, J. T., DiCerbo, K. E., Frezzo, D. C., & West, P. (2012). Three things game designers need to know about assessment. In D. Ifenthaler, D. Eseryel, & X. Ge (Eds.), *Assessment in game-based learning: Foundations, innovations, and perspectives* (pp. 59–81). New York, NY: Springer.

Mislevy, R. J., Behrens, J. T., DiCerbo, K. E., & Levy, R. (2012). Design and discovery in educational assessment: Evidence-centered design, psychometrics, and educational data mining. *Journal of Educational Data Mining, 4*, 11–48.

Mislevy, R. J., Corrigan, S., Oranje, A., DiCerbo, K. E., John, M., Bauer, M. I., . . . Hao, J. (2014). *Psychometrics and game-based assessment.* New York, NY: Institute of Play.

Mislevy, R.J., Haertel, G., Cheng, B.H., Ructtinger, L., DeBarger, A., Murray, E., . . . Vendlinski, T. (2013). A "conditional" sense of fairness in assessment. *Educational Research and Evaluation, 19*, 121–140.

Mislevy, R. J., Steinberg, L. S., & Almond, R. G. (2002). Design and analysis in task-based language assessment. *Language Testing, 19*(4), 477–496.

Morrison, B. (2013, November 19). Meaningful choice in games: Practical guide & case studies. *Gamasutra.* Retrieved from www.gamasutra.com/blogs/BriceMorrison/20131119/204733/Meaningful_Choice_in_Games_Practical_Guide__Case_Studies.php

Nakamura, J., & Csikszentmihalyi, M. (2002). The concept of flow. In C. R. Snyder & S. J. Lopez (Eds.), *Handbook of positive psychology* (pp. 89–105). New York, NY: Oxford University Press.

Newell, A. (1969). Heuristic programming: Ill-structured problems. In J. S. Aronofsky (Ed.) *Progress in operations research* (Vol. 3, pp. 361–414). New York, NY: John Wiley and Sons.

Newell, A., & Simon, H. A. (1972). *Human problem solving.* Englewood Cliffs, NJ: Prentice Hall.

NGSS Lead States. (2013). *4-ESS3-1 Earth and human activity.* Retrieved from www.nextgenscience.org/4-ess3-1-earth-and-human-activity

Perkins, D. N., & Salomon, G. (1989). Are cognitive skills context-bound? *Educational Researcher, 18*(1), 16–25.

Riconscente, M. M., Mislevy, R. J., & Hamel, L. (2005). An introduction to PADI task templates. *PADI Technical Report, 3.* Retrieved from http://padi.sri.com/downloads/TR3_Templates.pdf

Robinson, P. (2010). Situating and distributing cognition across task demands: The SSARC model of pedagogic task sequencing. In M. Putz & L. Sicola (Eds.), *Cognitive processing in second language acquisition: Inside the learner's mind* (pp. 243–268). Amsterdam: Benjamins.

Saxe, G. B. (1988). Candy selling and math learning. *Educational Researcher, 17*(6), 14–21.

Schalk, L., Saalbach, H., & Stern, E. (2011). Designing learning materials to foster transfer of principles. In L. Carlson, C. Holscher, & T. Shipley (Eds.), *Proceedings of the 33rd Annual Conference of the Cognitive Science Society* (pp. 300–305). Austin, TX: Cognitive Science Society.

Schmit, M. J., & Ryan, A. M. (1992). Test-taking dispositions: A missing link? *Journal of Applied Psychology, 77*(5), 629.

Schwartz, D. L., Bransford, J. D., & Sears, D. (2005). Efficiency and innovation in transfer. In J. Mestre (Ed.), *Transfer of learning from a modern multidisciplinary perspective* (pp. 1–51). Charlotte, NC: Information Age.

Schwartz, D. L., Chase, C. C., & Bransford, J. D. (2012). Resisting overzealous transfer: Coordinating previously successful routines with needs for new learning. *Educational Psychologist, 47*, 204–214.

Shaffer, D. W. (2007). *How computer games help children learn.* New York, NY: Palgrave.

Shavelson, R. J., Baxter, G. P., & Gao, X. (1993). Sampling variability of performance assessments. *Journal of Educational Measurement, 30*(3), 215–232.

Shavelson, R. J., Ruiz-Primo, M. A., & Wiley, E. W. (1999). Note on sources of sampling variability in science performance assessments. *Journal of Educational Measurement, 36*(1), 61–71.

Shute, V. J. (2011). Stealth assessment in computer-based games to support learning. In S. Tobias & J. D. Fletcher (Eds.), *Computer games and instruction* (pp. 503–524). Charlotte, NC: Information Age. Retrieved from http://myweb.fsu.edu/vshute/pdf/shute%20pres_h.pdf

Shute, V. J., & Ventura, M. (2013). *Measuring and supporting learning in games: Stealth assessment.* Cambridge, MA: MIT Press. Retrieved from http://myweb.fsu.edu/vshute/pdf/white.pdf

Shute, V. J., Ventura, M., Bauer, M. I., & Zapata-Rivera, D. (2009). Melding the power of serious games and embedded assessment to monitor and foster learning: Flow and grow. In U. Ritterfeld, M. Cody, & P. Vorder (Eds.), *Serious games: Mechanisms and effects* (pp. 295–321). Mahwah, NJ: Routledge, Taylor and Francis.

Shute, V. J., Ventura, M., & Kim, Y. J. (2013). Assessment and learning of qualitative physics in Newton's Playground. *Journal of Educational Research, 106*, 423–430.

Sikorski, T., & Hammer, D. (2010). A critique of how learning progressions research conceptualizes sophistication and progress. In K. Gomez, L. Lyons, & J. Radinsky (Eds.), *Learning in the disciplines: Proceedings of the 2010 International Conference of the Learning Sciences* (pp. 277–284). Chicago, IL: ISLS.

Stamper, J. C., Lomas, D., Ching, D., Ritter, S., Koedinger, K. R., & Steinhart, J. (2012). The rise of the super experiment. In *Proceedings of the 5th International Conference on Educational Data Mining* (EDM 2012) (pp. 196–200). Chania, Greece.

Sundre, D. L., & Wise, S. L. (2003, April). *'Motivation filtering': An exploration of the impact of low examinee motivation on the psychometric quality of tests.* Paper presented at the annual meeting of the National Council on Measurement in Education, Chicago, IL. Retrieved from www.jmu.edu/assessment/wm_library/Filter.pdf

Toulmin, S. E. (1958). *The uses of argument.* Cambridge: Cambridge University Press.

Tricot, A., & Sweller, J. (2014). Domain-specific knowledge and why teaching generic skills does not work. *Educational Psychology Review, 26*, 265–283.

Tukey, J. W. (1977). *Exploratory data analysis.* Reading, MA: Addison-Wesley.

Tukey, J. W. (1986). Data analysis, computation and mathematics. In L. V. Jones (Ed.), *The collected works of John W. Tukey: Vol. IV. Philosophy and principles of data analysis: 1965–1986* (pp. 753–775). Pacific Grove, CA: Wadsworth. (Original work published 1972).

Ventura, M., Shute, V. J., & Zhao, W. (2012). The relationship between video game use and a performance-based measure of persistence. *Computers & Education, 60*, 52–58.

Zapata-Rivera, D., & Bauer, M. (2012). Exploring the role of games in educational assessment. In M. C. Mayrath, J. Clarke-Midura, & D. Robinson (Eds.), *Technology-based assessments for 21st century skills: Theoretical and practical implications from modern research* (pp. 149–172). Charlotte, NC: Information Age.

Zwick, R., Zapata-Rivera, D., & Hegarty, M. (2014). Comparing graphical and verbal representations of measurement error in test score reports. *Educational Assessment, 19*, 116–138.

13

ON THE ROLE OF MULTILEVEL ITEM RESPONSE MODELS IN MULTISITE EVALUATION STUDIES FOR SERIOUS GAMES

Li Cai, Kilchan Choi, and Megan Kuhfeld

Introduction

A casual Google search these days would routinely return half a billion or more pages related to games for learning, exemplifying the enthusiasm in their development and use. Evaluating the effectiveness of games or other intervention strategies on learning outcomes would, however, require more serious discussions around design, measurement, and statistical analysis focusing on establishing causal inference, effect size determination, and statistical adjustments for confounding factors. During the past decade or more, federal educational research policy has shifted toward an emphasis on randomized experiments to examine the effectiveness of interventions. As a result, there has been a dramatic increase in the number of randomized trials in education during these years. Two branches of the Institute of Educational Sciences (IES)—the National Center for Education Evaluation and Regional Assistance (NCEE) and the National Center for Education Research (NCER)—have funded a large number of randomized trials to examine curricula, use of technology, and other interventions. According to a review of IES and NCER-funded randomized trials between 2002 and 2006, the majority were multisite cluster randomized trials (Spybrook & Raudenbush, 2009).

In multisite cluster randomized trials, clusters within a site are randomly assigned to one of two or more treatments, and this process is replicated at each site. For example, the sites in the experiment may be schools, and the clusters are classrooms which are assigned to either the treatment or control condition. The multisite trial enables a test of the generalizability of the treatment impact over the varied school settings in which the treatment may ultimately be implemented. In effect, a multisite trial allows for "mini-experiments" at each site, where each site provides an independent study of treatment efficacy (Raudenbush & Liu, 2000).

A multisite cluster randomized design in educational research typically includes a test-retest administration of (nearly) identical assessments of the outcome construct to the same group of individuals at two time points, before and after the intervention. For example, the outcome could be a measure of proficiency on a particular subject that the intervention is supposed to influence. The most commonly used method for scoring outcome measures is with the summed score (e.g., Curran, Bauer, & Willoughby, 2004; Curran & Bollen, 2001). The ubiquity of this approach stems from the straightforward method of scoring and the long history of classical summed-score-based test theory in the social and behavioral sciences. Researchers have increasingly utilized item response theory (IRT)-based approaches that rely on fitting IRT models to appropriately chosen calibration samples (Curran et al., 2008) and using the calibrated item parameters to estimate individual scaled scores such as with Bayesian expected a posteriori (EAP) or maximum a posteriori (MAP) methods (Thissen & Wainer, 2001).

While straightforward, these existing methods are not without their limitations. In the absence of including appropriate observed and latent variables as statistical controls in a measurement model, the observations of student performance on outcome items or tasks are correlated/dependent in four major ways: (a) the dependence between the outcome constructs at each occasion due to the longitudinal design; (b) the item-level residual dependence due to repeated (pre-post) exposure to the same set of measures; (c) the implausibility of assuming full exchangeability of individuals across treatment and control conditions, that is, the random variables associated with post-treatment individuals in the control condition cannot be exchanged without consequences with those in the treatment condition (see e.g., Lindley & Smith, 1972); and (d) the dependence of individuals due to their nesting in sites.

The dependence of latent constructs pre- and post-treatment leads to some ambiguities as whether the item calibration sample should come from pretest or post-test measures, or some combination (Curran et al., 2008). The item-level residual dependence, if unattended to, might lead to an overly optimistic estimate of the reliability of measurement for the target construct. The issue of full exchangeability across treatment and control conditions is particularly important, because failure to include important condition information (e.g., treatment assignment) in the measurement model will lead to inconsistencies in the subsequent inference about treatment effect. Finally, failure to account for nesting leads to the lack of congruence between statistical models used for measurement and impact estimation.

Thus, the traditional summed score approach (using classical test theory) or standard "off-the-shelf" IRT-based approaches have full exchangeability assumptions that are inconsistent with the conditional exchangeability implied and required by multisite randomized experimental studies with repeated measures.

In contrast, we propose a multilevel two-tier (MTT) item factor model that embraces conditional exchangeability and specifies model features that appropriately reflect the interaction of latent variable measurement models with the experimental design. In the following section, we describe the summed score approach and the MTT model in more detail, and explain why MTT modeling provides a superior solution to measurement and data analysis issues in multisite randomized trials.

Measurement Models

Summed Score Approach

The summed score approach is the most widely used method for scoring outcome measures. As can be seen in Equation 13.1, the summed score ($\hat{Y}_j$) for person j is calculated by adding the raw item scores, where y_{ij} represents the observed item scores (e.g., 0 or 1 for binary cases; 0, 0.5, or 1 for three partial-credit scoring categories, etc.) on item i. I denotes the total number of items.

$$\hat{Y}_j = \sum_{i=1}^{I} y_{ij} \tag{13.1}$$

This simple method, however, has critical disadvantages. Since this method simply adds up the item scores with equal weighting, differences in item difficulty, discrimination, and/or student guessing (among other psychometric characteristics) are completely ignored. Comparability problems arise when the numbers of observed items are different between tests or occasions, either by design or due to missing data, because direct total score comparison between pretest and post-test, for example, gain score, is less meaningful or often misleading in terms of true change in such cases. Yet another complicating factor is that preassigned item weights (often by fiat, e.g., giving partial-credit scored open-ended items more weight than dichotomously scored multiple-choice items) may lead to suboptimal reliability in that the total score may in fact be less reliable than the constituent subscores. Finally, inferences derived from the summed score distribution are sample-specific and dedicated linking/equating studies are required for generalization of the sample-based results to other populations.

Multilevel Two-Tier (MTT) Item Factor Model

In item factor models, an item can potentially load on one or more latent dimensions (factors). These factors may also be correlated, in the tradition of Thurston's (1947) multiple factor analysis. Bifactor model, a confirmatory item factor analysis model, has increasingly drawn interest among psychometricians (Gibbons & Hedeker, 1992). In a typical bifactor model, there is one primary dimension, representing a target construct being measured, and there are S specific dimensions that are independent conditionally on the general dimension, representing residual dependence above and beyond the general dimension. All items may load on the general dimension, and at the same time an item may load on at most one group-specific dimension.

Cai (2010b) proposed a two-tier item factor model for single-level data. It is minimally a more general version of the bifactor item factor model in which the number of general dimensions is not required to be equal to 1 and the correlations among these general dimensions may be explicitly represented and modeled. It may also be understood as a more general version of the Thurstonian correlated-factors multidimensional item response theory (MIRT) model that explicitly includes an additional layer (tier) of random effects to account for residual dependence (e.g., due to repeated measures).

In this chapter, we propose a synthesis of the two-tier item factor analysis model with multilevel latent variable modeling in a unified two-level modeling framework that is flexible in terms of its support for mixed item response formats, multiple groups, and repeated time points. This approach is a valuable analytic tool for game evaluation research which features different measures and items in pre- and post-test design, clustered randomized trial, and multisite clustered randomized trial. In a two-tier model for single-level data, two kinds of latent variables are specified, primary and group-specific (Cai, 2010b). This creates a partitioning of the vector of latent variables ϑ for individual j into two mutually exclusive parts: $\vartheta_j = (\eta_j, \xi_j)$ where η_j is a vector of (potentially correlated) primary latent dimensions and ξ_j is a vector of specific dimensions that are independent conditional on the primary dimension. All latent variables in the model are random effects that vary over the individuals.

The multilevel two-tier (MTT) model, on the other hand, considers hierarchically-nested data wherein individuals are nested within schools, for instance. Building upon the multidimensional item-level measurement model, such two-level nesting structure is explicitly modeled using within- and between-cluster models. In this model the latent variables for individual j in school k are partitioned into three mutually exclusive parts: $\vartheta_{jk} = (\theta_k, \eta_{jk}, \xi_{jk})$, where θ_k is the vector of level-2 (school-level) latent variables and η_{jk} and ξ_{jk} are the vectors of individual-level (level-1) primary and specific latent variables, respectively. The latent variables interact with item parameters to produce item response probabilities. For instance, a model that may work well with dichotomously-scored item responses is the following extension of the classical 2-parameter logistic IRT model (see, e.g., Reckase, 2009):

$$P\left(Y_{ijk} = 1 \mid \vartheta_{jk}\right) = \frac{1}{1 + \exp\left[-(c_i + a_i' \vartheta_{jk})\right]} , \tag{13.2}$$

where Y_{ijk} is a Bernoulli random variable representing the response to item i from individual j in school k, c_i is the item intercept, and a_i is a conformable vector of item slopes. The model represents the response probability of a correct response

($Y_{ijk} = 1$) as a function of these item parameters and the latent variables. Obviously $P(Y_{ijk} = 0 \mid \vartheta_{jk}) = 1.0 - P(Y_{ijk} = 1 \mid \vartheta_{jk})$. More complex item response models may be used depending on item types, such as the graded model for ordinal response data and the nominal categories model (see e.g., Cai, Yang, & Hansen, 2011). Continuous outcomes (e.g., conditional normal) or count outcomes (e.g., conditional Poisson) may be included as needed.

Given $i = 1, \ldots, I$ items, $j = 1, \ldots, n_k$ individuals in school k, and $k = 1, \ldots, K$ schools, the observed data (marginal) likelihood function may take the following form:

$$L(\gamma) = \prod_{k=1}^{K} \int \prod_{j=1}^{n_k} \left[\iint \prod_{i=1}^{I} P\left(Y_{ijk} = y_{ijk} \mid \vartheta_{jk}\right) f(\xi_{jk}) d\xi_{jk} f(\eta_{jk}) d\eta_{jk} \right] f(\theta_k) d\theta_k \quad (13.3)$$

where y_{ijk} stands for the observed response to item i from individual j in school k, and γ stands for the collection of freely estimated model parameters. Yang, Monroe, and Cai (2012) developed efficient dimension reduction methods for maximum marginal likelihood estimation with the Bock-Aitkin (Bock & Aitkin, 1981) EM algorithm. Alternatively, the Metropolos-Hastings Robbins-Monro (MH-RM; Cai, 2010a, 2010b) algorithm may also be used. Both algorithms are implemented in the flexMIRT® software (Cai, 2013).

A Latent Change Parameterization

Cai (2010b) noted that when an IRT model must be calibrated with longitudinal item response data, even if the measurement instrument may be unidimensional at each time point, the multivariate longitudinal item response data are inherently multidimensional. For designs with pretest and post-test, at least two occasion-specific primary latent dimensions are needed for each of the treatment or control groups to model the initial status and potential gains, as well as to investigate potential differences in the structure of measurement (e.g., shifts in location or discrimination of items) over time, if necessary. In addition, the responses to the same item in pretest (time 1) and post-test (time 2) from the same individual may be residually correlated, even after controlling for the influence of the primary dimensions. Thus, item-specific residual correlation factors are introduced to handle the potential residual dependence, and there are as many of them as the number of repeated items.

Multisite randomized experiments generally consist of two distinct groups—control and treatment—within each school. Thus, it is necessary to specify four within-school primary dimensions to represent the pretest and post-test status of treatment and control groups. This is akin to conditioning the latent outcome variable on the treatment assignment indicator. Our approach is more general because we allow both means and variances of latent variables to differ across treatment and control conditions, just as in a multiple-group model within each site. Finally, from the study design, it is clear that multisite randomized controlled trial data have a nested structure. Students (level-1 units) are nested within schools (level-2 units), where we assume further that the number of classrooms within a school is not large enough to consider classrooms as additional random components. More importantly, there are both control and treatment students within a school. Thus, both between-school and within-school variations in pretest and post-test latent variables need to be modeled.

Using conventional path diagrams, Figures 13.1 and 13.2 show an exemplary multilevel two-tier item factor analysis model. The MTT model can be employed with an assessment containing a large number of items at pretest and post-test, but only four pairs of common items are shown due to space constraints. The rectangles represent items, and circles represent latent variables. The four pairs of common items load on two between-school (level-2) primary dimensions, two within-school (level-1) primary dimensions, and four group-specific (level-1) dimensions in each condition.

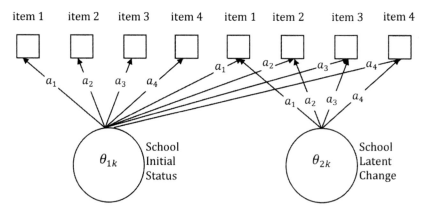

FIGURE 13.1 A multilevel two-tier item factor analysis model for multisite cluster randomized design with pretest and post-test design: Between-school model.

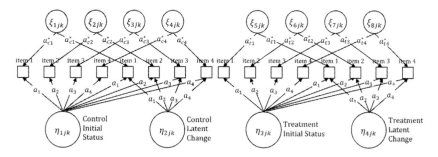

FIGURE 13.2 A multilevel two-tier item factor analysis model for multisite cluster randomized design with pretest and post-test design: Within-school model.

In terms of the factor pattern, the 16 × 14 factor pattern matrix corresponding to the model depicted in Figures 13.1 and 13.2 has the following form:

$$
\begin{pmatrix}
a_1 & & a_1 & & & & a^*_{c1} & & & & & & & \\
a_2 & & a_2 & & & & & a^*_{c2} & & & & & & \\
a_3 & & a_3 & & & & & & a^*_{c3} & & & & & \\
a_4 & & a_4 & & & & & & & a^*_{c4} & & & & \\
a_1 & a_1 & a_1 & a_1 & & & a^*_{c1} & & & & & & & \\
a_2 & a_2 & a_2 & a_2 & & & & a^*_{c2} & & & & & & \\
a_3 & a_3 & a_3 & a_3 & & & & & a^*_{c3} & & & & & \\
a_4 & a_4 & a_4 & a_4 & & & & & & a^*_{c4} & & & & \\
a_1 & & & & a_1 & & & & & & a^*_{c1} & & & \\
a_2 & & & & a_2 & & & & & & & a^*_{c2} & & \\
a_3 & & & & a_3 & & & & & & & & a^*_{c3} & \\
a_4 & & & & a_4 & & & & & & & & & a^*_{c4} \\
a_1 & a_1 & & & a_1 & a_1 & & & & & a^*_{c1} & & & \\
a_2 & a_2 & & & a_2 & a_2 & & & & & & a^*_{c2} & & \\
a_3 & a_3 & & & a_3 & a_3 & & & & & & & a^*_{c3} & \\
a_4 & a_4 & & & a_4 & a_4 & & & & & & & & a^*_{c4}
\end{pmatrix}
\qquad (13.4)
$$

where nonempty entries indicate free parameters. There are two between-school primary dimensions (item slopes in the first two columns above). The first dimension represents school k's initial status. The second dimension represents the potential post-test deviation from initial status for that school (e.g., due to exposure to business-as-usual instruction). For the control condition, the two within-school primary dimensions are in Columns 3 and 4. For the treatment condition, the two primary dimensions are in Columns 5 and 6. The interpretations of these dimensions resemble their between-school counterparts. Thus, there are a total of two between-school dimensions, four within-school primary dimensions, and eight within-school group-specific dimensions. Each residual dependence dimension is defined by an item pair within a condition. The constrained equal slope parameters on the item-specific residual dependence dimensions reflect an identification condition, as there is only one residual correlation per item pair. Note that Figures 13.1 and 13.2 and the corresponding factor pattern matrix display the model specification for a four-item assessment. If there were 20 items on the pretest and post-test, the size of the full factor pattern matrix would be 80 (20 pretest plus 20 post-test items, times 2 for both conditions) × 46 (2 between, 4 within primary, and 40 within residual dependence dimensions), which is a truly high-dimensional model. Note, however, that it is not necessarily the case that high dimensionality means a proliferation of parameters.

For a generic item i that appeared in both the pretest and post-test, the linear predictor portions of the item response models can be written as the following:

Pretest Control:

$$a_i\left(\theta_{1k}+\eta_{1jk}\right)+a_a^*\xi_{ijk} \tag{13.5-1}$$

Post-test Control:

$$a_i\left[\left(\theta_{1k}+\eta_{1jk}\right)+\left(\theta_{2k}+\eta_{2jk}\right)\right]+a_a^*\xi_{ijk} \tag{13.5-2}$$

Pretest Treatment:

$$a_i\left(\theta_{1k}+\eta_{3jk}\right)+a_{ti}^*\xi_{ijk} \tag{13.5-3}$$

Post-test Treatment:

$$a_i\left[\left(\theta_{1k}+\eta_{3jk}\right)+\left(\theta_{2k}+\eta_{4jk}\right)\right]+a_{ti}^*\xi_{ijk} \tag{13.5-4}$$

It is seen that each item has one overall discrimination parameter a_i and the various latent variables contribute to the item response in a systematic manner. The real additional parameters would come from the latent variable means and (co)variance components.

Specifically, two between-school latent variables θ_{1k} and θ_{2k} represent latent initial status and latent gain between pretest and post-test for school k, respectively. In addition, among the four within-school latent variables, the first two latent variables represent initial status (η_{1jk}) and latent gain (η_{2jk}) for student j in the control condition within school k, and the rest represent initial status (η_{3jk}) and latent gain (η_{4jk}) for student j in the treatment condition within school k. As such, the additional latent variables at post-test represent potential gains over the pretest level. Furthermore, the variation is decomposed at both pretest and post-test into between-school and within-school components. By allowing mean differences between η_2 and η_4 to be estimated, that is, the difference between latent changes between the treatment and control conditions within schools, potential effects of treatment on learning gain may be explicitly represented. This model is motivated by growth modeling developments as represented in Bock and Bargmann (1966), Embretson (1991), Cai (2010b), and McArdle (2009), among others. Upon estimating the item parameters, IRT-scaled scores can be computed for each of the latent variables as posterior means (expected a posteriori, or EAP, scores, Thissen & Wainer, 2001) or as multiple imputations (plausible values; see von Davier, Gonzalez, & Mislevy, 2009).

Advantages of the MTT Model

There are several new features of the MTT model that are particularly relevant to treatment impact evaluations. First, we estimate mean and variance of pretest and post-test latent variables separately for the treatment and control groups. This approach prevents us from the inadvertent bias induced by shrinking the individual posteriors of both treatment and control conditions to a common mean, when the treatment is expected to differentially impact the mean and variance in each condition. It is a standard practice in IRT modeling for off-the-shelf assessments that no information beyond the test items themselves (plus distributional assumptions about the latent variable, usually presumed standard normal) is used in estimating the scaled scores. Thus virtually all off-the-shelf IRT analyses and scaled outcome scores assume full exchangeability of the treatment and control participants. However, we argue that in an experimental context, the failure to include important conditioning information (e.g., treatment assignment) in the measurement model will lead to inconsistencies by shrinking outcomes in both treatment and control conditions to the grand mean, thereby diluting measured treatment impact.

It is interesting to note that this is not an entirely new observation. In the context of large-scale educational surveys, for example the National Assessment of Educational Progress (NAEP)—also known as The Nation's Report Card—researchers have long argued for the importance of including population conditioning covariate information into the measurement model so that estimates from student survey data are statistically consistent for the population comparisons of interest (Mislevy, 1991; Mislevy, Beaton, Kaplan, & Sheehan, 1992; Mislevy, Johnson, & Muraki, 1992; Schofield, Junker, Taylor, & Black, 2014). Similarly, when we adopt the widely held view among statisticians that all latent variables can be viewed as missing data (Dempter, Laird, & Rubin, 1977), we could not help but notice that this is exactly the same argument made in the multiple imputation literature for survey nonresponse (e.g., Little & Rubin, 2002) that important conditioning information from the data analysts' model must be present in the imputation model for the imputation-based inferences to be valid. In other words, key covariate(s) in the analyst's model should also be included when the multiple random imputations of missing data are produced. We take the conditional exchangeability one step further by including a range of observed and latent variables to make the measurement model commensurate with the research design.

Second, in the IRT model calibration stage, latent gain/change scores are represented explicitly in the MTT model. Notice that as opposed to the problematic use of observed gain scores, which tend to be less stable, the latent variables represent error-free components. Our approach is particularly effective when examining change from two-wave (pre-post) data, in that the variance of treatment latent gain scores is reduced by an amount proportional to the shared variance between pretest and post-test. In other words, the model utilizes the availability of a stable and randomly equivalent control condition where there should be (theoretically) only normative change in student post-test performance from pretest to decompose the observed variability in the outcome assessment into two components that may be provisionally termed latent prior knowledge factor and latent malleable factor. As soon as the model-based decomposition is achieved, we submit that the comparison between treatment and control groups should be focused on the latent malleable factors which are targeted to be changed in results of treatment. This is in stark contrast with the standard approach, whether summed score-based or IRT-based, in which the post-test outcome is used directly in impact estimation. We argue that the standard approach is less optimal because the variation in the post-test outcome conflates two sources of variance, that is, that of prior knowledge and that of potentially malleable difference. One direct consequence of our approach is that the resulting reduced variance in latent gain estimates may lead to substantially increased effect size of the treatment effect.

An Illustrative Example

An application of the MTT model comes from a large-scale randomized trial examining the instructional effects of video games with over 1500 students in 30 intervention classrooms and 29 comparison classrooms in 26 schools in nine districts. The serious games were developed by the Center for Advanced Technology in Schools (CATS) at the National Center for Research on Evaluation, Standards, and Student Testing (CRESST) to improve students' knowledge of pre-algebra topics such as rational number concepts. Students' mathematics learning outcomes were measured by items similar to pre-algebra mathematics standardized assessment items on rational numbers and fractions. Students in intervention classrooms played games on the topic of rational numbers and fractions, whereas those in the comparison classrooms played an alternative set of games on solving equations.

Eight games were developed for this study through the process of knowledge specification, software design and testing, teacher professional development, and assessment development. Two sets of knowledge specifications were developed: rational numbers/fractions, and solving equations. The knowledge specifications served as the design framework for the games. Four games covered fractions concepts (number line concepts, fraction addition, relationships among whole numbers and fractions using multiplication and division, direct variation) and four games covered solving equations concepts (integer operations, expressions, solving equations—conceptual, solving equations—procedural; see Vendlinski, Delacruz, Buschang, Chung, & Baker, 2010, for details on games and measures). Students in the intervention condition played the fractions games, and the solving equations games were comparison condition games.

The efficacy trial study which focused on estimating impacts of intervention by comparing outcome measures between treatment and control conditions required 12 instructional days (10 game play days and 2 testing days). In general, students played games for at least 40 minutes per game day. In general, teachers completed survey measures after the professional development session (feedback on games), on the pretest day (background), on game days (logs of student activities and problems), and immediately after the post-test (topics covered between game play and the post-test, and general comments on their study experience). Students were sampled from sixth-grade math classes. Of the total sample, 50% were female, 49% Hispanic/Latino/a, 24% White, 11% multiracial, 5% Black or African

American, 4% Asian or Pacific Islander, 2% American Indian or Alaskan Native, and 5% Other.

Twenty-four schools participated in this study, but one school was excluded from the analysis because the experiment could not be delivered due to a technical difficulty in that school. In each school, experimental and control classrooms were randomly assigned. Among the remaining 23 schools, 14 schools had both control and experimental conditions implemented, while the remaining nine schools had either only the experimental condition (six schools) or only the control condition (three schools). Note, however, that all the participating schools administered both the pretest and post-test measures of fractions knowledge as well as a brief post-test measure of solving equations knowledge. The pretest and post-test measures of fractions knowledge largely overlap, that is, the vast majority of items were repeated with just a few variant items.

The outcome measure of fractions knowledge was developed, tested, and refined during the game testing process. Vendlinski et al. (2010) reported that the outcome measure demonstrated high technical quality. The items were systematically developed from the knowledge specifications and were similar to items found in typical standardized assessments on those topics. Classical discrimination indices were adequate and the items were not overly easy or difficult for the target sample (proportion correct ranged from .4 to .7). The range of item to total score correlation was from .09 to .85. Classical reliability estimates were also moderate (.80).

Research Questions

The key research question in this analysis focuses on estimating the game's treatment impact on students' fractions knowledge learning outcomes. We conducted two different sets of analyses to compare two statistical approaches. Specifically, one analysis used the classical measurement approach in which raw summed scores of pretest and post-test items were calculated, while the other analysis utilized a multilevel two-tier (MTT) item factor model in which a latent gain score was estimated.

Results

Descriptive Results

We utilize the summed scoring method to establish baseline results for comparison purposes. In our study, the total numbers of items for pretest and post-test are, respectively, 22 and 23. Among 22 pretest items, 17 items are dichotomously scored (0 or 1), and the remaining 5 items are partial-credit scored: two items to 0, 0.5, or 1; two items to 0.3, 0.67, or 1; and one item to 0.25, 0.5, 0.75, or 1. Similarly, among 23 post-test items, 17 items are scored to either 0 or 1; one item to 0, 0.5, or 1; three items to 0, 0.3, 0.67, or 1; and two items to 0, 0.25, 0.5, 0.75, or 1. Note that there are 20 common items administered in both pretest and post-test.

Figure 13.3 presents descriptive statistics of raw summed pretest and post-test scores for control and treatment conditions. The dot and the vertical bar represent the mean and one standard deviation above and below the mean. The total numbers of students for control and treatment conditions used in our analyses are 763 and 808, respectively. For students who have both pretest and post-test scores, there are 709 students in the control group and 759 students in the treatment group. For the purpose of comparison between the two analytic approaches, we included only complete cases in both analyses. The pretest mean score for the control group is about 8 and its standard deviation (*SD*) is approximately 4. Similarly, the pretest mean score for the treatment group is 8 and its *SD* is 4.1. Although random assignment was at the classroom level within each school, highly similar overall pretest means across the two conditions provide another layer of assurance that the randomization indeed led to balance on pre-treatment differences in mathematics knowledge.

The post-test mean score is higher by approximately 1.5 points for the treatment group than for the control group. The observed post-test mean scores are 10.9 for the treatment group and 9.5 for the control group. This difference is approximately 0.3 pooled standard deviation of post-test.

We also examined the descriptive statistics of raw total pretest and post-test scores by schools and experimental conditions. As can be seen in Figure 13.4, there is some variability in pretest mean scores across schools. School 8 has a pretest mean of approximately 4 points, while School 9 has a pretest mean close to 13

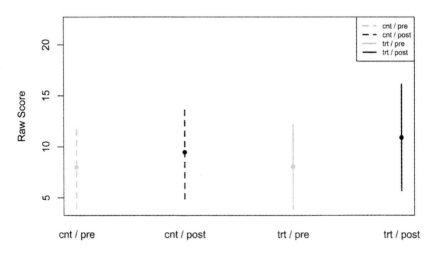

FIGURE 13.3 Descriptive statistics of raw total scores of pretest and post-test by experimental conditions.

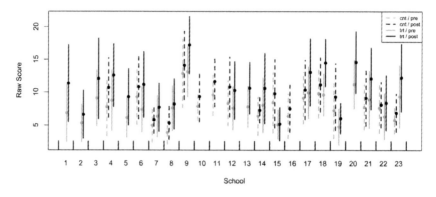

FIGURE 13.4 Descriptive statistics of raw total scores of pretest and post-test by schools and experimental conditions.

points. Except for these two schools, most of the rest of the schools have similar pretest mean scores. Within-school pretest difference between the control and the treatment, which is more important in a randomized trial, is not salient. Specifically, the pretest differences between the two groups in most of the schools range within a point and half, but three schools (Schools 8, 19, and 23) show differences of approximately 2.5 points or higher.

As for post-test mean scores, all the schools show higher post-test means than pretest means in both the control and treatment groups. This positive increase in mean scores is partly attributable to the fact that the post-test has one more item than the pretest. However, the differences in many schools are larger than one point, and the differences are larger for the treatment groups. For example, the difference between pretest mean and post-test mean in the treatment group in Schools 1, 4, and 18 is approximately four points. Furthermore, the differences between post-test mean and pretest mean are larger in the treatment group than in the control group for 10 out of 13 schools which have both treatment and control groups. These results indicate there may be positive treatment effects across schools.

Figure 13.5 displays descriptive statistics of the estimated latent pretest score and latent change score by experimental conditions. The means of latent pretest scores for both groups are very nearly 0 and the standard deviations are also close to 1. However, the latent change score means for the control and treatment groups are, respectively, 0.022 and 0.341. Thus, the observed difference is equal to 0.319. The outstanding pattern is that the standard deviation of the latent change score is far smaller than the standard deviation of latent pretest score. The standard deviation of the latent change score for the control is 0.335 and for the treatment is 0.448. The pooled standard deviation is about 0.40, which is only 40% of the latent pretest score's standard deviation. This potentially leads to increased effect size as elaborated in detail in later sections.

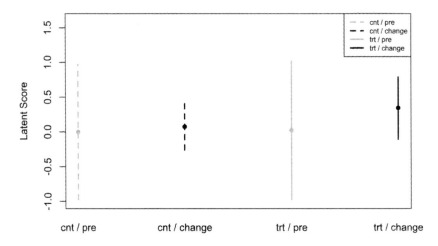

FIGURE 13.5 Descriptive statistics of latent pretest scores and latent change scores by experimental conditions.

This reduced variance of latent change score is necessitated by the fact that the latent post-test score can be viewed as a sum of initial status and latent gain (Equation 13.5-1 to 13.5-4). In other words, if we treat the total variance of latent post-test as constant, the latent change score is equal to the latent post-test score minus the latent pretest score, so the variance has to be smaller. When we view the gain score variance, say, in the control condition as representing the variability of the malleable factor distribution in the population of interest, it becomes the more natural unit of comparison for computing standardized effect sizes.

We also plot the means plus/minus one standard deviation for the latent initial status and latent gain scores for each condition within a school (see Figure 13.6).

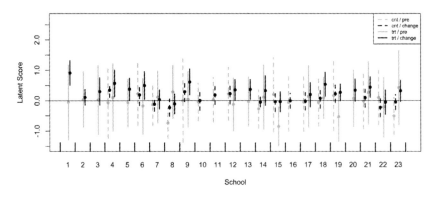

FIGURE 13.6 Descriptive statistics of latent pretest score and latent change score by schools and experimental conditions.

The most noticeable effect is that almost all the schools now show positive change. But such positive change is larger and statistically significant for the treatment condition in contrast to the control condition. In addition, the standard deviation of the latent change score is significantly smaller for the standard deviation of the latent pretest score.

Impact Model: Two-Level Hierarchical Model

Having completed the measurement model, we employ a standard two-level hierarchical model to estimate the treatment effect in multisite cluster randomized trial design. The model (Model 1) in Equation 13.6 specifies a model with outcome variable Y_{ij}, the raw total post-test score, for student i in school j, as a function of treatment indicator variable Trt_{ij}. Note that the treatment indicator variable takes a value of -0.5 for the control condition, and 0.5 for the treatment condition within each school j. By virtue of this coding, β_{0j} represents the mean post-test score for school j and β_{1j} represents the expected difference in the outcome between treatment and control conditions in school j.

$$
\begin{aligned}
Y_{ij} &= \beta_{0j} + \beta_{1j} + Trt_{ij} + \varepsilon_{ij}, \quad \varepsilon_{ij} \sim N(0,\sigma^2) \\
\beta_{0j} &= \gamma_{00} + u_{0j} \quad u_{0j} \sim N(0,\tau_{00}) \\
\beta_{1j} &= \gamma_{10} + u_{1j} \quad u_{1j} \sim N(0,\tau_{11})
\end{aligned}
\tag{13.6}
$$

The level-1 error term σ^2 is assumed to be normally distributed with mean 0 and variance σ^2. At level 2, β_{0j} and β_{1j} are modeled as a function of the grand means and the random effects around the means, u_{0j} and u_{1j}, respectively. The regression coefficient γ_{10} represents the overall treatment effect. The two random effects are assumed to be bivariate normal with variances τ_{00} and τ_{11}, and covariance τ_{01}.

In addition, we specify another two-level HLM (Model 2) which includes observed pretest summed score as a covariate. This variable is group-mean centered so β_{0j} still represents the mean post-test score for school j. The key parameter of interest β_{1j} becomes the expected difference in post-test score between the two groups in school j, holding pretest constant.

$$
\begin{aligned}
Y_{ij} &= \beta_{0j} + \beta_{1j} * Trt_{ij} + \beta_{2j} * \text{Pretest}_{ij} + \varepsilon_{ij}, \quad \varepsilon_{ij} \sim N(0,\sigma^2) \\
\beta_{0j} &= \gamma_{00} + u_{0j} \quad u_{0j} \sim N(0,\tau_{00}) \\
\beta_{1j} &= \gamma_{10} + u_{1j} \quad u_{1j} \sim N(0,\tau_{11}) \\
\beta_{2j} &= \gamma_{20} + u_{2j} \quad u_{2j} \sim N(0,\tau_{22})
\end{aligned}
\tag{13.7}
$$

Results using raw scores

Using those two models above, we analyzed two data sets: total raw pretest and post-test scores, and MTT scaled scores. The results from total raw scores are presented in Table 13.1. The grand mean of raw post-test total score post-test (γ_{00}) is approximately 10.1 and the expected overall difference between treatment and control (γ_{10}) is 1.4, which are all statistically significant. This expected difference, 1.4, is about 0.23 of pooled standard deviation of post-test raw score. Also, the variance of the treatment effect across schools is 5.7 and its 95% interval of the expected differences across schools ranges from −3.28 to 6.05. Note, however, that this variability does not take the pretest differences into account.

In the second panel of Table 13.1, we present the result from Model 2 as specified in Equation 13.7. The pretest score is positively associated with the post-test (i.e., one unit change of pretest leads to a 0.93 increase in post-test). After controlling for pretest difference, the overall treatment effect is approximately 1.1 and its variance is 1.3, which becomes much smaller than the corresponding variance in the previous unconditional model. The lower and upper ends of the 95% interval of the treatment effects across schools are −1.05 and 3.43, respectively.

Figure 13.7 shows each school's empirical Bayes (EB) estimate of treatment effect from Model 2. The middle bar in each school (x-axis) represents the EB estimate and the vertical line represents its 95% confidence interval. The solid horizontal line represents the overall treatment effect ($\gamma_{10} = 1.119$), whereas the dotted horizontal line is the reference line whether each school's treatment effect is statistically significantly different from zero. Ten out of the 23 schools show intervals that do not cover 0, which means that students in these schools

TABLE 13.1 Impact Model Result: Raw Total Pretest and Post-test

Fixed effects	Model 1: Unconditional			Model 2: Pretest as covariate		
	Estimate	SE	p value	Estimate	SE	p value
Intercept (γ_{10})	10.062	0.489	< .001	10.334	0.486	< .001
Trt (γ_{10})	1.388	0.636	.029	1.119	0.332	.001
Pretest(γ_{20})				0.930	0.026	< .001
Variance components	Estimate	SE	p value	Estimate	SE	p value
Level-1 (σ^2)	19.914	0.728	< .001	7.919	0.298	< .001
Intercept (τ_{00})	4.723	1.634	.002	5.178	1.646	.001
Trt (τ_{11})	5.669	2.436	.010	1.307	0.686	.029
Pretest (τ_{22})				0.005	0.298	< .001

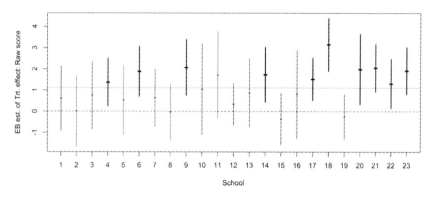

FIGURE 13.7 Empirical Bayes estimate of treatment effect by schools: Conditional model result with raw total score.

performed statistically significantly better in the treatment than those in the control conditions. Nine of the remaining 11 schools (the exceptions are Schools 15 and 19) have a positive EB estimate, but their treatment effects are not statistically significant as their 95% intervals cover a value of 0.

Results using MTT scaled scores

We also fit the previously specified multilevel models to the latent gain scaled scores obtained from the MTT model. Note that the outcome of the analysis is the latent change scores instead of the post-test score. As can be seen in Table 13.2, the overall difference in the latent change score between the treatment and control group is 0.243 and its variance is 0.013. The resulting 95% interval estimate of the differences between the two conditions across schools ranges from 0.466 to 0.021. Interestingly, the overall treatment effect does not change much even after controlling for latent pretest score in the model, indicating that the MTT model has already partialed out the initial status differences. The coefficient (γ_{10}) in Model 2 is 0.236 and its variance reduced to 0.008. The overall treatment effect is approximately equal to 0.58 standard deviation unit of the latent change score.

Finally, we present the EB estimate of the treatment random effects and the 95% confidence intervals based on Model 2 for each school in Figure 13.8. The horizontal line represents the overall treatment effect, which is 0.236. The most noteworthy thing in this figure is that 22 schools' lower 95% confidence limit is above zero. This indicates that the treatment effects in 22 schools except for one school (School 8) are statistically significant.

TABLE 13.2 Impact Model Result: Latent Gain Scores From the MTT Model

Fixed effects	Model 1: Unconditional			Model 2: Pretest as covariate		
	Estimate	SE	p value	Estimate	SE	p value
Intercept (γ_{00})	0.199	0.042	< .001	0.207	0.042	< .001
Trt (γ_{10})	0.243	0.035	< .001	0.236	0.029	< .001
Pretest(γ_{20})				0.107	0.009	< .001
Variance components	Estimate	SE	p value	Estimate	SE	p value
Level-1 (σ^2)	0.119	0.012	< .001	0.110	0.004	< .001
Intercept (τ_{00})	0.038	0.008	.001	0.037	0.012	.001
Trt (τ_{11})	0.013	0.004	.049	0.008	0.006	.094
Pretest (τ_{22})				0.000	0.298	.423

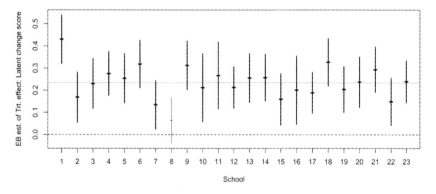

FIGURE 13.8 Empirical Bayes estimate of treatment effect by schools: Difference in latent change score between the treatment and control groups.

Effect Sizes

Effect sizes (ES) are reported and used extensively in randomized trials as they provide more meaningful standardized interpretations of treatment effect estimates. We calculated ES of the treatment effect obtained from multilevel impact Model 2. Three different effect sizes were calculated as follows:

- Cohen's δ (Cohen, 1992) γ_{10}/SD of outcome
- Hedges's ES (Hedges & Rhoads, 2010) = γ_{10}/sqrt ($\sigma^2 + \tau_{00} + \tau_{11}$))
- Conditional ES (Spybrook, Raudenbush, Congdon, & Martinez, 2011) = σ^2)

TABLE 13.3 Effect Sizes

Outcome scores	Est. (γ_{10})	Post-test SD	Lev-1 var (σ^2)	Lev-2 Int var (τ_{00})	Lev-2 Trt var (τ_{11})	Hedges's ES	Cond. ES	Cohen's δ
Raw/summed	1.139	4.986	19.914	4.723	5.669	0.207	0.405	0.228
Latent change	0.236	0.419	0.110	0.037	0.009	0.615	0.705	0.579

Cohen's δ is colloquially referred to as "the ES" and is calculated by dividing the treatment effect coefficient by the standard deviation of the outcome. Thus, the treatment effect is phrased in terms of the standard deviations of the outcome measure. Hedges's ES is comparable to Cohen's δ except for the fact that it uses a model-based standard deviation of the outcome. In other words, the square root of the sum of all the variance components in an unconditional two-level hierarchical model for the multisite randomized trials is placed in the denominator instead of the standard deviation of outcome in the case of Cohen's. Lastly, Spybrook et al. (2011) introduced the conditional ES in their Optimal Design software, which is by far the most popular software program for conducting statistical power analysis for various cluster randomized design studies. Conditional ES uses only level-1 variance which is reduced after pretest score is included so it is generally bigger than either Cohen's δ or Hedges's ES.

As we see in Table 13.3, the raw score model yielded an ES of roughly 0.2. Although a 0.2 ES is viewed as a small effect size, given the short duration and low frequencies of treatment, it should be considered as a fairly sizable effect. Furthermore, our MTT latent change score model produces an ES of approximately 0.6. In addition to the results in Figure 13.8 that display statistically significant treatment effects for 22 out of 23 schools in the sample as compared to 10 out of 23 schools in the raw score model, the MTT latent change score model also significantly improves the ES estimate compared to the raw score model ES.

Discussion

This chapter proposed a multilevel two-tier (MTT) item factor model as a generalizable solution to measurement error and multilevel modeling issues in multisite randomized trials. We argued that the traditional measurement approaches using either raw summed scores or "off-the-shelf" IRT-based scaled scores ignored the plausibility of certain inherent exchangeability assumptions. Appropriately integrating measurement modeling with treatment impact modeling in multisite randomized studies with repeated measures requires the careful specification of model features that serve to explain (a) the dependency between the latent outcome variables at each occasion; (b) item-level residual dependence due to repeated measure; (c) lack of full exchangeability of participants between treatment and control conditions; and (d) individual nesting within sites. In contrast, we illustrated how the multilevel two-tier item factor model may be used to address each of the four aspects mentioned above, as well as contain many other desirable features.

The MTT item factor model for calibrating and scaling pretest and post-test item responses is developed for multisite cluster randomized designs with test-retest administration. By estimating the mean and variance of pretest and post-test latent variables separately for the treatment and control groups, the MTT model avoids shrinking the individual posteriors of both treatment and control conditions to a common mean. In this model, the assumption of "conditional exchangeability" holds, that is exchangeability within experimental groups. This assumption is much more appropriate for multisite cluster randomized designs than full exchangeability.

Additionally, we note that the particular factor pattern of the MTT model (both between and within schools) lends itself to another interpretation that may be useful to some. The latent gain score dimensions are effectively a specific dimension (as in a bifactor model) if the latent initial status dimension is regarded as the primary dimension, albeit with additional equality constraints. Adopting the standard bifactor or hierarchical item factor model interpretation, the specific dimensions represent residualized variation above and beyond the pretest variation (Reise, 2012). As such, they isolate that part of the post-test individual differences in performance that is specific, after controlling for prior knowledge. In contrast, the standard approach of using post-test scores (observed or scaled latent variable estimates) as an outcome conflates two sources of variance, that is, that of prior knowledge and that of malleable difference. As a result, the latent gain score dimensions from the MTT model are more sensitive measures for targeted interventions than the observed outcome scores (see e.g., Gibbons et al., 2008, p. 365).

The MTT model was demonstrated with data from a randomized cluster controlled trial assessing the instructional effects of video games on pre-algebra math topics. When the outcome data were analyzed with the standard approach using post-test summed scores as the outcome variable, results indicated a positive and statistically significant (but small) effect size (.23 Cohen's d). When the outcome variable is constructed from a multilevel multidimensional latent variable modeling approach, the effect size improved to medium to large range (approximately .6). The new latent variable modeling-based outcome measure was more sensitive to instructional intervention than standard measurement approaches. When interpreted more broadly, this research highlights the importance of integrating design, measurement, and impact analysis when evaluating the effectiveness of interventions. Recent developments in multidimensional and multilevel item response theory can isolate components of outcome variation that represent malleable factors, thereby potentially increasing the sensitivity of statistical tests and reducing the sample size requirements because of the improvements in sensitivity. More research on model specification and conditions under which the models are applicable is also needed.

Author Note

Part of this research is supported by the Institute of Education Sciences (R305C080015 and R305D140046). The views expressed here belong to the authors and do not reflect the views or policies of the funding agencies.

References

Bock, R. D., & Aitkin, M. (1981). Marginal maximum likelihood estimation of item parameters: Application of an EM algorithm. *Psychometrika, 46,* 443–459.

Bock, R. D., & Bargmann, R. E. (1966). Analysis of covariance structures. *Psychometrika, 31,* 507–533.

Cai, L. (2010a). High-dimensional exploratory item factor analysis by a Metropolis-Hastings Robbins-Monro algorithm. *Psychometrika, 75,* 33–57.

Cai, L. (2010b). Metropolis-Hastings Robbins-Monro algorithm for confirmatory item factor analysis. *Journal of Educational and Behavioral Statistics, 35,* 307–335.

Cai, L. (2013). flexMIRT: Flexible multilevel item factor analysis and test scoring [Computer software]. Seattle, WA: Vector Psychometric Group.

Cai, L., Yang, J., & Hansen, M. (2011). Generalized full-information item bifactor analysis. *Psychological Methods, 16,* 221–248.

Cohen, J. (1992). A power primer. *Psychological Bulletin, 112*(1), 155-159.

Curran, P., Bauer, D., & Willoughby, M. (2004). Testing main effects and interactions in latent curve analysis. *Psychological Methods, 9,* 220–237.

Curran, P., & Bollen, K. (2001). The best of both worlds: Combining autoregressive and latent curve models. In L. Collins & A. Sayer (Eds.), *New methods for the analysis of change* (pp. 105–136). Washington, DC: American Psychological Association.

Curran, P., Hussong, A., Cai, L., Huang, W., Chassin, L., Sher, K., & Zuchek, R. (2008). Pooling data from multiple longitudinal studies: The role of item response theory in integrative data analysis. *Developmental Psychology, 44*(2), 365–380.

Dempter, A. P., Laird, N. M., & Rubin, D. B. (1977). Maximum likelihood from incomplete data via the EM algorithm. *Journal of the Royal Statistical Society – Series B (Methodological), 39,* 1–38.

Embretson, S. (1991). A multidimensional latent trait model for measuring learning and change. *Psychometrika, 56,* 495–515.

Gibbons, R. D., & Hedeker, D. R. (1992). Full-information item bi-factor analysis. *Psychometrika, 57*(3), 423–436.

Gibbons, R. D., Weiss, D. J., Kupfer, D. J., Frank, E., Fagiolini, A., Grochocinski, V. J., . . . Immekus, J. C. (2008). Using computerized adaptive testing to reduce the burden of mental health assessment. *Psychiatric Services, 59,* 361–368.

Hedges, L., & Rhoads, C. (2010). *Statistical power analysis in education research* (NCSER 2010-3006). Washington, DC: National Center for Special Education Research, Institute of Education Sciences, U.S. Department of Education.

Lindley, D. V., & Smith, A. F. M. (1972). *Journal of the Royal Statistical Society – Series B (Methodological), 34,* 1–41.

Little, R. J. A., & Rubin, D. B. (2002). *Statistical analysis with missing data* (2nd ed.). New York, NY: John Wiley.

McArdle, J. J. (2009). Latent variable modeling of difference and changes with longitudinal data. *Annual Review of Psychology, 60,* 577–605.

Mislevy, R. J. (1991). Randomization-based inference about latent variables from complex samples. *Psychometrika, 56,* 177–196.

Mislevy, R. J., Beaton, A. E., Kaplan, B. K., & Sheehan, K. M. (1992). Estimating population characteristics from sparse matrix samples of item responses. *Journal of Educational Measurement, 29,* 133–161.

Mislevy, R. J., Johnson, E. G., & Muraki, E. (1992). Scaling procedures in NAEP. *Journal of Educational Statistics, 17,* 131–154.

Raudenbush, S. W., & Liu, X. (2000). Statistical power and optimal design for multisite randomized trials. *Psychological Methods, 5*(2), 199–213.

Reckase, M. (2009). *Multidimensional item response theory.* New York, NY: Springer.

Reise, S. P. (2012). The rediscovery of bifactor measurement models. *Multivariate Behavioral Research, 47,* 667–696.

Schofield, L. S., Junker, B., Taylor, L. J., & Black, D. A. (2014). Predictive inference using latent variables with covariates. *Psychometrika.* Advance online publication. doi:10.1007/s11336-014-9415-z

Spybrook, J., & Raudenbush, S. W. (2009). An examination of the precision and technical accuracy of the first wave of group-randomized trials funded by the Institute of Education Sciences. *Educational Evaluation and Policy Analysis, 31*(3), 298–318.

Spybrook, J., Raudenbush, S. W., Congdon, R., & Martinez, A. (2011). *Optimal Design for longitudinal and multilevel research: Documentation for the Optimal Design software Version 3.0.* Available from www.wtgrantfoundation.org

Thissen, D., & Wainer, H. (Eds.). (2001). *Test scoring.* Mahwah, NJ: Erlbaum.

Thurston, L. L. (1947). *Multiple-factor analysis.* Chicago: University of Chicago Press.

Vendlinski, T. P., Delacruz, G. C., Buschang, R. E., Chung, G. K. W. K., & Baker, E. L. (2010). *Developing high-quality assessments that align with instructional video games* (CRESST Tech. Rep. No. 774). Los Angeles: University of California, National Center for Research on Evaluation, Standards, and Student Testing.

von Davier, M., Gonzalez, E., & Mislevy, R. (2009). What are plausible values and why are they useful. *IERI Monograph Series, 2,* 9–36.

Yang, J., Monroe, S., & Cai, L. (2012, April). *A multiple group multilevel item bifactor analysis model.* Paper presented at the annual meeting of the National Council on Measurement in Education, Vancouver, Canada.

INDEX

Note: bold page numbers indicate figures and tables.